Becoming Lincoln

Standing Lincoln, by Augustus Saint-Gaudens, 1887,
Lincoln Park, Chicago

Becoming Lincoln

✦

William W. Freehling

UNIVERSITY OF VIRGINIA PRESS
Charlottesville and London

University of Virginia Press
© 2018 by the Rector and Visitors of the University of Virginia
All rights reserved
Printed in the United States of America on acid-free paper

First published 2018

1 3 5 7 9 8 6 4 2

Library of Congress Cataloging-in-Publication Data

Names: Freehling, William W., 1935– author.
Title: Becoming Lincoln / William W. Freehling.
Description: Charlottesville, VA : University of Virginia Press, [2018] |
Includes bibliographical references and index.
Identifiers: LCCN 2017061669 | ISBN 9780813941561 (cloth : alk. paper) |
ISBN 9780813941578 (ebook)
Subjects: LCSH: Lincoln, Abraham, 1809–1865. | Lincoln, Abraham,
1809–1865—Political career before 1861. | Lincoln, Abraham, 1809–1865—
Political and social views. | Presidents—United States—Biography.
Classification: LCC E457.35 .F74 2018 | DDC 973.7092 [B]—dc23
LC record available at https://lccn.loc.gov/2017061669

Cover art: Standing Lincoln, by Augustus Saint-Gaudens, 1887,
Lincoln Park, Chicago. (Photograph by Frank Dina)

FOR

Alison Goodyear Freehling
Alison Freehling Johnson
William Goodyear Freehling
Unbelievable Trio

Contents

Illustrations

FIGURES

Maps

Becoming Lincoln

Standing Lincoln, by Augustus Saint-Gaudens, 1887, Lincoln Park, Chicago

Introduction

A superb statue introduced me to Abraham Lincoln. During my teenage years, our apartment overlooked Chicago's Lincoln Park. One day, when wandering in the park, I came across Augustus Saint-Gaudens's *Standing Lincoln*.[1] On this and later visits, I wondered about the hero towering above his patriotic eagle chair—and especially about his agonized head. Some tormenting questions obsessed him. What could make a great victor so sad?

My answers, three score and seven years later, suffuse this tale of Abraham Lincoln's epic prewar rises and falls. Our greatest president endured a dismal youth after a sunny start. His presidency came after no experience as governor, four failed terms as a state legislator, a sole frustrated term in the U.S. House of Representatives, two defeats for the U.S. Senate, and a lost pursuit of the vice presidency. A wretched bankruptcy and a difficult marriage mixed in. A murderous war would top it off.

Lincoln's reversals made him ever more detached, yet engaged. He grew increasingly melancholic, yet determined to laugh away sadness. He became a classic self-helper, yet adept at attracting help. He suffered excruciating failures, yet scored historic triumphs. His plunges and recoveries offer more than an important personal tale, replete with lessons for all who stumble. His uneven odyssey also illuminates defining American mid-nineteenth-century turning points, including the development of the republic's first national market economy and the causes of its Civil War.

The tale starts with Lincoln's early plummets and comebacks, as a youth and during his formative economic/political struggles. A ferocious Unionist endured, determined to save the national republic as it had rescued him.

That unionism shaped Lincoln's extreme caution about antislavery. Yet this ultrapractical politician also aspired to do something for suffering humanity.

His resulting prewar statecraft crept behind his party's antislavery radicals. He especially shunned antislavery forced on the South. He only twice tested his cherished alternative—that moderate northerners could some distant day ease moderate southerners toward consent to abolition, without a civil war. As a lame-duck congressman, he deep-sixed his first attempt—so deeply that his fleeting innovation still remains unknown. A dozen years later, as a beginning president, he tried again. He hoped his appointed southern Republicans could (very gradually) convert Dixie's most northern, least enslaved outposts to manumission—and without a civil war.

Key secessionists preferred disunion to that fantasy. Abraham Lincoln preferred war to severed Union. As my epilogue briefly illustrates, halfway through the president's war for Union, victory demanded a radical abolitionist. Yet the newly coercive emancipator's doubled reward, Union reborn and abolition secured, cost more lives than the prewar Unionist had shuddered to contemplate. This is the saga of why Saint-Gaudens's *Standing Lincoln,* to ring true, had to mold joy and horror into a harrowing image of human becoming.[2]

A Puzzling Inauguration

Near the end of his first presidential term, Abraham Lincoln would famously promote the U.S. Constitution's Thirteenth Amendment, banning slavery from the Union. Yet as his presidency began, Lincoln's First Inaugural Address cheered a seemingly opposite Thirteenth Amendment, barring congressional emancipation.[1] Congress had approved this Thirteenth hours before. The Civil War would stymie all but six states' ratification. But why would an eventual Great Emancipator celebrate outlawing a powerful means of emancipation? This and other difficult questions made President Lincoln's inauguration a puzzling prologue.

1

During the four months between the Illinoisan's November 1860 popular election and his March 4 inauguration, seven of the fifteen slave states formed a new Confederacy, dedicated to the insistence that no President Lincoln would govern them. Rumors abounded that rebels plotted to murder the president-elect during the inauguration. The assassination would kill more than an incoming president. A republican essential, the peaceful transfer of power, would also perish.

On Inauguration Day, Lieutenant-General Winfield Scott, the U.S. Army's highest officer since George Washington, turned Washington, DC, into a warriors' camp. Scott stationed sharpshooters in the Capitol Building's windows, overlooking inaugural ceremonies, and on Pennsylvania Avenue roofs, above the inaugural parade. Scott also positioned mounted "flying artillerymen" on Capitol Hill, primed to descend on disturbances. He ordered more soldiers to mass around the president-elect's carriage the moment Lincoln came into public sight.

In 1861, the inaugural parade came first, then the inaugural address, then the swearing in. The outgoing president customarily collected the incoming chief executive at high noon, to begin the parade toward the Capitol Building. On March 4, 1861, outgoing president James Buchanan arrived a trifle late at Lincoln's temporary residence, the Willard Hotel. This sprawling structure consumed the corner of Fourteenth Street and Pennsylvania Avenue, near the Executive Mansion (renamed the White House at the dawn of the twentieth century).

Immediately after emerging from the Willard's Fourteenth Street entrance, Buchanan and Lincoln stepped into a barouche (a four-seat horse-drawn carriage, usually open to public view). Before Lincoln took his seat, mounted troops surrounded the conveyance. The procession then turned left from Fourteenth Street and proceeded down wide, dusty Pennsylvania Avenue.

When the barouche reached the Capitol, Buchanan and Lincoln stepped inside, to Lieutenant-General Scott's temporary relief. The incoming and outgoing presidents strode to the U.S. Senate's chamber, where Vice President–elect Hannibal Hamlin of Maine took his oath of office. In the golden age of U.S. senators, service in this hall had been Lincoln's fondest dream.

That ambition had recently been thrice thwarted. In 1855, six years after his single failed term in the U.S. House of Representatives, Lincoln had lost his first U.S. Senate election. In 1856, he had finished second again when the Republican National Party's convention balloted for a vice-presidential nominee (who, if elected, would become the Senate's presiding officer). In 1858, Lincoln had stumbled yet another time, vanquished for the Senate by his Illinois nemesis and northern Democrats' star, Stephen A. Douglas.

Now, having sped past Douglas in the 1860 presidential election, the president-elect advanced from the site of his highest ambition toward higher office still. When Lincoln stepped into public view on the temporary inauguration stand along the Capitol's East Portico, General Scott's apprehensions swelled again. Sharpshooters could hardly pick off every potential conspirator among some thirty thousand observers.

The pre-presidential Lincoln had thought he spotted a different conspiracy. U.S. Supreme Court Chief Justice Roger B. Taney had written the 1857 majority decision in the Court's infamous *Dred Scott* case, outlawing Congress from abolishing slavery in prestate territories. Taney would next deploy his *Dred Scott* logic, Lincoln had alleged, to outlaw abolition in states (including in Lincoln's Illinois). The Illinoisan had added that Senator Douglas plotted to help Taney with the follow-up decision, nationalizing slavery. Now the accused pair would witness their accuser's ascension.

Oregon's U.S. Senator Edward D. Baker would be a happier witness. Before migrating westward, Ned Baker had been among Lincoln's favorite Illinoisans. The native Englishman had also been one of Lincoln's most successful Whig rivals. Baker had won the party's nomination for an Illinois seat in the U.S. House of Representatives two years before Lincoln captured the prize. The Englishman had also been considered the better prairie orator.

The magnanimous Lincoln had never begrudged his friend's success. He had even named his late son Edward Baker Lincoln. Now Edward Dickinson Baker's lilting English accent commenced the inauguration ceremony: "Fellow citizens, I introduce you to Abraham Lincoln, president-elect of the United States of America."

Magnanimity multiplied as the president-elect stepped toward the narrow rostrum. After removing his signature black stovepipe hat, Lincoln saw no place to park the eight-inch addition to his six-foot, four-inch height. Stephen A. Douglas, nicknamed the Little Giant and a foot shorter than Lincoln, came forward to hold the troublesome article—to become his conqueror's temporary valet. The gesture symbolized that these two bitter rivals on slavery issues had merged on the issue of the hour—on whether southerners could fracture the Union.

Abraham Lincoln's dress marked the comer who had arrived. His newly purchased shiny cashmere suit fit his sprawling frame somewhat better than the ungainly frontiersman's previous attempts at city splendor. He placed his lovely ebony cane over a corner of his inaugural address, protecting the script from afternoon breezes.

Lincoln's only occasionally lovely expressions showed that his oratory, like his policies, remained in a state of transition. His post-1854 verbal artistry had excelled his earlier efforts. His advancing eloquence had helped fuel his comeback from political oblivion. Few still considered Ned Baker the superior wordsmith. But the 1861 Lincoln could not yet muster the secular poetics of his 1863 Gettysburg Address or the Christian depth of his 1865 Second Inaugural Address.

In his First Inaugural Address, only saving the Union inspired memorable phrases. "We are not enemies," Lincoln soothed secessionists, and we must not become "enemies. . . . The mystic chords of memory, stretching from every battle-field and patriot grave to every living heart, . . . will yet swell the chorus" for "Union, when again touched . . . by the better angels of our nature."[2]

But how would better spirits preserve the currently nonangelic Union, especially without a civil war? A brothers' brawl would most likely start at

Fort Sumter in South Carolina's Charleston harbor or at Fort Pickens near Pensacola, Florida. Those two piles, the last important federally held properties on Confederates' claimed soil, symbolized the Union majority's claimed power to govern the secessionist minority.

Both exposed forts, to remain in federal hands, required sterner stuff than symbols. Their Union commanders begged infusions of men, materiel, and food. Yet reinforcing the forts could provoke war. Combat would start disastrously for Lincoln if his provocations included firing the first shot. Some or all of the remaining eight southern states in the Union would then likely join their seven precipitous brothers. Lincoln would be saddled with winning a much more difficult civil war—or losing the Union.

On the inauguration stand, Lincoln did not say how he would avoid the appearance of provoking civil war and still hold precarious forts. Nor did he say how he would handle the gap in his party between his moderate antislavery policy and Radical Republicans' program. Radicals laid out explicit plans to abolish slavery in U.S. territories as a prelude to crushing the Peculiar Institution in southern states. Moderate Republicans, in contrast, seldom linked their insistence on stopping slavery's expansion in territories with bondage's "ultimate extinction" in states. Unlike their radical brethren, most moderates favored that proposed Thirteenth Amendment, forbidding congressional emancipation in states. Yet if an "irrevocable" amendment against congressional emancipation triumphed, how would the insistently moderate president become some Great Emancipator?

Lincoln's First Inaugural Address left the answer as uncertain as his strategy to save Forts Sumter and Pickens without firing first shots. Behind him, the unfinished Capitol Building epitomized unfinished policy. The structure's old wooden dome had been removed. Cranes, thrusting from the cavity, had not yet lifted the new iron dome into position. A statue of liberty, intended to crown the dome, still listed on the ground. This incomplete backdrop was as if designed to question whether an inexperienced crisis manager's indistinct plans for his forts and for slavery's "ultimate extinction" could solve republicanism's killing crisis.

After completing his address and swearing to uphold the Constitution, Lincoln would possess power to advance solutions. After his constitutional nemesis, the wizened Chief Justice Taney, reluctantly muttered the prescribed oath, Lincoln vigorously repeated the enabling words. The empowered president then strode safely back into the domeless Capitol. General Scott's warriors had secured the peaceful transfer of power. But could the endorser of the first version of a Thirteenth Amendment and the infrequent, vague proponent of slavery's "ultimate extinction" become the statesman to secure endangered forts, majority rule, perpetual Union, and blacks' freedom?

1

The Rising Lincolns and
the Kentucky Plummet

❧❦❧

During his multiple plunges before rising to the presidency, Abraham Lincoln knew that previous Lincolns had significantly climbed. That understanding helped him psychologically balance an American anomaly: currently plummeting Lincolns.

1

The initial American Lincoln, the future president's great-great-great-great-grandfather Samuel Lincoln (1622–1696), migrated in 1637 from East Anglia, hotbed of English Puritanism, to Massachusetts, capital of the American variety. Samuel Lincoln's radical move, a three-thousand-mile migration, sought a conservative purpose. He would save the English Puritan Revolution.[1]

Samuel Lincoln dropped heavy anchor after his transatlantic gamble. He settled in the Plymouth Colony town of Hingham and never left. To his rootedness in his first American home he added another stabilizing tradition: a protective community of family members surrounded him. Samuel Lincoln had crossed the ocean with his two brothers. By 1680, 25 percent of Hingham's 240 adventurers bore the name Lincoln.

Samuel's son Mordecai (1657–1727) moved only twice. Nine miles separated his three homes. His son Mordecai Junior (1686–1736) remained on Plymouth Colony terrain until 1720, almost a century after Grandfather Samuel arrived. When thirty-four years old, the grandson moved southwest in two short bursts, totaling 120 miles and ending in the Reading, Pennsylvania, area. Mordecai Junior migrated in the traditional Lincoln style, accompanied by his brother Abraham and a bevy of kinsmen and friends. The New England migrants built a mid-Atlantic fortune in ironworks.

Junior's son John (1716–1788) moved farther after waiting longer for his major migration. At age fifty-two, "Virginia John," as posterity calls him, traveled down the Great Philadelphia Wagon Road, then down the Virginia Road to Rockbridge County in Virginia's Valley. Four brothers joined his settlement, near the lovely Blue Ridge Mountains.

"Virginia John's" son, Abraham Lincoln (1744–1786), emulated his father's single far-flung movement. Near the end of the American Revolutionary War, this Abraham Lincoln trekked with his famous distant cousin Daniel Boone and a coterie of Boones and Lincolns through the Cumberland Gap to that rumored land of western plenty, Kentucky. In the Louisville environs, he bought thousands of virgin acres.

The landed titan, the future president's grandfather, never learned whether he had purchased wisely. In May 1786, a Shawnee brave, infuriated that whites had seized tribal terrain, ambushed the new Kentuckian. As the slain pioneer's eight-year-old son Tom, the future president's father (1778–1851), sobbed by the corpse, the assailant seized the screaming boy and dashed.

Tom's oldest brother, age fourteen and yet another Mordecai Lincoln, moved faster. He rushed to the family compound, seized a rifle, and fired. The bullet mortally wounded the Shawnee, missing Tom Lincoln by inches.

Destiny's inches not only saved a father to sire a president. The shot also bestowed a fortune on the rescuer. Because of Kentucky's primogeniture and entail laws, this latest Mordecai, as eldest son, received the entire estate. He lived with his extended family in the Louisville environs throughout the famous Abraham Lincoln's pre-adult years, raising blooded horses and prospering.

The future president knew almost nothing about successful Lincolns before Uncle Mord. But he cherished this star of the family's rendezvous with a Shawnee. Balanced against Abraham's eventually ashamed sense of his father, his admiration for Uncle Mord gave him that rarity for a poor man: family pride.

The pride honored not just his father's savior but also the rescued family's traditions, established centuries since by Samuel Lincoln and carried on by Uncle Mord. The latter-day Mordecai and Abraham retained their forbearers' sense that risks, while occasionally necessary, needed to be tempered. Uncle Mord's famous nephew would move his adult habitat hardly at all. Like the founding American Lincoln, he would become a conservative who slowly led a carefully hedged social revolution.

2

The future Great Emancipator's colliding sense of familial shame swelled from his father's reversal of the ancestral trajectory. As a penniless twelve-year-old, Tom Lincoln became a wanderer. The restless migrant lived in many temporary shelters before he was twenty-one, then in six more dwellings as an adult.[2]

The wanderer still decently prospered until his late thirties, partly by honoring another family commandment. He remained near helpful relatives. His father's cousin Hannaniah Lincoln (in Springfield, Kentucky) and Uncle Mord's brother Isaac (in eastern Tennessee) assisted the apprentice teenager's scrambles.

When the sojourner came of age, he long stayed in the Louisville environs, especially Elizabethtown, the center of his murdered father's extended network of fellow migrants from Virginia. In Elizabethtown, Tom Lincoln, a young adult with significant carpentry skills, erected cabins, fashioned coffins, and crafted furniture. Examples of his crude corner cabinets still survive.

By age twenty-eight, when he married Nancy Hanks, niece of a carpentry mentor, Tom Lincoln had become a modest property holder. He owned two Elizabethtown lots, with a log cabin on one and his 238-acre farm nearby. In 1807, eight months after he married Nancy Hanks, the couple's first child, Sarah, was born in their Elizabethtown log cabin.

Tom Lincoln then resumed wandering, yet within range of his extended family. In December 1808, after selling his first farm, he bought and moved to 345-acre Sinking Spring Farm (named after a lovely spring bubbling up from a deep cave). He had to erect his latest log cabin hastily. On February 12, 1809, a future president was there born.

3

The latest Abraham Lincoln's mysteries begin, appropriately, with this birthplace. Other American nineteenth-century politicians celebrated such log-cabin credentials (or fibbed to acquire the boon). In an egalitarian democracy where candidates craved identity with commoners, a log-cabin birth magically connected aspirants and voters. Why, then, runs this Lincoln puzzle, would America's classic self-made man shun the classic magic?

The mystery becomes more telling because Lincoln paraded later aspects of his climb from the bottom. In New Haven in 1860, he proudly recollected that a quarter century ago, "I was a hired laborer, mauling rails" and working "on a flat-boat—just what might happen to any poor man's son!" Four years later, speaking to three Union regiments, the president declared that only American "free government" offers "an open field and a fair chance" for "the humblest and poorest" to attain "the highest privileges and positions." While "temporarily" occupying this "big White House," he was "living witness that any one of your children may look to come here, as my father's child has."[3]

Yet the master politician hid his log-cabin birth and his first seven years. In 1860, when campaign advisors begged for romantic recollections of his beginnings, the presidential candidate reluctantly afforded sparse remembrances. He seemed "painfully impressed," wrote his campaign biographer, "with the extreme poverty of his early surroundings" and with "the utter absence of all romantic and heroic elements." When pressed harder for fetching memories, Lincoln protested against the "great piece of folly" in attempting "to make anything out of my early life" except "a single sentence . . . in Gray's Elegy: 'The short and simple annals of the poor.'" "That's all you or anyone else," Lincoln glared at prying allies, can "make . . . of it."[4]

Few Lincoln quotes are more famous. None is more misleading. In his first log cabin, Lincoln hardly suffered a stricken existence. For seven years, he enjoyed a relatively happy Kentucky childhood. Through the gloom of his later childhood, he could hardly remember the earlier interlude—much less consider his log-cabin birthplace a romantic springboard for rising.

4

His selective memory measured the severity of his family's Kentucky plunge. Five years before disaster and two years after Abraham's birth, his father again successfully moved inside the Elizabethtown environs. The wanderer leased 30 acres of the nearby 228-acre Knob Creek Farm.

The place briefly became a family haven. True, the parents lost their third and last child, Thomas Jr., after only a few days of life. But the survivors— mother, father, son Abraham, and daughter Sarah—formed a model nuclear family surrounded by a model extended family. A bevy of aunts, uncles, and cousins, all survivors of Grandfather Abraham Lincoln, resided within a day's travel from Knob Creek Farm.

Tom Lincoln farmed a few acres of limestone bluffs (knobs) above Knob Creek. While father worked, Abraham and Sarah swam in the creek's clear waters or played hide-and-seek among overhanging knobs. In this natural playground, with no necessity for his son to labor, Tom Lincoln ranked in the top 15 percent of Hardin County property owners.

Sarah's playmate ranked higher still among his classmates. During Abraham's scattered few months in Kentucky's so-called blab schools, pupils learned by blabbing different texts aloud, simultaneously. The boy's scant later Indiana schooling would feature the same din. The grand total of his Kentucky and Indiana "formal" schooling: twelve months of blabbing.

This constricted exposure to a "primitive" mode of learning proved revealingly valuable. In schools, Abraham learned his lifelong blab method. Beyond classrooms, he blabbed for hours to startled squirrels. The self-helper would lie on his back, feet propped on trees, reading aloud from favorite texts. He seldom had to recite what some teacher forced him to memorize. He instead could blab his way through any book that struck his fancy. His favorites included great tales of great heroes: William Shakespeare's epic dramas of historic kings, the Bible's riveting sagas of struggling saints, and John Bunyan's inspiring allegories of *A Pilgrim's Progress*. These volumes filled his voice with wonders and his dreams with ambitions.

As his orations would prove, his voice turned written words into spoken magic. He was, he told Joshua Speed, "slow to learn." But once a text mouthed its way into his memory, he was equally "slow to forget." He compared his "mind" to "a piece of steel, very hard to scratch any thing on it and almost impossible after you get it there to rub it out."[5] After voice and eyes labored together to get it in, he deployed visual imagery to make beautiful sounds out of books' silent descriptions. It would be a long way from frontier blabbing to the exquisite Gettysburg Address. But both depended on that combination of eye and voice that blab schools helped an innately gifted orator to master.

The young blabber lived on a stimulating American avenue. The Cumberland Trail, on the National Road between Nashville and Louisville, passed near Knob Creek Farm. Over the wide dirt, slaves, slaveholders, farmers, merchants, peddlers, and evangelicals streamed past. A spectator felt not frozen on a farm but part of a moving nation, booming on ribbons of travel. Abraham Lincoln would not need to learn to be a nationalistic advocate of internal improvements. The Knob Creek locale made that Whig gospel as instinctive as blabbing the written word.

With education as with everything else, the positive side of Lincoln's adult personality—the confident, forbearing, magnanimous, Uncle Mord side—bloomed on Knob Creek Farm. True, the future president's father was only a lower-middle-class aspirant, not even owning Knob Creek Farm. But with Tom Lincoln's modest farm yields and occasional carpentry commissions, the hardscrabble frontiersman helped turn Abraham Lincoln's first seven years into a positive experience.

During these crucial years for growing toward productive adulthood, the boy experienced neither "poor white trash" financial rages nor shattered families' emotional sores. He had no harsher daily assignment than frolicking with his sister and visiting successful Lincolns. One-third of his way through his childhood, he stood tall, psychologically as well as physically, unknowingly armed to survive his next fourteen ravaged years and the many crushing blows to follow.

5

The ravages started less suddenly than Abraham Lincoln remembered. His father's undoing had been imminent for months, outside the boy's sight. Tom Lincoln's laborious advance teetered on quicksand: Kentucky's property laws. The state never surveyed Kentucky lands. Imprecise boundaries plus unsuspecting land purchasers yielded vulnerable rustics. Years after a purchase, crafty salesmen could claim that victimized farmers had purchased nothing valid.

Thrice in 1815–16, Kentucky's land title morass ensnared Tom Lincoln. When sharks challenged his titles, he dabbled with lawyers, then shrank from the legal cost, then recoiled from Kentucky. In the fall of 1816, Tom Lincoln left his wife and two children temporarily behind while he explored neighboring Indiana.

He found that Indiana pioneers received surveyed federal land for pennies. Tom Lincoln ultimately enjoyed clear title to eighty Indiana virgin acres for two dollars per acre (about fifty-three dollars per acre in twenty-first-century cash), paid over ten years (or four pennies a day). The U.S. government's sales of surveyed Indiana tracts, compared to private sales of unsurveyed Kentucky lands, reinforced Abraham's observations of the Cumberland Trail. The Union never seemed an abstraction to a frontier lad who had watched national roads and national land policies offset local governments' inactivity.

Yet Tom Lincoln's new frontier also threw up frightening obstacles. Indiana had entered the Union only six months earlier. The virgin land contained only sixty-five thousand pioneers, or one settler per four square miles. To explore the barely populated frontier, Tom Lincoln had to travel alone from Kentucky down the Ohio River, disembarking in Troy in southernmost Indiana. The seeker then jolted nine miles down a primitive wagon road before disappearing into a dense wilderness. He hacked through towering underbrush, seven more miles into habitats of few humans and many creatures. Slightly south of Little Pigeon Creek, sixteen miles north of the Ohio River, he found an ideal (he hoped) locale for a comeback from Kentucky catastrophe. He claimed his U.S. government prize by piling brush in four corners and burning notches in each corner's trees. Then he struggled down to the great river and sailed against the currents back to his evicted Kentucky family.[6]

Before winter struck in 1816, Tom Lincoln and his three dependents forever fled Kentucky. Abandoning Samuel Lincoln's imperative, echoed by five later generations of Lincolns, they chanced migration without a saving group of compatriots. The quartet of soon-to-be-isolated Lincolns separated themselves from Uncle Mord and dozens of relatives who had helped each other survive an Indian's slaughter of their patriarch. The four fleeing Lincolns forfeited Tom Lincoln's carpentry customers. They abandoned a lush Kentucky bluegrass carpet dotted with few trees and many farms. They instead dared a tangled forest with no clearings, no customers, no neighbors, no kin, no shelter, nothing except whatever their grunt labor could fashion. By the end of Abraham Lincoln's first exhausting day in his antiplayground, the seven-year-old's grunts indicated the depth of his plummet—and why he never considered his Kentucky log-cabin birth his springboard to triumph.

2

The Indiana Plunge

⁂

"At once" upon entering the Indiana forest, Abraham Lincoln recalled in his third-person 1860 autobiography, he "had an ax put into his hands." Until "within his twenty-third year, he was almost constantly handling that most useful instrument."[1] Equally constantly, his father drove the productive lad to swing the adult weapon.

1

Why did a seven-year-old rookie swing an ax more productively than most adults? Only his unusual height marked a frontier he-man. Unlike some Paul Bunyan, that other legendary frontier rail-splitter, no bulging biceps or thick thighs or massive chest marked this prodigy. His gangly frame featured overly long arms extending to overly long fingers that reached unusually far down unusually long legs. His overly long feet were flat, barring heel-to-toe movement. Neither his clumping stride nor his ill-fitting pantaloons, short of his ankles by six inches, hinted that this motley fellow could exert coordinated grace.

His peculiar length, however, made him too naturally gifted at axing for his own good. The longer an axman's frame, the greater his potential to maximize the ax's advantage: its leverage. To understand why leverage made Lincoln's ax especially auspicious, try (or imagine!) a little experiment. Unfasten an ax's blade from its handle. Grasp the seven-inch-long blade, a rectangular amalgam of iron and steel, by its noncutting edge. Then thrust the blade's cutting edge at a tree. The impact will sting the hand but hardly dent the tree, with only a smidgeon of bark flying.

To experience the contrast, reattach the blade to its thirty-three-inch hickory handle. Then, after grasping the handle at its nonblade end, swing again. As the indeed "most useful instrument" explodes past the bark and tears into the tree, chunks will leap and your hands will but tingle. That's leverage.

Even as a seven-year-old, Abraham had the ideal body to expand his ax's leverage. His long arms extended the ax handle's length. His long feet anchored his force. His inability to move from toe to heel here for once proved auspicious. A wise axman keeps his feet still, out of harm's way. With his feet planted, Lincoln in motion no longer looked ungainly. At the perfect moment, he simultaneously snapped his wrists, shifted his weight, and rotated his hips as he slammed his ax home.

Bulging Paul Bunyan types could not believe that this slim lad's heave sounded like two of theirs. To a despairing father, no sound could be sweeter than the crash of Abraham's ax. With his son's help, the Indiana forest might compensate for his Kentucky disaster.[2]

2

The father turned his previously frolicking lad into an exhausted assistant. Delights at besting his sister at hide-and-seek gave way to shocks at confronting a frightening environment. The family's first forest shelter offered scant protection against fright. This so-called half-faced camp, amounting to less than half of a crude log cabin, slanted from its anchors, two corner trees, downward toward its back "wall," a single thick log. No way could even Abraham's short sister Sarah stand tall toward the rear.

Up front, the half-faced camp risked an open face to the wilderness. At the center of the nonwall, a fire required constant resupplying. Sometimes, merciful winds kept smoke from billowing inside. While inhabitants slept, a blaze helped keep wolves outside. Their eyes, gleaming like ice amid the fire's leaping flames, hinted at more daunting creatures hovering about. As Abraham Lincoln wrote some two decades later,

> When first my father settled here,
> 'Twas then the frontier line:
> The panther's scream filled night with fear,
> And bears preyed on the swine.[3]

Tom Lincoln enjoyed hunting less ominous beasts. His son recoiled from such sport. After killing a wild turkey at age eight, the boy vowed never again to murder a creature. He also detested his daily task: struggling the one and a half miles to the nearest source of drinking water, a bubbling spring, and then straining back, hauling two loaded buckets.

Clear water, wild meat, and a half-faced dwelling sustained life that first winter, until spring bloomed in the Indiana forest. Then, amid dogwoods' multicolored hues, the wild forest had to be axed into a farmer's sanctuary. After axmen downed mammoth black walnut or red oak or shagbark hickory trees, they hacked the corpses into remnants.

Worse was the underbrush, pricking, infecting, and sometimes killing. Giant trees could not fend off the tyrant of the underbrush: wild grapevines. These obstructers crept up from the ground, with thin, string-like green tendrils leading their march. Once their tendrils grasped branches, grapevines leapt from one tree to the next, weaving contorted shapes above human heads. The initial underbrush, now overbrush too, made swarms of trees look like underwater grottoes.

Inside grapevine tangles, the poison sumac's blood-red stems piled as high as young Abraham Lincoln's shoulders. At his feet, poisonous snakes slithered under vines. The slinking reptiles would later become the mature Lincoln's favorite symbol of a malignity that could not be assaulted without risking healthy children.

"Foxed" jeans would later become the boy's shield against the underbrush. Frontier matrons would cover leggings with animal skins, usually foxes' coats. The armor protected torn skin from grapevines and burning itches from sumac.

But when Abraham Lincoln first fought the underbrush, he suffered the battlefield before anyone foxed his jeans. His knives sometimes disappeared into vegetarian tangles. Although axing down grapevines offered the best of poor alternatives, tangled vines left no room for leveraged swings. A cramped lunge only uncovered inches of ground and sky.

Massive trunks littered even a "cleared" forest acre. Axmen carved these survivors into useful chairs. Less helpfully, stumps became targets for vines' tendrils. The Lincolns could only plant between the stumps, and only if constant vigilance prevented vines' comeback. From young Lincoln's perspective, poorly cleared farmland, the reward for horrendous toil, compared dismally with the hills and streams of Knob Creek Farm, beset only by land speculators that a lad never saw.

3

His father scarcely eased the boy's transition. Tom Lincoln regaled other males with coarse humor and bawdy stories. But he did not amuse his child when demanding labor. The insistent chief stood five feet, eleven inches tall, five fewer inches than his son's mature height. In later years, Tom's stubby body, thick neck, and black hair gave off an ironic illusion. He would look more like Stephen A. Douglas than like Abraham Lincoln.

The irony epitomized the cavern between father and son during their long, frigid, undeclared war. In the manner of cold wars, the struggle rarely blazed. Under his father's lashes and curses, Abraham's resentment usually silently simmered.

During scarce time off from labor, the boy most often sought not chances to play but opportunities to read. Lincoln sometimes pursued his self-education after hours, beside the family fire or up in his loft. But nighttime family bustle in close quarters distracted an exhausted day laborer. Oil lamps up in rafters added perils more than illumination. Young Lincoln's reading had to be mostly in daylight, at rare moments when his father relented from commands to hustle.

Upon finding his son stretched out beneath a tree, reciting his latest volume as if in blab school, the illiterate father would rage about wasted time and lazy offspring. The lad would pick up the ax, mutter if at all beneath his breath, and search for another few minutes to filch from grunt labor. Only during an occasional month did his father allow Abraham to attend Indiana blab schools. "I hain't got no eddication," Tom later explained, "but I get along far better than ef I had."[4] To which his son still later answered that his taskmaster "taught him to work but never learned him to love it."[5]

No one needed to teach Abraham Lincoln to love Shakespeare's cadences or biblical sagas. The language's haunting rhythms, decorating great tales of great men accomplishing great feats, instinctively appealed to a loather of battle against vines and snakes. The father loudly cursed his son's bookish preoccupations as the essence of irresponsibility. The son silently denounced his father's contempt for education as the essence of mindlessness.

This usually bloodless civil war hardened Lincoln's most distinctive personality trait: a persona divided. As he swung his ax, the grunting youth would barely hear his father's taunts. His world featured only his blackened thoughts. Then Abraham would break beyond his retreat, cracking filthy jokes and becoming less distinguishable from fellow frontiersmen (including Tom Lincoln).

Abraham's divided consciousness flirted with psychic danger. When his attentions swerved inward, they came saturated with melancholy, befitting his bleak situation. When blackness outside overwhelmed the inner brooder, as when a loved one died, he harbored suicidal thoughts. At less extreme times, his inner obsessions could create obliviousness to the world beyond his head. Then he could seem like an uncaring companion and spouse. His was not the personality for deep friendships with men or exotic affairs with ladies.

But his was the personality, when he properly balanced it, to act in the world and watch himself acting—the actor coolly judging his passionate action. The capacity turned his duality not into pathology but into health. Inside his thoughts, he drew the sting from his father's criticisms, formulated a persona opposite from the tormentor's, and reconsidered how he might refashion the universe. It was all a little grandiose for an overworked, cornered youngster. It was also the birth pangs of a fabulous statesman.

4

Outside his imagination, Lincoln's source of warmth, during his initial Indiana trials, usually glowed from his mother and sister. The absence of other genial humans eased a year after his arrival. Then Elizabeth and Thomas Sparrow, Abraham's mother's aunt and uncle, migrated from Kentucky along with their adopted eighteen-year-old son, the illegitimate Dennis Hanks. After the relatives arrived, Abraham and Tom built a log cabin for their nuclear family, while the Sparrows occupied the half-faced camp. With Kentucky kin in residence and a Kentucky-style log cabin as home, the gulf between the boy's past and present lives slightly shortened.

A year later, the gap intolerably lengthened. The culprit: again the Indiana underbrush. A shade-loving plant, the white snakeroot, shared the forest floor with snakes, grapevines, and sumac. The snakeroot's brilliant white clusters of tiny flowers decorated the plant in September and October.

The virginal appearance deceived. Cattle, after snacking on the flower, suffered debilitating tremors. Humans, after drinking the sufferers' milk, developed lethargy, then trembles, then stomach agonies, then grotesquely swollen tongues, then vomiting, comas, and death. The cycle consumed three weeks. Frontier doctors knew no cure.

In September 1818, when Abraham Lincoln was nine years old, Elizabeth and Thomas Sparrow succumbed to this so-called milk-sick. Then Lincoln's mother suffered the affliction. On October 5, she found release. The son, as usual laboring beside his father, fashioned the pegs that held together the boards that lined the crude coffin.

And then the boy helped lower Nancy Hanks Lincoln into the earth. The funeral came months later, when a minister happened upon the hamlet. The gravestone came a century later, when antiquarians memorialized the spot (they hoped) of Lincoln's mother's unmarked grave.

Only once did Lincoln hint at his heartbreak. During the Civil War, the president told a bereaved child that he had experienced the same horror. We both have seen, Lincoln wrote, that when "sorrow comes . . . to the young, it comes with bitterest agony, because it takes them unawares."[6]

5

Tom Lincoln's recovery from his wife's death temporarily removed him physically, as he had long been absent emotionally. Months after Nancy Hanks Lincoln perished, her bereaved husband roamed back to Kentucky in search of a replacement bride. Months later still, on December 2, 1819, he married his second wife and Abraham's second intimate Sarah, Sarah Bush Johnston Lincoln.

Until the new couple returned to Indiana, twelve-year-old Sarah and her ten-year-old brother, with some help from Dennis Hanks, had to survive forest perils. Their new stepmother found her new non-offspring to be exhausted, tattered, filthy, terrified.

The older Sarah shoved her new husband into a labor new to him: making his crude home more than a shelter. She insisted that he whitewash the ceiling, install wood flooring, and smear daub into cracks between logs. She added her furniture to the repaired cabin.

She also merged her three offspring and Tom's two children into a somewhat repaired family. She demanded that her new husband allow her new stepson an occasional hour to read and a spare month in blab school. Abraham

Thomas Lincoln

Sarah Bush Johnston Lincoln

revered her. He later bought the couple their final home, perhaps hoping more for his stepmother's comfort than for his father's. Tom Lincoln, perhaps in response to his son's relative affections, favored his nonbookish stepson over his sired bookworm. Not even so superb a substitute mother as Sarah Bush Johnston Lincoln could smooth over all rough edges inside that log cabin.

6

Shortly after his mother's death and his father's remarriage, Abraham's new chore offered relief from a subjugating homestead. With the forest in partial retreat and axing no longer constant, primitive mills for grinding corn came to the forest, creating possibilities for culinary delicacies. Raw corn could be ground into cornmeal, and then cooked into corn pone, corn grits, corn bread, and corn griddle cakes.

Abraham relished bringing bags of raw corn to Gordon's Mill, two miles distant. The nonchore carried him delightedly away from Tom Lincoln. He moved toward hours of gossiping, joking, and pranks. Meanwhile, a horse performed the labor, plodding in a circle and thereby empowering the mill that ground the corn.

Once, however, the lad overly lashed the begrudging nag whose reluctant strides slowly moved the grinding wheel. The animal kicked back. Its hoof smashed into Abe's forehead. The boy dropped, "apparently killed for a time,"[7] as he later wrote. Tom Lincoln was summoned. Fears of yet another family burial loomed.

Hours later, Abraham Lincoln awoke, remarkably undamaged. If the horse's blow had crashed into his skull in a slightly different spot, the son would have shared his mother's unmarked grave. It was all too reminiscent of the scant inches that had spared Tom Lincoln at about the same age, when Uncle Mord's bullet had slain the Indian kidnapper. Coincidences as well as deep causes do drive human epics.

7

During the decade after his hours of deathless sleep, Abraham relished his expanding chances to escape his father's glare. Tom Lincoln now needed his son less to labor at home and more to earn pennies abroad. The father, his fortunes slipping again, increasingly relied on his son's wages to keep land sharks away from land titles.

During Abraham's years of roving around the Little Pigeon Creek environs, in search of temporary employment, he never earned more than three cents an hour. His jobs never lasted more than a few weeks. He usually lived with momentary employers, less often with neighboring friends, less often still at home. The absentee continued to hand his sparse wages, minus his slight expenses, over to his father, as the law required until he became twenty-one.

His later description of his father as a "wandering laboring boy" now fit Abraham uncomfortably closely. More uncomfortably still, at least Tom Lincoln had a specialty: carpentering. As a day laborer, Abraham specialized in nothing. His lean muscles were hired to perform all frontier menial tasks imaginable. On farms, he split logs, built fences, cleared fields, managed swine, and pulled fodder (usually hay). More happily on the Ohio River and its tributaries, he built rafts, ran ferries, marketed goods from flatboats. Always folks noticed the dual attitude that had enraged his father. He ever displayed distracted laziness (so others called it) during his physical tasks, concentrated passion during his reading moments.

The son's passion illuminated the father's violation. In frontier America, a minor's requirement to hand wages to his father was a pre-adult's honorable as well as legal obligation. Lincoln possessed a deep sense of personal honor. But puritan fathers also had honorable obligations, especially to prepare sons for adult advancement. Peculiarly in America, Lincoln later emphasized, free labor meant freedom to transcend work for others.

Youthful education served that adult opportunity. Many a desperate frontiersman, while insisting on his offspring's heavy labor, also honored his children's right (a *right* most Americans considered it) to years in school. Tom Lincoln little honored such children's rights. Throughout Abraham's Indiana years, the father's regime left the son scant time for reading and less time for schooling. That educational opportunity denied, more than pennies handed honorably to his father, likely felt most insufferable to Abraham Lincoln.

8

The Indiana ordeal's final blow struck deeper than the underbrush or the educational deprivation. In 1826, Sarah, Abraham's nineteen-year-old sister, married Aaron Grigsby, son of a neighboring wealthier family. Young Lincoln and the groom's brother, Nathaniel Grigsby, relished each other. The families' alliance could help elevate more Lincolns than Sarah.

No such Indiana luck ever eased Abraham Lincoln's youthful melancholy. A month before her brother's twentieth birthday, Sarah perished when giving birth to a stillborn child. Of the four Lincolns who had fled their confiscated Kentucky terrain, the mother and sister were dead and the father oblivious (or worse) to the son's needs. When Abraham revisited the scene fifteen years later, he lamented that

> I range the field with
> pensive thread,
> And pace the hollow rooms,
> And feel (companion of the dead)
> I'm living in the tombs.[8]

His family viewed Sarah's tomb with fury as well as grief. The Lincolns conceived that the Grigsbys had killed Sarah by failing to call a doctor in time. The Grigsbys responded (or so it seemed to the Lincolns) with a shrug, as if saying that superiors need not notice inferiors' criticisms.

Then came the climactic insult (as the Lincolns saw it). The Grigsbys invited all Little Pigeon Creek folk, except the Lincolns, to a neighborly celebration of the joint marriage of Reuben and Charles Grigsby (two brothers of Aaron and Nathaniel) to the Hawkins sisters. The supposed snub provoked Abraham Lincoln's first literary production, "The Chronicles of Reuben," an unpublished extended verse that spread its crudities beyond Little Pigeon Creek.

The piece, couched as a biblical tale, claimed that Charles and Reuben, on their mutual wedding night, each blundered into the wrong sister's virginal bed. Then, the lascivious fable climaxed, Billy, another Grigsby brother, lacked the equipment to bed Betsy, another Little Pigeon Creek damsel. While "Reuben & Charles have married 2 Girls," went the bawdy rhyme, "Billy has married a boy," for

> betsy She Said . . .
> My Suiter you never Can be, . . .
> Your low Croch proclaims
> you a botch and that
> never Can ansor for me.[9]

Billy Grigsby answered by challenging Abraham to a fight. Lincoln retorted by calling Billy too unmanly for a brawl. Insultingly, Abraham offered up his weaker stepbrother as the appropriate fighter. After Billy pummeled the substitute, young Lincoln threw this Grigsby to the ground. Then other members of the clans had at each other.

This version of the Hatfields versus the McCoys, when compounded by "The Chronicles of Reuben," illuminates how incredibly far Lincoln's self-made verbal dexterity had already progressed, a decade before he found better use for his stylistic flair (and for his jocular crudity). The brawl also showed how far his emotional control would have to develop, lest his inner distress impede rather than fuel a self-made man's triumphs.

More broadly, the Grigsby-Lincoln melee between haves and have-nots showed that in America, glory from rising remained precariously balanced against shame from falling. American economic abundance helped sustain white men's climbs from outhouses to executive mansions. But when opportunities soured, whether from bankruptcies or Indian raids or white snakeroot or land sharks, angry victims abounded. When those who had reached the heights lorded it over those mired in the mud, resentments swarmed like grapevines. Stir in a mourner's grief and add "The Chronicles of Reuben." From that shocking stew, unknown in his frolicking first seven years, flamed Abraham Lincoln's melancholy and his first brothers' war, that melee with arrogant Grigsbys.

9

In early 1830, with Tom Lincoln still stuck in the Little Pigeon Creek mud, the underbrush staged its latest comeback. Another epidemic of milk-sick struck. Simultaneously, the Lincolns' Hanks cousins bragged about the better, healthier possibilities that they had found in frontier Illinois. Listening to their rosy descriptions, the patriarch decided that his record of thirteen years in one cursed place needed to be shattered.

Before Tom Lincoln's latest wandering began, Abraham celebrated his twenty-first birthday. The new adult was now legally free to go his own way. He need only stay in Indiana after the wanderer departed. But might honor require a final trip with father?

3

The Illinois Crash

❖❖❖

Upon joining his father's migration to Illinois, Abraham Lincoln could hardly foresee an important consequence. He had no inkling that Stephen A. Douglas existed, much less that opposing Douglas in Illinois politics would provide a national ladder to the top. If Abraham had stayed in Indiana, his campaigns against that state's less prominent Democrats could have provided no such boost. Chance or destiny? As with Uncle Mord's cosmic bullet and the mill horse's noncosmic kick, Lincoln's tale constantly featured that puzzle.

1

A more mundane puzzle: Why did Lincoln continue as his father's unpaid helper a year longer than frontier custom or law required? Posterity can only guess. While Abraham's resentments called for severance, his family's traditions discouraged going it alone. While the son owed nothing more to the father legally, puritan obligation stirred felt responsibilities. While sister Sarah's death shriveled family affections, snapping the last tie may have been unsettling.

In March 1830, with whatever reasons and apprehensions, Abraham Lincoln, a month past his supposedly liberating twenty-first birthday, drove one of the two rickety wagons, each behind two oxen, carrying Tom Lincoln's family and possessions away from Indiana. On their two-week, 225-mile exodus, they crossed the Wabash River at Vincennes, then rolled by swollen streams and saturated soil to central Illinois. Twelve miles west of the tiny hamlet of Decatur, they arrived at the U.S. government's ten acres that cousin John Hanks had urged them to try, before they purchased the homestead.

The squatters' landed sliver lay at a juncture of prairie and forest, on a bluff above the north side of the Sangamon River. In central Illinois, the Sangamon provided the unofficial dividing line between predominantly northern and largely southern settlers. By settling north of the river, the Lincolns symbolically aborted "Virginia John's" attempt to carry the family's New England legacies to the South. Abraham Lincoln, destined to tip the central Illinois balance slightly northward (and thus the state's balance and the nation's too), veered slightly to the Yankee side when he squatted for his first night.

At the juncture between not only North and South but also between prairie and forest, the Lincolns chose a prairie homesite, providing better distance from milk-sick contaminations. Then they chose the forest's downed corpses, contributing better building material for house and fence. Beyond their prairie fence, grass clumps twisted their rows of corn.

That summer of 1830, irregular rows yielded sparse kernels. In contrast, swarming mosquitoes brought abundant malaria. Tom Lincoln, shaking from fever and hunger, thundered that he wanted out of this phony Eden. Before he could lead another departure, winter trapped his family inside a nightmare.

Horrified residents labeled it The Winter of the Deep Snow. An inch of ice atop six feet of snow created murderous conditions. Then more snow piled on. Cows starved. Carcasses froze. Young Lincoln had a new calling. He begged neighbors for corn kernels.

When winter broke, the elder Lincolns retreated toward Indiana. Friends stopped their eastward flight in Illinois's Coles County, halfway between Decatur and the Indiana border and just south of Illinois's Charleston. After experiencing three more Coles County homes in the next six years, Tom's exasperated wife barred further uprooting. The beached patriarch, having been in the top sixth of his Kentucky county's yeomen, plunged into the bottom fourth of Illinois farmers.

The father's departure liberated the son. Tom Lincoln need not have fled the family's new Decatur home. The Winter of the Deep Snow was past history. The house and fence crowned rich soil. A promising springtime dawned. By picking this moment to quit, the elder Lincoln left the disgusted offspring with no thought of sharing another family migration.

2

Abraham's sense of filial duty would remain. He would buy his father and stepmother a dwelling. He would loan them money to ward off bankruptcy. He would occasionally visit their Coles County home. But he would never welcome them to his house. He would never introduce them to his wife or children. He would not witness the patriarch's death, or attend the funeral, or observe the grave.

Abraham would dutifully follow the family tradition of naming a son after the grandfather—but only after the grandfather perished. Even then, Abraham Lincoln would finesse having to call his son "Tom." He would nickname the latest Thomas Lincoln "Tad" at birth. Only Tad Lincoln, among Abraham Lincoln's flock, would possess a nickname that hid the given name.

In his 1860 autobiography, Lincoln would hide his resentments as poorly. His father, he would write, was "litterally without education." (Abraham did not have to add "litterally.") The parent could only "bunglingly sign his own name." (The son did not have to pile on "bunglingly.")[1] These addendums, written a quarter century later, signaled angry residue from a bitter experience.

The same wounds had earlier generated Abraham's protective secrecy, hiding aspirations that his father despised. When the son became an adult, his secret life generated a visible tower of non–Tom Lincolns: nonhunter, nonfisherman, nonilliterate, nonfarmer, noncarpenter, non–manual laborer, non–husband of an uneducated, penniless bride, non–demanding parent, non-Democrat, non–church member, and especially nonwanderer. Non–Tom Lincoln soon became non–Stephen A. Douglas. Throughout the pre–Civil War years, Abraham's almost every political move battered Douglas's latest initiative.

3

Lincoln called himself "a sort of floting Drift wood" during his first year away from his living parent.[2] The image pictured free will negated—humans (alias driftwood) at the mercy of forces beyond their control. Yet Abraham's first choices, like many to follow, would turn his loose determinism into a half-truth. In his first decision after his father's farewell, he chose a river identity.

During Abraham's early Kentucky years, the National Road, almost touching Knob Creek Farm, had been his first window onto a wider world. During the ensuing Indiana years, he had instead seen the Ohio River, connecting to the Mississippi River and flowing within sixteen miles of his Little Pigeon Creek house, as the avenue leading beyond his locale. Then, during his first Illinois year, he had observed the Sangamon River as it meandered below his father's log cabin, carrying people and commerce down to the Illinois River and on to the Mississippi.

He had spent his most despised Indiana and Illinois hours away from rivers, grubbing for pennies from landed labor. He had enjoyed his most cherished youthful moment when he rowed halfway across the Ohio River, ferrying two stranded travelers to their steamboat. His customers had each tossed a shiny half dollar into his meager vessel. The would-be river rat later called this "a most important incident in my life. . . . The world seemed wider and fairer before me."[3]

The river world had seemed still wider during his adventure as a nineteen-year-old. He had been commissioned to build a flatboat, load it with Indiana farm produce, and float it down the Mississippi. Near Baton Rouge, a brutal fistfight with seven enslaved black robbers had punctured the river voyage. Outraged observation of a New Orleans slave auction had ensued. Whatever his horror at seeing the worst of slavery, Lincoln still aspired to trade eye-opening watery adventures for dreary landed toil. That aspiration helps explain why an irresponsible dreamer captured his attention that first year on his own.

4

Denton Offutt, four years older than Lincoln, had also been born in Kentucky's bluegrass region. But where Lincoln's lower-middle-class log-cabin birth had transpired in the Louisville environs, Offutt had begun life amid upper-class Lexington surroundings. Where the Lincolns had landed in Kentucky after generations of movement south and west from the Boston area, the Offutts had long been raising, taming, and selling blooded horses in the Border South.

After Denton Offutt's father died, a lush inheritance and a commercial dream propelled this eccentric capitalist to central Illinois, about the same time Abraham Lincoln arrived. Offutt meant to buy animals and produce from Illinois pioneers, then sell his purchases in New Orleans. As middleman between the new Midwest and the best Old South port, he would ride the productive (he dreamed) Sangamon toward a trading empire beyond the fantasies of even Erie Canal merchants.

Offutt's soaring ambition required overcoming Illinois's crabbed inner rivers. Flatboats rode river currents downriver. But without self-propulsion, vessels could not return against the current. All the Prairie State's inner rivers except the Illinois were too choked and/or shallow for self-propelled steamboats, unlike the blessedly wide, deep rivers marking the state's edges: the Wabash, Ohio, and Mississippi.

Offutt started with floating temporary flatboats downriver, to be broken up and sold along with the produce they conveyed. The vision obsessed a stocky little man with outlandish costumes, comic grammar, and wild projects. Lincoln, lover of ridiculous tales, found him hilarious. When thirty Offutt hogs balked at boarding a flatboat, the boss ordered their eyes stitched shut. That lunacy failed. Onlookers, especially Lincoln, tittered.

Offutt had the answer—better hijinks. After collecting five dollars to quiet an ungovernable steed, Offutt whispered sweet nothings in the wild animal's ear. That "craziness" worked! Lincoln understood perfectly. In a splendid exchange after Lincoln rose in politics, Offutt sent the imminent great man word "to quit his damned politics and go into some honest business, like taming horses." That "sounds like Offutt," roared Lincoln.[4]

The joshing companions first met when Offutt, searching for Sangamon River helpers, stumbled upon an unemployed lad, freshly on his own and seeking river adventures. In early 1832, Offutt's inquiries around Decatur led to John Hanks, who suggested that Offutt also sign up cousin Abraham. Lincoln suggested Dennis Hanks as a further collaborator.

Offutt charged the three lads with voyaging from Decatur to Springfield to load his temporary flatboat with wares. They should then float his craft down the Sangamon River, then the Illinois, and finally the Mississippi to New Orleans. Upon arrival, Offutt would sell the flatboat's cargo while his employees would break up the vessel and sell the wood. Then all would rendezvous back in Springfield, ready to float downriver on Offutt's next transient flatboat.

In March 1831, Lincoln and his two compatriots looked up Offutt in Springfield. They found no flatboat and an inebriated boss. A contrite Offutt offered each fellow twelve dollars to help build the missing craft. So instead of floating downriver toward excitement, Abraham Lincoln shouldered his ax again, downed timber again, floated logs to the local sawmill, and lashed the emerging wood planks into an eighteen-by-eighty-foot flatboat.

On the monster raft, the sailors briefly enjoyed a respite from their river's usual inhospitality. Their flatboat, upon leaving Springfield, would have usually meandered in the Sangamon's shallow waters and tepid currents. But in the spring of 1831, the normally sluggish Sangamon featured gushing waters, thanks to lavish melt from The Winter of the Deep Snow. Offutt and his three employees floated speedily from Springfield down the swollen Sangamon to tiny New Salem.[5]

There, twenty miles below Springfield, townsfolk had built a so-called milldam across the river. The harnessed water better drove spinning wheels of local grist- and sawmills. Previously, plodding nags had generated limited power (and almost killed young Abraham Lincoln).

The more modern power left Offutt's primitive flatboat powerless when the craft stuck atop the New Salem milldam. New Salem folk, sprinting toward the spectacle, had no idea that they would witness a major turning point in a great man's life. They saw only a tall stranger with a low-slung, beat-up straw hat (no soaring top hat yet for Mr. Lincoln!) and jeans that stopped six inches short of his boots. The twenty-two-year-old stripped off his ratty workman's hickory shirt, plunged into the river, and sought to push the vessel across the milldam.

The flatboat resisted. Water seeped aboard. In desperation, Abraham transferred the craft's rear-end load to nearby boats. Then he drilled a hole in the front end. The flatboat pitched slightly forward, water drained toward the hole, and just as the boat escaped over its milldam prison, the rescuer plugged the opening.

After Lincoln freed Offutt's conveyance from the New Salem milldam, Offutt thought he saw providence's plan. Here he should build a general store, erect a landing, lease grist- and sawmills, graduate from flatboats to steamboats, hire crews to clear and deepen the Sangamon, and more permanently employ that transient miracle worker, Abraham Lincoln. With Lincoln solving unforeseen problems, Offutt would turn New Salem into Illinois's Cincinnati.

Whatever Lincoln thought of this vision, he agreed to further the escapade. His initial assignment, to run Offutt's new general store, soon doubled into also directing his employer's leased mills. The employee would have preferred a third assignment: becoming Offutt's steamboat captain. But at least New Salem landed adventures would be part of the river commercial world and would involve more than menial labor. And just maybe, the big-talking employer would turn his favorite employee into a river tycoon.

The thought was less outlandish than it sounds. Illinois's huge prairies and minuscule towns invited a metropolis to develop, akin to Cincinnati or Louisville or St. Louis. With railroad development expensive, most inhabitants thought the interior marketing center would be on a river, flowing to the Illinois and then to the Mississippi. So which spot on which choked central Illinois river would triumph?

If New Salem had only 150 inhabitants, Chicago had no more. If the Sangamon had too shallow a bed, the Chicago River sometimes flowed the wrong way, east toward Lake Michigan rather than consistently west toward the Illinois and the Mississippi. If southern Illinois's Vandalia was Illinois's capital city, its river, the Kaskaskia, veered too sharply south and west to serve most central Illinoisans. New Salem seemed as likely a future prairie monarch as Springfield or Peoria or Galena or Dixon's Ferry or Jacksonville or Petersburg—or Chicago.

The flighty Denton Offutt was not the man to turn New Salem, situated on the contrary Sangamon, into *the* commercial colossus (if anyone could!). Goods for his New Salem store arrived tardily in the early fall of 1831. With funds sparse, Offutt built a store for the merchandise far from town customers. Then he bought one thousand hogs and three thousand bushels of corn before building any place to hold them.

Before the spring of 1832 dawned, Offutt's inheritance vanished. So did Offutt. Two years later, his creditors would rout him from hiding. After his imprisonment for debt, his jailbreak, and his final bolt from Illinois in December 1834, his whispering to horses would more successfully dominate his ventures.

5

While the eccentric had absconded, his dreams for New Salem lingered, kept alive in part by his favorite employee. Abraham Lincoln conceived that daffiness alone had undermined his employer's strategies. As if to strengthen Lincoln's diagnosis, an apparently responsible local entrepreneur charged, almost at the moment when the irresponsible Offutt first disappeared.

On February 19, 1832, Vincent A. Bogue made the announcement of the decade in the semi-isolated Sangamon River world. His 150-ton leased steamboat, Bogue bragged, would finally link Springfield and New Orleans. His initial voyage, he proclaimed, would feature the first steamer to chug *up* the Sangamon, against the current to Springfield. He would start at Beardstown (where the Sangamon River flows into the Illinois, which flows into the Mississippi). He would steam upriver to his mills, fifteen miles beyond New Salem, then proceed five more miles to Springfield.

Subsequently, he would turn his steamer around, then voyage easily downriver to Beardstown and on to New Orleans. His ship's name invited good luck: *The Talisman*. With a little luck, Bogue dreamed, his experiment would prove that steamboats could tame the Sangamon, that Springfield could become Illinois's Cincinnati, and that he could become the next Cornelius Vanderbilt.

Lincoln, with dreams of becoming a lesser Bogue, bought (with borrowed money) a New Salem warehouse. There he hoped to store the goods soon to pass to and fro Springfield and New Orleans. He then hustled down to Beardstown to join a crew charged with clearing river obstacles hindering *The Talisman*'s historic upriver journey.

On March 9, 1832, Bogue's (hopefully) game-changing steamboat arrived at Beardstown. There the shallow Sangamon threw up its habitual spring obstacle: ice. After four days, Lincoln and compatriots smashed enough ice so *The Talisman* could start upriver. Two weeks later, after Lincoln and compatriots axed away logs and debris at every river twist, the apparently charmed ship arrived at Bogue's mills, only five miles short of Springfield, amid wild celebrations.

There, *The Talisman* proved false to its name. The river suddenly dropped (1832 was a year after The Winter of the Deep Snow!). With no room to turn around, the endangered steamboat crawled backward, with Lincoln now an assistant pilot. The retreat stalled (where else!) atop the New Salem milldam. The sticking point had to be half demolished before the stricken ship could limp toward Beardstown, where it arrived fatally smashed. Lincoln's warehouse failed soon thereafter.

6

Once again, Lincoln believed that he had merely hitched his river dreams to the wrong dreamer. Vincent Bogue had hoped that private workers could clear the river for *The Talisman*. Instead, Lincoln speculated, maybe a government, state or national, would deepen and disentangle the Sangamon. Furthermore, maybe a general store for local settlers could meagerly profit until governmental internal improvements brought steamboats.

Wisely thinking small, after a year of experiencing Offutt and Bogue, Lincoln started a tiny retail enterprise in the late summer of 1832. Then, after several months of skimping by, the nouveau merchant wondered if bigger might be better. He struck a partnership with a competitor, William Franklin Berry, two years younger and a Kentucky reverend's son. Berry brought to the partnership some goods from his own store, some cash, and some local connections.

The partners saw that too many New Salem storeowners served too few settlers. Consolidation seemed the key to profitability. By taking over faltering competitors, Lincoln-Berry's store could become a finalist of two surviving stores. Then the partnership might crush the rival.

Preliminaries worked as planned. Whenever a competing store fell in late 1832 and early 1833, Lincoln and Berry bought the goods, always on credit, going, Lincoln reported, "deeper and deeper in debt."[6] Then only two stores endured. Samuel H. Hill unfortunately owned the other.

Hill, a New Jerseyite, had opened the first New Salem country store in 1829. In 1839, after New Salem collapsed, he would move his wares downriver to Petersburg. He would retire at midcentury, worth millions in early twenty-first-century dollars. Along the way, in the spring of 1833, this undefeated local titan routed the novice Lincoln-Berry duo.

Or, as Lincoln put it, our store "winked out." When alcoholic binges killed Berry in early January 1835, Lincoln shouldered the store's entire debt. The burden (ever after Lincoln called it the "national debt") amounted to $1,100 (approximately $31,000 in early twenty-first-century dollars).[7] No one would have then believed that this incautious entrepreneur would become America's favorite self-made man—and an obsessively careful politician!

As Lincoln began slowly to reduce his "national debt," he eschewed two commonplace quick fixes. He could use bankruptcy to slice his obligation. Or he could flee his creditors. A month before William Franklin Berry's death in January 1835, Denton Offutt had bolted from debtors' prison, then from Illinois.

Lincoln scorned such "dishonor." He pledged to pay every penny of the Lincoln-Berry debt. His commitment exacted a crushing price. He later called his debt "the greatest obstacle I have ever met" (which was saying a mouthful). Paying off $1,100 seemed to him "the work of a lifetime."[8]

It turned out to be the work of more than a decade. It also turned out to enable a life's work. The repute of an utterly "Honest Abe," so rare in this capitalistic casino, would be politically golden. Lifting his burden, however, "galled him and hastened his wrinkles," his law partner later reported.

Lincoln, being Lincoln, saw no choice. During years of development in many areas, Abraham Lincoln did not have to develop into following honor's call, any more than he had to develop into loathing slavery's depravity. The son, unable at age twenty-one to forget filial obligations, could not at age twenty-five duck a debtor's obligations. His pledge to repay had been his bond and his entrance ticket to the capitalistic chase. The chase's losers had no right to flee the winners.

Later, Lincoln thought that voters' pledge to obey election winners provided entrance tickets to the polls. Neither families nor capitalism nor democracy could endure if individuals flouted their vows. "Honest Abe" could no more allow secession in 1860–61 than emulate Denton Offutt in January 1835.

8

His first crash demonstrated that the American land of opportunity honed a two-edged sword. The midwestern frontier offered an especially promising field for the penniless. But it often viciously closed upon the impoverished. Indians had slaughtered Lincoln's grandfather. Land sharks had decimated his father's Kentucky opportunity; the underbrush had killed his mother; the shortage of doctors had slain his sister; and perils of credit had closed his store.

To escape affliction with honor intact, a menial toiler could work the prairie sod, if he could abide that grind (and Tom Lincoln's son loathed the thought more than most pioneers). Or he could join zany entrepreneurs in seeking more credit to try more reckless enterprises. In 1832–35, Abraham

Lincoln had helped himself to these shortcuts—and had collapsed more swiftly than most.

After collapse, revival required the humility to blame one's erring self, plus the intelligence to see better ways forward, plus the sense to eschew quick fixes in a debt-haunted economy, plus the patience to persevere the slow, steady way. Abraham Lincoln had succumbed to ordinary American ways to fall. He now looked for extraordinary ways to regroup.

4

The New Salem Recovery

❦

In the late nineteenth century, Horatio Alger Jr.'s 125-plus books, selling some 20 million copies, famously celebrated Americans' rises from rags to riches. Alger dedicated his 1883 Lincoln volume, *The Backwoods Boy, Or How a Young Rail-splitter Became President*, to Alexander Henriques, vice chairman of the New York Stock Exchange. The dedication appropriately affirmed Lincoln's conjunction of economic and political rises. Still, Lincoln's *political* climbs made him the supreme Alger.

1

Lincoln issued his first political notice after his first economic setback. In early 1832, when Denton Offutt's debacle canceled Lincoln's initial New Salem employment, the plebeian blamed the Sangamon River more than Offutt. Until governmental internal improvements intervened, Lincoln believed, choked rivers would doom more sensible central Illinois enterprises than Offutt's.

Lincoln so argued in his March 9, 1832, "Communication to the People of Sangamon County," announcing, at age barely twenty-three, his precocious candidacy for the state legislature.[1] He had lived in New Salem for only a year. He had little schooling, scant money, and no job. Yet he begged Sangamon County voters for a state legislature seat.

My quest, he conceded, is "more presuming than becomes me." A "great degree of modesty . . . should always attend youth." He had been "born and have ever remained in the most humble walks of life." If he lost, he had "been too familiar with disappointments to be very much chagrined."

Yet his "peculiar circumstances" during "the last twelve months" spotlighted central Illinois's predicaments. Alluding to his misadventures at New Salem's milldam and Offutt's debacles as river merchant, Lincoln urged easier conveyance, to export surplus products of our "fertile soil" and to import "necessary articles from abroad." Too much "drifted timber," too "zigzag" a "course," too "low" a level, and too much ice in "freezing weather" snarled the Sangamon River. While railroad alternatives heat "our imaginations," construction costs will "shock" our "heart." Our state government, however, can afford the "vastly important . . . improvement of the Sangamo River."

A month after this appeal, the *Talisman* disaster reemphasized the problem. But would New Salem folk select a novice to provide the cure? And would Sangamon County voters beyond New Salem, having never heard of Abraham Lincoln, support the village rookie?

2

Jackson-era victors required personal as much as ideological appeal. Lincoln's frontier charm attracted all New Salem residents, whether rich or poor. His swift rise in esteem started among poorer citizens. To attract scruffy ruffians, Abraham commenced with that rarity, a boon from his father. Tom Lincoln spun hilarious tales. His stories emphasized the raunchy and ridiculed the pompous.

As master of ridicule, the son went one step beyond the father, with the oldster's unintended help. Tom Lincoln was a devout churchgoer. His less-than-devout offspring trailed along to gather comic material. After Sunday services, Abraham famously gathered the fellows. Upon mounting a stump, he delivered a perfectly memorized, outrageously taunting rendition of the latest pulpit performance, complete with the right exaggerated gestures at the right sidesplitting moments.

His language embellished his postures. While he later learned the King's English, he always retained a rustic's dialect. "Aren't" was always "ain't"—as in "ain't you a fine fellow." "One" was always "own"—as in "ain't that own pretty lady." "One of them" was always "own of em"—as in "ain't that own of em swell fellas."

Not-so-gentlemanly dialect well served ungentlemanly jokes. Although Lincoln sometimes turned sexual material into comic smut, his favorite off-color stuff featured farting or defecating. An admirer of his humor asked why he failed to publish a collection of his tales. "Such a book," Lincoln declared, "would stink like a thousand privies."[2] He wrinkled his nose as he portrayed a fat old squire, struggling to carve an immense turkey. "I'll see if I can't cut up this bird," announced the hacker, "without farting."[3]

Lincoln's most famous ridicule of privy smells irreverently starred George Washington. The humorist claimed that English hosts teased an American traveler by hanging Washington's portrait in an outhouse. "Nothing will make an Englishman SHIT so quick," retorted the American, "as the sight of Genl Washington."[4]

Comics often make puns at their own expense. Lincoln's long, lean, arguably homely face offered the perfect backdrop as he told about the alleged time that a stranger handed him a mysterious jackknife. Upon hearing that the unfamiliar blade was surely his, the confounded Lincoln asked how the fellow figured. The answer: A lady asked me to return the knife to its true owner, who would be uglier than all others. So Lincoln was "fairly entitled to the property."[5]

Lincoln as jokester improved the joke. He started with a dreary expression. As the fun developed, his visage relaxed. Wrinkles descended from his eyes to his nose, his cold gray eyes sparkled, and as the punch line approached, guffaws shook his towering frame. At the climax, the butt of the joke, Lincoln's supposedly homely face, became, of all things, handsome.

This unassuming giant's fabled honesty proved even more seductive. The moniker "Honest Abe" commenced during the fleeting days of Denton Offutt's store. Lincoln famously walked two miles to deliver a half pound of tea, inadvertently left behind, or 6¼ cents, inadvertently overcharged.

Less winsomely, a widely floated tale claimed that upon visiting a prostitute, Lincoln agreed to a five-dollar fee before shedding his clothes. Then he discovered that he had only brought three dollars. His almost-purchased damsel said no matter; his credit was fine. But Lincoln donned his jeans. He would not enjoy without instantly paying.[6]

If the tale failed as factual truth (and the jury will always be out, even though close friend Joshua Speed claimed to check it out with the damsel), its crudities captured winning Lincoln qualities. He was so loaded with integrity, so earthy, so physical. He proved all that in his famous Jack Armstrong brawl.

A few miles southwest of town, the unruly Clary's Grove Boys hung out. The toughs' chief bore the all-American nickname "Jack" (really John) Armstrong. The leader, unlike the gaunt Lincoln, sported a short, stout body, bulging biceps, and trunk-like legs. Armstrong's endowments discouraged reckless challenges at that gauge of frontier might, a wrestling match.

Denton Offutt, reckless adventurer, thrust a reluctant Lincoln where sensible New Salem lads feared to tread. Offutt bragged around the village that his clerk was the mightiest stud. He would bet five dollars on it. The Clary's Grove Boys appointed Armstrong to win the wager.

How could the gangly Lincoln throw the thick Jack Armstrong, Illinois's first little giant? For the same reason that Tom Lincoln's son had thrust an ax deeper into trees than most adults: leverage. Frontier wrestling in a standing position, with the two protagonists required to retain their initial hold until one heaved the other, demanded perfect coordination of limbs in one explosion of power (like axing).

As legend has it, Jack Armstrong, surprised at Lincoln's power when their bodies locked, cheated by breaking the hold and then throwing the opponent. The downed Lincoln responded with just the grace that he could not summon three years earlier, in his brawl with Billy Grigsby. This time, the question was pettier than whether a beloved sister's life had been irresponsibly shortened. It was whether the irresponsible Denton Offutt deserved five dollars. Lincoln answered by bounding up, calling the bout a draw, praising Jack Armstrong as a splendid wrestler, and shaking the little giant's hand.

Everyone won with this gesture (except Denton Offutt, who learned nothing in New Salem except new ways to lose). Lincoln secured Armstrong's gratitude and the Clary's Grove Boys' adoration (plus their votes, even when he opposed Jacksonian candidates, usually the pack's favorites). Meanwhile, Jack won a lifelong friend (and later, as we will see, his son's best chance to escape prison).

During adventures with the Clary's Grove Boys, Abraham repressed his brooding side. He never seemed cut off, as if his fellows were not there. He was always there to prove he could jump higher, run faster, swim swifter, and out-wrestle most anyone, even if he looked comically gawky. His legendary feats included lifting a thousand pounds with a harness. He could hold a seven-pound ax by one hand, with the arm perpendicular to his body, for minutes without limb or weapon flickering. He would pull off that trick for amazed Executive Mansion coworkers in the last year of his presidency. Always he excelled without bragging, never pushing compatriots' noses into the wounding fact of their physical inferiority.

Laughter helped. Everything always reminded him of a story, often sending the Boys into hysterics. Remember the time, he would ask, when the drunk thought he was pumping water for washing? He was actually pumping another drunk's arm, who covered the pumper with vomit. When the first reeking drunk was later asked, "what in the world is the matter," the imbiber replied that "you ought to have seen me before I was washed" up.[7]

Lincoln comically acted out his words. He was the drunk who pumped; he was the drunk who was pumped; he was the crowd that held its nose. Alone among America's greatest statesmen, he started out as a towering wrestler and a champion distributor of proletariat smut.

But Lincoln was hardly a Clary's Grove Boy. His other necessary partisans, the town's wealthier members, also relished him. Lincoln rarely drank, never smoked, seldom cursed, and infrequently ate with gusto. Like his Puritan forebearers, he was a prudish ascetic in many ways but with this crucial difference: He never rubbed sinners' faces in their outrages. The Boys felt he was never their critic. The establishment felt he was never Jack Armstrong. It was the way to be puritanical—and widely popular—on the egalitarian, yet not-so-equal frontier.

Upper-class admiration started in the same place as underclass affection: with shocked appreciation of unexpected skill. Just as plebeians never thought that the ungainly newcomer could toss their little giant, so the refined never thought that Lincoln's twang would contest cultivated opinions. The first startled convert and New Salem's cofounder, James Rutledge, relished his Literary and Debating Society. The somewhat sophisticated Rutledge had never dreamed that a passionate wrestler and crude comic would enter his society's doorway.

He instead witnessed the rustic ambling inside. The newcomer asked to speak. With permission reluctantly granted, Lincoln gave them not the expected (and dreaded) "humorous story." Instead, he presented an "argument so pithy and forcible that all were amazed." More filled "Abe's head than wit and fun," Rutledge told his wife that night. "He lacked" only "culture."[8]

The young New Salem shopkeeper coveted his own version of the missing boon. When not tending to Offutt's properties or regaling the Boys with yet another tale, the blab-school product pursued higher learning, astonishing the town's few high school graduates. In the open air, he absorbed borrowed volumes blab-school style, slowly reading and speaking, rereading and repeating, until he laboriously learned and never forgot the strange words.

Lincoln had some help with the strangest words from the perfectly named Mentor Graham, the local schoolteacher and only a few years older than his prize "pupil." Graham later exaggerated his role in the apparent country bumpkin's mounting cultivation. Abraham accomplished most of the learning by himself, miles from Graham's out-of-town door, giving "self-made" yet another illustration.

The self-education never soared far into the highest culture. Lincoln almost never read novels, then a rising form of sophisticated expression. He read few plays, with the exception of Shakespeare's (whose characters' brooding soliloquies fit uncannily with Lincoln's gloomy meditations). He did relish romantic poetry (Burns was a special favorite), and he wrote a bit of it himself. But music was never a passion, nor fine arts, nor history beyond the American political epic.

When he became a lawyer, he evolved into a fine practical attorney, not a deep legal philosopher. When he contemplated his well-read Bible, he little heeded doctrinal disputes. The exception: He sometimes brooded over whether fate determines practical men's actions. More often he pled for practical learning. He urged semi-literate farmers to study advanced agricultural tactics. Their grimy labor would then yield richer fruits.

Mentor Graham told him that sound grammar led to sounder rhetoric. So Lincoln secured a copy of Samuel Kirkham's *English Grammar* (1829) and dutifully memorized the tome. Grammar's severe rationality appealed to Abraham's logical practicality and gave his persistent "aints" a more coherent persuasion. James Rutledge and fellow upper-crust New Salemites took notice.

Within months of arriving in New Salem, Lincoln had become a universal charmer. With no affectation or even strategy, he had found the ideal of an aspiring frontier politician. He was from but not of the rednecks, increasingly of but never from the cultivated. He courted the smelliest while never, ever, condemning their smell. He impressed the smartest while never, ever calling them better.

He happened upon his ideal place to impress when he wandered into the local New Salem courtroom, Justice of the Peace Bowling Green presiding. Green, perhaps the heaviest man in town ("Pot" was his nickname), carried his legal knowledge as lightly as Lincoln displayed his grammar. Green's contempt for pretentiousness was as soaring as his half brother's (Jack Armstrong!).

"Pot" was also Lincoln's unofficial brother as frontier humorist. New Salem's justice of the peace found this devotee of his courtroom hilarious. Lincoln would listen to a court proceeding intently and capture its gist immediately. When Green asked, his new pet would pronounce a slang version of the court's proper judgment in his high-pitched twang, while his gestures perfectly mimicked earnest lawyers. It was just the way, with just the same impact, that he had perfectly imitated a Sunday sermon. Bowling Green could not get enough of the fellow.

Soon, "Pot" was not just laughing. Lincoln became, with Green's permission, poor pleaders' unpaid "attorney." "Honest Abe" drafted deeds, composed receipts, and distributed legal advice. Between chuckles from the learned judge and gratitude from uneducated Jack Armstrongs, Lincoln had found his first way to become more than non–Tom Lincoln. In his first courtroom, he became Abe Lincoln, Everyman's Lawyer.

Bowling Green became among the first to urge Abraham to become everyman's candidate for office. "Pot" was delighted when Lincoln ran for the legislature with a largely internal improvement platform, seductive to all New Salem residents. Yet how could this newcomer, dazzling in the tiny town but unknown beyond it, win a Sangamon County election?

4

Providence here intruded on Lincoln's biography for the first time since the future hero inadvertently landed in Stephen A. Douglas's future state. The precipitating event could have occurred anytime. But the Sauk and Fox Indians picked this moment, six weeks after Lincoln had announced his candidacy for the state legislature and four months before the election, to provoke the so-called Black Hawk War with the U.S. government. In April 1832, Native American warriors, having angrily departed their U.S. lands, returned to Illinois, Iowa, and Wisconsin, seeking a fairer settlement. When militiamen massed against the "invasion," Lincoln joined the army and spread his political potential beyond New Salem.[9]

Each local militia regiment, with around seventy men enrolled, elected its own captain. The election featured a *non*-secret ballot. The regiment's volunteers lined up behind their favorite candidates (as if choosing teams in a latter-day softball game). At the insistence of Jack Armstrong and the Clary's Grove Boys, Lincoln ran against Bill Kirkpatrick, a Springfield mill owner whose imperious attitudes annoyed scruffy folk.[10]

Of the two candidates, Kirkpatrick owned $^{19}/_{20}$ of the possessions. But on April 21, 1832, Lincoln received three-fourths of the votes. The victor would win plusher offices. But no "success," he later declared, "gave him so much satisfaction."[11] In his first election, he had stumbled upon his second way to become more than non–Tom Lincoln: Abraham Lincoln, Popular Politician.

Impressed Black Hawk War compatriots comprised a who's who of coming Illinois notables and a few imminent national figures too. National comers included Zachary Taylor, whom Congressman Lincoln would be among the first to nominate for the presidency; Robert Anderson, commander of Fort Sumter during President Lincoln's first Civil War decision; and future Confederate president Jefferson Davis, who would order Anderson to be blasted out of Lincoln's Fort Sumter.

Local movers and shakers who here first noticed Lincoln included his first two law partners: John Todd Stuart and Stephen Logan; his most powerful future Illinois Whig allies: John J. Hardin, Joseph Gillespie, and Edward Baker; the men who would soon hire him as Sangamon County deputy surveyor: John Calhoun and Thomas Neale; and two titans in Springfield, his future hometown: the physician Jacob M. Early and the capitalist Elijah Iles.

Many an American aspirant has climbed on the basis of such early connections, formed in secondary schools and colleges. The Black Hawk War was Lincoln's Harvard, Yale, or Princeton. By the end of the war, New Salem's precocious champion had met and impressed practically all the key players in his imminent local ascent.

Lincoln's contributions to swamping Native Americans had no such significance. His most famous Black Hawk War fight was with a white wrestler (he lost that one). Mosquitoes, he remembered, drew more blood than Black Hawk's warriors. He more vividly recalled burying several scalped whites, victims of the intruders' fury.

But mostly he spent some eighty days marching bloodlessly about. For his wartime service, the federal government paid $125 (plus 160 Iowa acres later). His heirs would still later sell his Iowa lands for $1,800 in late nineteenth-century cash (about $47,000 in early twenty-first-century dollars). Captain Lincoln's maiden electoral race had netted not only his first wider political notice but also his fledgling materialistic climb up Horatio Alger's ladder.

5

But could the twenty-three-year-old parlay his Black Hawk War captaincy into a Sangamon County legislative seat in the August 6, 1832, elections? On July 10, 1832, when Major Robert Anderson mustered his future commander out of the federal army, Lincoln had only twenty-six days left to race home plus campaign beyond New Salem. Yet the state's primitive conveyances, the reason for his transportation schemes, precluded speed over the 240 miles.

When Lincoln belatedly arrived, he had less than two weeks left to campaign. His message was as curtailed as his canvass. "I am humble Abraham Lincoln," he said, and "my politics are short and sweet, like the old Woman's dance."[12] Shorter still were his opportunities to speak about Sangamon River improvements beyond New Salem.

The election results demonstrated his intense but largely local following. In his village, he captured 277 of 300 votes (92.3 percent). Beyond New Salem, he won only 380 of 8,015 ballots (4.7 percent). With his wider weakness undercutting his local strength, he finished eighth of thirteen Sangamon County candidates. Only the top four aspirants secured state legislative seats. Still, few twenty-three-year-old beginners ever suffered so promising a political loss.[13] In contrast to future dispiriting shortfalls in political conventions and state legislatures, Honest Abe would never again suffer defeat when folk who knew him best balloted at local crossroads.

Less auspicious than the twenty-three-year-old's only local election setback was his investment of his first governmental paycheck. He unwisely poured his $125 from the Black Hawk War into that retail partnership with the inebriated William Franklin Berry. More unwisely still, the partners thrust their New Salem country store into that competition with Samuel Hill's established enterprise.

A year earlier, the Black Hawk War had rescued Lincoln from Denton Offutt's debacle. Now his entrepreneurial conqueror, Samuel Hill, suffered a governmental setback that invited Lincoln's economic comeback. Hill had become New Salem's postmaster for a typical American rural reason. Provincial post offices best thrived as part of general stores. But Hill spent too much energy devastating the Lincoln-Berry store and too much time peddling liquor to New Salem males. His female post office customers especially protested.

Hill resigned as postmaster shortly after the Lincoln-Berry store collapsed. On May 7, 1833, Lincoln, unemployed Whig, secured appointment to Hill's old post from a Democrat, President Andrew Jackson! No willing Democrats surfaced, in this Whig-dominated tiny community, to forestall Lincoln's appointment. With Hill shedding his unhappy governmental career and Lincoln dropping his disastrous merchant career, New Salem's ultimately two most successful men, now good friends and mutual admirers, straightened out their respective roads ahead.

Lincoln averaged $45 yearly during his three years as New Salem postmaster. The pittance (about $1,450 yearly in early twenty-first-century dollars) required supplementary income. Lincoln clerked a little in Hill's store, swung his ax a little for rural friends such as "Uncle Jimmy" Short (Mentor Graham's neighbor), and earned a few more government nickels (a dollar here for clerking at elections, $2.50 there for taking tally sheets to Springfield).[14]

The postmaster's greatest reward from delivering the mail came not from slight salaries but from educational opportunities. His post office duties consumed only an hour or so, two days a week. That left more time to read than he had enjoyed as a store clerk. Better still, his post office received some choice reading material: America's newly booming political newspapers.

A revolution in printing methods had furthered cheap publications for the masses. This so-called "penny journalism" cost voters only pennies for partisan amusements. The mails brought penny sheets from all directions. Postmaster Lincoln read many papers before delivering them. His favorites included all Whig newspapers and especially the local Whig sheet, the *Sangamo Journal*. By the end of 1833, New Salem's consumer of everyone's newspapers stood self-educated enough to pursue higher political posts.

His new "uniform" signified his new direction. Seldom seen now were his ax and the foxed britches that clung six inches above his ankles. Predominate now became the gentleman's stovepipe hat that ascended eight inches above his head. New Salem's new postman stuffed his new hat with letters and newspapers. Soon, legal briefs and state papers would line this "briefcase." Increasingly, his hat would become his symbol. The giant, no longer appearing to be all legs, now looked closer to all head, largely self-trained to tower.

6

His cerebral promise won him a governmental promotion toward the end of 1833, six months after he became New Salem's postmaster. The county surveyor, John Calhoun, and his assistant, Thomas Neale, needed an adjutant to help survey roads, woods, and hamlets in Sangamon County's suddenly (and briefly) booming northern portion. Since no trained surveyor could be found, Calhoun and Neale needed a quick learner of the required geometry and trigonometry.

Calhoun and Neale, both Democrats, knew no local Jacksonian who aspired to conquer the skill. But they did know Whigs' Lincoln from—where else?—the Black Hawk War. Lincoln assured them that he could quickly learn surveying. So for the second time, Andrew Jackson's appointment gave Jacksonians' ultimately most feared opponent a leg up.

Sangamon County's new deputy surveyor trained himself remarkably quickly. He devoured Robert Gibson's thick, detailed *The Theory and Practice of Surveying* and Abel Flint's thin, demanding *Geometry and Trigonometry, Together with a Treatise on Surveying.* Once again, Mentor Graham helped the self-learner a little (and bragged about his exaggerated aid a lot). But once again, Lincoln mostly blabbed the strange new language, alone and aloud, slowly memorizing it. After mastering the odd jargon in six exhausting weeks, Lincoln bought the strange sixty-six-foot chains, staffs, and compasses and stepped upon a promising path toward economic success—and political triumph.

During the several boom years before the Panic of 1837, when a landowner purchased settled acres or an unsettled domain, value partly depended on precise boundaries. Tom Lincoln had suffered Kentucky bankruptcy partly because much of "his" nonsurveyed land turned out to be others' possessions. His son's surveys helped preclude Illinois versions of the peril.

At this brief economic moment, a fortune depended on which impeded Illinois river would be improved enough to make which Illinois village the next Cincinnati. Travelling salesmen offered East Coast purchasers a potential midwestern bonanza. Today, buy a little town plot in "New Boston" for pennies, chanted tempters in places like old Boston. Tomorrow, internal improvements could make your guess worth thousands. As with the Black Hawk War, Lincoln had chanced into the right passing phenomenon.

In the first half of 1834, the cry for surveying in Sangamon County became overwhelming. The Democrats' John Calhoun had chosen the right Whig to meet the demand. After mastering the exacting surveying science almost overnight, the inexperienced surveyor had the other experience necessary to put abstract theory into precise practice. The terrain in central Illinois, as Lincoln and his father had discovered, half-resembled Indiana forestland. Few Illinoisans had spent so many hours dodging forest burrs and briars (and snakes!).

Lincoln's first survey netted him the fixings for yet another new "uniform," the one he painfully remembered that he would need. In early January 1834, he surveyed Russell Godbey's spread, six miles north of New Salem. Godbey paid him with two buckskins. Lincoln took the payment to Hannah Armstrong, Jack's wife. Mrs. Armstrong used the tough skins to "fox" Lincoln's jeans.

Now familiarly clad, Abraham Lincoln was back laboring in the woods, albeit this time excelling with his brains and compasses rather than with his leverage and axes. Farmers gladly paid the expert woodsman to show where trespassers must not hack their timber. Land speculators gladly paid still more to show where squatters must not invade their lot.

From January 1834 onward for three years, Lincoln laid out Huron, Petersburg, Bath, Albany, and New Boston. Still, his largest reward, as for his post office services, was not in dollars earned but in political prospects advanced. Just as the mails brought him a treasure of political newspapers, so the surveying gave him a wealth of political contacts. Lincoln needed votes beyond New Salem to win his second try for a Sangamon County legislative seat.

An untimely economic setback almost precluded attempting to reverse his political loss. Because of his "national debt," that clinging legacy of his misadventures with William Franklin Berry, he had had to borrow cash to buy surveying equipment. In early 1834, a frontiersman, holding his note, demanded immediate repayment. A court thrust the hapless debtor into bankruptcy. An auctioneer sold his surveying tools.

Lincoln's popularity in New Salem saved him. "Uncle Jimmy" Short, one of Russell Godbey's and Mentor Graham's neighbors north of town, could not bear Abraham's plight. Short bought Lincoln's surveying equipment and presented it back to the debtor. The temporarily defrocked surveyor repaid "Uncle Jimmy" soon and much more later. In 1861, new President Lincoln would hand "Uncle Jimmy" a patronage plum worth one thousand dollars per year. Of such little deals are big American political tales spun.

With his compasses and chains restored, Lincoln spent the first half of 1834 accumulating Sangamon County surveying commissions and political chits. Armed by new acquaintances beyond New Salem, at midyear Lincoln announced his legislative candidacy. While he still urged state internal improvements, he conducted, he reported, "more of a hand-shaking campaign than anything else."[15] Beyond shaking hands, the campaigner plunged into the July fields, helping to pick and shuck corn. He picked twice as fast as even such an expert as "Uncle Jimmy."

He found that potential voters relished his jokes even more than his labor. Have you heard, he would ask, the one about the two boys who chased a bear? The boldest lad clutched a hind leg. His companion climbed a tree. After quite the "tussle," the "exhausted" warrior "cried out in alarm, 'Bill, for God's sake come down and help me let this darned bear go!'"[16]

This physical giant was so natural, so rustic, so devoid of airs. Yet this sparsely educated humorist had mastered difficult surveying so quickly. In 1832, few voters beyond New Salem had heard of the newcomer. In 1834, rich and poor folk throughout Sangamon County marveled that they could elect a prodigy.

At the August election, the four highest vote gatherers won Sangamon County legislative seats. Lincoln finished second with 1,376 votes, more than double his 1832 tally. He collected only fourteen fewer votes than the leader.[17] Merely twenty-five years old (he would be the second-youngest legislator), he had become a one-man New Salem government—postmaster, surveyor, and now legislator too. These positions combined paid him around $450 yearly ($50 for delivering the mail, approximately $150 for surveying, $250 as a legislator—something like $12,000 annually in early twenty-first-century dollars).[18] After entrepreneurial failure, he had traveled the political road toward economic competency.

7

This prototype American self-made man remained a sport among Horatio Alger achievers. Few were as self-educated—or as hampered by a father's contempt for schooling. Fewer had suffered such a business catastrophe. Most had triumphed as entrepreneurs before they gave politics a thought—if they ever conceived of joining the (as many thought) lesser calling.

Only unusual circumstances gave Lincoln his rare political (and thus economic) chance. Even on the frontier, few American communities were as underdeveloped as Lincoln's fleeting New Salem. Few displayed such a scant hierarchy or so few promising lads. Elsewhere, few Democrats had to fill offices with Whigs or fill mentally demanding positions with scantily educated youngsters.

The timing of Lincoln's opportunities proved equally exceptional. If the Black Hawk War had occurred a year earlier, Lincoln would have missed his precocious army captaincy and its political boost. If his surveying had transpired several years later, the Panic of 1837 would have precluded the frontier craze that multiplied his 1834 voters beyond New Salem.

If he had been a late eighteenth-century politician, aristocratic elitism would have precluded a commoner's soaring. If he had been a late nineteenth-century politico, the highly developed two-party system would have stymied an impoverished stranger's lonely vault. Instead he enjoyed the beginning years of crassly popular politics, when President Andrew Jackson proclaimed every Tom, Dick, and Harry a potential governor. No Jacksonian better fit that Jacksonian ideal than New Salem's Whig plebeian.

The conjunction of right place with right time helps explain why Lincoln swiftly transcended his first adult crisis. But not many Americans in any era have been superior in so many ways and so uncommonly modest too; so physically powerful and so mentally precocious; such a talented jokester and so superb a popular campaigner. Because he had fit himself skillfully into an unusual time and place, the new legislator might now further his dream for American self-achievers. He could help public government develop the infrastructure that would open opportunity for private climbers.

5

The Rise and Fall of a State Legislator

❖❖❖

Abraham Lincoln's eight years in the Illinois legislature, often slighted and even called a hack's folly, assuredly came streaked with failure. His legislative mission, establishing state-aided canals and railroads, crashed so painfully that six years would pass before he again achieved political office. That failed quest for local internal improvements may seem unimportant compared to his later achievement of a Union saved and emancipated. But the lessons learned from his first political debacle guided his strategies toward latter-day triumph. Moreover, his fumbling first attempts for state railroads and canals throw perspective on his subsequent sure-handed quest for a national economic transformation. That pivot would become a key reason, second only to his redirections on saving Union/ending slavery, why a much longer Age of Lincoln would replace the shorter-lived Age of Jackson.

1

On December 1, 1834, the twenty-five-year-old rookie legislator, decked out in his first businessman's suit, strode into sleepy Vandalia's fraying state hall, the southern Illinois site of fifteen years of past legislative inaction.[1] The initial contact between vigorous newcomer and fading stage anticipated the legislative drama two years hence. Then Lincoln and other young sports would prod tired veterans into a monster debt for state internal improvements and a productive move of the state capital to Springfield.

Abraham's suit on his first legislative day, like his stovepipe hat when he became New Salem's postmaster, confirmed a new identity, beyond non–Tom

Lincoln. Lincoln had borrowed sixty dollars for the attire from Coleman Smoot, New Salem justice of the peace.[2] The new lender epitomized richer fellows who joined poorer citizens in speeding the Clary's Grove Boys' playmate into the ruling class.

The new debt illuminated why the impatient debtor experienced initial wild rides. Lincoln's weakness for borrowing, always a dangerous temptation for aspirants who cannot wait, had helped fund, then had helped destroy, his New Salem store. That same appetite for debt would nourish, then sabotage his thrust as Illinois legislator. Only this time, the gambling entrepreneur who had crashed against Samuel Hill's store would learn every inch of the folly.

Never again would Lincoln be confused with a plunger. Always his future story would feature precise location of the center of the road. His misadventures as a careless legislative spender would especially inform his care as a rising antislavery moderate.

2

Lincoln's future law partner, William Herndon, called his colleague's determination to rise a "little engine that knew no rest."[3] Strike that "little." Then you have it.

The young Lincoln craved, he told his best friend, Joshua Speed, not material wealth but linking his "name with the events transpiring in" his "day." He especially desired some accomplishment "that would redound to the interest of his fellow man." After his January 1, 1863, Emancipation Proclamation, he and Speed would share a sublime moment, remembering what had long ago been said and what had at last been painfully achieved.[4]

Before, during, and after antislavery battles, the Whigs' Lincoln saw nothing sublime about Andrew Jackson's conventional American wisdom: The best government governs least. Lincoln wanted more than a government that punished "crimes" and "non-performance of contracts." Even if "all men were just," they would "need government" to do what individuals "can not do *at all* or . . . *so well* . . . for themselves."[5]

Illinois's woeful interior transportation exemplified individuals' inability to do enough for themselves. As Lincoln had learned aboard *The Talisman*, no private entrepreneur could untangle the Sangamon River. Dependence on an ornery river limited even so experienced a capitalist as New Salem's Samuel Hill and doomed the inexperienced Abraham Lincoln.

Since entrepreneurs could not do it all, government had to help build canals and railroads. Then the masses and the capitalists would flock. Lincoln meant to be the rags-to-riches politician who helped backwater Illinois to spawn

American wealth and leaders. It was an incredible ambition, considering that in 1830, Illinois ranked only eleventh in northern population, with fewer people than all but two southern states and equally trifling national politicians.

Lincoln, Whig to his heels, expounded the Illinois version of a new nationalism for an age of transportation revolution. His economic nationalism was thicker than the Founding Fathers' variety. In their age, the nation's economy had been too fragmented, men's consciousness too localized, pride in provincial accomplishment too overriding for national economic programs beyond the rudimentary.

The Founding Fathers' thinner nationalism changed little even after being dangerously exposed. England almost reclaimed its former colonies in the War of 1812, after weak national sinews almost doomed the young republic. Still, Jeffersonians' swift return to state's rights comforts aborted their corrective 1816–17 nationalistic legislation. Their national tariff to protect infant American industry barely survived the 1820s. Their Second National Bank of the United States perished in 1836. Their national program of internal improvements dribbled out in the 1840s.

Climactically, their incomplete National Road mocked John C. Calhoun's February 4, 1817, exhortation that Congress "perfect" a national "system of roads and canals." The nation, cried South Carolina's very temporary high nationalist, must "conquer space."[6] Fifteen years later, Calhoun, arch nullifier, would lead his generation's retreat to local space.

At midcentury, only state governments had significantly conquered space. The first epic conqueror, New York's Governor DeWitt Clinton, presided over the Erie Canal in 1825. This 363-mile waterway between Albany on the Hudson River and Buffalo on Lake Erie, finished in eight years, collected enough tolls to pay for its $7 million construction during the ensuing nine years.

Tolls comprised a minuscule fraction of the canal's dividends. The artificial waterway provided the missing avenue between New York City's Hudson River and the Midwest's Great Lakes. The new national trade connections rained wealth on the state's merchants, cities, towns, and farmers. New York City became a national economic titan. Migrants poured into the nationalized state to share the nationalized bounty. The ensuing canal craze also boosted wealth in Pennsylvania, Massachusetts, Indiana, and Ohio.[7]

Interior states without canals lagged, including Illinois. Some great national waterways—Lake Michigan, the Wabash River, the Ohio, and the Mississippi—connected the eastern, southern, and western edges of Lincoln's state to national markets. Except for the Illinois River, however, waterways in the state's center barely touched the lifeblood on the extremities. The Sangamon River, a typical example, lurched from an isolated midstate beginning

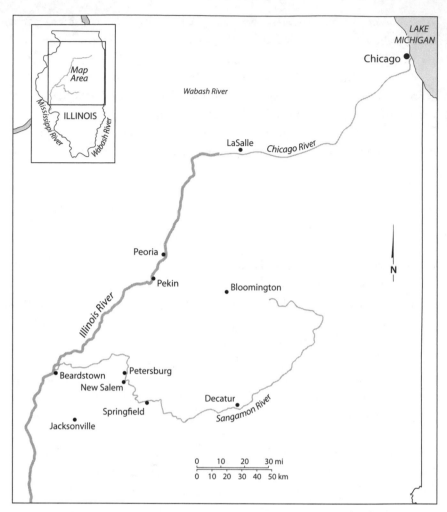

The crippling Chicago and Sangamon Rivers, before internal improvements.
(Compare maps on pages 62 and 126.)

and splayed in many directions before staggering into the easily navigable
Illinois River and then into the supremely navigable Mississippi. So, too,
the Chicago River could not decide which way to course in its fitful journey
between Lake Michigan and the Illinois River, thus crippling Chicago's pre–
internal improvements economy.

Central Illinois's nonconnections with national commerce afflicted Lincoln's Sangamon River environs as severely as Chicago. The sluggish Sangamon had moored Lincoln on New Salem's milldam. The river's meandering
course to the Illinois River and its nonconnection with the Wabash had
poorly enriched his New Salem store. Settlers had scantily peopled the central

Illinois plots that he surveyed. The do-little legislature had little improved the disconnected infrastructure.

In the face of central Illinois's transportation poverty (and thus its backwater stagnation), young Lincoln meant to assault legislative inertia. Illinois's *"fertility* of soil," he told fellow legislators shortly after joining them, "surpasses every other spot of equal extent upon the face of the globe," endowing us with a greater potential for "agricultural wealth and population." The boon will make the "burden" of paying for government-boosted internal improvement systems "of no sort of consequence." By making Illinois of great consequence, he later told Josh Speed, he meant to be his state's DeWitt Clinton.[8]

That Clinton indeed! Precanal-era New York had been one of the richest northern states. Post–Erie Canal Illinois was one of the poorest. Illinois's annual state budget was seventy thousand dollars. Its annual deficit was twelve thousand dollars. Canals and railroads that could bind it into national commerce would cost many millions. How could the strapped state legislature afford even baby steps toward creating America's newest Empire State?

3

Lincoln's first legislature, 1834–35, debated two solutions. Illinois could borrow the money. Or the Prairie State could beg federal funds. Lincoln, Whig nationalist, introduced a resolution that asked the federal government for at least one of every five dollars received from selling its Illinois lands.[9]

Other legislators preferred to sell ex-federal acres that the state already owned. In 1822, as the Erie Canal connection westward from the Hudson River to the Great Lakes neared completion, the federal government had offered Illinois a huge landed expanse (ultimately 284,000 acres) to help the state build a canal westward from Chicago and Lake Michigan. That artificial waterway could bypass the contrary Chicago River and thus at last viably connect the Windy City to the Illinois River and the Mississippi.

For twelve years, the state dithered about how its federal acres could finance the watery connection. Few acres could be sold until buyers believed a canal would be dug. No digging could begin until the state raised seed money. Little cash came into the coffers when the state offered its bonds without guaranteeing payment of interest and principal.

Lincoln's first legislature broke this logjam with its Illinois and Michigan Canal Act. The "Michigan" referred to Lake Michigan, lapping the heels of barely populated Chicago on the contrary Chicago River. The "Illinois" referred to the fast-flowing Illinois River, joined by the erratically flowing Chicago River and subsequently joining the mighty Mississippi.

Thanks to the Erie Canal, the five midwestern Great Lakes, including Lake Michigan, enjoyed an open watery avenue to New York City. Thanks to its connection with the Mississippi River, the Illinois River enjoyed an equally open path to New Orleans. But Illinois's interior waterways' chocked connections to the Illinois River were a commercial disaster.

Witness the inadequate Sangamon and exasperating Chicago Rivers. If, however, a canal could bypass the wayward Chicago River between Bridgeport (near Chicago) and La Salle (on the Illinois River), a jackpot rivaling the Erie Canal's might lift the Illinois heartlands. With eyes on that prize, the 1835–36 legislature approved a five-hundred-thousand-dollar bond issue to finance the Illinois and Michigan Canal's initial digging.[10] This time, the state guaranteed payment of the bond's interest and principal. Sangamon County's freshman legislator cherished the apparent breakthrough.

Lincoln's first legislature also chartered the first state bank, to help sell Illinois and Michigan Canal bonds and to help finance sixteen other new internal improvement companies. The incorporated companies included a three-hundred-thousand-dollar Beardstown & Sangamon Canal, projected to make central Illinois's twisting Sangamon at last a straight arrow toward Beardstown on the Illinois River. Lincoln, having steamed up the choked Sangamon from Beardstown on that ill-fated *Talisman* adventure, introduced the bill.

With the act of incorporation in his pocket, the internal improvement apostle sped from the legislative hall to Petersburg, several miles down the dawdling Sangamon River from dwindling New Salem, hoping to sell shares in the new canal company. Lincoln told Petersburg folk that their dollars for shares would avert New Salem's plight. If locals made the Beardstown & Sangamon Canal Company their concern, he claimed, their river would be straightened, steamboats would chug up to Springfield and down the Illinois, and migrants would flock to the new El Dorado.

The orator put a speck of his scant money behind his huge prophecy. With one dollar down, Lincoln bought a five-dollar share in the Beardstown & Sangamon Canal Company. Then he purchased seventeen virgin acres in Huron, the empty town he had surveyed downriver from sleepy Petersburg.

Lincoln here played public and private parts in his model Horatio Alger drama. In the legislature, he helped secure the Beardstown & Sangamon Canal Company's incorporation. Then he advertised the shares and purchased one himself, along with land that would boom if settlers came.

He had created only a paper company. The Beardstown & Sangamon Canal Company, despite his oratory, received only seventy-eight dollars from only sixty-five investors. Although the company had been chartered for three hundred thousand dollars, engineers estimated that straightening the wandering Sangamon, all the way to the Illinois, would cost eight hundred thousand dollars. Lincoln had unfortunately illustrated his own dictum. The public purse had to open very wide before private enterprise could even narrowly flourish.

His first legislature's sole success, the Illinois and Michigan Canal, proved his theory even more convincingly. The company's state-guaranteed bond sold well. Investors also sought the company's cache of long-since-granted federal acres along the canal route. In no longer scarcely populated Chicago, land that had sold for nine thousand dollars per acre early in 1835 brought twenty-five thousand dollars by the end of the year. Illinois land sales, stalled at under a third of a million acres in 1834, leapt to 2 million–plus acres in 1835. The speculations that state-guaranteed borrowing would start infrastructure, and that new settlers would seek new land, and that more land sales would finance more canal miles, and that still more migrants would pour into disappearing empty spaces—well, who would now bet against a seemingly proven fantasy at a mid-1830s moment when the national economy shot up?

4

Not the delighted legislature, and not its enchanted sophomore leader. During his freshman term, Lincoln had realized that his best legislative foot forward must be a step delayed. Before older legislators would follow, he must learn their trade. The freshman's presence had been significant only for a scotched prayer for federal aid and an empty gesture toward a Sangamon River canal. Yet there he stood, from the first moment of his second term, 1836–37, at the forefront of the most important Illinois deliberations until the 1858 Lincoln-Douglas showdown. How had the sophomore put himself in position to seize this moment?

He had risen politically the eccentric Lincoln way. Until his last (1864 presidential) election, Lincoln never rode governmental accomplishments to greater power. Instead, his extraordinary oratorical skills fueled his emergence from obscurity and his comebacks from failure.

His best forward marches came when a series of debates against more famous opponents afforded oratorical opportunities to leapfrog those who underestimated his prowess. So it would be in the 1858 Lincoln-Douglas Debates. So it was in the 1836 Sangamon County election campaign for state legislature, here dubbed the Cavalcade after its special nature.

Fortuitous timing had again handed Lincoln an election opportunity. In 1832, the Black Hawk War had coincidently transpired right after Denton Offutt's New Salem affairs collapsed and right when Lincoln needed notoriety, to make a promising (although losing) first stab at a legislature seat. So, too, the 1836 Cavalcade Debate innovation coincidently came just when Lincoln needed legislators' admiration, to transcend his (1834–35) freshman position on legislative back benches.

The Cavalcade affair, never seen before or after in Lincoln's Illinois, involved horsemen from both parties pounding together across Sangamon County, searching for the next place to dismount and debate. The nine Whigs together comprised the Long Nine. Each Long Niner stood at least six feet tall. Long Niners and shorter Democrats braved hungry mosquitoes in the morning, howling wolves at night, and cutting barbs in afternoon debates.

They stopped first on July 16 in a town displaying a name with a proper historic ring, Athens. They stopped finally on July 30 in a town about to enjoy a large history, Springfield. Sangamon County Whigs and Democrats agreed that the next legislature ought to replace Vandalia with Springfield as state capital. Concurring on little else, they slashed each other in every little village or large farm where they dismounted and voters appeared.

Lincoln, the longest Long Niner in height and among the shortest in previous repute, soared to the top in Whigs' esteem (and Democrats' fury) with each Cavalcade stop. Exchanges between rivals had to be short, so everyone had an oratorical moment. The necessity precluded Lincoln's oratorical weakness—his tendency to wander in longer speeches. The format also maximized his oratorical strengths: his quick tales, swift repartee, and lightning capacity to strip an issue to its essence.

During the Cavalcade, he swung particularly sharp verbal elbows. He denounced Jacob Early, his commander for a month during the Black Hawk War, as a scurrilous demagogue. He slashed Richard Quinton, one of Illinois Democrats' favorites, as a scandalous politico. He disparaged Martin Van Buren, imminent U.S. president, as Andrew Jackson's toady. All the while, he called a Whiggish activist government the savior of a nation and a state in dire need of economic development.

As usual in his surges, his unexpected talents made his leaps seem higher. Having been a usually silent nonfactor in his first legislative session, he now looked as nonconsequential. His high-pitched voice was squeaky, his gestures jerky, and his clothes floppy. Yet his verbal blows stung more than anyone else's.

At the Springfield climax, Cavalcade Democrats asked a noncandidate to quash their chief tormentor. Springfield's George Forquer, fifteen years older than Lincoln, had once been an upstart himself. In the 1820s, when he favored Whig solutions, Forquer had been successively Illinois secretary of state and attorney general. In the early 1830s, still a Whig, he had become an important state senator, especially as a precocious champion of state internal improvements.

George Forquer had lately quit the legislature and switched political parties. Almost immediately, the Democrats' President Andrew Jackson had given the turncoat his reward. When the ex-Whig assumed office as the register of the Springfield U.S. Land Office, he swept up the state's largest federal sinecure, worth three thousand dollars yearly (about seventy-nine thousand dollars yearly in early twenty-first-century dollars).

On July 30, Forquer finished his new Democratic mates' Cavalcade campaign. "This young man," thundered the veteran while pointing at Lincoln, "must be taken down." While claiming to be "sorry that the task devolves upon me," Forquer ridiculed the silent Whig, calmly standing with folded arms ten feet away. Revenged (they thought) Democrats roared approval.

Lincoln came prepared. When riding toward Springfield the previous day, he had happened upon a novelty. Atop Springfield's best frame house soared the county's first lightning rod. Lincoln asked how this safeguard worked and who might be the owner? It happened to be George Forquer.

Lincoln knew that nothing beat an unforgettable physical symbol to make an unforgettable oratorical point. Twenty-two years hence, he would declare, immediately prior to the Lincoln-Douglas Debates, that "a house divided cannot stand." He now made Forquer's lightning rod the high point of the Cavalcade extravaganza.

Forquer had "commenced his speech," recalled the Whig counterpuncher, "by saying that this young man would have to be taken down." I am indeed a "young man," affirmed the twenty-seven-year-old, in a politician's "tricks and trades." And he "would rather die now" than, like his elder, change my political party to receive an office worth three thousand dollars per year, and then "have to erect a lightning rod" over my house, "to protect a guilty Conscience from an offended God."[11]

Two days later, Sangamon County voters confirmed their new leader. While every Long Niner won reelection, Abraham Lincoln received the most ballots.[12] He now dreamed of becoming, as a legislative sophomore, as precocious a lawmaker as he was a Cavalcade orator—and at the moment when his favorite internal improvement laws might triumph.

5

That dream swiftly frayed. In the first December days of the monumental 1836–37 legislative session, a younger legislator stole the show. Stephen A.

Douglas, age twenty-three and a freshman representative, moved to seize the internal improvement issue that Lincoln aspired to own.[13]

Douglas had the background to leapfrog older opponents. A Vermonter and briefly a New Yorker before moving to Illinois at age twenty, Douglas had experienced a preteen's three months per year in common school, a teenager's two years in an academy, and an almost-adult's six months of study in a New York State law office. Having arrived in Illinois almost as penniless as Lincoln, Douglas thought of himself as a self-made man. A resentful Lincoln thought of the five-foot, four-inch Little Giant as born with a silver spoon in his mouth.

The more polished migrant could soon afford more than silver spoons. Upon arriving in Illinois, Douglas endured only a few weeks, where Lincoln suffered many months, as a frontier bottom-dweller. Securing his law degree at age twenty-one, the Little Giant won election as a $250-per-year state's attorney at twenty-two and as a freshman state legislator at twenty-three.

The freshman was instinctively the better legislator than the sophomore Cavalcade hero. Douglas had no intention of emulating Lincoln's rookie term on the back benches. The Little Giant waited only a week into the legislative session to present a resolution, initiating the term's biggest issue.

His initiative called for three integrated internal improvement projects.[14] Douglas urged completing the Illinois and Michigan Canal, thereby connecting Lake Michigan (and thus Chicago) with the Illinois River (and thus with the Mississippi River's New Orleans). Then he would build two railroads, crossing each other at center state. The first, to be called the Illinois Central Railroad, would run the long way down the state's length, connecting the Illinois and Michigan Canal (and thus Chicago) up north with the Ohio River down south. The second, to be called the Northern Cross Railroad, would cross the short way across the state's width, uniting the Mississippi River on Illinois's western extremity (and thus St. Louis) with the Wabash River on the state's eastern edge. He would thereby fuse every disconnected corner of the state (and its especially unconnected center) into a national transportation network.

Two months later, when lawmakers passed an unsystematic version of Douglas's systematic design, the package of decrees came to be called the System.[15] The misnamed February 27, 1837, enactments included authorization for eight railroads with 1,350 total miles of track, blown up from Douglas's two railroads with 600 miles. Where Douglas would improve two rivers, lawmakers leapt to seven. Where Douglas proposed little else, legislators piled on a $250,000 mail highway and $200,000 to be divided between the sixteen (of sixty) counties untouched by the System's internal improvements.

Worse, where Douglas's blueprint ran from one established center (Chicago) to another (St. Louis), following DeWitt Clinton principles, Illinois's would-be Clintons, including the new pride of Sangamon County, sought to make village nonentities into Illinois competitors. The legislators' projected railroad would bypass both Chicago and St. Louis, in the futile effort to blow tiny Galena and Alton into Mississippi River centers. Their decentralized nonsystem authorized any community anywhere near a projected eventual route to start building state-financed transportation.

To pay for this grab bag, the legislature authorized $10 million in new state-guaranteed bonds. The Illinois and Michigan Canal, retaining independent status, received permission to issue another $500,000 bond. The state's debt soon approached $15 million (about $400 million in early twenty-first-century wealth).

I have "never for a moment," protested Douglas, "dreamt of such a wild and extravagant scheme."[16] Still, on the final roll call tally, the Little Giant reluctantly voted for the extravagance. Lincoln, with no reluctance, also voted aye.

Lincoln's enthusiasm for a mountain of debt belied his 1836 campaign letter. He there had urged federal rather than state funding. He had wished to distribute "proceeds of the [federal] sales of the public lands to the several states, to enable our state, in common with others, to dig canals and construct railroads, without borrowing money and paying interest."[17]

That campaign pledge echoed his 1834–35 resolution as freshman legislator, asking the federal government for one-fifth of its proceeds from selling Illinois acres. Throughout his acceptances of more and more state debt, he believed that internal improvement dollars ought to come more and more from federal funds. Why then did Lincoln help lead the scramble to overload Douglas's streamlined craft with swamping state debt?

He fell for Illinois's public borrowing partly because private borrowing had been his signature early-adult weakness, partly because the laissez-faire President Andrew Jackson rejected federal boosts to individual states, and partly because more state funding would boost Springfield's new dream. By spreading benefits to more counties than Douglas proposed, the Long Niners collected support for Springfield as the state's new capital. Their winning legislative tactic has been saddled with a nonwinsome label: "logrolling." According to posterity's ugly definition, logrolling means you vote for my bill, I'll vote for yours, and the two laws will serve both our interests (and no one else's).

That scoff at "logrolling," however, distorts the word's original meaning and Lincoln's intent in 1836–37. The word commenced as a description of frontier neighbors' aid to each other. You help roll my log to my homesite, went the understanding. Then I'll help roll your log to your homestead. Thus we will together transform our non-neighborhood of homeless frontiersmen into a neighborhood of log homes.

Lincoln had the original meaning of "logrolling" in mind when he gave his vote to another county's internal improvements and sought its vote for his capital location. He conceived that with the new capital at Springfield, in the dead center of both the state and the System, Illinois's underpopulated core would fill with eager frontiersmen. Douglas, residing in Jacksonville, situated on no river, cared little about making the Sangamon River flow faster or Springfield the state capital. He still cared enough about creating state transportation to accept, reluctantly, Lincoln's bloated System.

These two eventually epic antagonists thus started as brothers, sort of. The uneasy brotherhood lasted only as long as the System seemed viable, which was only two years longer than Douglas's one term in the legislature. While the System collapsed, Douglas raced from his brief legislative interlude to become George Forquer's successor as register of the Springfield U.S. Land Office, then to a seat on the Illinois Supreme Court, then to the U.S. House of Representatives.

Meanwhile, Lincoln remained mired in the state House of Representatives, attempting to repair his devastated System. The failed repairman came to nurse a bitter jealousy of Illinois's most triumphant youngster. The Lincoln-Douglas epic, like everything else in Abraham Lincoln's plunges and recoveries, hardly started with slavery issues or came disassociated from internal improvements.

6

Abraham Lincoln became the most important casualty of the System, even though he was far from the only midwife. In 1837, at least two dozen legislators fought for its passage as hard. If Lincoln had happened to fall fatally from his horse during the Cavalcade campaign, the same System would have swept through the legislature (and the same designation of Springfield as capital would have been approved).

Lincoln's designation as arch advocate of a disastrous legislative scheme would come after the System became a calamity. But signs of Lincoln's vulnerability abounded even when most legislators considered the System invulnerable. While more than three-fourths of the legislators joined Lincoln in the act of creation, more than half his most prominent future rivals had qualms akin to Douglas's. The early critics included, among Democrats, not only Douglas but also his future chief U.S. Senate lieutenant, William Richardson, and among Whigs, future congressmen Edward Baker and John Hardin plus future U.S. senator Orville Browning. Abusing the miscalled System, cried Hardin, "was like abusing a horse after he was dead and commenced stinking."[18]

Since the System did not stink on arrival, Lincoln briefly did not need to defend its excesses against his more prophetic rivals. The Panic of 1837, first devastating New York and other northeastern markets, commenced three months after Illinois's improvements act passed. Initially, midwesterners felt the Panic's impact much less. Only the follow-up Crisis of 1839, more crushing in the Midwest than anywhere, sunk the Illinois System.[19]

During Illinois's 1837–38 economic interregnum, Lincoln's political stock rose with the System's first successes. In August 1838, Lincoln again finished first in the Sangamon County election for legislators.[20] In November, he rode in triumph over the Northern Cross Railroad's first eight miles of track from the Illinois River, toward Jacksonville and Springfield. *The Experiment*, America's first Mississippi Valley locomotive, hauled the celebrants. The trip seemed an incredible vindication. Lincoln's legislative efforts had apparently bypassed the likes of *The Talisman*. His bitter memories of that shattered steamer, doomed on the ornery Sangamon, gave way to elation about *The Experiment*'s breeze over virgin terra firma.

A month after the heartwarming breeze, Whigs ran Lincoln for Speaker of the House of Representatives. Lincoln, if victorious, would have been America's youngest state Speaker. He lost by only five votes.[21]

Then, in 1839, the economy, the System, and Lincoln's political standing all plummeted. Illinois railroad bonds sold for pennies on the dollar. The canal's lands languished unsold. The state barely managed to pay interest on its bonds. In dozens of Illinois locales, railroad tracks and canal ditches halted in midstride.

In the emergency, Lincoln proposed that the legislature offer the U.S. Treasury twenty-five cents per acre for all its still-owned Illinois acres. He would then have the state sell its new turf for $1.25 per acre. The one-dollar-per-acre profit, he prayed, might save the System. Fellow legislators approved his proposed begging in Washington. But federal authorities rejected the beggars.[22]

Other Lincoln remedies proved equally futile. He proposed to give the System to a private joint stock company, with the state holding some shares and interested Illinoisans buying the rest. But legislators, recalling fiascoes such as the Beardstown and Sangamon Canal Company, doubted that private investors would buy the paper company. Lincoln also proposed raising taxes on the richest private lands, owned by the richest men. "The wealthy can not *justly* complain," Lincoln declared, and anyway, "they are not sufficiently numerous to carry the elections."[23]

His tax-the-rich proposal passed. But the insufficient dollars collected could not bail out Illinois. As America's worst depression yet swamped the System, most legislators favored judicious retreat. They would suspend interest payments, suspend canal digging, and suspend railroad construction. They would cancel suspensions only when the economy recovered.

Lincoln answered that temporary suspension meant permanent surrender. "We are now so far advanced," he warned deserting compatriots, that "retreat" will bring "disgrace or great loss." Stopping "work on the Canal" would resemble "stopping a skiff in the middle of a river—if . . . not going up, it *would* go down."[24]

Just as he had felt honor bound to repay his "national debt," states seemed to him honor bound to redeem their bonded pledges. The very way the System had passed, he warned, would double suspension's dishonor. The link between a System for all counties and a capital for Springfield, Lincoln had thought, exemplified logrolling at its moral best. Severing that link— continuing the capital's benefits for Sangamon County while deserting the System's benefits for everyone else—would display logrolling at its ethical worst. My *"Sangamon County,"* Lincoln publicly soared, "though not *legally* bound, . . . is *morally* bound to adhere to that System, through all time to come!"[25]

"All time to come!" For the highest achievements, politicians must seek perpetual goals. But statesmen must know when to advance and when to stall. Extremists never learn that lesson. The Lincoln who insisted that morality required more debt *now,* whatever the awful timing, had yet to learn that requirement for great statecraft.

7

Sangamon County's formerly favorite legislator publicized his fall from grace by losing his specialty, a humorous joust.[26] On February 26, 1841, he urged the legislature to save the System from suspension by adding $3 million in new bonds to the $10.5 million in bonds already issued. The Democrats' Wickliff Kitchell shot back that plunging "still deeper" in debt to cure a state "prostrated by debt" reminded him of an Arkansas drunkard. "Every experiment to cure him," winked Kitchell, "was of no avail."

Then "a neighbor . . . recommended some *brandy toddy.* The insensible man" shot up. He called the recommended medicine just "the stuff." Just so does "the gentleman from Sangamon," climaxed Kitchell, always consider that "more debt would be for the better."

Lincoln, allegedly the frontier's best spinner of the self-serving anecdote, thought he saw how to regain supremacy. Wickliff Kitchell reminded him, Lincoln said, of an "eccentric old bachelor who lived in the Hoosier State."

Like Kitchell, the Indianan saw "*big bugaboos* in every thing." One day, the alarmist fired "as fast as possible" at "the top of a tree." When asked what drew his bullets, the Hoosier replied, "a squirrel."

The bachelor's brother, seeing no squirrel, examined the eye that peered through the gun sight. On one of the hunter's "eye lashes," Lincoln chuckled, "*a big louse*" crawled about. Kitchell also "imagined" seeing "squirrels every day, when they were nothing but *lice.*"

Lincoln's decreasing supporters cheered the (they thought) killing hit. In contrast, his increasing doubters thought that his tale illuminated why his stock plunged. Wickliff Kitchell's anecdote about the drunk from Arkansas had its devastating appropriateness. Lincoln's weakness for more debt bore comparison with a drunk's weakness for more toddy. But Lincoln's proposed huge new bond issue hardly resembled a squirrel or a louse. The would-be mainstream legislator, joking about a $3 million additional debt, epitomized extremists who would not bide their time.

Before his 1840–41 legislative time mercifully ended, the Northern Cross Railroad leased its scant tracks, built at a cost of $436,000, for two thousand dollars per year. In July 1841, the state suspended payments on its System debt. In February 1842, the State Bank folded.

The Illinois and Michigan Canal meanwhile suspended digging, to resume in the mid-1840s. The artificial waterway between Chicago and the Illinois River opened operations in 1848. Mules, plodding alongside the man-made stream, gave ships a surer and faster ride than the exasperating Chicago River. Yet the primitive watery improvement could boost Chicago only so much— and much less than suspended railroads promised.

No railroad dream sparked completion by 1850. The Northern Cross Railroad had been designed to run from Springfield east to the Wabash and west to Quincy (on the Mississippi). At midcentury, the company's westward rails from Springfield had only reached Meredosia (on the Illinois River). No tracks yet ran eastward from the new state capital. Meanwhile, Chicago's dream of iron horses racing to the Mississippi at Alton and at Galena had yielded only slightly useful local connections to Elgin and Aurora.

All the crippling railroad suspensions would give way at midcentury to strenuous resumption (though it would take the state until 1880 to retire the old debt). Resumptions of the System would vindicate all but one of Lincoln's theories. The exception: his conviction that a temporary suspension would preclude a timely renewal.

He paid dearly for the exception. In Sangamon County's legislative election of 1840, he finished last among the winners, after doubting that he

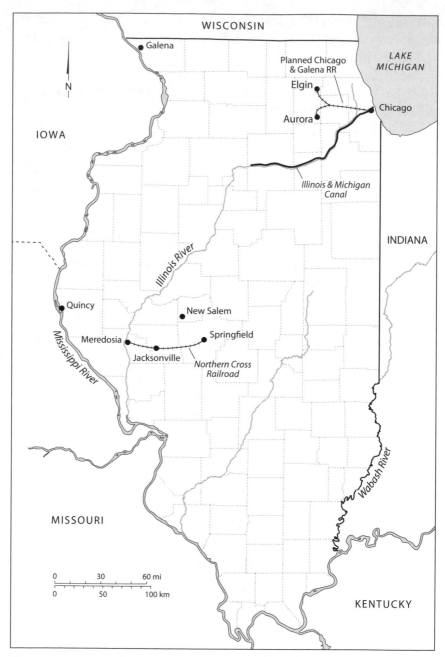

Illinois internal improvements, as of 1850. (Compare maps on pages 50 and 126.)

would even be nominated.[27] In 1842, the Whig Party nominated his senior law partner, Stephen Logan, for his seat, with Lincoln's blessings. Logan, uncontaminated by the System's rise and fall, saved the position for the fallen legislator's party.

8

On March 1, 1841, Lincoln's final term as state legislator ended. As the discarded lawmaker sought to cope with his frustrations, he spent years glooming over why such promise had turned to such ashes. As always, his melancholic ponderings yielded a survivor's strength. He was adept at learning from plunges. His contemplations would eventually yield acute understanding of extremism's perils and timing's imperatives. The resulting differences between his fall as internal improvement zealot and rise as antislavery moderate would be historic. But given the cost of his rebirth—a depression deeper and more sustained than his usual melancholy—he fortunately still enjoyed the day job that had commenced in the blasted System years.

6

The Rise and Limits
of a Pre-1850s Lawyer

❧❧

Lincoln's rise as a lawyer slowly turned his "national debt" into an ugly memory. But this largely self-educated attorney hardly proved that in Horatio Alger's America, unaided self-helpers could always soar. Lincoln's first legal opportunities came in limited forms, at a fleeting time, and at a vanishing place. Furthermore, three indispensable mentors early helped lift him to achievements he might not have attained alone. Equally indispensable U.S. government and state infrastructure would later help enable his financial ascent.

1

Soon after happening upon New Salem in 1831, it will be remembered, Lincoln wandered into Justice of the Peace Bowling Green's courtroom. Before "Pot" Green's bench paraded frontier commoners with their vexations—debts, divorces, slanders, robberies, murders—that twisted everyday life. A physically huge commoner presided. "Pot" Green's costume announced his egalitarianism. His single suspender kept his rough-hewn pants around his three-hundred-pound girth.

Bowling Green invited the village newcomer to guess at imminent court verdicts. When Lincoln's guesses proved accurate, the judge asked the non-lawyer to write plebeians' legal forms. When the forms proved perfect, Green advised his admirer to become an attorney. Lincoln shuddered. How could you study something so grand when you had barely studied anything?

Two years later, Russell Godbey, a rising farmer in "Uncle Jimmy" Short's neighborhood, almost tripped over the answer. Godbey came upon the twenty-four-year-old Lincoln "astraddle . . . Jake Bails's wood pile," blabbing a tome's words into the open air.

"Abe—what are you studying?" Godbey asked.

"Studying law."

"Great God Almighty."[1]

New Salem folk had so exclaimed ever since Lincoln arrived. Great God Almighty, the gawky newcomer seeks to outwrestle Jack Armstrong! Great God Almighty, the relic of Denton Offutt's folly aspires to be our Black Hawk War captain! Great God Almighty, the ex-captain wants to be our state legislator! Great God Almighty, the bankrupt fellow trains to be our assistant surveyor!

And now he would be our lawyer, despite shattering customs for legal studies. He would study law before attending (no matter graduating, not even attending) a college or a precollegiate academy. He would study outside a law school, outside a law office, all by himself, blabbing on a woodpile!

Lincoln also disbelieved it until a cultivated squire seconded Bowling Green's motion. John Todd Stuart, scion of the haughty Todds, possessed credentials to make plebeians believe. God, went the saying, settled for one *d*. But the Todds flaunted two.[2]

Two years older than Lincoln, Stuart grew up in Lexington, Kentucky. Henry Clay and sundry Todd cousins (including the future Mary Todd Lincoln) resided nearby. John Todd graduated from Centre College near Lexington. In 1828, he studied in a prominent Kentucky law office, migrated to Springfield, and hung out his shingle.

The elegant squire meant to tower above frontier rustics. But four years after the dandy arrived, he recognized that one commoner was not so common. Stuart met Abraham Lincoln on Black Hawk War battlefields. Springfield's self-appointed aristocrat noticed how naturally Lincoln got himself elected captain. Ever after, Major Stuart promoted the achiever whom he congratulated himself on discovering.

Opportunity for a Lincoln promotion arrived in 1834 when Stuart, now in his second legislative term, welcomed the rookie to the Vandalia statehouse. There "Jerry Sly," as disgusted Democrats called the Whig wire-puller, guided the novice through legislative back rooms. Stuart then advised Lincoln to study law. He lent his protégé the necessary books and implored him to get to work.

Lincoln naturally took to studying what he was excitedly crafting. Writing law in Vandalia seemed to him even more magical than preparing the downtrodden for Bowling Green's courtroom. Why not master Green's and Stuart's profession, while deserting axes and foxed jeans forever?

So there Russell Godbey spied Lincoln in 1834 after the legislature adjourned, startling squirrels with facts blabbed from *The Revised Statutes of Illinois,* Sir William Blackstone's *Commentaries on the Laws of England,* and James Kent's *Commentaries on American Law.* Scant months of blab school had surprisingly prepared Lincoln for this higher learning. Reading "aloud," explained the student, marshals "two senses. . . . First I see," and "second I hear." Therefore "I . . . remember . . . better."[3] Beyond the library, when sunlight highlighted Jerry Sly's tomes, he could best see and say legal details, say and see legal procedures, see, say, and memorize a few cases.

That fresh-air education enabled admission to the frontier bar. Six months after Judge Stephen A. Logan of the Sangamon Circuit Court certified to the candidate's good character (no examination required), two Illinois Supreme Court judges declared Lincoln qualified to practice (only a half-hour oral exam required). These slight requirements help explain why a law education without law professors could score after several months of blabbing.

Lincoln might have long been a lawyer without sufficient clients except for Jerry Sly. On April 15, 1837, Springfield newspapers advertised the new firm of Stuart & Lincoln. Days earlier, Lincoln had quit dying New Salem and moved to awakening Springfield.

Weeks earlier still, Representative Lincoln had led the successful legislative charge to make Springfield the state's new capital. American politicians customarily became lawyers first. Abraham Lincoln first entered the legislative arena. There he helped promote his imminent new town into the capital. He thereby helped expand residents who might require his legal services.

The move to Springfield served not only a politician who needed law clients but also a son who repudiated his parents' wanderings. Before Tom Lincoln, five generations of successful American Lincolns had each made only a single significant move. Abraham Lincoln moved from New Salem only after he ensured Springfield's promise. He would not migrate again until he moved into Washington's Executive Mansion.

2

A novice frontier lawyer needed as slight legal knowledge to practice as to qualify. Lincoln's early endeavors with John Todd Stuart repeated the tiny range of petty cases he had watched Bowling Green determine: disputes over pigs, cows, fences, insults, divorces, and debts—especially debts. Seventy percent of Lincoln's first decade of cases involved IOUs.

Those ragged slips of paper provided currency in underdeveloped Illinois. Scant gold or silver coin circulated. Folk often paid with promises to pay (unless they paid with animal skins or other such frontier bounty). Recipients of paper pledges paid their bills with IOUs received, as did subsequent recipients of the original promises.

The paper pledges advanced the primitive economy until someone reneged on a promise. Then lawyers stepped in. With his characteristic five-dollar fees from handling small debts (and from handling equally petty divorce, slander, and criminal cases), lawyer Lincoln slowly paid off his "national debt." By the mid-1840s, he could take an ex-debtor's next capitalistic step. He lent his few extra dollars, often gleaned from unreliable debtors, to reliable debtors at 10 percent interest.

3

His political skills helped secure early court triumphs. Juries settled most suits. Before jurors as before voters, Lincoln remembered how the lowly communicate. He used short and familiar words, terse and active sentences, unadorned and simple logic. "Aim lower," he instructed Billy Herndon, "and the common people will understand you." But "if you aim too high," you will "only hit . . . the educated and refined, . . . who need no hitting."[4]

In court as on the stump, the selective legal striker looked like a commoner conversing with commoners. His disheveled hair and slovenly dress matched his customers' appearances. His dusty pants fell inches short of his worn shoes. His tattered green carpetbag and broken yellow umbrella seemed a tramp's possessions. One potential client rejected his services, sniffing that he seemed a "country rustic on his visit to the circus."[5]

Amid the circus-like atmosphere of court day, provincial jurists relished being addressed by one of their own. They inwardly cheered when he cut short an opponent's endless drawl by declaring, "I reckon I must be wrong." He reckoned that the opposition's point after point was right as his adversary pounded already conceded arguments at bored jurymen.

Then suddenly he snapped up, as if from a nap, squeaking in his high-pitched voice, "I reckon that one is ridiculous." With rustics wide awake, he briefly summarized a nub of the matter. Any sleepy lawyer "who took Lincoln for a simple-minded man would very soon" awaken with "his back in a ditch," observed one admirer.[6] Nothing was simple about aiming low without condescending, nor about eliminating fluff and stressing essentials, nor about employing mimicry, sarcasm, and ridicule without insulting opponents, nor about using hilarious anecdotes, often of the barnyard variety, without mocking the serious atmosphere.

The off-color jokes resist recapture, since no stenographers recorded court arguments. Yet omitting poorly reported ribald poorly recaptures Lincoln's courtroom genius. Better to note what this jokester allegedly said and add that if he didn't say that one, he often recounted similar backwoods whoppers.

According to one story, Lincoln told a favorite joke during a recess, outside the courtroom but within earshot of jury members. Jurors "by chance" overheard about a farmer's lad who rushed up to his father. "The hired man and Sis," panted the youngster, are "in the hayloft—she's a liftin' up her skirts and he's apullin' down his pants and fixin' to pee all over the hay." The father chuckled that the son had his facts right but his conclusion wrong.[7]

Later in court, Lincoln told the jury that the opposing lawyer's correct facts supported a wrongheaded conclusion. That was the Lincoln way to victory: with simplicity and a smile. Even if he lost the case, he won plebeians' affection for the next case—or the next election.

4

When partnering with John Todd Stuart, Lincoln spent more time on the next election than with the next jury. John Todd had hoped his junior partner would run the office while the senior partner ran for Congress. The junior partner preferred to share political escapades. Both partners found campaign trails especially captivating in 1838, when Stuart ran for Congress against *that* Stephen A. Douglas.

Occasionally, Lincoln stood in for his partner. These first (alas unrecorded) Lincoln-Douglas debates would hardly be the last. Nor was this initial campaign encounter with Douglas any less bitter or close than the finale. Stuart secured the 1838 congressional seat by only 36 votes (1/1,000th of about 36,000 ballots).

The election's bare winner lost the campaign's final brawl. While Stuart had arrived in Illinois as a disdainful Kentucky patrician—a Todd with two *d*'s to his heels—he had quickly seen that such airs would not do. As "Jerry Sly," he had become a political operator and exhibit #1, alongside his law partner, that in frontier politics, Whigs must be as small *d* democrats as Jacksonian Democrats.

In his climactic encounter with Douglas, Stuart went beyond Lincoln as a belligerent populist. Furious at some unrecorded accusation, Stuart slapped his arm around the Little Giant's head and dragged the squirming victim through a public square. Douglas retaliated by biting Jerry Sly's thumb. The wound swelled with infection. Ever after, Lincoln and Stuart had only to glance at the scar to reinvigorate their loathing of Stephen A. Douglas.

More troubling than Stuart's scarred thumb was the partnership's slim profits. With the senior partner absent most of the time (and providing direction little of the time), the graduate of Jake Bails's woodpile struggled to keep up with cases. "We have been in a great state of confusion," Lincoln confessed to a colawyer at the beginning of the 1838 political campaign, and "we beg your pardon for our neglect."[8] In 1841, when Stuart departed for his second congressional term, the neglectful firm dissolved.

Lincoln's second senior partner, Stephen A. Logan, had been the circuit court judge who certified the blabber for the bar. Like John Todd Stuart, Logan came from a pedigreed Kentucky family, enjoyed a Lexington education, and met Lincoln on Black Hawk War battlefields. There the similarities ended. Where Stuart was suave and tall, Logan was a quenched-up little man, snappish and ill-dressed, with tobacco squirting from his lips. Where Stuart rather ignored his law practice and coveted political office, Logan resigned his judgeship to procure legal fees. Where Stuart paid little heed to Lincoln's initial legal limitations, Logan meant to bring his junior partner up to snuff.

The ex-judge knew that hard work on arcane precedents sometimes turned around even simple cases. He also knew that intense legal scholarship earned more complex cases with more lucrative retainers. Under Logan's tutelage, Lincoln mastered complicated tactics for his several hundred Illinois Supreme Court cases.

In his 1850 "Notes for a Law Lecture," Lincoln implicitly scorned his pre-Logan self. "Young lawyers," he warned, commit no "more fatal error . . . than relying too much on speech-making." Exceptional "powers of speaking" provide no "exemption from" legal "drudgery." Lawyers' "leading rule" must be "diligence," whereas "negligence" assures "failure in advance."[9]

His "blabbing" way of studying, while perfect for mastering legal details, did not encourage legal philosophizing. His "general knowledge of law was never very formidable," Logan noted. Lincoln's legal friend Ward Hill Lamon added that he "reasoned almost entirely from analogous cases previously decided" rather than from the law's "great underlying principles." But after conquering a "case in hand," summarized Logan, he could "make about as much of it as anybody."[10]

One Logan habit personified his contribution to Lincoln's tactics. The sour, dour, picky legal scholar usually fingered a penknife and a raw stick. As Logan preached the doctrine of narrow research on slight cases, he would whittle, whittle, whittle at the stick, until he carved the sharpest edge.

Lincoln would ever after whittle, whittle, whittle at his law brief (or political speech) until the superfluous disappeared. The Great Emancipator would later relish, in a wonderful irony, the spare rhetoric of the proslavery apologist

John C. Calhoun. Stephen A. Logan's ceaseless whittling and John C. Calhoun's unadorned logic would help move Lincoln slowly toward his masterpieces of complex simplicity, his Gettysburg and Second Inaugural performances.

5

In 1844, when Stephen Logan departed to partner exclusively with his son, Lincoln graduated from mentors. Bowling Green had died two years earlier. Lincoln had given the funeral oration. Tears had streamed down his face as he eulogized the first, heaviest, dearest of the three Illinois attorneys who had boosted his climb. His tears had expressed not just grief but also thanks—thanks for the man, for his aid, and for the self-help culture that expected no man to do it all for himself.[11]

Abraham Lincoln became a poster child for Horatio Alger triumph. No one fell lower or rose higher. Yet no one better illustrated that American self-help culture naturally generated not only opportunities but also aid for the aspiring. Like Green, Stuart, and Logan, the successful often delighted to help the promising. They resembled latter-day baseball scouts, proud of spotting raw talent and prouder still of pushing the promising to the next level. Not even Abraham Lincoln, supreme self-made man, soared exclusively on his own talents, not in a civilization that turned on its irony of expecting self-help and often providing a sustaining hand.

As unsettled frontier areas disappeared and established hierarchies domi-nated, the unconnected and undereducated found fewer opportunities than Lincoln had enjoyed. But no later self-helper seized opportunities more adeptly. Abraham Lincoln, having proved worthy of the right time and the right place and the right helpmates, commenced at age thirty-five to take his turn at boosting his own chosen newcomers.

6

The new senior partner selected the promising, deferring, and lighthearted Billy Herndon as his junior partner. Where the impoverished Lincoln took his eccentric route to learning law, the well-off Herndon followed the conventional path. Billy's father, a successful Springfield merchant, sent him to the best town schools, then to neighboring Jacksonville College, and on to studying law in a prominent practice, Logan & Lincoln. Three years later, when Logan withdrew from the partnership, Lincoln promoted the student to the junior partner chair.

Where Logan was nine years older than Lincoln, Herndon was nine years younger. Where Logan exuded learned stiffness, Billy projected debonair

Four Illinois legal compatriots: John Todd Stuart (*top left*), Stephen Logan (*top right*), William Herndon (*bottom left*), and Judge David Davis (*bottom right*)

relaxation. Herndon's prized patent leather shoes added a wisp of elegance to the partnership's sprawling one-room office on the third floor of Springfield's Tinsley Building, near the courthouse. A bedraggled long table, scarred with whittling marks, served as desk. A tattered long sofa, too short for a full Lincoln sprawl, collided with a wall that provided a footrest. A stuffed envelope on the desk was labeled, "when you can't find it anywhere else, look in this."[12]

While looking for something missing, the senior partner often blabbed newspapers and repeated jokes. Billy suffered such distractions, not least because Lincoln split partnership proceeds evenly (Logan had given his junior partner only a one-third share). Still, Lincoln's junior partner knew where frontier equality ended. He was always "Billy." His senior partner was always "Mr. Lincoln."

For Mr. Lincoln, the change from Logan to Herndon reduced drudgery as well as adding camaraderie. Billy researched most of the cases. From these arrangements in the 1840s, each partner collected around $1,500 yearly (about $40,000 in early twenty-first-century coin). That income approximately matched Lincoln's yearly average with Logan and around doubled his harvest with Stuart. In the 1850s, when the transportation revolution brought some big railroad cases, the partners each usually received in the area of $4,500 annually.[13]

7

Proceeds would have shrunk without the Circuit. For twelve weeks every spring and again every fall, attorneys toured the Eighth Judicial Circuit's fourteen county seats with Judge David Davis. At each stop, travelers held court for as many days as necessary. The Circuit recalled Sangamon County's Cavalcade of 1836, where the Long Nine had won election and Lincoln had leveled George Forquer with a lightning rod. Just as politicians had to scramble throughout a sparsely inhabited county to find enough voters, so lawyers had to traverse the Circuit to find enough fees.

Judge Davis and his merry followers faced trying challenges as they covered some eleven thousand square miles, sprawled across central Illinois from the Wabash to the Illinois River. During the spring's snowmelt, lawyers called their ordeal the Mud Circuit. As entourages crept along sloppy roads in decaying carriages or atop aging nags (including Lincoln's Old Tom), lawyers remembered moving faster when strolling a dry city block.

Nightly accommodations rarely matched city hotels' spaces. Only three of this Circuit's county seats contained more than a thousand folk. In the other ten destinations, tiny inns, largely uninhabited except when the Circuit came around, sometimes had to be stuffed with three attorneys to a bed and six beds to a room. With food poor and moonshine raw, most itinerants fled home on many weekends.

Not Lincoln. As usual, he abstained from hard drink and barely noticed tasteless food or barest lodging. But he relished other compensations. While Stuart's contacts had provided some early customers, local attorneys, seeking

Lincoln's help, supplied many Circuit clients. While Herndon's research reduced Lincoln's drudgery, the Circuit cut that bore toward zero. Cases were simple, time short, and law libraries often nonexistent.

Best of all, where the office's laborious work and only occasional visitors reduced Lincoln's chances for storytelling, the Circuit's many fellow travelers and long hours after labor expanded occasions for tales. "Remember the time," he would start. When his audience egged him on, he would remind the fellows, for example, of times when crowded inns forced female strangers to sleep in men's beds. Each sex's head discreetly lay at the opposite end of the mattress. A gent might tickle a foot. A lass might slide down a trifle. A fella might tickle a speck higher. A gal might slide a tad lower. And then what happened, Mr. Lincoln? To great guffaws, the humorist would add not a word.[14]

Nine of his Circuit words proved most legendary. When Ward Hill Lamon, Lincoln's best Circuit friend, split his pants before a court appearance, too much of Lamon could be seen. Lamon's amused colleagues started a fund for new pants. Each subscribed an absurdly small sum for the large size required. Lincoln had the last laugh: "I can contribute nothing," said the jokester, "to *the end in view.*"[15]

After he delivered a zinger, Lincoln would often withdraw without leaving. He would lean his chair against a wall, put his feet on the chair's rail, clasp his hands around his knees, tip his hat forward to shield downcast eyes, "and drawn up within himself as it were," appear "the very picture of dejection and gloom."[16] Minutes or hours later, he would suddenly rejoin joshers and contribute another side-splitter.

Even when the jokester returned to this society, he maintained a defining aloofness. As Judge David Davis described the limited intimacy, "his Stories—jokes" were "done to whistle off sadness." They provided "no evidence of sociality." Instead, Lincoln "was the most reticent" and "Secretive man I Ever Saw." He had "no spontaneity, . . . no Strong Emotional feelings for any person," not even on the "Circuit," the "place" where "Mr. Lincoln" was "as happy as *he* could be."[17]

The oft-times loner among friends here displayed one rare attribute of a statesman. He could remain inside situations yet outside them, connected with his fellows yet detached from them, poised to reconsider a mistake, whether someone else's or his own. That talent, as ideal for a justice as for a comer bent on self-improvement, encouraged David Davis to appoint Lincoln a substitute judge in more than three hundred Circuit cases. The substitute displayed aloof perspective on furious pleading. He would be no different when he became an ever-improving politician.

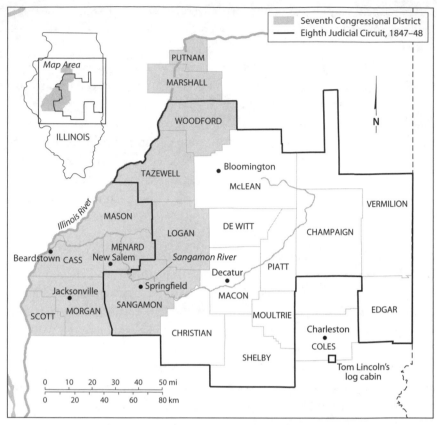

Lincoln's Eighth Judicial Circuit and Seventh Congressional District.

The Circuit contributed even more voters than customers. As a surveyor, Lincoln had befriended many citizens beyond New Salem. As a Circuit rider, he amassed an especially dense crowd of admirers in the four counties included in both the Eighth Judicial Circuit and the Seventh Congressional District. That quartet of counties voted 75 percent for Lincoln when he ran for Congress, compared to 52.3 percent in the congressional district's other counties.[18]

His fellow Circuit riders eventually dominated Lincoln's presidential campaign team. The campaigners' captain, Judge David Davis, towered physically no less than legally. Judge Davis's three hundred pounds required two horses to pull his carriage around the Mud Circuit. His weightier credential, his degree from Yale Law School, blew away competition in these provinces. In 1860, when Judge Davis summoned Circuit cronies to battle for their favorite humorist, they eagerly massed behind the Executive Mansion aspirant.

Perhaps the eagerest, Ward Hill Lamon, of split-pants notoriety, became President Lincoln's Washington, DC, bodyguard. David Davis became the president's appointment for U.S. Supreme Court justice in 1862, then his executor after the assassination. Circuit brotherhood, a mercy for the melancholic lawyer, served him to the end and beyond.

8

Lincoln revered the law for more than slim fees, good camaraderie, and a campaign team. Lawyers, he preached, must stabilize the Founding Fathers' republic. Attorneys must encourage bad suits to be dropped, churlish antagonisms to be compromised, and imperfect claims to be settled. If no pretrial armistice could be procured, proper legal procedures had to ease violent disagreement toward peaceful settlement.

As supplier of soothing remedies, Lincoln would represent whoever asked first. He argued for and against debtors and creditors, slanderers and the slandered, wives and husbands, slaves and slaveholders. Everyone deserved the best defense, he reasoned; and the better the opposing lawyers' logic, the better would be judges' decisions. The lawyer safeguarded the republic as much as protected his clients. With scrupulous legal procedures omnipresent, the democratic state could endure nasty disputes—and avoid deadly slavery controversies.

This gospel dominated Lincoln's first formal public oration, delivered on January 27, 1838. His title, "The Perpetuation of Our Political Institutions," proclaimed the oration's conservative aim. His locale, the Young Men's Lyceum of Springfield, signaled the orator's youthful age for such foreboding conservatism.

The Lyceum's precocious speaker, two weeks short of his twenty-ninth birthday, had not yet experienced Stephen Logan's pruned language. Lincoln's resulting overblown oratory (Billy Herndon called it "highly sophomoric")[19] turned epic warnings feverish. "In the great journal of things happening under the sun," began the grandiloquence, "we the American People," in "the nineteenth century of the Christian era," must "transmit" our "civil and religious liberty," greater "than any" in "former times," to the final "generation that fate shall permit the world to know." Then, trumpeted Lincoln's conclusion, *"the gates of hell shall not prevail against"* our "temple of liberty."[20]

Between the introduction and conclusion, Lincoln pressed his overriding point: "Reverence for the constitution and the laws" must save the Union. No external force—not "all the armies of Europe, Asia, and Africa combined"— could "crush" our national democratic destiny. "Never! . . . If destruction" will be "our lot, we must ourselves be its author."

He warned against an "ill-omen amongst us." Substitutions of "wild and furious passions" for "sober judgments of Courts" augur our national "suicide." Mob outrages, hardly peculiar to the southern land of "pleasure-hunting masters, . . . pervaded the country." The national disease had lately felled the abolitionist editor Elijah Lovejoy, slaughtered by a mob in free-soil Alton, Illinois; white gamblers, hung by vigilantes throughout Mississippi's gallows-strewn countryside; and the mulatto boatman Francis L. McIntosh, roasted alive after he slit a St. Louis deputy sheriff's throat.

Lincoln especially dwelled on Mississippi. Lynchings there, he shuddered, had slain white gamblers, then "brutalized" negroes suspected of "insurrec- tion," then massacred "white men," allegedly leagued "with the negroes," then murdered "strangers from neighboring states." Dead men dangled "from . . . trees upon every road side," rivaling "Spanish Moss" as "drapery of the forest."

An abolitionist, unlike this Lyceum speaker, would have added that slavery caused the worst atrocities to bedevil the Deep South. Lincoln indicted his nation, not the other section. His silence on the morality of black slavery contrasted with his ferocity on the iniquity of white violence.

Whether "abolitionism" is "right or wrong," he emphasized, "mob law" is neither "justifiable nor excusable." Under "fearful . . . mobocratic spirit, . . . good men" will "grow tired" of "seeing their property destroyed; their fami- lies . . . endangered; and their persons injured." Then bad men will rally the disaffected against republican Union.

Destructive demagogues, Lincoln worried, sprang naturally from Amer- ica's postrevolutionary generation's frustrations. The Founding Fathers' gen- eration had won immortal glory. The inheriting generation ached for equal fame. Amid that hothouse atmosphere, the unscrupulous could bid for noto- riety, whether by "emancipating slaves or enslaving free men."

To preclude evil choices and honor his generation's obligation, Lincoln urged "every American . . . lover of liberty" to swear "never to violate . . . the laws of the country; and never to tolerate their violation by others." If "rev- erence for the laws . . . becomes" our "national political religion," if "cold, calculating, unimpassioned reason" overcomes unruly passion, if mobs fade and courts flourish, America will remain "free to the last."

The Lyceum Address raised the ante of Lincoln's petty local cases. He placed attorneys and judges in the vanguard of the nation's postrevolutionary saviors of liberty. He also turned preserving the *national* republic into the critical salvation. Not a word in the Lyceum Address made saving *local* repub- licanism the prime American obligation.

Here soared, in Lincoln's first great oration, an insistent national Whig, con- testing the terrain where Andrew Jackson's state's rights democracy reigned.

Here also thrived the unyielding national Unionist, unwilling to allow southern localists to abandon ship. But could scrupulous attorneys and icy judges save national Union's troubled glory?

9

The orator's concept of local courts as saviors of national republicanism especially triumphed when Lincoln *lost* arguably his most important case, the famous *Matson* affair.[21] In the early 1840s, Robert Matson, owner of Kentucky slaves plus Kentucky and Illinois acres, sent some of his Kentucky slaves to work his Illinois spread. Matson cynically evaded Illinois's emancipation law by distinguishing between "domiciled" and "in transit" slaves. "Domiciled" enslaved blacks permanently lived in a region. "In transit" bondsmen temporarily passed through the area. Many northern states (including Illinois) granted masters an exemption from laws liberating "domiciled" slaves, if their human property was "in transit."

For years, Kentucky's Matson shoved slaves through Illinois's loophole. In the early 1840s, he brought his Kentucky slaves to his Illinois farm in the spring, swore to a witness that they were "in transit," and returned them to Kentucky in the fall. When this subterfuge worked, he grew bolder. In the mid-1840s, he skipped the farce of returning allegedly "in transit" Illinois slaves to their alleged Kentucky "domicile." He instead annually swore to witnesses that his enslaved domestics would never be permanently "domiciled" in Illinois.

The ruse worked until his domestic situation twisted against him. The unmarried Matson lived in Kentucky with a white woman, Mary Corbin, mother of at least one of his children. The tempestuous Ms. Corbin distrusted her lover's relationship with his female slaves. Perhaps to relieve her suspicions, Matson sent five of his Kentucky slaves, Jane Bryant and her four children, to his Illinois farm. There Anthony Bryant, Jane Bryant's black husband, had long served as foreman (so long that even Matson no longer considered Anthony "in transit" and thus still a slave).

For the next two years, Matson continued his annual charade of declaring Jane Bryant and her four children to be "in transit." Then his jealous white mistress closed the loophole. Mary Corbin suspected that her lover had sired Jane Bryant's imminent fifth baby. The angry Corbin let it be known that the pregnant mother and her children might indeed be soon "in transit"—sold away to the Lower South, far from Anthony Bryant.

In mid-August 1847, the alarmed Bryant led his family to the protective home of Dr. Hiram Rutherford, a neighboring physician. Robert Matson countered by securing a jailing of the escapees until courts decided their fate.

The family remained imprisoned for two months, pending an October 6–7 circuit court hearing.

Dr. Rutherford asked Abraham Lincoln to represent the Bryants at the historic hearing. Lincoln replied that the Matson side had tentatively contacted him. If ongoing negotiations with the slaveholder yielded a confirmed hire, he would have to represent the party that first hailed him, according to lawyers' informal "cab rule."

Lincoln cared most not about "cab rules" or about which side he defended but about participating in the epic (and perhaps about earning a retainer). When his negotiations with Matson collapsed, he came back to Hiram Rutherford, asking to represent the slaves. When the unforgiving doctor rejected the turncoat, Lincoln turned back to Matson. This time, the slave owner hired the future Great Emancipator to lead his suit to reenslave the fugitives. The spectacle would transpire in the Coles County Courthouse, ten miles north of Lincoln's father and stepmother's log cabin.

In keeping with the importance of the showdown, the presiding Coles County Circuit Court judge, Illinois Supreme Court Chief Justice William Wilson, asked a Supreme Court colleague, Judge Samuel Treat, to help decide the case. Before these high-powered judges paraded high-powered attorneys. Congressman-elect Abraham Lincoln and a former Illinois state attorney pled for the master. Congressman Orlando Ficklin plus a state senator pled for the slaves. Spectators jammed the courtroom. Not until the Lincoln-Douglas Debates would an Illinois showdown exude such Shakespearean atmosphere.

Abraham Lincoln, Shakespeare fancier, especially looked forward to this enactment of his Lyceum script. Law and order, as determined by fine judges after hearing fine pleadings, must here save the Founders' republic from apparently imminent riot. Beyond the courthouse, a white Matson employee paraded the streets, twirling the rope he hoped to use to drag the black Bryants back to Kentucky (and then God knows where). Hiram Rutherford's supporters massed on horseback, poised to rescue the slaves. Against these lawless plans, Lincoln sought soothing legal procedure, his savior of national republicanism.

As the courthouse spectacle commenced, even Matson conceded that slaves permanently "domiciled" in Illinois must be freed. But according to the Illinois Supreme Court's *Willard* verdict (1843), Illinois courts must honor slave owners' "right of transit with a slave." Matson had thus continually announced his intention to "transit" his temporary Illinois residents back to Kentucky.

The two Supreme Court justices dismissed Matson's announcements. Chief Justice Wilson called Matson's "declared intentions" hardly the dominant "fact." The slaveholder had "domiciled his servants here for two years or upwards," with no "transit" back to Kentucky.

Lincoln, knowing the flimsiness of the "in transit" dodge, added a procedural technicality. He urged that liberating these slaves required a full-fledged writ of habeas corpus hearing. Judge Wilson, indicating as little tolerance for the technicality as for the dodge, asked Lincoln if he had anything more to argue. Matson's attorney did not. The exchange illustrated what Lincoln knew very well—that arguments for this slaveholder had little chance under these judges.

After initial fury, Robert Matson and unruly supporters outside the courthouse accepted his slaves' liberation. Perhaps the court had liberated the master as well as the slaves. A year after Robert Matson lost the blacks who had tormented Mary Corbin, the two whites married.

Abraham Lincoln also won by losing. True, he lost recompense for his services. Matson stormed away without paying his lawyer. But the court, by liberating the slaves, may have also liberated Lincoln from a tormented conscience, if he had won six Bryants' permanent enslavement. The losing lawyer may also have been spared a future political problem. If he had helped lock Bryants forever in chains, Free-Soilers might have later called him damaged antislavery goods, unfit to be the prime Republican.

More surely, the court's decision against Matson vindicated, for the moment, Lincoln's Lyceum way to save the Founders' republic. He had urged that rational decisions by the best judges, after hearing the best lawyers' arguments, would preclude mobs from savaging the republic. Along with all attorneys and all judges in arguably the most important trial in antebellum Illinois history, Abraham Lincoln, vanquished lawyer, had followed his Lyceum script and helped avert a riot. Thanks to attorneys on and below the bench, damage to the Union, all too possible amid demagogues exploiting slavery's tensions, had this time not exploded from the Founders' rawest unsolved problem.

A critical national case, a decade later, would offer a less pleasant perspective. Lincoln's Lyceum way to save Union gambled on judges to make the right decision. But what if judges issued the wrong decision, shattering to the republic? In 1857, judges in the *Dred Scott* case would toss this killing evidence at the Lyceum Address, turning an enraged Lincoln toward very different salvations for Union.

Theoretically, the *Matson* case might seem as threatening to the Lyceum logic and its author. Any lawyer who contended for a dubious master against heroic fugitives risked *winning* the case and becoming known as some Great Enslaver. Lincoln, however, likely considered the gamble slight. He knew Justice Wilson's and Treat's scruples, from arguing before them many times.

Abraham Lincoln likely felt that defending the indefensible here came almost cost-free. He could live up to the narrow lawyerly creed that the worst client deserves the best defense, participate in a great event, pick up a few dollars, watch slaves being rightly freed, revel in the avoidance of riots over the wrong verdict, and thus feel the glory of his Lyceum argument's vindication.

Still, the slight risk that his pleas might have enslaved Matson's fugitives will never make posterity fonder of A. Lincoln, Esquire. Even his most disappointed latter-day critic, however, must admit that he had become a cagier gambler than the young legislator who threw wild dice at the "System." He had paid for that folly by spending six anguished years in the political wilderness, contemplating when to take what risks. A month after the *Matson* case, he would be journeying to Congress and harder tests of how much he had learned.

7

The Rise and Turbulence of a Marriage

⋯≒⊱≓⋯

Before migrating to Springfield, Abraham Lincoln slept in countless frontier shelters. Changing beds almost as often as jobs, he wandered between Indiana huts as a teenager and New Salem cabins as a young adult. Then, in mid-April 1837, the twenty-eight-year-old bachelor quit New Salem and wandering. He hoisted two stuffed saddlebags atop a borrowed horse and rode to Springfield's courthouse square. To secure his own bedding for the first time, he stopped at the town's leading general store.

1

A part owner, Joshua Speed, also from Kentucky but four years younger and many times richer, offered to sell a bed and furnishings for seventeen dollars. As "small as the sum was," answered the newcomer, he "was unable to pay it." Speed "never saw a sadder face." Taking pity, the Kentuckian offered "to share 'my' large room with a double bed up-stairs." "Where is your room?" asked the stranger. Speed pointed at the spiral stairs. Lincoln bounded up, dropped his bags, and sped down. "Beaming with pleasure," he "exclaimed 'Well Speed, I am moved.'"[1]

He would move again only when Speed returned to Kentucky, four years later. During their some 1,400 nights in their large bed, the two friends often shared their large room with store clerks and other comrades. Billy Herndon, before studying the law, slept there for months. When the amiable roommate decided to become an attorney, Lincoln advised Billy to study under Stephen

Logan. Thus did Logan & Lincoln's rigorous legal classroom lead to Lincoln & Herndon's genial law office.

As Lincoln's storytelling notoriety spread in Springfield, young bucks gathered nightly above Speed's store to hear his whoppers. Then listeners would try to outdo the master. Speed called the zany competition "The Social Club."[2] Nights on the Circuit could have had the same nickname.

Lincoln secured board in Springfield the same way he found shelter. Before moving to Illinois's imminent capital city, Lincoln had ridden back from the Vandalia legislative session with William Butler, clerk of the Sangamon County Circuit Court. When they stopped for the night, Lincoln tossed and turned in bed. Bill Butler asked what ailed his fellow traveler. "I am in debt," Lincoln despaired, and "don't know what to do."

Butler beseeched the agitated compatriot to share our family's dwelling before returning to New Salem. Later, when the ex–New Salem resident settled in Speed's room, Butler urged Lincoln to share our meals. The debtor dined gratis at the Butlers' table for several years.[3] Complimentary room from Speed, complimentary board from Butler—shades of "Uncle Jimmy" Short buying Lincoln's surveying tools at auction and presenting them to bankruptcy's victim.

Again and again, Lincoln's rise from impoverishment illuminated not just the relative openness (for white males!) of relatively unformed frontier society, not just his capacity to blab toward higher learning, but also his amiability with male comrades. Fellow frontiersmen, loving his company, hated to see him sink. Thus did this Horatio Alger continually prove that self-helpers' skills must include aptitude for luring assistance.

2

Luring eligible Springfield females proved more difficult. Before Springfield, Lincoln had experienced no fancy table manners, no cultivated dancing, no clever bon mots, no chaste rules about what to say or where to sit or how to dress or how to bare the soul. He charmed tough frontier matrons. But delicate upper-class maidens, not so much.

His aspiration to rise, domestically as well as politically, invited his vulnerability. He could not abide becoming another Tom Lincoln. So he would not settle for a clone of his mother, sister, or stepmother. He desired a mate with more—more education, more refinement, more ambition, more money. His "mores" pushed him toward refined society's definition of "better" females—a realm where he fit like a square peg into round holes.

Abraham's bawdy tales, males' delight, had to be shunned among polished damsels. Demonstrations of his physical prowess, famed in the open air, were unwelcome in refined drawing rooms. Ladies favored dancing. Lincoln's two flat feet had to do the prancing. He could not anchor his feet, swing his arms, and rotate his hips, as when axing or wrestling. He had to clump, clump, clump as he spun around the dance floor, with his female partner's toes at his mercy. "I want to dance with you in the worst way," he implored his future bride. And that is the way he danced, chuckled the future Mrs. Lincoln—in the worst way.[4]

His better way was to sit, gazing up adoringly, at the feet of a belle. He was "not sufficiently Educated & intelligent in the female line" to "hold a lengthy Conversation with a Lady," reported his future sister-in-law.[5] "Quick, lively, gay" belles invited his uncomfortably passive admiration.

3

Before Lincoln chanced Springfield society, Ann Rutledge had for many months stalled off the difficulty. This New Salem maiden, Lincoln's first fiancée, was no cultivated belle, with manners that made a rough frontiersman squirm. She was of a world higher than Tom Lincoln's (always that requirement), yet not with upper-class manners and expectations (always, after Ann, the difficulty).

Lincoln probably met Miss Rutledge in 1831, soon after landing in New Salem. She was then eighteen, he twenty-two. Her father, James Rutledge, had moved from South Carolina to an Illinois village that at first existed only in his imagination. The town father had erected early log cabins (reserving the biggest for himself), built and co-owned that New Salem milldam, inaugurated the town debating society, and established the town tavern. He was the big man in town. His eldest daughter, who managed the tavern, was the big catch.

Neither James nor Ann Rutledge looked down on poorer customers. Their unpretentious airs helped make their tavern a capital spot for frontier plebeians. The founder's daughter was genial, charming, fairly well educated, with auburn hair, blue eyes, and skills at frontier domestic arts—knitting, sewing, cooking. She had, said "Uncle Jimmy" Short, a near neighbor, "a moderate education, and without any of the so called accomplishments." John McNamar, "Miss Ann's" fiancé before Lincoln, treasured her as "a gentle, Amiable Maiden, without any of the airs of your city Belles."[6]

If she seemed Abraham Lincoln's ideal match, she was also the least available. She had agreed to marry McNamar, Sam Hill's entrepreneurial partner. But later that year, McNamar postponed the nuptials by temporarily returning to his native New York State, to patch up family troubles. He promised to return shortly and to write often.

He stopped writing after a year. He had not returned after another year. Ann and the Rutledges gave up on the apparent conniver. Her door opened for other admirers.

By early 1835, Abraham Lincoln became the second man whom Ann Rutledge agreed to marry—but this time with a condition. Marriage must be delayed until she could tell her ex-fiancé, to his unwelcome face, why she had moved on. Her new fiancé, who conceived that honor demanded repayment of his "national debt," admired that morality. He also relished their decision to finish their studies, he in law and she at a neighboring female academy, before undertaking household burdens.

They never had that opportunity. In August 1835, Ann Rutledge sickened of typhoid fever. She lingered for weeks. Then she became the third beloved female that the twenty-six-year-old Abraham had lost to frontier fevers: first his mother, then sister Sarah, now this. As a teenager, he had reacted to sister Sarah's death with the obscene "Chronicles of Reuben." This time, the more mature young adult internalized the rage. His friends, on a suicide watch, hid his razors.

4

The ensuing two candidates for the raw frontiersman's hand, each coincidently named Mary, both offered less comfort and more cultivation. Lincoln's first potential aristocratic bride, Mary Owens of Green County, Kentucky, came to New Salem to visit her married sister. Their father, Nathanial Owens, the richest man in the county, had raised his girls to be belles in Lashfield, his brick, Georgian, two-story plantation house.

Mary Owens's older sister Betsy had happily traded elegant life in Lashfield for married life in a New Salem log cabin. Betsy thought that a similar swap would benefit her visiting sister. The matchmaker recommended Abraham Lincoln.

Both Lincoln and Mary Owens saw a case for the match. The Kentucky lady's lively mind, confident personality, and superb education (and possible dowry) enticed the ambitious frontiersman. In turn, she relished his naïve sweetness and fierce self-improvement. But she feared that "Mr. Lincoln was deficient in those little links which make up the great chains" of female "happiness." His "different . . . training" threatened a "congeniality which would have otherwise existed."[7]

An oafish (she thought) act epitomized her apprehensions. On a horseback frolic with several couples, they came upon a wide stream. The other male riders guided their ladies' horses across the watery divide. Lincoln blithely rode ahead. "When I rode up beside him," reported Mary Owens, "I remarked, 'You are a nice fellow; I suppose you did not care whether my neck was broken or not.' He laughingly replied, (I suppose by way of compliment) that he knew I was plenty smart to take care of myself."[8]

As Lincoln saw it, he here appropriately praised a smart horsewoman. He extended his notion of compliment during another petty drama that made Mary Owens bristle. One day, after the pair joined Hannah (Mrs. Jack) Armstrong for a stroll, Hannah lugged her infant up a hill. Lincoln, carrying nothing, did not offer to haul the child. The Kentucky heiress told him he would not "make a kind husband," for he lacked "smaller attentions." As for the rough frontiersman, he saluted Hannah Armstrong's lack of helplessness.[9]

Despite tensions over his manners, the wary couple crept toward an alliance. Finally, Lincoln thought that honor required him to dare the question. In early May 1837, he had just moved to Springfield. When proposing that she join him, he warned, "I am afraid you would not be satisfied." Springfield displayed "a great deal of flourishing about in carriages." You "would . . . be poor without the means of hiding your poverty." He would "be much happier with you." But in "my opinion," he squirmed, "you had better not do it."[10]

A final overture doomed any doing. "I am now willing to release you," went the plebeian's climactic proposal, if "you wish it." He also remained "willing, and ever anxious to bind you faster." But she must first convince him "that it will, in any considerable degree, add to your happiness."[11]

Instead, Mary happily returned to Kentucky. There, an eager fellow swept her off to a Missouri marriage. As for Abraham, he asked Betsy ex-Owens "to tell your Sister that I think she was a great fool, because she did not stay here and marry me."[12]

The failed suitor sought to purge his feelings in a spoof about the debacle. With humorous (so he thought) exaggeration, he described Mary Owens as an "old maid," for no one so "full of fat" could have "reached her present bulk in less than thirty five or forty years." After he "had delayed" an understanding with the colossus "as long as I thought I could in honor do," he "made the proposal . . . again and again," and "shocking to relate, she answered No," with ever "greater firmness." He then "verry unexpectedly found myself mortified almost beyond endurance," having been "actually rejected" despite "all my fancied greatness; and to cap the whole, I then, for the first time, began to suspect that I was really a little in love with her."

The insulted lover's "conclusion": He must "never again think of marrying." No one "block head enough to have me" would be satisfying.[13] The better conclusion: This unsophisticated frontiersman and a cultivated heiress, if sufficiently mutually satisfied to marry, would likely suffer bad moments.

Two years after Mary disappeared, Lincoln, now age thirty, confronted the same problem inside the same drawing rooms. Mary Todd, almost twenty-one when she entered the social apex of Illinois's new capital city, arrived from one of Lexington, Kentucky's most cultivated parlors. The newcomer's grandparents, Robert Parker and Levi Todd, had been among Lexington's founding fathers. They had built two of the area's most sumptuous brick houses. They had also championed the town's most pretentious motto—here thrives Transylvania University, "The Athens of the West."[14]

Levi Todd's son, Robert Smith Todd, topped his father's wealth with banking and manufacturing triumphs. He also added to Transylvania's "Athens of the West" illusion, serving as trustee of Lexington's "Harvard." The state senator helped stuff his town mansion on West Main Street with offspring and twice his father's possessions.

Robert Smith Todd's business trips cost Mary Todd a resident father over half the time. His accumulation of children also cost Mary a caring mother. Robert's first wife died giving birth to her seventh child in twelve years. His second wife, from Mary's perspective the classic wicked stepmother, survived nine childbirths, also in a dozen years.

As a teenager, Mary Todd happily escaped this stuffed household. The future Mrs. Lincoln boarded for years at Shelby Female Academy, then at Mentelle's for Young Ladies. Charlotte Mentelle, the formidable headmistress of the refined school on well-named Rose Hill, raised her daughter to marry Henry Clay's son. She also taught Robert Smith Todd's daughter French conversation and European letters. One day, according to legend, Mary Todd announced in Henry Clay's parlor that she meant to reside in Washington's Executive Mansion.

After Rose Hill, the cocky heiress instead resided with her infuriating stepmother. Then, at age twenty, Mary Todd again escaped West Main Street. Her eldest sister, Elizabeth, wife of Ninian Edwards, asked her to come live in their Illinois home, Springfield's finest on Quality Hill. Mary's sister Frances had lately parlayed a similar invitation from sister Elizabeth into marriage to Dr. William Wallace, Springfield's pharmacist. With Frances's room empty, Elizabeth urged Mary to come husband-hunt amid Quality Hill's quality candidates.

When Mary Todd traded Lexington's Rose Hill for Springfield's Quality Hill, her new town sported not only Robert Smith Todd's three oldest daughters but also three promising politician cousins: John Hardin, John Todd Stuart, and Stephen Logan. At the society's lead was not a Todd but Elizabeth's husband, Ninian Edwards. That haughty squire bore the same name as his father, one of Illinois's first governors and U.S. senators. The younger Ninian and Elizabeth Edwards staged Springfield's so-called Coterie's plushest parties. Into these exclusive gatherings, whether for tea or dinner or dancing, the Edwardses' brash and witty new houseguest fit perfectly, while searching for a husband fit for her political ambitions.

When choosing the most likely future president, Mary Todd may have considered Stephen A. Douglas (whether he considered her is an unanswerable question). Many months passed before Mary Todd thought Abraham Lincoln might be the true comer. With his legal and political ties to her Todd cousins, Lincoln apparently belonged at Coterie festivities and inside Mary Todd's calculations.

Yet what a social misfit! In Quality Hill's best drawing room, he was the most economically indebted, the least formally educated, the most incorrectly attired, the least socially connected, and the most conversationally inept. But he raptly listened while Mary Todd poured out bon mots. He also instinctively realized how to push this belle's buttons. Instead of flowers, Lincoln gave her his victorious election returns, tied with a red ribbon.

Mary relished the political obsession that the gift symbolized. Like the male talent scouts (including cousin John Todd Stuart), she guessed that this awkward, gawky fellow had potential. Her guess impelled heavier risk. Stuart bet only on an easily replaced junior partner. She would have to wager her life—or at least the only life she desired to live—on her choice of political husbands. Once she decided to place the bet, she differed in the crucial way from her man's previous Mary. She meant to have Abraham Lincoln.

But did he mean to have her? On the one hand, he cared that she weighed seductively less than Mary Owens. He liked them pleasantly plump, not blown up to the proportions of his previous Mary. He also noticed happily that the present much younger Mary (by ten years) displayed even better education, far more spice, much more wealth—and incomparably more interest in politics. "Save me from" being "a *political woman,*" Mary Owens had exclaimed.[15] Save me from political unimportance, Mary Todd would have retorted. That version of salvation could make her Lincoln's welcome bride.

But her drawing room finesse made her seem foreign. Her fiery temper made her seem threatening. Her aristocratic tastes could increase his "national debt" faster than Mary Owens's lesser material desires. The socially awkward frontiersman valued control, caution. The socially gifted heiress cherished impulsiveness, irreverence. As Coterie gossips celebrated her drawing room flamboyance, "she could make a bishop forget his prayers." But could she make a drawing room lightweight forget his qualms?

As he wavered, her sister and brother-in-law told "Lincoln and Mary . . . more or less, directly . . . not to marry." The potential bride and groom "were raised differently and had no feelings . . . alike."[16] Perhaps this admonition pulled the comer back from the heiress. Perhaps also Abraham's flirtations with a beautiful Quality Hill newcomer, Ninian Edwards's cousin Matilda Edwards, fed his doubts about whether he loved Mary Todd enough.[17]

More certainly, with both his Marys, the closer he came to matrimony, the more he quailed at the risk. This time, it was Abraham rather than a Mary who decided to end the wavering. In late December or early January 1840–41, he broke off a promised engagement to Miss Todd with a tender word and a kiss.

He then fell into weeks of the same severe melancholy that he had last suffered after Ann Rutledge's death, six years earlier. He called it the "hypo" (for hypochondria). John Hardin's sister termed it "two cat fits and a duck fit." Ninian Edwards described him as "Crazy as a *Loon.*" Joshua Speed again hid his razors. Abraham disappeared from legislative cronies for almost a week. He called himself "the most miserable man living—I must die or get better."[18]

A month later, he felt better, aided by Dr. Anson Henry's potions. A year later, however, he still harbored guilt about his retreat from promises to wed Mary Todd. Partly because of his unusually sharp sense of honor, with results akin to his repayment of every penny of his "national debt,"[19] the couple resumed their tortuous explorations. This time, they shunned Quality Hill, her family, and the Coterie. Instead, they met secretly in Dr. Henry's drab parlor.

Appropriately, a political adventure fueled their final decision. Lincoln had entered a political war of words with State Auditor James Shields. This Irish Democrat was as short as Illinois's Little Giant. Like Douglas, Shields frequented the largely Whig (and seldom Irish) Quality Hill receptions.

The Whiggish Coterie considered the misplaced Shields a conceited dandy. Lincoln wrote Whig lampoons of the Irishman, published anonymously in the *Sangamo Journal.* According to the spoof's heroine, the "Widow Rebecca," Shields had declared it "distressing" that "I cannot marry" all you ladies. "I know how much you suffer." But "do do remember, it is not my fault that I am so handsome and so interesting."[20]

The enraged Shields, after uncovering "Rebecca's" creator, challenged Lincoln to a duel. Before he answered, Mary Todd and her friend Julia Jayne (soon to become Mrs. Lyman Trumbull) joined the skirmish. The ladies anonymously published their own "Rebecca" letter, with the "Widow" offering peace if Mr. S. "will . . . squeeze my hand as hard as I squeezed the butter." He can even marry me, for "isn't marryin' better than fightin', though it does sometimes run into" more "fightin'." But I know he would "rather fight than eat," and I get "the choice of weapons." I choose "broomsticks or hot water or a shovelful of coals." He can choose whether "I shall wear breeches" or he shall wear "petticoats."[21]

This latest "Rebecca's" mockery further enraged Jimmy Shields. He demanded a duel more insistently. Lincoln chose a deadly weapon (from the short Shields's perspective): long swords, which could slice the little Democrat before he could touch the lengthy Whig.

Since Illinois barred dueling, the duelers traveled to well-named Bloody Island in the Mississippi River. The island rose closer to Missouri (where dueling was legal) than to Illinois. There, Mary Todd's cousin John Hardin arranged an honorable compromise before Bloody Island became newly bloodied.

After Lincoln arrived back on Illinois shores intact, he appreciated how Molly, as he called Mary, had helped play "Rebecca" in this political farce. A bit more lubrication could now ease the uneasy couple toward marriage. Lincoln had eight months earlier helped Joshua Speed creep toward nuptials. He now wrote his friend, asking whether you are "in *feeling* as well as *judgment*, glad you are married? . . . Please answer . . . quickly."[22] After Speed's speedy affirmative, Molly could have her man.

The question-and-answer exchange with Speed, like the almost duel with Shields, had its revealing absurdity. As if Joshua's "feelings" with his Fanny had any bearing on whether a wedded Abraham would feel right with Molly! The felt necessity of the exchange speaks loudly about Lincoln's uncertainty about a match loaded with promise and perils.

Ever since his own "national debt" and the System's state debt, he had shied away from such gambles. But on November 3, 1842, he finally dared the question, almost two years after he had kissed Mary good-bye. The next morning, the thirty-three-year-old would-be groom rushed over to the Reverend Charles Dresser's dwelling on Eighth and Jackson and secured his agreement to officiate that very night.

Simultaneously, Molly asked her reluctant sister to stage the sudden nuptials on Quality Hill. In the evening, Lincoln slipped on Molly's finger a ring with a hastily engraved prayer, "Love is eternal." Procrastination had ended not with resolution of clashing upbringings but with determination to escape the agonizing delay, before another day passed.

6

The birth of Robert Todd Lincoln (Bobby), nine months minus three days after the ceremony, epitomized the courtship's hurried finale. Hurry and those merely three days did (and still do) make cruel tongues wag. But whether or not Bobby's conception broke the premarital logjam, the baby's arrival partially compensated for marital tensions. The couple mutually cherished their newborn son and the three who followed. Edward Baker Lincoln (Eddie) arrived in 1846. William Wallace Lincoln (Willie) emerged in 1850. Thomas Lincoln (Tad) appeared in 1853.

Conversations about the boys and politics best connected the awkwardly matched mates. Lincoln exemplified the new age of playful parenting. Mother (no longer Molly) reveled in the joy of Father (no longer Abraham) as he rolled across their floors with their boys in a bear hug.

Yet some of his signature qualities undermined his parenting. His thirst for advancement yielded many departures from home. Bob remembered Father best in those years as a packer of carpetbags. When not physically absent, Lincoln could psychologically wander. Witness the melancholy lawyer brooding half the time on the sidelines during joshing Circuit evenings.

One day, Father packed his younger lads into a wagon and pulled them through the Springfield streets. He then ascended into one of his oblivious trances just before they tumbled out of the wagon. The two boys' screams fell on two deaf ears as he pulled the lightened load for blocks, as if cargo remained aboard.[23]

Cronies on the Circuit shrugged off Lincoln's psychological departures. His wife instead found his nonresponses insulting, infuriating. When she lashed out, he didn't hear, or ambled out of the room, or departed for the office, or left for the Circuit, or plunged into campaigning. His exits, his sister-in-law Elizabeth Edwards thought, signaled "a cold Man," with "no affection."

Mary Lincoln put it more charitably. "When he felt most deeply," the wife wrote, "he expressed the least," for he "was *not* a demonstrative Man." Or as she wrote in an intriguingly ambiguous sentence, "if her husband" stayed "at home more," she "could love him better."[24]

Tight quarters magnified tensions between an unusually undemonstrative husband and an unusually effusive wife. While Abraham had become accustomed to Speed's large room and Mary to the Edwardses' palatial house, they cohabited at first in a drab eight-by-fourteen-foot bedroom, upstairs in the second-class Globe Tavern. Mary, whose romantic sense featured Madame Mentelle's Rose Hill, saw nothing appealing in the meagerness.

Several months after Bobby's August 1, 1843, birth, the strapped couple dared a slightly less meager rented house at 214 S. Fourth. Here, Robert Todd visited his namesake grandson and took pity on his daughter. In early January 1844, with Todd funds partly propelling Lincoln, he again knocked on the Reverend Charles Dresser's door on Eighth and Jackson. This time, Lincoln sought not an officiator at his wedding but the home of the minister. Dresser agreed to sell the Lincolns his five-room, one-and-a-half-story bungalow for

$1,200 in cash plus a land parcel (appraised for $300 at the late April 1844 settlement).

Lincoln had feared that Mary would bridle at constricted spending, inside whatever crabbed house he could provide. Instead, Robert Smith Todd funded part of the original house purchase (and, as we will see, all of the bungalow's eventual reconstruction). Meanwhile, Mary usually economized and scrimped, as if she were trained to be Ann Rutledge.

Occasionally, she would succumb to a buying binge, alarming to her husband, before she stopped, lest she spend them back to the Globe Tavern. Her emotional binges more often roiled domestic tranquility. Cousin Stephen Logan warned her that Lincoln "is much too rugged for your white hands to attempt to polish."[25] But Madame Mentelle's prodigy could not leave crudity unpolished. She nagged Lincoln to brush his unruly hair, to stop reading on the floor, to cease eating butter off his knife, to forbear from answering the door in his shirtsleeves and stocking feet, and to desist from telling visitors that he would "trot out the women folk."[26]

Occasionally, she would more than nag, and not always inside the house. Whenever her corrections provoked him, he shrunk into aloofness rather than lashing back. Sometimes his emotional exodus climaxed in physical departure. She was then known to explode out the door in hot pursuit of the infuriating retreater. Some claimed to see her on occasion wielding hot tea to throw in his face, fireplace logs to slice his nose, or brooms to slap his back.[27]

It was all too eerily like Mary's imagined "Widow Rebecca," who had suggested that Mr. Shields should duel not with pistols but "broomsticks or hot water or a shovelful of coals." But in the Springfield streets, Illinois males' favorite humorist saw nothing funny about his occasionally broom-wielding matron. On one occasion, he picked up his assailant and carried her back, kicking and screeching, into their anger-laced bungalow.

These infrequent embarrassments formed the public face of the Lincolns' private unease. Yet two huge positives usually prevailed. The couple mutually cherished their children and his political advances. Politics had paved their uneven road to marriage. Political success smoothed their jagged path toward domestic peace.

With one word on the climactic occasion, this political man captured an unmixed blessing in a marriage of mixed elements. On the night after the November 6, 1860, presidential election, Abraham Lincoln examined the returns for hours. In the early morning, wearily realizing that he had triumphed, he marched on Eighth and Jackson. Upon opening the door, he burst out, "Mary! Mary! *WE are elected!*"[28]

8

A Congressional Aspirant's Rise

⊰ЭЬ⊱

For half a decade after the demoted state legislator suffered relegation to private life, he and his wife dreamed of a revival in Congress. He might then secure federal rescue of Illinois's System. She might star in the capital's drawing rooms. The irretrievably political couple dared hope because in Illinois, only Lincoln's Seventh Congressional District usually elected a Whig.

1

Two Seventh Congressional District Whig stars blocked Lincoln's way. Both Edward (Ned) Baker and John Hardin, when state legislators, had trimmed Lincoln's internal improvement excesses. Both were also more popular campaigners.

Hardin, a year younger than Lincoln, migrated to Illinois's Morgan County, one county west of Lincoln's Sangamon, shortly after graduating from Kentucky's Transylvania University. John Hardin and Stephen A. Douglas both practiced law in Morgan County's Jacksonville (then Illinois's most populated village, with more people than Chicago!). The shared locale gave Hardin an 1830s version of Lincoln's 1850s opportunity. As Jacksonville's leading Whig, Hardin could advance by *almost* besting Douglas, the most unbeatable Democrat in Illinois's majority party.

In 1834, Hardin came within four votes of blocking the Little Giant's quest to become the state attorney. Then, in 1836, only Hardin survived the Douglas-led Democratic Party's sweep of Morgan County's legislative seats. This sole Morgan County Whig who stood tall against the Little Giant was appropriately as physically imposing as Lincoln: soaring, muscular, hand-some—and a more popular wielder of Whig polemics.

The also more popular Ned Baker migrated from England to Lincoln's Sangamon County. This superb and charming orator, prematurely graying and balding, became known as the "Gray Eagle." Where Lincoln stymied Democratic foes with George Forquer's lightning rod, Baker famously presented a special gift to Whig colleagues, visiting from Chicago. He promised that the present—a caged bald eagle—would soar in celebration the second it heard that the Whigs' 1840 presidential candidate, William Henry Harrison, had won Washington, DC's Executive Mansion.[1]

As if in proof, the patriotic beast spread its wings and shrieked upon hearing "Harrison." Some observers thought they saw Baker pull "tail feathers" right before "the spectacular effect." No one ever saw Hardin (or Lincoln) pull off such hijinks.

Against the ultrahandsome Hardin's hard-edged charisma and the ultraplayful Baker's fetching charm, the struggling Lincoln possessed only one advantage. His outflanked state party needed an organizer to match Democrats' electioneering. Baker and Hardin found political maneuvering a bore. Lincoln savored party building. By erecting a Whig state party organization, Lincoln could win compatriots' gratitude and maybe his turn in the Seventh District congressional seat, at least after Hardin and Baker took their turns.

Illinois Whigs, like counterparts elsewhere, had lagged behind Democrats in building partisan organizations. Lincoln's snobby brother-in-law, Ninian Edwards, typified old-fashioned Whigs' disdain for patronage, demagoguery, and electioneering. Edwards's old-wave Whig sneer lost the snob his legislative position. Lincoln's new-wave Whig popular campaigning could win the political organizer a congressional post.

Democrats scoffed that Whigs remained too undemocratic for democratic campaigning. Lincoln responded with a variation on his "lightning rod" putdown of George Forquer. His tormentor this time, Democrats' Colonel Richard Taylor, mocked Honest Abe's egalitarian postures. The phony Lincoln, Taylor sneered, married on Quality Hill and in Ninian Edwards's parlor!

In response, Lincoln snuck up on his tormentor. He jerked Colonel Taylor's vest. Out tumbled "Dick's ruffle shirt," his "gold chains," and his "gold watches." Amid "uproarious laughter," Lincoln recalled that he had entered Illinois as "a poor boy," atop a "flatboat" with "only one pair" of "buckskin . . . breeches." Sopped breeches, after shrinking, left a "blue streak around my leg," visible "to this day." If this is "aristocracy," Lincoln climaxed, "I plead guilty to the charge."[2]

He pled innocent to Democrats' wider accusation: that Whig policies favored the rich and wellborn. What is undemocratic, Lincoln asked, about

Four Illinois political compatriots: Edward Dickinson Baker (*top left*), John J. Hardin (*top right*), Norman Judd (*bottom left*), and Lyman Trumbull (*bottom right*)

using the nation's lands and funds to bring lush transportation and therefore poor emigrants to prairie opportunities? And what is undemocratic about raining productive National Bank loans on impoverished developers of mandatory infrastructure?

Lincoln's questions illuminated an important (and still underappreciated) fact. While Democrats came first to the American mid-nineteenth-century populist feast, Whigs soon flocked to the table. The "Age of Jackson" swiftly became an age of two-party populism, with the Abraham Lincolns as egalitarian as the Andrew Jacksons.[3]

Democrats still called their program more democratic than Whigs' proposals. By killing the National Bank, Democrats meant to end the deposit of the people's governmental funds in a monster bank, supposedly benefiting only rich stockholders. Democrats would instead deposit the people's funds in a so-called Subtreasury System, meaning nonbank vaults underneath the Treasury Department. Whigs retorted that the people's coin would then rust uselessly in subterranean iron boxes. The Abraham Lincolns hoped a revived National Bank would loan the people's funds to develop the people's economy.

Development was the key to the Whig worldview, whether the issue involved National Bank loans to local entrepreneurs or federal grants to state infrastructure. The federal government held far more dollars and the lion's share of states' unsold land. After the System's demise, Whigs urged, only federal resources could finance a transportation boom for central Illinoisans.

Why, Lincoln asked, had the people voted against Whigs' more democratic policies? His answer: Democrats deployed better electioneering organizations to spread a feebler message. His solution: improved Whig organizations to rouse mass conviction and voting.

Lincoln likened a coordinated party canvass, seeking to persuade voters and deliver the persuaded to the polls, to an organized military campaign. When organized English invaders faced unorganized Americans in 1812, he noted, our forebearers belatedly "organized—met—conquered—killed." Now, a concentrated Democratic Party came "armed . . . with falsehood, slander, and detraction." A disorganized Whig Party must again out-organize our "country's enemies."[4]

Whig organizers, urged Lincoln, must begin by fashioning layer upon layer of nominating conventions. Otherwise, Whig candidates will fight each other before voters. Then a single Democratic Party candidate will win.

Instead, a statewide Whig conclave must nominate the party's single ticket for governor and presidential electors. Then, in each congressional district, Whig conventions must choose a single candidate, selecting between each county convention's lone selections. After these conventions decreed, no loser should appeal to a higher convention or to the voters.

To his controlled convention nominations, Lincoln would add a controlled campaign hierarchy. At the top, the statewide Whig convention must select a statewide Central Committee, which must appoint and oversee congressional district Whig Committees, which must appoint and oversee Whig County Committees, which must appoint county captains, who must appoint precinct captains, who must appoint section captains, who must "see each man of his Section face to face" and make sure that each visits the polls.[5]

Political warriors must also scrutinize neighbors, seeking potential converts. Captains must keep "CONSTANT WATCH on the DOUBTFUL," handing them "such documents as will enlighten and influence them."[6] Each captain must additionally raise fifty to one hundred dollars to finance Whigs' statewide newspaper.

Oral appeals must supplement written arguments. Since custom forbade nominated presidential candidates from addressing rallies, candidates for Electoral College posts toured often. Lincoln, a habitual Whig Electoral College candidate, lavished weeks on campaign trails every four years, as did Democrats' Little Giant. The two orators spent dozens of afternoons trading verbal blows before their 1858 showdown.

Election Day exertions, urged Lincoln, must finalize campaign efforts. We must know who will vote for us and convey our fanciers to the polls. "Our solemn conviction" is that Whigs, while a minority in recent elections, are a silent "majority of this nation" and will triumph, whenever we arouse "all" our partisans.[7]

Here as everywhere, understanding the eventually famous Lincoln requires appreciating the earlier obscure partisan. In "union is strength," cried the Union's subsequent savior, two decades before the Civil War and with only his disorganized Whig Party in mind. "A house divided cannot stand," urged the future Republican, a decade and a half before the Great Debates with Douglas and with only his disorganized Illinois Whig Party in sight.[8]

In the mid-1840s, to gain the elusive Whig congressional nomination in a district where two more popular titans made him odd man out, Lincoln became the esteemed reformer of old-fashioned Whigs' antiparty snobbery. In the mid-1850s, to earn Illinois Republicans' senatorial and then favorite-son status for vice-presidential and presidential nominations, he would become the supreme architect of the new state party. In early 1861, to stimulate antislavery politics in the Border South, the new president would use patronage appointments to encourage a native Republican Party.

The many Americans who hate partisan politicians—a curious trait in a nation infatuated with democratic politics—can never fully appreciate the ladder Abraham Lincoln ascended toward the top. "A free people," Lincoln declared in his 1852 eulogy of Henry Clay, his favorite politician, "naturally divide into parties." A would-be statesman "who is of neither party is not—cannot be—of any consequence. Mr. Clay therefore was of a party."[9] So was the never more consequential Mr. Lincoln, as the first secessionists would emphasize when fleeing a patronage-sustained southern Republican Party.

In the 1840s, Lincoln's payoff for partisan organizing depended on his convention system. Grateful politicians in a Seventh Congressional District convention could give him the Whig congressional nomination, sparing him from facing the more charismatic Baker or Hardin in popular primaries. But county, then district, conventions could crush his hopes. In the aftermath of the ruined System, Lincoln, the most extravagant System spender, became a likely Whig loser.

Lincoln's ladder of conventions led to his first post-System defeat, occurring in his county convention before he even reached the district convention. On March 20, 1843, after seven ballots, the Sangamon County Whig Convention narrowly selected Ned Baker over Lincoln as its favorite son for the Whig congressional nomination. Baker partisans then begged the loser to champion the winner against John Hardin in the district showdown between Sangamon and Morgan Counties' candidates for Congress.

Lincoln unhappily agreed to become Baker's district convention spokesman. He felt, he complained, like a best man supporting a groom who "has cut him out and is marrying his own dear 'gal.'"[10] But after Hardin thumped Baker in the Seventh Congressional District's so-called Pekin Convention, the loser's best man spied a way to become a future groom. Lincoln would seek to cajole the convention that favored Hardin to favor Baker the next time around. Then it might be Lincoln's turn the following time. Posterity calls Lincoln's hoped-for arrangement "rotation in office." Lincoln called it "turnabout is fair play."

Hardin called it foul play. Why should a popular winner agree to retire two years hence, before serving an hour? So Lincoln needed to present more ambiguous language about future elections to the 1843 district convention, after it anointed Hardin for the upcoming race. Lincoln's solution revealed that the impatient advocate of the System had evolved into a patient manipulator of political language—a formidable addition to his patient erection of party organizations.

On May 1, 1843, Lincoln finessed Hardin's district convention into resolving that Baker would be "a suitable" Whig nominee for Congress next time. This Pekin Agreement did not preclude the 1844 congressional district convention from calling someone else (including Congressman Hardin!) most "suitable." The 1846 convention could also select Hardin or Baker, not Lincoln, as most "suitable." But the Pekin Agreement bore some implication that the district's three Whig luminaries, in the interest of party unity, should each serve one congressional term, until all had had a turn.[11]

Ned Baker rode the implication to Congress in 1844. But when Lincoln sought the same ride in 1846, Hardin questioned Lincoln's (self-serving) rule that a district convention must choose a party's congressional candidate. Hardin sought an equally self-serving alternative. Voters in primary elections, instead of politicians in stuffy conventions, should elevate their favorite Whig candidate. Hardin, likely the people's favorite, apparently intended to seek a Whig district primary's vote for another election to Congress, whatever a district convention preferred and the Pekin Agreement implied.

In retrospect, Hardin's populist menace is hard to appreciate, for posterity knows that Lincoln ascended and Hardin disappeared. But never read history backward. In 1846, Hardin and Baker remained the Seventh Congressional District's most popular Whigs. Lincoln's best hope to catch up remained that politicians in convention assembled, grateful for party service delivered, might read the Pekin Agreement his way.

In early 1846, the desperate Lincoln tried to shame Hardin away from a congressional race. He wrote his nemesis one of his longest, most convoluted letters, comprising 2,600 words of exasperation, hurt feelings, and special pleading.[12] But his labor for the party, not his anguished plea, ultimately deterred the potential rebel. After asking around, Hardin realized that Lincoln's political chits, plus violations of the Pekin Agreement's unifying objective, could split the congressional district's Whigs and thus elect a Democrat.

Rather than fighting Lincoln and the Pekin Agreement, Hardin decided to bide his time until the agreement no longer weakened his hand. In the interim, Hardin patriotically enlisted to fight the Mexicans—a truly fatal decision. Colonel John J. Hardin perished in the Mexican War's Battle of Buena Vista, February 23, 1847. The tragedy dimmed the history of perhaps the most promising Illinois leader you have never noticed.

Hardin's death also removed the Illinois Whig that Abraham Lincoln had least mastered. Had Colonel Hardin survived (or better still, come home as a war hero), Lincoln would perhaps never have emerged as *the* central Illinois Republican politician, destined to take on Douglas. Shades of what could have happened if Abraham Lincoln had bid his father good-bye in Indiana, or if that Indiana mill horse had kicked him an inch higher, or if Ann Rutledge had lived years longer. The story of this relentless climber does raise questions about the fates.

3

How appropriate, then, that after Lincoln's Whig convention nomination and Hardin's unhappy surrender to the verdict, only the Springfield leader's youthful outbursts on fatalism could block his congressional election.

Democrats nominated the Reverend Peter Cartwright to oppose Lincoln.[13] The fiery preacher had routed Lincoln for the legislature in 1832.

Fourteen years later, Peter Cartwright could only repeat the victory by playing the fatalism card. Both candidates thought slavery wrong, abolitionism counterproductive, the National Bank passé, and internal improvements mandatory. But Cartwright, twenty-three years older and a Sangamon County resident seven years longer, remembered that as a new settler, Lincoln had ridiculed preachers, rejected church membership, and speculated that impersonal fate determined men's actions and thoughts. Should such an infidel, Cartwright asked during the 1846 campaign, become our congressman?

Lincoln answered in his "Handbill Replying to Charges of Infidelity," July 31, 1846.[14] These some four hundred words comprised the future president's fullest explanation of his complicated fatalism. How, voters wanted to know, could he believe *both* that his opinions could lead to different outcomes *and* that fate determines all outcomes?

The "Handbill" hemmed and hawed. Lincoln denied that "I am an open . . . scoffer at Christianity." (But "open" aside, did Lincoln privately scoff?) He had never "spoken with intentional disrespect of religion." (But "intention" aside, had disrespectful words slipped out?) "True, . . . in early life I was inclined to believe" in "the 'Doctrine of Necessity.'" But I advocated fatalism, he wrote, only in private, only with "one or two or three" compatriots, and never within the last "five years." (But did he now believe the doctrine?)

He had "never," he added, "denied the truth of the Scriptures." (But did he believe in said truth?) "Several . . . Christian denominations," Lincoln noted, preached determinism. (And did he?) I could never "support . . . an open enemy of and scoffer at religion," Lincoln affirmed. (But is he secretly said enemy?) And what about that overarching theological question, missing in his denials: How can a human, devoid of free will, willfully choose Christ?

That "higher matter of eternal consequence," Lincoln answered, is solely between a man "and his Maker." This election, he implied, solely involves a lower matter of secular consequence: Will Whigs or Democrats best serve central Illinois's interests? That political criterion doomed Peter Cartwright's theological attack. The reverend's unpardonable political sin, in this Whig district, remained his Democratic Party allegiance. By the middle of the campaign, the Democrat haplessly stopped campaigning.

At the end of the canvass, August 3, 1846, Lincoln received a record 56 percent of the Illinois Seventh District's vote for Congress. He amassed four percentage points more than Hardin won in 1843 and three more than Baker collected in 1844. As usual, Lincoln scored particularly heavily in the four Seventh Congressional District counties also included in his Eighth

Judicial Circuit. There he had greeted and served many folk semi-annually. His political exile from office had finally ended—or had he received but a temporary reprieve?

4

He had for sure only temporarily escaped the big issue of the campaign and the biggest riddle of his mentality. The "Handbill," Lincoln's best explanation of the free-will puzzle, remained a blur. Then again, "blur" best describes Lincoln's position on fatalism. "Mr. Lincoln told me once," reported Joseph Gillespie, a close Illinois Whig friend, "that he could not avoid believing in predestination." But "he considered it a very unprofitable field of speculation because it was hard to reconcile" fatalism with "responsibility for one's acts."[15]

Right *there* was Lincoln's intellectual predicament. He believed in predestination, and especially that men stood squeezed between inescapable internal "motives" and equally inescapable external propulsions. Yet he equally believed that men must responsibly choose honor's dictates. He could live with both choice and inevitability only by thinking long and hard about how and when he might slightly move huge forces in moral directions.

If he exerted his willpower at inexpedient times and/or with inexpedient pressures (as when sticking by the doomed System), he would be crushed. Yet if he exerted his slight force at a rare timely moment (as when inventing turnabout is fair play and cornering more powerful politicians into yielding to his invention), he might tease the inexorable. After the System years, no politician acted more slowly, more carefully, more ponderously, always testing each item's power in a slew of theoretically irreconcilable beliefs.

But on the many occasions when this activist wavered uncertainly, he would not forever wait to be sure. To imagine him frozen against ever taking a stab is to misunderstand him utterly. Theoretical fatalists in the Marxist vein, such as Lenin, can as little be understood as passively waiting for some predetermined opening.[16]

Lincoln's semi-fatalism allowed him, as a practical politician, to face an individual's normal lack of control unusually squarely. He remained equally able to pounce at abnormal moments when he glimpsed a possibility. He would, for example, become the Great Emancipator only after the slowest inching beyond his twenty years of antislavery silence, picking scant instants to creep slightly when he might somewhat matter.

Before the slavery issue, he had strayed too unthinkingly to the side of his personal sway. He had thus fatally exposed his overambitious economic program to an overwhelming economic panic. His comeback had featured a shrewder calculation of how much he could do, and when. Bowing before Baker's and Hardin's temporarily unbeatable force, he had slowly built up party power and party rules for future use. After four hard years, he had deployed his partisan creations at just the right moment to wedge himself into a congressional seat. But in Congress, could his little personal force budge a nation's huge impersonal propulsions—and with the results he intended?

9

The Congressional Fall

A two-year congressional term included long and short sessions. Abraham Lincoln's long session, running from early December 1847 to mid-August 1848, included the future Great Emancipator's futile efforts to avoid slavery issues. The futility helped cause Whigs' loss of his congressional seat in the August 7, 1848, Illinois election. After doing too little about slavery to be politically viable in the long session, Lincoln attempted too much in his short session (early December 1848 to early March 1849). Thereafter, the bruised ex-congressman fruitlessly sought a Washington, DC, patronage position. He would not return to the nation's capital for eleven years.

1

On December 2, 1847, Mary, Bobby, Eddie, and Abraham Lincoln arrived in Washington with high expectations for the long session. They rented a small second-floor bedroom in Ann Sprigg's boardinghouse, erected on part of the future site of the Library of Congress. Mrs. Sprigg's first-floor dining-room windows overlooked Capitol Park and the Capitol Building. The epic view highlighted new worlds to conquer. The claustrophobic bedroom suggested the Globe Tavern revisited.

While the husband escaped during his long workday, the wife hoped for fresh prominence after hours. Mary Lincoln could not vote or serve. But she could captivate and charm. Her drawing-room prowess, she hoped, could indirectly influence Capitol titans. Then, in daytime, she could cross the park to watch her Abraham become Washington's new lion.

The lioness became the first disillusioned Lincoln. Few luminaries invited Washington rookies much less their families to drawing rooms. Few congressmen brought their wives much less their children to town. Mrs. Sprigg's boarders sometimes disliked Mary and her rowdy boys. Within weeks, the thwarted spouse and rambunctious sons retreated to the Todds' Lexington, Kentucky, home.

After Mary's angry 1848 departure, three-plus months of Abraham's long session remained. This separation of husband and wife generated their most revealing surviving correspondence. When the exchange began, Lincoln reported that housemates on "decided good terms" with you "send their love. . . . The others say nothing."

Before you left, the fledgling congressman continued, I resented you "some" for "hindering" my "attending to business." Now, "nothing but business . . . has grown exceedingly tasteless." He hated "to stay in this old room by myself." He winced that Bobby and Eddie might "forget father."[1]

When Mother offered to return with their fellows, Father responded, "I want to see you, and our dear—*dear* boys very much." So "if" you will "be a *good girl* in all things, . . . then come . . . as *soon* as possible."[2]

The wife delayed returning east until his long session ended. Washington snubs still rankled, as perhaps did his "good girl" line. The husband, almost ten years older, could be woundingly condescending with his "child bride." Then again, she had been woundingly condescending about his parlor foibles. When either braved the other's comfort zone, the misfit struggled while the mate cringed. Escape from the other's presence provided relief. But loneliness spoiled the separation. Only shared delight in his politics and their children built serene bridges.

2

In Lexington, Mrs. Lincoln suffered her father's absences and her stepmother's frost. In Washington, Mr. Lincoln savored a haven for drawing-room misfits. During the 1840s, chattering politicians relished a bowling lane near Mrs. Sprigg's boardinghouse. Congressmen took turns rolling the ball. Then they gossiped while others hurled.

Lincoln's banter made up for his hurling. An accurate heave of the weighty ball required three coordinated steps forward. Lincoln, superb axman when standing still, erratically hurled when thrusting forward.[3] His latest stumbles on his flat feet resembled his former Quality Hill dancing. This time, bowling gutters rather than belles' toes took the punishment.

This time, the giant giggled at his gaucheries. His appealing ability to chuckle at his lurches also generated his guffaws at his whoppers during breaks between gutter balls. "I suppose you city boys never saw the time," started one of the rural wit's favorites, "when the Irish bull quizzically stared at new American boots outside his stall. 'I shall nivir git em on,' the Old World relic seemed to be muttering, 'till I wear em a day or two and stretch em a little.'"⁴

The frivolity won Lincoln the same leg up in Washington that his pioneer tales had earned in New Salem. Word that he was story-telling led folks to descend on the bowling alley, recalling the "Social Club" in Joshua Speed's large bedroom after store hours. But to ascend further in Washington, DC, the frontiersman would have to add a statesman's depth to a commoner's comedy. Did Congressman Lincoln bring auspicious programs?

3

The Whig had packed a speech on the tariff. His maiden oration instead supported national internal improvements, even in local areas. Years after leaving the state legislature in semi-disgrace, he better understood the System's collapse. Legislators had too much relied on Illinois resources, too recklessly gambled on governmental debt, and too heedlessly defied economic panic.

Lincoln arrived in Congress at an auspicious time for a new departure. With the recession easing, Illinois had scored a breakthrough. The Illinois and Michigan Canal, pushed forward with national land grants despite running in only one state, had been completed in April 1848. Chicago now sat on a vital link (with the help of the new canal) between the Illinois River (and thus the Mississippi) and Lake Michigan (and thus the eastern seaboard). A month before the watery bonanza opened, construction commenced on the Galena and Chicago Union Railroad, seeking greater speed between the Windy City and the Mississippi River.

Now that the federal purse might open, President Andrew Jackson's closure, his 1830 so-called Maysville Veto, loomed larger. The president's veto message had declared federal projects unconstitutional, when built in only one state. But what if a project exclusively in one state could link many states and the single state could not afford the linkage (as before Illinois's new canal)?

In his June 20, 1848, congressional oration, Lincoln's answer included belated caution. Five words emphasized his evolution: "I would not borrow money." We must "do *something*" but not "too much." At each session, Congress should "first determine *how much* money can, for that year, be spared for improvements."

That newly judicious nationalism accompanied his Whiggish motto that the "local and partial" could be "general" and national. Lincoln conceded that Illinois's lately completed canal between the Chicago and Illinois Rivers benefited his state more than any other. But one state's artificial waterway also boosted many states' national market. Sugar grown in Louisiana could now be profitably shipped from the Mississippi through the Illinois River and Illinois's new canal to the Great Lakes and on to eastern states. Louisiana planters received more for the treat, and Yankee consumers paid less for the sweetener. A "final crisis" now loomed, climaxed Lincoln, over national support despite local advantage. We must "battle manfully" or "surrender" nationalizing improvements.[5]

He battled manfully over the wrong crisis at the wrong time. In the state legislature, his poorly timed insistence on mammoth System funding had defied economic cycles. In Congress, his badly timed appeal for federal aid to transportation construction, even if the project only ran through one state, flouted political cycles. During the Mexican War's aftermath, national attention veered from old Whig/Democrat tiffs over local projects to new North/South fury over slavery's expansion (and especially the Peculiar Institution's potential in lately acquired Mexican territories). Viable statesmen had to swerve equally swiftly.

Lincoln would not budge from silence on provocative slavery issues. Yet the same politician, half a decade later, would give historic orations against slavery's extension. Why did he remain mute on this pregnant subject in 1848, when he longed to score an oratorical breakthrough and providence had delivered a golden opportunity? The answer requires a detour into Lincoln's extended speechlessness on America's most distressing subject.

4

Ever since "I can . . . remember," President Lincoln would write in 1864, I have believed that "if slavery is not wrong, nothing is wrong." The national hypocrisy, he had declared nine years earlier, "continually exercises the power of making me miserable."[6]

More than the republic's abstract hypocrisy generated his misery. Slavery's horrors came up close and personal. On a steamboat trip southward from Louisville in 1841, he had shuddered when seeing "twelve negroes . . . chained six and six together, . . . like so many fish upon a trot-line. In this condition, they were being separated forever from . . . fathers and mothers and . . . from wives and children." Tyrants coerced them southward, "where the lash of the master is proverbially more ruthless and unrelenting." Yet the victims daily strummed "the fiddle," played "cards," and "cracked jokes."[7]

Lincoln never called blacks "Sambos." But he winced at this behavior, akin to what a later generation would term "Sambo-ish." He remained uncertain whether "cheerful" appearances matched inner selves. Or did unfortunates only play the "happy" black to deter punishment? At any rate, they seemed hapless, hopeless, mocking America as a supposed haven of equal opportunity. Fourteen years later, the memory remained "a continual torment" to Lincoln, for "I see something like it every time I touch" a "slave-border."[8]

Yet he applauded "the great body of the Northern people" who "crucify their feelings" by remaining silent, "to maintain . . . the constitution and Union." Except for slavery, he believed that the Founding Fathers had erected a republican "City upon a Hill" for an undemocratic globe to emulate. "The world's best hope," he concurred with Henry Clay, "depended on the continued Union of these States." We must be "ever . . . watchful for the slightest tendency to separate."[9]

His master passion to save the Founders' flawed republic would swell. But his initial determination needed no expansion to dominate his statecraft. He considered the national republic a treasure. He called saving the gem his generation's great responsibility. If the national republic shattered, the world would be shown that democracy poisons large nations. But if his generation accomplished their mission as well as the Founding Fathers' generation had wrought theirs, inspired men everywhere would erect vast national democracies, based on the great truths that all men are created equal, that the lowly can vault as high as the lordly, and that central governments can further egalitarian progress in local provinces.

He also revered the Founders for deploring slavery and for working slowly toward, he and they thought, the only safe cure. Our Fathers, Lincoln noted, sought to preclude their Union's further contamination by barring more slaves from entering the republic. They also prohibited slaves from infecting America's vast free labor sprawls. Their national Northwest Ordinance (1787) banned enslaved migrants from the great Midwest. Their Missouri Compromise (1820) barred slavery in the huge Louisiana Purchase terrain north and west of enslaved Missouri.

While containing enslaved U.S. regions, cheered Lincoln, the Founders had slowly, safely commenced voluntary, consenting, nondisruptive manumissions. When the '76ers revolted from England, every state, North and South, still suffered from slavery. By 1830, when Lincoln came of age, almost every Yankee state had slowly eased slavery away. New York, once containing an approximately 15 percent slave population, had finally abolished the increasingly peculiarly southern institution in 1827. By 1850, more than a hundred thousand Border South slaves had been slowly manumitted, with Maryland almost half along on the limping progress and Delaware seven-eighths finished.

In another generation, hoped Lincoln, decontamination, with masters' agreement, would be finished everywhere above the South, including in still-infected Illinois.[10] Lincoln would settle for continuation of the Fathers' incremental, voluntary, nondisruptive road toward "ultimate extinction," even if the crabbed improvement took another century. He deplored outside "fanatics" who would not wait for insiders' necessarily gradual progress.

He feared that impatient Yankee do-gooders would destroy blacks' no less than whites' democratic destiny. Where would harm to white democracy end, he wondered, if the Founders' republic dissolved into severed pieces? How would redemption for slaves begin if the unfortunates were torn out of freedom's imperfect Union and imprisoned in a perfected slaveholders' Union? Both races would more surely benefit, he answered, if moderates preserved the so-called Great Republic, incrementally shrunk the area of enslavement, gradually converted slaveholders to peaceable change, and hoped that Yankee fanatics did not goad enraged southerners into destroying freedom's best hope.

Other answers to Lincoln's questions loomed. John Brown in Harpers Ferry would tomorrow precipitate peacetime violence. Lincoln himself would someday lead wartime coercion. If the North had earlier gone for abolitionism, sooner provoked secession, and faster won a civil war, blacks would have escaped their chains sooner. Many latter-day Americans, if transported back to the nineteenth century with twenty-first-century mentalities intact, would have joined abolitionist extremists, crusading for faster progress from the 1830s onward.

Lincoln, profoundly a mainstream politician, saw no way latter-day glory could begin in such far-out ways. In his opinion, the heavily racist northern mentality, prone toward African colonization and fearful of civil war, would scorn premature extremism. He saw that Radical Republicans could win scant elections in his own Border North (and not that many more in John Brown's Upper North) before civil war. The only practical way forward, long thought the someday Great Emancipator, was to seek pacific solutions, attempt incremental reforms, avoid wartime slaughter, and avert the risk of turning America's democratic City on the Hill into a devastated republican inferno. Only after all else failed would he accept terribly swift swords, with ultimate tears of joy for the blacks, horror for the dead, and anguish for sinning humanity.

5

As Abraham Lincoln started his long attempt to avoid what he considered disaster, his wariness about inflaming southerners toward disunion flowed from his apprehensions about human irrationality. He winced at memories of his potentially killing street fight with the Grigsbys and his almost murderous duel with James Shields. He wished his wife would control her temper. He watched supersensitive southerners, including his Kentucky in-laws, storm at Yankee do-gooders.

His 1838 Lyceum Address had denounced wild emotions as democracy's downfall. Lincoln had derided disruptive demagogues as republican villains. He had celebrated sober judges and lawyers as democracy's saviors. He had prophesized that unless courts' rationality eliminated demagogues' chaos, irrational citizens would overturn law, order, and Union. He prayed that a Union of sympathetic northerners and soothed southerners might some distant day consent—his most crucial word on emancipation—*consent* to "ultimate extinction."

His one-word step for saving endangered Union now and southern *voluntary* emancipation someday—HUSH—defined his statecraft for almost two decades. "I bite my lip and keep silent," he wrote in 1855.[11] He equally well could have penned that accurate self-portrait in 1837 or in 1848.

As Lincoln proved in 1837 when first confronting the issue as a state legislator, he would not even speak enough to detail his sparse written reason for silence. In reaction to abolitionism's first stirrings, the 1837 Illinois legislature resolved "that we highly disapprove of . . . abolition societies and . . . doctrines." The "General Government," continued the resolutions, "cannot abolish slavery in the District Of Columbia" or in "the slave-holding States" without residents' "consent."[12]

On January 20, the Illinois House of Representatives accepted these resolutions, 77–6. Five days later, the Senate concurred, 32–0. Together, the two chambers voted 109–6 (or 94.5 percent) that southern consent must precede federal emancipation and that abolitionists should hush.[13] The vote demonstrated that Border North public opinion would have to change mightily, before some "North" would rise to compel abolition in some "South."

Representative Lincoln (silently) cast one of the six votes against the anti-abolition resolutions. His dissent remained unexplained for six weeks, lest he irritate potential supporters of moving Illinois's capital to Springfield. Only after he had helped secure his new hometown's boon did he enter a noise-less explanation of his vote. With fellow Long Niner Dan Stone, he placed a "silent Protest" in the *House Journal.*

Stone and Lincoln's written protest seconded the legislature's opinion that Congress could not abolish southern slavery and should not free the District of Columbia's slaves without residents' consent. Lincoln and Stone also agreed with legislators that abolitionists tend "to increase" rather "than to abate" slavery's "evils." The two dissenters only protested that the legislature's anti-abolition resolutions should also have denounced slavery's "injustice and bad policy."[14]

These few words revealed nothing about how abolitionists made slavery's evils worse. Nor did the protest reveal how antislavery would ever prevail, if slaveholders had to consent to abolition. True to his commitment to muzzling himself, Lincoln waited five years to issue a one-sentence hint at his answer.

7

The lonely hint came in his February 22, 1842, Address to the Springfield Washington Temperance Society. The oration featured a plea that temperance reformers renounce holier-than-thou tirades. Lincoln hoped the renunciation would ease drunkards toward consent to repudiate demon drink. He condemned the "lordly judge" whose "thundering . . . denunciation" derides drunkards as "moral pestilences" and "authors of all . . . vice and misery and crime." Those insulted will never "join . . . a hue and cry against themselves." Instead, self-righteous denouncers will prod self-righteous sinners "to meet denunciation with denunciation . . . and anathema with anathema."

In contrast, unassuming persuasion might evoke no screaming fit between reformer and sinner. Instead, an encouraged fellow republican might liberate himself from liquor's despotism. Compare that external encouragement and internal reconsideration, urged Lincoln, with hysterical wars to smash the sinners, yielding only worlds hysterical to smash the critics.

Quiet temperance appeals could instead produce the "tyrant" liquor "deposed," with "no . . . orphans starving, no widows weeping." Uninsulted sinners might consent to self-improvement. Better still, went Lincoln's only pre-1849 sentence on how black slavery might be ended, when a properly reforming "Reign of Reason shall be complete, . . . there shall be neither a slave nor a drunkard on the earth."[15]

That barely spoken hope for a conquering antislavery consent had to suffice. Listeners had to see for themselves the similarity between the converted drunkard and the converted slaveholder. In both cases, righteous critics wrought havoc. Instead, discreet allies might achieve agreement. So the future Great Emancipator maintained almost two decades of silence on slavery, as the issue of his lifetime swelled uncontrollably.

8

Abraham Lincoln's special locale furthered his refusal to speak about slavery. This native of the Border South had landed in a Border North state—indeed in the Yankee borderland state that extended farthest south and contained the most surviving northern specks of the 1776 national institution.

Southern pioneers had crossed the Illinois border to dominate the lower third of the state. Some had brought black so-called "indentured servants." Supposedly, such laborers had "voluntarily" consented to serve "masters" for an allegedly confined period of time.

Other so-called French slaves in southern Illinois suffered black bondage without consent or time limits. The unfortunates descended from perpetual slaves that French settlers brought to Illinois *before* Congress passed the 1787 Northwest Ordinance. That ordinance barred *new* slaves' entrance. But the Founders, here as everywhere, left local populations free to decide about slaves already in an infected area. Hence Illinois's previously arrived "French" slaves (and often their issue) remained enslaved until the mid-nineteenth century.

Black serviles, whether indentured servants or "French slaves," together numbered some five thousand unliberated southern Illinois laborers during the 1820s and 1830s. Many southern Illinois masters and white neighbors wanted more bondsmen. The southern Illinois campaign for welcoming slave importations climaxed with a referendum on calling a state constitutional convention in 1824.

Northern Illinois citizens, almost all of them from northern free labor states, massed against southern Illinoisans' call. Central Illinois, where ex-southerners comprised over 40 percent of voters, narrowly opposed a potentially enslaving convention. The state's 57 percent vote against the convention signaled that overall, the Border North's Illinois leaned against the Border South. At that critical Illinois juncture, Abraham Lincoln was an observant fifteen-year-old.

Thereafter, most central Illinois politicians avoided leaning either way. State demography encouraged ultracautious antislavery men. No American answered the moderate call more continuously than the long-silent aspirant at central Illinois's vital center.

9

At home, southerners operated a classic closed society, where slavery was concerned. Heretics' pleas for abolition suffered repression, lest slaves or slaveless whites acquire dangerous ideas. If that silencing of democratic debate seems un-American, the censorship struck most southerners as America's salvation. They would combine the globe's most powerful enslavement of blacks with the world's most widespread free institutions for whites. With so-called gag rules against slavery debate, in the South and in Congress, they would guard their color line against incendiary opposition, however loudly Yankees screeched that democracy requires open debate on *everything*.

Many Yankees loathed gagging in a republican Congress. But many southerners insisted on congressional silence, no less than silence in their states, about their antirepublican institution. A fraction of northern congressmen supported the South's insistence, whether to keep the national peace or to save their national party. Thus commenced the first extended congressional slavery crisis during Lincoln's adulthood, starting in 1835 when a congressional gag triumphed and ending in 1845 with the silencer's rout.[16] Understand this preliminary contest between despotism's and democracy's political requirements and you begin to comprehend why history's worst civil war erupted fifteen years later.

Abraham Lincoln, detesting antirepublican gags almost as much as antirepublican slavery, voted against several newly proposed congressional silencers three years after the last gag perished. But he wanted no part of provoking the South out of the Union. So this future Great Emancipator said nothing about the congressional gag—the issue that dominated his first slavery tumult.

10

At the same 1845 moment when the congressional majority deserted gag rules, Texas Annexation demonstrated why slavery convulsions could no longer be hushed. A Texas crisis had been brewing since 1835, when American settlers led the revolution against Mexico and the establishment of a slaveholding Texas Republic. Revolutionaries claimed that their new republic's terrain extended south of the Nueces River, to the Rio Grande River (the current U.S./Mexican border). Mexican authorities countered that illegitimate revolutionaries had the least right to terrain between the Nueces and Rio Grande.

In 1845, outgoing American president John Tyler engineered U.S. annexation of the Texas Republic, adding some quarter-million square miles to the Union. In 1846, President James K. Polk's troops crossed the Nueces and marched southward toward the Rio Grande, provoking the Mexican War, 1846–48. American rout of the Mexicans yielded the Mexican Cession in 1848, adding another half-million square miles to the United States. The gigantic twin acquisitions, comprising fruits of both the Texas Revolution and the Mexican Cession, together doubled the Union's geographic size, provoking swollen controversies over whether slavery could enter new U.S. domains.

In Springfield at the time of Texas Annexation, Abraham Lincoln, two years short of becoming a congressman, deplored the new slavery controversy. "I never could very clearly see," he wrote, "how . . . annexation would augment the evil of slavery." American "slaves," he reasoned, "would be taken" to Texas "in about equal numbers, with or without annexation. And if more *were* taken because of annexation, . . . so many the fewer" would be "left where they were taken from."

He saw clearest folly in ignoring his signature plea. "I hold it to be a paramount duty of us in the free states," he warned, "due to the Union . . . and perhaps to liberty itself (paradox though it may seem) . . . to let the slavery of the other states alone."[17] Lincoln saw superb benefits for white liberty in preserving democracy in Union. He saw less hope for black liberty in provoking slaveholders toward forming their own despotic Union.

For North Americans of all races to enjoy a peacefully liberated republic, Lincoln believed in 1845, as long before and after, northerners must cease provoking insulted tyrants toward furious disunion, thereby perhaps dooming blacks to perpetual prison. Yankees must instead gently coax southern brethren over many years to apply the 1776 temple's lessons of liberty to all Americans.

11

Three years later, during his 1847–49 long congressional session, Lincoln silently indicated what he would say if he ever spoke on slavery expansion. Several times, he voted for the so-called Wilmot Proviso, barring slavery from all land acquired from Mexico after Texas Annexation. But he would no more now raise his voice against slavery in the Mexican Cession than he had lately campaigned against Texas Annexation or gag rules.

He remained determined to make a difference in his single congressional term, before "turnabout is fair play" returned him to Springfield obscurity. But few congressmen wished to hear about his internal improvement urgencies, and he dared not speak about others' antislavery urgencies. To make his splash, he would have to orate about some nonslavery aspect of the Texas convulsion.

Lincoln had lately chanced into a potential topic. He had visited his Todd in-laws in Lexington, Kentucky, en route to Washington. He had happened to be in town to hear Henry Clay lecture on November 13, 1847.

The Whigs' Clay attacked Democrats' President James K. Polk for marching American troops southward past the Nueces River and toward the Rio Grande, thus precipitating an allegedly unnecessary war. Now, the Great Compromiser warned, American slavery might infect many previously uninfected spots between the two rivers. Polk's march toward the Rio Grande, Clay concluded, caused all the following travail.[18]

In his infamous Spot Address to Congress, January 12, 1848, Lincoln dropped Clay's mention of slavery's expansion onto ex-Mexican spots. The Illinoisan instead exclusively damned the Polk administration for marching onto disputed spots and thus provoking a counterproductive war. Lincoln thereby aimed to make national patriotic waves without stirring nation-shattering slavery controversies.

Lincoln argued that Mexico had rightly claimed spots south of the Rio Grande River. The Texas Republic (and after annexation, the United States) had equally rightly claimed spots north of the Nueces River. But who rightfully owned the some one hundred miles between the rivers?

That depended, Lincoln answered, on which nation's inhabitants had settled and controlled which spot. Mexicans had occupied the spot between the rivers that Polk's soldiers invaded. Therefore U.S. invasion had caused the war.

The invasive President Polk, diagnosed Lincoln in the Spot Address, because "deeply conscious of being in the wrong," hopes "to escape scrutiny by fixing the public gaze upon . . . military glory." Meanwhile, Polk futilely gropes to end the war that he immorally commenced. His mind, "tasked beyond its powers," runs "hither and thither, like some tortured creature on a burning surface, . . . bewildered, confounded, and miserably perplexed."[19]

The words brimmed with Lincoln's usual Whiggish vitriol against Democrats. But did firebrands about past Jacksonians' errors illuminate present policy? The potential irrelevance received confirmation two weeks later when Mr. Polk's treaty ended the war that Lincoln had called beyond the supposedly "bewildered" president's capacity to finish.

So where was Lincoln's oratorical passion about what the war had produced—the slavery expansion controversy that threatened Union? And where was his patriotic celebration of compatriots who had died for their country, especially central Illinois's John J. Hardin? Lost, many Illinoisans lamented, in an empty oratorical spree over milk long since spilled. Some Illinois Democrats even called Lincoln's criticism of his nation's war traitorous, while young Americans fought, bled, and died.

"Traitor" Lincoln was not. He voted to supply the soldiers who fought a supposedly needless war. His criticism of a dubious war in progress set courageous precedent for republican inquiry during a national crisis.

His hometown critics still thought that he was battling the wrong crisis at the wrong moment. Critics included not only Democrats, eager to assault, but also Billy Herndon, keen to applaud. Illinois voters wanted to know not whether their republic had started an immoral war two years ago but whether slavery could spread to all that new U.S. soil *now*.

Illinois bipartisan criticism of the Spot Address threatened Whigs' customary retention of the Seventh Congressional District seat. Before the August 1848 election, Whigs' candidate for the lame-duck Lincoln's post, none other than Stephen Logan, had to overcome more than his former junior partner's Spot Address. The sour, dour whittler lacked the charismatic power recurring in Hardin to Baker to Lincoln. Logan also faced an unusually formidable Seventh Congressional District Democrat, the Mexican War hero Thomas L. Harris.

The whittler lost by 106 votes. The tiny margin indicated that a better candidate could have survived Lincoln's missteps. But the same numbers indicated that if "Spotty" Lincoln had not provoked dissent, Logan might have won. The unpopular little lawyer also might have won if Lincoln had given an inspiring eulogy for Hardin, the congressional district's fallen hero. A patriotic Lincoln oration in turnabout-is-fair-play style, praising a former Whig rival for final sacrifice to beloved Union, might have blunted Thomas L. Harris's war hero appeal. But Lincoln's wrong oration at the wrong moment had helped lose Illinois's only previously safe Whig congressional seat.

12

Lincoln likely concurred with that widespread verdict. Witness his fast self-correction. Usually, his recalibrations came slowly. This time, his reconsideration came scarcely a month after Stephen Logan's defeat.

After his long session adjourned, Lincoln enjoyed a September tour around the Northeast with his belatedly returned wife and sons. In Boston's Tremont Temple, Lincoln heard New York governor William H. Seward's oration. "I reckon you are right," the future president told his future secretary of state after the speech. Whigs must "give . . . this slavery question . . . much more attention . . . than we have."[20] Or as Lincoln should have put it, "*I* must find an early opportunity to give antislavery action my first attention."

Two weeks into Lincoln's ensuing short congressional session, New York congressman Daniel Gott provided the Illinoisan's opportunity. On

December 21, Gott introduced resolutions, calling sales of humans "contrary to . . . fundamental principles" and "notoriously a reproach to our country throughout Christendom." The New Yorker's resolutions would end the District of Columbia's slave trade.

On January 10, 1849, in the House of Representatives, Lincoln announced his intention to introduce substitute resolutions, which he read without comment. His intended substitutes would delete Daniel Gott's condemnation of southerners and outlawing of slave sales. The Illinoisan's resolutions would instead use federal dollars to lure Washington, DC, residents toward consent to liberate their slaves.

In this maiden antislavery effort, Lincoln usually shunned extremism, fatal to his fight for an internal improvement System in the state legislature. Seeing that silence on slavery had become equally fatal, he sought middle ground, far right of Yankee extremists. At midcentury, these forerunners of Radical Republicans meant to force slavery and the slave trade out of Washington, DC, terminate the interstate slave trade, obliterate slavery in the federal territories, bar acquisition of new enslaved terrain, and ban new slave states. Their "ring of fire" around the Old South, they promised, would drive slavery toward "ultimate extinction."

The Lincoln of 1849, nine years short of even mentioning ultimate extinction, would compel no one to free an adult. His resolutions would require only the District's black children to be freed, only at an (unspecified) grown-up age and with compensation to owners. To free current adults, the Illinois congressman would instead *entice* slaveholders toward voluntary manumissions. District residents would be paid "full cash value" to consent to their human property's freedom, after congressional and District majorities consented to the plan. This triple consent of the governed, Lincoln prayed, would revive the Founding Fathers' tactic for slow removal of bondage, always with the liberating area's agreement.

His intended conservatism met a firestorm against supposed radicalism. Angry critics called him an irresponsible fanatic. He would allegedly incite both sections and provoke a national bloodbath. Within the week, his dozen original supporters melted away. He never introduced his resolutions. His silence about slavery resumed for five more years.

Perhaps because the apprehensive antislavery rookie caved so quickly, those thundering against his alleged extremism never spotted his only radical bit. Nor has the revealing speck since been recognized. The undetected half sentence in his District resolutions was as understated as the equally understated single sentence in his temperance lecture, connecting conversion of drunkards and slaveholders. The scant words this time would have offered "full cash value" for any slave "now" living "within" the "District . . . *or now owned by any person or persons now resident within said District.*"[21]

Lincoln's here-italicized words swept beyond the some 4,600 slaves who labored in the capital. Washington residents sometimes owned many slaves who lived and worked beyond the District. Most such slaves toiled in the northern reaches of the South, fairly near the District. There, slaveholders formed small minorities and had been slowly manumitting slaves. There, gentle pleas and federal payments might hasten a consenting process already incrementally begun.

By potentially freeing slaves living beyond the District, Lincoln's intended resolutions embodied slaveholders' feared "entering wedge"—the federal action on federal terrain that could advance antislavery inside southern terrain. Abraham Lincoln, native of the Border South and husband of a Border South heiress, knew all about the slaveholders' fear that democratic agitation against so undemocratic an institution could creep inside the South, especially undermining slaveholders in the region's most northern, least consolidated outposts. In 1849, however, he was not yet the man nor his North yet the section to stand firm against a screeching South, sure to demand, upon first discovery, that federal payments to divide the most vulnerable southern region be buried alive.

Until his earliest presidential decisions, no further federal proposals to transform slaveholders' inner domains would inform this moderate's statecraft. Lincoln's 1854–60 antislavery thrusts would all deploy strategies of defense, aimed at blocking slaveholders from destroying Yankees' treasures beyond the South. Then, in 1861, the new president would try a better version of his undiscovered 1849 strategy, again seeking federal encouragement of consent to antislavery inside the least southern South. This time, the most reactionary slaveholders would notice, Lincoln would not quail, and the explosion would be historic.

13

After his short session adjourned, Abraham Lincoln, dismayed at leaving federal office as much a political nonentity as when he arrived, sought a Washington patronage position. He hoped to benefit from his dogma that patronage must reward the party's most successful campaigners. Otherwise, the best partisans would skip the party's next warfare.

As the only rookie representative and one of only two northerners in a gang of seven Whig congressmen, calling themselves the Young Indians, Lincoln had helped launch the presidential candidacy of the Mexican War hero

Zachary Taylor. After the general became the Whigs' presidential choice, Lincoln had led Taylor's Illinois popular canvass. With President Taylor entering the Executive Mansion as Lincoln exited Washington, the ex-congressman hoped for his deserved (he thought) reward. If appointed to an executive branch patronage position, he could return to Washington haunts before former congressional colleagues came back to town.

He especially wished to become the General Land Office's commissioner. The post, stationed in the Interior Department's new Washington office, paid three thousand dollars yearly—more than he had annually earned as a lawyer. The commissioner could influence federal land grants to railroads, even if they ran in only one state—Lincoln's panacea, along with the Illinois and Michigan Canal, for rescuing Illinois's System. The Taylor administration wished an Illinoisan to be the commissioner. Lincoln pitched his case as the most deserving Illinoisan to William Ballard Preston, the Virginian and fellow Young Indian who had become Taylor's secretary of the navy.

Unfortunately for Lincoln, Taylor officials thought a healthy party should open new ground, not just reward old warhorses. They also preferred a commissioner who had not lately flamed out in Congress. They especially meant to rally Whiggery in burgeoning Chicago. The Windy City's Justin Butterfield became their nominee, although he had initially favored Clay and had seldom campaigned for Taylor. Lincoln's victorious presidential choice had defied the Illinoisan's strategy for continued party victory.

14

In 1849, no one foresaw that in a dozen years, the failed Illinois congressman, after losing twice for the U.S. Senate and once for the vice presidency, would be president on the eve of civil war. Nor did any prophet envision that memories of his Taylor patronage fiasco would continue to distract a victor who had leapt miles beyond that setback. Taylor's lieutenants, however, did foresee that Lincoln would be absent from Whig action for years, unless they assuaged his disappointment. They thus asked the sulking ex-congressman to become secretary to Oregon Territory's governor. Shortly afterward, the administration offered the governorship itself.

By accepting the Oregon appointment, America's prime Horatio Alger would embrace a widespread Alger strategy: migrate toward opportunity. The migration tactic particularly enticed frontiersmen, including Lincoln's prime rivals. A couple of years before Lincoln pondered his migratory opportunity, Stephen A. Douglas moved from Jacksonville to Chicago and a fortune as railroad entrepreneur.

Meanwhile, Ned Baker, like Lincoln, could not be easily reelected to their Seventh Congressional District seat. "Turnabout is fair play," the Whig mantra that had advanced them both, arguably limited each to one turn as this district's congressman. Baker responded by moving to Galena, Illinois, on the Mississippi River, where he claimed another district's congressional seat. Thereafter, Baker traveled toward (failed) railroad gambles in Panama, then toward (failed) flings in California, then toward triumphs in Oregon, where he won a U.S. Senate seat in under a year.

Lincoln, in contrast, shuddered at migration. He would not become another Tom Lincoln, forever wandering after greener pastures. Nor did his cultivated wife wish to preside over supposedly uncouth Oregon drawing rooms. They both preferred that he reject President Taylor's invitation to the provinces, anchor in Springfield, revive his law practice, and think about why his congressional forays had yielded only crushing disappointments.

10

The Union's Economic Rescue

✦⊰⊱✦

Abraham Lincoln rose financially soon after plunging politically. The Illinois Central Railroad, flush with the Union's largesse, wrought an Illinois economic revolution during the early 1850s. The transformed transportation tied a provincial state into the national market and lifted Lincoln toward modest wealth. Then, several years after economic Union provided the Illinoisan's ladder beyond financial strain, political Union offered a road beyond backwater stagnation. The doubled ascension turned a grateful striver into an ever more fanatical Unionist.

1

In 1848, Lincoln's brief holiday between congressional sessions highlighted limitations of even the most navigable midwestern waterway. After his long congressional session (where few heeded his appeal for national internal improvements), and after his postcongressional swing around the eastern seaboard (where William H. Seward suggested speaking up on slavery), he took Mary and their boys to Buffalo. Either on this trip or in 1857, the would-be national commercialist visited nearby Niagara Falls. There an awed Lincoln, usually stuck on a river lacking enough navigable water, wondered where all that tumbling water came from.[1]

On his 1848 trip home, Lincoln marveled at more water still, spread from horizon to horizon. Since Mary wished to "travel the lake route home," he purchased tickets on the *Globe,* the new luxury steamer cruising the Great Lakes between Buffalo and Chicago. After arriving in the Windy City, the family

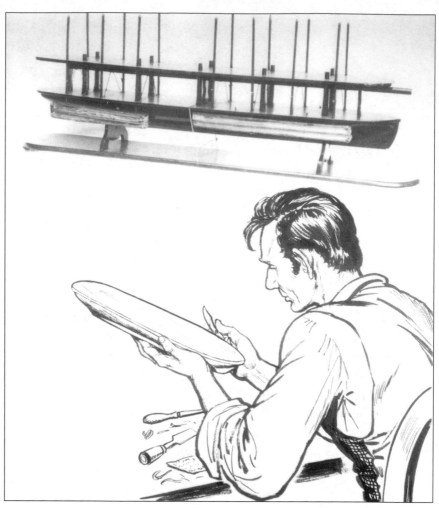

Lincoln whittling, Stephen Logan style, at his riverboat brainchild

would travel the newly finished Illinois and Michigan Canal down to the Illinois River. Then, even these unusually good (for central Illinois) waterways required a landed supplement, with the Sangamon River offering no way to speed upstream. So the family would hail the stagecoach to Springfield.

From Buffalo, the *Globe* had conveyed the Lincolns westward on Lake Erie, then northward on Lake Huron, then southward on Lake Michigan to Chicago. Almost always, broad, easily navigated waterways dominated the lake landscape. The major exception: the narrow, choked, twenty-eight-mile-long Detroit River, uniting Lakes Erie and Huron.

In contrast with the Great Lakes' oceanic sprawl and Niagara Falls' broad torrents, the river's crabbed flow had left the steamboat *Canada* marooned

Lincoln showing off the eighteen-inch model of his self-rescuing vessel to quizzical Springfield residents with John Francis Rogue's state capitol dominating the background

on a sandbar before the *Globe* arrived. The Lincolns watched western muscle men heave her cargo overboard and shove crates under her keel. Rescuers liberated the *Canada* only after the *Globe* passed on.

The turmoil recalled Lincoln's salvaging of Denton Offutt's flatboat, stuck on the New Salem milldam. The crippled *Canada* made the Detroit River seem another Sangamon, the culprit that snagged central Illinois in a penny-ante economy. Cramped water in the rivers, endless water in the Great Lakes and at Niagara Falls: Man's ingenuity needed to transcend nature's imbalance.

Upon his return to Springfield, Lincoln imagined a way to turn frustrating rivers into helpful streams. A marooned vessel, he speculated, might rise atop its own balloons. Empty "buoyant air chambers," he thought, could line a steamer's hull until needed. In an emergency, elaborate ropes and pulleys could force air into the chambers. Then bulging balloons would lift the vessel up and over milldams or sandbars.

In Springfield, Lincoln spent hours whittling away, Stephen Logan style, at an eighteen-inch model of his projected self-rescuing vessel. On his return to Washington, the lame-duck congressman applied for a federal patent. Soon after his short session, the Federal Patent Office granted him Patent #6469, for "Buoying Vessels over Shoals." No other president, before or since, has received a patent. No one else could now use his patented balloons to overcome rivers' snares.[2]

2

The ink had scarcely dried on Lincoln's patent before the Union's government made the Illinoisan's newest attempt at a central Illinois watery rescue irrelevant. A huge U.S. land grant for a "Central Railroad" in Illinois stimulated tracks and locomotives to sprout like prairie grass. With iron horses racing over regions where watery crafts crept, an avalanche of settlers and customers lifted Lincoln's central Illinois into the nation's economic and political forefront.

For two centuries, Americans had seen waterways, whether oceans or lakes or rivers, as keys to commerce. Lincoln had epitomized Americans' water-obsessed mentality. His teenage awareness of the outside world had commenced on the Ohio, matured on the Sangamon, and climaxed on the Mississippi. His first campaign document, seeking election to the legislature at the ripe old age of twenty-three, had pleaded for Sangamon River improvements.

The youth had reasoned that railroad substitutes would be too expensive. Two decades later, when traversing the Illinois and Michigan Canal, the thwarted middle-aged striver had hoped that the System's sole triumph, connecting Chicago to the west by an artificial waterway, would rescue the Windy City from its contrary river. Now railroads pushed Chicago's trade beyond the useful but limited canal, teaching midwesterners (and especially ex–river rat Lincoln) that commerce need not require water.

In Springfield, the lesson seemed to transform a town legend. River folk often see human characteristics in their vital streams. Central Illinoisans' personalization of the Sangamon resembled a classic river image.

In ancient Greek lore, Acetous, god of the nation's longest freshwater river, sired three beautiful daughters with voluptuous singing voices, all banished to a rocky Mediterranean island. In revenge, the nymphs lured seaborne voyagers with scanty dress. They then gleefully sang when sailors wrecked on the

rocks. Their ditty became notorious as the Sirens' Song. They entered Western literature as prototype femmes fatales.

Lincoln and fellow sufferers on the Sangamon did not need to read the
ancients to recognize their river's similarity to a temptress. Ever since the
Sangamon had impaled Lincoln on a New Salem milldam, he had fought
the river, in and out of icy streams, in and out of hapless legislatures, lamely
seeking to strengthen the exasperating flow. Throughout his two decades of
flailing, his river had seemed full of promise, fuller of denials, and fullest of
indifference to his frustration. Then as railroads suddenly opened central Illinoisans' possibilities and imaginations, the choked and choking Sangamon
took on another classic form. In the new world of iron horses, the river
seemed like a bypassed old maid.

3

Stephen A. Douglas's U.S. Senate maneuvers delivered the railroad breakthrough. Lincoln's lifetime rival, although four years younger, had always
seemed a provoking step ahead. In mid-1830s Illinois legislative proceedings,
Douglas had introduced a limited version of the System, while Lincoln went
politically broke chasing an extravagant version. At the beginning of the
1840s, Douglas became an Illinois Supreme Court justice, while Lincoln prepared to leave the state legislature in semi-disgrace. In 1842, Douglas vaulted
into the national House of Representatives, while Lincoln had to wait his
turn behind John Hardin and Edward Baker. In 1846, Douglas bounded into
the U.S. Senate (where he would remain until his death in 1861), while Lincoln squeezed out one dismaying term in the national House.

Lincoln's jealousy first became bitter in 1850. Then he sank from congressional powerlessness into Springfield isolation, while Douglas rose from senatorial back benches to national fame. In the Senate of 1850, Douglas secured a
North-South coalition for the Compromise of 1850. Then he forged an East-
West internal improvement coalition for Illinois's primary benefit.

Douglas's coup amassed 2.5 million federal acres to finance Illinois's
"Central Railroad." His projected behemoth would traverse the state's long
length, brushing western Illinois towns where the Illinois and Ohio Rivers
joined the Mississippi, with an added branch running eastward to Chicago.
"If any man ever passed a bill," the Little Giant bragged with the cockiness
that drove Abraham Lincoln wild, I enacted "one of the most gigantic enterprises of the age."[3]

Douglas prevailed by precluding rifts in his coalition. Democrats normally opposed Whigs' national aid to state improvements. But the Illinois

Democrat used his allies' state's rights convictions to forge a unique partnership with economic nationalists. Under state's rights provisions of Douglas's bill, the state legislature would decide both how to construct the nationally financed railroad and how to sell the enabling national land. Subsequently, legislators would determine how to tax and regulate the constructed rails.

To avert fears of an unbalanced federal budget, Douglas's bill gave states not scarce dollars but languishing federal acres. To rally southwestern states behind an Illinois jackpot, the Little Giant's legislation added land grants to Alabama and Mississippi, enabling rails to be constructed from the Central's southern Illinois terminus southward to the Gulf of Mexico. To bring a midwestern rival behind Illinois's lucre, the Douglas bill required the Central to build a bridge over the Mississippi River, from its Illinois northwestern terminus westward to Iowa.

To allay eastern distrust of the western measure, Douglas told some northeasterners, holders of worthless Illinois bonds, that his state would likely use its new tax proceeds to redeem its old paper. Rescued debtors, hinted Douglas, might even become new millionaires. The state might hand the Central's charter to eastern financers.

Most easterners still opposed the western extravaganza. But the Illinois senator had shrunk his opponents to a national minority. A year earlier, Congressman Lincoln had failed to secure a House majority for a few transportation dollars. Douglas's 2.5-million-acre land grant, in contrast, sailed through the Senate and later the House, with three-fourths of westerners defeating most easterners. The Whigs' President Millard Fillmore signed the Democrat's bill into law on September 20, 1850, the day after Congress finalized the Compromise of 1850, partly another Douglas coup.

4

Illinois received its federal largesse on the condition that railroad construction begin within two years and finish within ten. No problem. Inside five months, the legislature awarded eastern capitalists the federal land and a corporate charter. Within another two months, the Illinois Central Railroad Corporation commenced construction. During the ensuing fifty-five months, the company finished all 705 projected miles. In September 1856, this longest railroad in the world connected most of Illinois to the Mississippi (and thus to the South) and to Chicago (and thus to the East).

The swift completion showered bounties on the corporation and its governmental partners. The federal government profited from selling its retained half of the acres in the railroad's zone. The retained spread, unsalable at $1.25

per acre before Douglas's law, sold out for $9 million before the railroad's completion. The U.S. government later gleaned more millions from discounted rates when using the railroad.

The Illinois government profited even more. Its tax on the Central, starting at 5 percent of gross proceeds, swiftly ballooned to 7 percent. Within three decades, tax receipts paid off the state's $16 million debt from the System debacle (as Douglas had predicted).

Also as Douglas had predicted, the corporation's eastern investors received an immediate bonanza. Partners had to put up only $2 million of the railroad's $25 million startup costs. Capitalists received the remaining 92 percent by selling some federal acres and using the remainder as collateral to sell bonds. Within a few years, the railroad retired the bonds. Shareholders, out of pocket only $2 million for a $25 million railway, collectively averaged a $2 million yearly income during their gold mine's first twenty years.

In 1850, Illinoisans had enjoyed only 111 miles of railroad track (1.2 percent of the nation's). In 1860, almost 3,000 miles of track crisscrossed the state (9.2 percent of the Union's and more railroad miles than any state except Ohio). During the transforming decade, ten companies together built three times more Illinois tracks than the Illinois Central's. To the Central's rails up and down the state's length (plus one track to Chicago), newcomers added nine lines across Illinois's width, running from sundry Mississippi River towns to and from Chicago.

The Windy City, with its only westward line creeping only a little toward Galena in 1850, enjoyed ten finished lines to and fro the Mississippi in 1860. At Chicago, new rails joined many lines running toward and from the eastern coast. Or to repeat the astonished conclusion in Abraham Lincoln's central Illinois, now that rails connected Illinoisans and Americans in all directions, who needs the Sangamon?

5

Illinois's resulting economic takeoff vindicated Lincoln's theory about preconditions for American abundance. His viewpoint collides with latter-day theories that raw resources necessarily made Americans "a people of plenty" or that raw frontiers necessarily produced economic egalitarianism. Without human (and especially governmental) intervention to add transportation, Lincoln believed, natural riches would lie fallow. But after man-made infrastructure beckoned settlers to nature's riches, America could be Horatio Alger's terrain. It followed that Lincoln's age of national politicians, in the years before emancipation brought them even greater glory, hardly produced

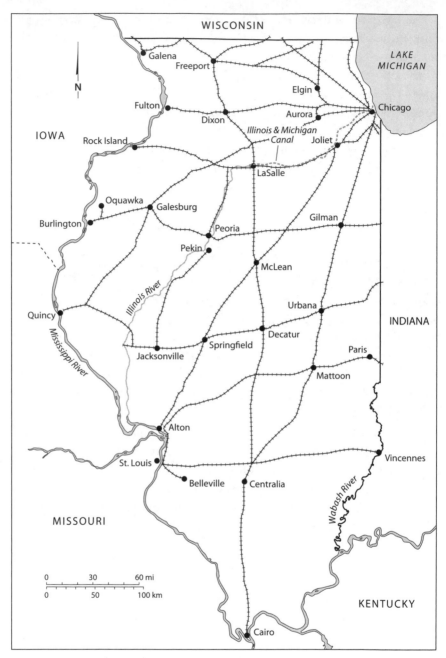

Illinois internal improvements, as of 1860. (Compare maps on pages 50 and 62.)

hackwork. They provided governmental keys to an economic opportunity that became a nation's signature.

Before the railroad revolution, Illinois contained only 851,470 inhabitants. In 1850, that population stagnated at eleventh in the nation, third in the Midwest and trailing five southern states. By 1860, the state's inhabitants had doubled to 1,711,951. The population then ranked fourth in the nation, second in the Midwest, and ahead of every southern state.

Most Illinois newcomers settled in the countryside. New farmers helped double the state's corn production during the 1850s, triple its wheat output and improved acres, and multiply its tobacco crop seven times. Cities also boomed. Lincoln's Springfield doubled its population. Douglas's Chicago quadrupled its peoples.

The world's longest railroad became the globe's best colonizer. The Illinois Central's advertisements, trumpeted throughout Europe and America, urged the ambitious to come build rails, then till farms near the tracks. Save a portion of your construction wages, went the lure. Then, with our cheap mortgages, you can buy our cheap acres in the country's best farmlands, featuring splendid access to national markets.

The largest industry in Chicago demonstrated how railroad, countryside, and city intermeshed to generate extravagant growth. Chicago's McCormick Harvesting Machine Company commenced in the early 1850s, when the new Illinois and Michigan Canal provided Chicago's only large-scale transportation to its hinterlands. Farmers along the new waterway relished the company's new aid to harvesting. But reapers were heavy and users along the canal scarce.

Then railroads transformed Illinois. Farmers near the tracks multiplied, seeking improving reapers. The McCormick Company produced 1,730 reapers in 1849, 6,229 in 1855, and 12,000 in 1860. Thus did Douglas's federal land grant spawn the Central Railroad, which attracted supplementary railroads, which beckoned the farmers who brought the factories to Lincoln's previously underpopulated, underdeveloped frontier.

6

Surging state population meant swelling national political power. After the booming 1850s, Illinois's number of congressmen shot from nine to fourteen. Its presidential electors leapt from eleven to sixteen. In 1860, the state's two favorite sons vied to occupy the nation's favorite house.

After Stephen A. Douglas's national coming-out party in the 1850 U.S. Senate, few denied his presidential potential. But after Lincoln's debacles in the 1847–49 U.S. House of Representatives, few saw Executive Mansion possibilities. During his 1849–54 involuntary withdrawal from politics, the ex-congressman's dividends from Illinois's railroad revolution had to be exclusively financial.

Materialistic uplift he abundantly received. During the 1850s, the lawyer's income tripled to around $4,500 annually. After paying off the final dribbles of his "national debt," the longtime debtor became a locally significant lender. Supposedly, the New York Central Railroad offered him a (rejected) ten-thousand-dollar annual retainer. Demonstrably, the Illinois Central paid him a handsome annual salary plus a five-thousand-dollar bonus for one case.

Despite Lincoln's occasionally large railroad retainers, his legal career still largely limped down prerailroad ruts. He still spent half the year on the Circuit. Both on the grimy road and in his messy Springfield office, he still largely chased paltry fees for fleeting attention to petty cases.

Only 4 percent of his 1850s cases involved railroads. His legal forays still usually concerned individuals facing slander, divorce, property damage, and debt (half the time debt). His 1850s railroad cases usually involved iron horse versions of noncosmic contentions, including trespassing, killing animals, or damaging fences. His predominance of petty cases, railroad or otherwise, indicated how railroads most boosted his earnings. The railroad revolution doubled the number of Illinoisans, which doubled the number of squabbles, which doubled the number of attorney fees, which, when you usually averaged only ten dollars per dispute, significantly fattened your wallet.

Because Lincoln's big fees for big cases remained exceptions, his fresh affluence still left him outside his town's upper class. In 1860, 28 percent of Springfield's residents owned more property. Seventy-one percent of the city's lawyers exceeded his net worth.[4] When he left for Washington in 1861, he owned some five thousand dollars' worth of choice real estate (including his Springfield home and 160 Iowa acres). He also had $9,378 out on well-secured loans.

A half decade later, he would leave Mary an $83,344 estate (the equivalent of near $2.2 million in early twenty-first-century cash). He would gain almost 80 percent of his 1865 fortune from saving 66 percent of his twenty-five-thousand-dollar annual presidential salary.[5] For this seeker, politics always came first. Having started as a politician before he became a lawyer, the resurrected politician would amass a wealthy man's estate from political salaries after becoming an ex-lawyer.

During his presidency, Lincoln cared nothing about becoming the equivalent of a modern millionaire, if he even noticed. He had long only sought middle-class comforts for his family and political advance for himself. In the 1850s, the Union's economic surge, lifting him into Springfield's upper middle class, had given him the necessary materialistic boon at just the right political moment, when climactic slavery controversies called for heroics.

His gratitude for economic ease multiplied his devotion to Union. In important contrast, Lower South squires little relied on the Union for better transportation, more migrants, and richer markets. Deep in the South, easily navigable rivers flowed speedily in the right direction, blacks provided much labor, and ocean ships carried produce, especially cotton, to international markets. In the Cotton Kingdom, enthusiasm for other ideals than Union galloped at the same time that Yankee Horatio Algers such as Abraham Lincoln rode a Unionist surge.

7

After triumphs, all Horatio Algers face a proverbial fork in the road. Some formerly impoverished sufferers, dazzled by fresh possibilities, become nouveau riche squanderers and/or speculators. Others, more repelled by old travails and less enticed by new spending, become wary purchasers and/or careful investors. Because of his monkish indifference to monetary extras and his repellent memories of poverty's agonies, Abraham Lincoln became the classic post-Alger guardian of the rewards of climbing. He would preserve his wealth and his Union with the same tight-fisted determination.

The newly comfortable lawyer kept embarrassing recollections of early discomforts carefully hidden. The rare occasions when he lifted the guard illuminated bitter memories. His "Almanac" case, *People v. Armstrong* (1857–58), one of only twenty-six times Lincoln defended an accused murderer and the only time he wept in a courtroom, offers an affecting example.[6]

The revealing incident began when Hannah Armstrong, widow of Jack Armstrong, Lincoln's wrestling foe a quarter century ago in New Salem, begged him to save Duff Armstrong from jail. Along with other youths in their twenties, Hannah and Jack's son had lately abused evenings at religious camp meetings, defying lessons daily preached under the revival tent. After one of their drunken sprees, one of their fellows, "Pres" Metzker, suffered a fatal broken skull.

A grand jury indicted James Norris for allegedly smashing Metzker's head from behind with a yoke, ripped from an ox cart. Another grand jury indicted Duff Armstrong for supposedly lashing a *slung* shot into the victim's eye from in front. (No *sling* shot this: Duff's supposed weapon was a leather-wrapped missile, the same shape as modern baseball's hardball, but harder, attached to a leather strap that could be whipped like a modern pitcher throws, but faster.)

The victim's savaged head bespoke terrible weapon(s). At James Norris's trial, occurring before Duff Armstrong's, the jury accepted the manslaughter case for yoke versus skull. The convicted Norris suffered eight years in prison.

James Norris's prior conviction helped Lincoln defend the alleged slung shooter. A doctor testified that Norris's blow from *behind* sufficed to kill "Pres." Since Norris is a convicted murderer, Lincoln asked, must Duff Armstrong, with his blow from in *front*, also be guilty of the murder, beyond reasonable doubt?

Although Abraham Lincoln thought this his best argument, posterity often considers his more colorful "almanac" gimmick more persuasive. A prosecution witness claimed to have seen, by the light of a gleaming moon, Duff savage Metzker with the slung shot. The defense attorney coaxed the eyewitness to repeat his allegation several times. Then Lincoln produced an almanac, indicating that at the fatal hour, the dim moon could highlight no slung shots.

Still, Duff and several observers thought that Lincoln's closing fifteen minutes of pleading, with moons scarcely mentioned, most captured the jury. As Lincoln began his climactic plea, his handsome snow-white suit and broad black cravat anticipated another cleaned-up frontier humorist, Mark Twain, a quarter century hence on the Lyceum lecture circuit. As Lincoln's jury address climaxed, he stripped off the fashionable coat and tie, rolled up both sleeves, threw down one suspender, "Pot" Green style, and seemed to regress into his afflicted self, a quarter century before.

Lincoln in his white suit at the "Almanac" trial, May 7, 1858

Lincoln told the jury about arriving in New Salem like "a sort of floting Driftwood," a "strange, friendless, uneducated, penniless boy."[7] In New Salem, he continued, his wrestling match with Jack Armstrong had earned his first public notice. Subsequently, his rapprochement with his foe had earned his entrance into the strapped Armstrong family's protective circle. In their crude cabin, Lincoln fondly recalled, Jack's wife, Hannah, had fed him coarse victuals, foxed his surveyor pants against bristles, washed and repaired his torn shirt, and smiled at the spectacle of the giant rocking baby Duff's cradle.

Now Jack had died, the defense attorney winced, leaving his widow impoverished and his son an accused murderer. I have come to Duff's rescue gratis, Lincoln explained, out of reverence for Hannah and affection for Jack, to beg that their son receive the mercy they gave me. You can break an angel's heart, his choked voice whispered as tears moistened his cheeks. Or you can give her boy a reprieve.

The jury swiftly gave Duff another chance. The public only saw Lincoln sob on one other occasion. He broke down when eulogizing "Pot" Green, that rotund New Salem judge who had given an uneducated lad a chance as a legal assistant.[8] A secret sufferer with these memories, long desperate about his "national debt," could not abide squandering either his new dollars or his beneficent Union, after the nation's railroad era had lifted him into the upper middle class.

8

Lincoln's miseries with his father, before his New Salem travails, added another bar to post-Alger risk taking. This time, the deterrent's emotional power became obvious in tears *not* shed, on the most common teary occasion.

In mid-1849, Abraham had rushed to Tom Lincoln's Illinois bedside, three hours distant, upon hearing that death beckoned. He had found a recovering patriarch. A year and a half later, upon receiving the same summons, this time appropriate, Abraham had skipped the scene. He had also skipped the funeral and trips to the grave. He had previously skipped introducing his wife and sons to Tom Lincoln.

Since helping his father and stepmother move to Illinois, the son/stepson had sporadically visited them. He had twice rescued them from eviction. But after ugly Kentucky/Indiana times, the son reserved his warmth for the stepmother. His icy determination not to be Tom Lincoln defined his many roles rejected and their opposite embraced: the nonfarmer who became an attorney, the nondisciplinarian who became his boys' rollicking companion, the nonilliterate who sent his son to Harvard, the former provincial who became a cosmopolitan statesman, and the wandering father's son who only moved from Springfield once after 1835—into the president's house.

9

Nonmoving averted a post–Horatio Alger tightwad's most likely financial crisis. Movement into a new dwelling especially imperils domestic budgets. Lincoln's antimigratory compulsion instead invited a domestic showdown.

The problem first surfaced when Abraham Lincoln and Mary Todd courted. He doubted that an heiress could bear his frugality. She doubted that a human could so shun creature comforts.

Yet she thought his hand worth living his way rather than hers. Fourteen months after their marriage and five months after son Robert arrived, it will be remembered, the Lincolns purchased a Springfield bungalow from the Reverend Charles Dresser, who officiated at their marriage. The bungalow on Eighth and Jackson stood a convenient few blocks from Lincoln's office.

But it inconveniently contained only five tight rooms. Here, for eight striated years, Mary lived up to her marital bargain. She scrimped, sewed, cleaned, cooked, and tended to son Bobby, then to son Eddie, in the style of her husband's ideal yeoman's wife. The heiress had seemingly become Ann Rutledge's clone.

But Mary could no longer bear playing Ann after the bungalow seemed to shrink. On February 1, 1850, Eddie, three years old, died from tuberculosis. Six weeks later, the Lincolns conceived a replacement, William Wallace Lincoln (Willie), born December 21, 1850. Then arrived a playmate for Willie, Thomas Lincoln, born April 4, 1853. Father instantly nicknamed the latest arrival "Tad," as if unwilling to call him "Tom" except on the birth certificate.

New arithmetic doomed the old bungalow. One of two older sons surviving, plus two new male urchins born, netted three rambunctious boys, jammed with a large husband, a live-in housekeeper, and a frazzled heiress into tight quarters. Mary, with migraines pounding amid the uproar, suffered acute claustrophobia. With Abraham's income doubled, why couldn't they move? Rather than answer, he stalled.

More arithmetic disarmed the procrastinator. In September 1854, Mary sold a dowry gift from her father: eighty choice Sangamon County acres. She received $1,200, four-fifths of the bungalow's purchase price and sufficient to purchase a doubled dwelling. Abraham still stalled. How to reconcile a husband allergic to relocation and a wife repelled at remaining?

Easy! You blow off the roof. In April 1856, after Lincoln left for three months on the Circuit, laborers removed the bungalow's roof, built a second

Mary and Abraham (with his new beard) approaching their rebuilt Springfield house, December 1860, with seven-year-old Tad leading and nine-year-old Willie chasing. (Bob, seventeen years old, is at Harvard, finishing his first semester.)

floor above the first, enclosed the old and new spaces in a handsome brown Georgian facade, and nailed down a red cedar shingle crown. Lincoln returned to a lovely panacea for both a suffocating wife and an unmovable husband, with Mary's late sale of her dowry paying for all but one hundred dollars of the transformation.

One neighbor claimed to recollect that a shocked Lincoln, upon first encountering a towering house where a bungalow had squatted, asked, pray "tell, . . . where" does "old Abe Lincoln" live? He used to live "around these parts." Or as another neighbor claimed to recall, Abraham told Mary that "you remind me of . . . the fellow who went to California and left one baby at home." Upon returning three years later, he found three. "'Well Lizzie,' the gent said, 'for a little woman and without help, you have raised thunder amazingly.'"[9]

Few Lincoln items are more amusing—or perhaps more fanciful. The two neighbors' reports, recorded decades after the event, could have been embroidered, maybe concocted, like much early Lincoln lore. Instead of being surprised at his first sighting, Lincoln may have partly planned the remodeling. After Mary provided the cash, so savvy a politician might well have switched to influencing a project that he could no longer block. So dedicated a jokester might also have aspired to play henpecked husband.

Yet even if Lizzie's tale never passed Lincoln's lips, it passes muster as a classic example of his frontier parables, often combining provincial charm and universal veracity. This inspired parable also illustrates essentials about Lincoln. The roof raising highlights the couple's usually veiled tension over spending, destined to recur with headline-making consequences in Washington's Executive Mansion. The nonrelocation also illuminates Lincoln's post-Alger cautiousness with more than money, throughout his road to the presidency and on to Appomattox.

10

Lincoln's post-Alger investing was as careful as his spending and his slavery politics. Many Illinois middle-class contemporaries speculated in land, railroads, and factories—sinews of the booming new midwestern economy. Douglas, for example, bet his fortune on railroads and enjoyed several more fortunes.

One modest fortune sufficed for Lincoln. After the System, he had had more than enough of sprees. He bought two shares in one railroad (his adopted town's bid to share the unprecedented infrastructure). Otherwise, he financed others' secure land purchases at 10 percent (or more) interest.

His biggest loan illustrated his constant prudence. He lent his largest railroad retainer to Norman Judd, his economic and political colleague as well as Chicago's wealthiest railroad attorney. Lincoln's collateral: Judd's Iowa acres, purchased in part with the loan and wonderfully situated on the projected transcontinental railroad route that the two lawyers had lately furthered. Lincoln took care to know the collateral as well as the borrower. He inspected the choice parcel out in Council Bluffs, across the Missouri River from Omaha, Nebraska.

A more speculative investor would have bought the Iowa land for himself, gambling on a future gain. Lincoln, allergic to speculation, preferred a surer, smaller profit. He figured to receive regular interest payments from Judd, an ultrasuccessful professional, with sterling security that interest would be paid until the loan was retired. If payments unexpectedly disappeared, Lincoln could seize the lush land and/or Judd's numerous other prime assets.

Nothing is risk free in American capitalism, much less in frontier capitalism. But no investments could be more gilt-edged than Lincoln's sober lending. On the eve of the Civil War, this spendthrift survivor of huge debt, now on the other side of the American lending game, had almost ten thousand dollars out on loan. Not a penny was lost. After Lincoln's death, Norman Judd repaid the estate double what he had borrowed. The payoff climaxed Abraham Lincoln's illustration of the ultracautious fork in the post-Alger road.

11

His climb from rags to tightly guarded wealth punctures one classic mistake in Horatio Alger legends. The error holds that the self-made man thrives whenever intrusive governments and officious philanthropists keep hands off. Lincoln instead demonstrated that no one rises altogether unaided.[10]

Lincoln's surveying road to a legislative seat came thanks to "Uncle Jimmy" Short's rescue of his surveying tools at a bankruptcy auction. His start in the law came thanks to Bowling Green. His first law books arrived courtesy of John Todd Stuart. His climactic law lessons came thanks to Stephen A. Logan. He could commence practicing law in Springfield because Josh Speed provided shelter and Bill Butler donated dinners. He remained mired in the lower middle class until a huge federal government land grant financed a railroad revolution. His rise demonstrated that philanthropic uplift of the desperate and governmental partnership with capitalists were both as American as, well, Abraham Lincoln's degree of self-helping.

Lincoln saw a more precise moral. Union, he cheered, especially enabled the rising Alger, adding economic to political democracy in the civilization where all men were (supposedly) created equal. Just as the Union government's land grant had brought the transportation that liberated a shackled Illinois, so the Union's migrants had rushed in to seize advantage and the Union's markets had reached in to enrich newcomers.

The "leading object" of our government in this "People's contest" for "Union," President Lincoln would tell Congress on July 4, 1861, "is to elevate the condition of men—to lift artificial weight from all shoulders—to clear the paths of laudable pursuit for all—to afford all an unfettered start, and a fair chance, in the race of life."[11] There was the vital connection between the Alger who tightly guarded his middle-class winnings and the politician who saved his treasure, Union.

11

Three Climactic Railroad Cases

✣

In the mid-1850s, Abraham Lincoln's legal career rose toward (but never quite to) the top. With his three climactic railroad cases, his courtroom success reached its height and limits. To rise higher, Lincoln would need to star in politics, especially with slavery issues.

1

In over half of Lincoln's railroad suits, this supposed "railroad lawyer" argued against carriers. Even when railroads' stakes rose highest, railroads' foes could purchase his talents. Before one important railroad suit, he asked his preferred potential client to offer "something near as much as I can get from the other side." Then you can "retain me." But "justice to myself" requires a guaranteed fee during "the largest law question . . . in the state."[1] Five years earlier, justice to himself had required representing a master chasing fugitive slaves.

As in that *Matson* case, lawyerly ideals sometimes compelled arguments against his preferred verdict. Opposing attorneys, he continued to think, bore responsibility only to perfect their clients' positions. Then judges or juries could best see how to sooth distraught citizens. Witness the *Matson* case. In that disruptive drama, judges had rightly called Lincoln's best legal rationalization for the master wrong, thereby pacifying a riled community.

Illinois Supreme Court proceedings demanded the most sophisticated rationalizations. Lincoln here starred more than four hundred times— almost a tenth of his court appearances. Here commonplace pleas gave way to important contests, staged in an architecturally superb arena.

As a Long Niner in 1837, Lincoln had helped convince the legislature to move the capital to Springfield. The new building for legislators and supreme court justices still shines almost two centuries later. Now called the Old Capitol Building, the antique features local Yellow Sugar Creek limestone, clothing a replica of an ancient Greek temple. A snow-white cupola and a fiery-red dome complete local architect John Francis Rogue's majestic design (see drawing, page 121).

The supreme court's chamber, consuming almost half the first floor, exemplifies the building's epic aura. The courtroom sweeps sixteen feet in height, one hundred feet in length, and seventy feet in width. The room's statue of an American eagle matches the proportions of its European prototype: towering eagle pulpits in aged cathedrals. The chamber's red curtains, covering the front wall from floor to ceiling, provide a soaring canopy over the chief justice's chair.

In this highest state chamber, Lincoln advanced his education in pruning bloated arguments. He "studied . . . harder," Judge David Davis remarked, when "he could not" easily remove "the rubbish of a case."[2] Stephen A. Logan, his second law partner, had started his training in whittling swollen briefs to cutting truths. The tactic fit the pupil's natural inclinations. Lincoln's tight control of turbulent emotions nurtured admiration for reducing angry disputes to icy simplicities. His intellectual hobby, memorizing Euclid's geometry, featured messy reality shrunk to precise formulas.

Sometimes, Logan's pruning tactic was inappropriate, as in jury trials such as the "Almanac" trial. Then all manners of pleas might strike a chord with rough-and-ready jurists. But especially in complicated state supreme court cases before learned judges, Lincoln specialized in excising lower courts' procedural errors, tangled precedents, and misleading perspectives. By stripping away rubbish, he laid bare the decisive—a move that usually swept the highest court's decision. This apt training for winning complex cases, plus his seven times more frequent appearances in the state supreme court than arguing anywhere for or against railroads, established his most accurate label: not "Railroad Lawyer" but "Supreme Court Attorney."

2

His first important railroad case, *Barret v. Alton & Sangamon Railroad* (1851–52), appropriately climaxed in the state supreme court chamber.[3] His triumph required his whittling specialty. His client had received a legislative charter to bypass the choked Sangamon River with tracks and trains between Springfield and Alton, arguably Illinois's most promising Mississippi River port.

Later the legislature, as the company requested, revised the charter to shorten the journey. A few original shareholders, objecting to the revision, refused to pay the remainder due on their shares. When the company sued for payments, recalcitrant shareholders answered that a legislative charter is an inviolable contract and changes cancel an unchangeable document.

The supreme court confrontation matched Abraham Lincoln, holder of two shares in the railroad and opponent of defaulting shareholders, against James Barret, holder of thirty shares and defaulting on his payments after his investment suffered "illegal" change. Colliding investment purposes impelled these two shareholders. Lincoln and other Sangamon County developers hoped that a railroad connecting Alton and Springfield would form "a link in a great chain" of railroads, uniting "Boston and New York with the Mississippi."[4] After the charter revision, Lincoln told the Illinois Supreme Court, the twelve miles shorter, more direct tracks would improve the link.

Barret answered that "his" company's original route, before being "illegally" revised, would have provided tracks (and thus purchasers) hard by his unsold four thousand–plus Sangamon County acres. The new route, he protested, would miss his land by several country miles.

Victory required Lincoln to chop away potential procedural loopholes, then to reduce Barret's argument to its suspect essence. Lincoln first had to demonstrate that the Alton & Sangamon had properly received 5 percent down from its subscriber, had properly registered Barret on its books, and had properly called for his remaining 95 percent. Having stripped away the petty, Lincoln assaulted the interesting: James Barret's thesis that the sanctity of contracts *always* forbade charter revisions.

Lincoln reduced "always" to "usually." He cited precedents, in and out of Illinois, for court approval of charter revisions, if occasional changes enhanced both the charter's purpose and the public's benefits. Illinois Supreme Court justices eventually concurred with Lincoln that in the *Barret* case, "a few obstinate" shareholders' loss of some "incidental benefits" must not "deprive the public" of a "superior and less expensive route."[5]

The winning attorney's *Barret* tale ended on a lower note. Twice in the later 1850s, Lincoln defended a defaulting stockholder against the *Barret* precedent. His efforts to overturn himself lost, then lost again. He remained, even at his impressive heights as a practicing lawyer, a hired gun, willing to argue against his own previous and preferred brief, in exchange for a fresh retainer.

In contrast to *Barret,* Lincoln's second major state supreme court railroad case, *Illinois Central v. McLean County* (1853–56), arrived in the high court's chamber barren of procedural trivia.[6] The parties had agreed to appeal only *McLean*'s main issue to the highest court.

The Alton & Sangamon would have lost only several thousand dollars if the court had declared that revising original charters cancels original shareholders' obligations. In contrast, the state of Illinois might have lost millions of dollars (and perhaps its whole new System) if the court had declared Illinois Central's charter unconstitutional.

The *McLean County* case pitted the Illinois constitutional requirement for uniform county property taxes on "the value of property" against the Illinois Central's doubly eccentric charter. This singular document required the company to pay unprecedented *state* taxes on gross proceeds, in exchange for unprecedented exemption from *county* property taxes. Legislators cherished the trade-off. Thanks to the Central's unparalleled relief from county taxes on property, the company could afford its exceptional state tax on proceeds. Thanks to its tax bonanza from the Central, Illinois's government could retire its colossal debt from the System.

McLean County officials responded that the trade-off unconstitutionally eliminated *our* county's property tax proceeds. The state's constitution, the county's lawyers pointed out, *always* mandated "uniform taxes" on the "value of property." Abraham Lincoln, retained by the Central, again used his supreme court whittling specialty to trim "always" to "usually."

In *Barret,* the court had concurred with Lincoln that charters could occasionally be changed. Now he asked the same judges to concur that Illinois property taxes could occasionally be less than uniform, if the exception again served the widest public interest. In *State Bank v. People* (1843), he reminded Illinois Supreme Court judges, they upheld the Illinois State Bank's unprecedented exemption from property taxes. In other states too, Lincoln demonstrated, courts had sanctioned occasional exceptions to constitutionally imposed tax rules.

The court's response cited Lincoln's out-of-state precedents and his take on Illinois's exceptions. Our Founding Fathers, declared Chief Justice Walter B. Scates's majority opinion, never intended uniform taxes to be "an inflexible universal rule," with no "exceptions." The legislature's unique exception for the Illinois Central promoted "a vital power of government": to benefit the public interest in unique ways under unique circumstances.[7]

Having saved the Illinois Central from potentially ruinous county property taxes, Lincoln asked the company for a five-thousand-dollar bonus, beyond his two-hundred-dollar retainer. When refused, he sued. The McLean County jury might have been expected to reject Lincoln's bonus, a reward, after all, for depriving *their* county of property taxes. Instead, the jury approved Lincoln's five thousand dollars.

Then the Central might have been expected to appeal Lincoln's huge bonus. Instead, the railroad company added a yearly retainer throughout the 1850s to Lincoln's one-time five thousand dollars (about $132,000 in early twenty-first-century dollars). The attorney, after all, had spared the company from millions in property taxes, just as the company's state taxes eventually spared the commonwealth from $16 million in System debt (about $420 million in early twenty-first-century coin). Thus did this unique retainer, piled atop unique taxes, create that rarity after bruising courtroom contentions: smiles all around. *That,* one can almost hear the Lyceum Address orator gloating, is how republican courts need to work.

4

Lincoln's final major railroad case, *Hurd et al. v. Rock Island Bridge Company* (1857), transpired not in Springfield's sumptuous Illinois Supreme Court Chamber but in the state's tiniest courtroom, squeezed into the top floor of early Chicago's most sprawling building.[8] As if anticipating the city's latter-day Merchandise Mart (that unusually wide architectural sport in a landscape starring unusually tall skyscrapers), the three-story Saloon Building had consumed the corner of Clark and Lake since the Windy City's early village days. The structure's sprawl had once contained Chicago's first city hall. It still housed the city's most extravagant arena for public entertainment and its most lavish offices and stores—everything except an American saloon!

The Saloon Building's title referred to nothing American. To name the building after its disproportionate space for performed spectacles, early Chicagoans adopted Londoners' term for vast vestibules in opulent opera houses and theaters. That provincial use of sophisticated language invited guffaws at nouveau Chicago. Yet the building's theatrical name appropriately announced that one of the most melodramatic events on the Lincoln trail here was staged.

A spectacular explosion on America's most celebrated river led to the historic courtroom drama. On May 6, 1856, Jacob Hurd's new steamboat, the *Effie Afton,* smashed into the new Rock Island Railroad Bridge's critical element, its drawbridge. When the bridge's draw opened, steamboats could proceed on the Mississippi River. With the drawbridge section closed, trains could cross above the river.

A steamboat's passage required a skilled captain to manage treacherous waters after the bridge's draw opened. The feat particularly challenged pilots their initial time through. The *Effie*'s captain lost control when first braving the perils. The crash ignited the steamer and part of the bridge. The enflamed structures fused into a giant fireball that floated haplessly downriver.

Two sorts of onlookers cheered the sight. Antirailroad boatmen whooped for the demise (they prayed) of railroads' challenge to Mississippi River steamboats. In contrast, prorailroad southerners celebrated the end (they hoped) of Yankees' effort to build the first railroad bridge over the Mississippi (and thus secure a head start in the race for the first transcontinental railroad).

Until the crash, the Rock Island location had seemed to offer an auspicious place to bridge the wide river. The limestone island's length bifurcates the Mississippi for miles, while its width extends halfway across the river. Railroad tracks across the island's width could connect to tracks on two short bridges, one running eastward to Rock Island City, Illinois, and the other westward to Davenport, Iowa. Train tracks could here half-cross the Mississippi on terra firma, eliminating half the expense of a long bridge exclusively above water.

Before construction began, a key southerner sued to block the creation. Mississippi's Jefferson Davis, U.S. secretary of war, sought a court injunction against railroad tracks over "his" island. The War Department, the secretary noted, still owned Rock Island, site of its abandoned Fort Armstrong. Davis urged the court to oust iron horse intruders, thus saving the island for a federal arsenal.

The Mississippian's suit, despite seeking to stymie Yankees' transcontinental railroad advantage, was not altogether a cynical southern ploy. In the 1880s, the island would harbor the federal government's main arsenal. The renamed Arsenal Island still has that raison d'être.

The future aside, Davis, past Mexican War hero and present southern transcontinental railroad enthusiast, blended U.S. military and southern commercial visions. Alas for Davis, the presiding judge, Ohio's U.S. Supreme Court Associate Justice John McLean, preferred Yankee commercial visions. McLean ruled that the nation's no-longer-used land could properly further the nationally beneficial first railroad bridge over the Mississippi.

Nine months later, on April 22, 1856, the locomotive *Des Moines* pulled the initial train over the great river. With trans-Mississippi America now connected to the "Atlantic Seaboard," celebrated the *Davenport Daily Gazette,* locomotives will soon speed "onward to the Pacific."

Or so northern visionaries dreamed during the two weeks before the *Effie* savaged the new bridge. Jacob Hurd blamed the drawbridge's alleged obstructions for his expensive vessel's disaster. He sued the Rock Island Bridge Company for two hundred thousand dollars. His victory could bankrupt the bridge company, at least temporarily reanoint riverboat men as kings of Mississippi River commerce, and doom Yankees' hopes to race ahead in the transcontinental railroad sweepstakes.

In contrast, Jacob Hurd's defeat could refresh the bridge's prospects, revitalize the railroad's quest to turn steamboats into dinosaurs, and reinvigorate the northern dream of controlling the initial continent-wide transportation extravaganza. No wonder that folks stuffed the tiny third-floor courtroom in the mammoth Saloon Building for three weeks in September 1857. This judge and jury might determine whether Chicago's railroad revolution would retreat or advance—perhaps advance all the way to mastering the main avenue across American spaces.

5

While the *Hurd* case has come down to posterity as Lincoln's, Norman Judd was the bridge's lead attorney. Judd would soon depend on Lincoln for favors, including an appointment to Civil War office and a loan to buy Iowa land. But during the *Hurd* case, Lincoln's court opportunity depended on Judd's favors (as, in part, would Lincoln's later opportunity to become Republican presidential nominee).

Judd, a veteran Chicagoan (he had arrived before the Saloon Building), had enjoyed sixteen years as the city's state senator. He had thrived still longer as a senior partner of the Windy City's most prominent law firm. More recently, Judd had served as regular attorney for the Rock Island Bridge Company.

After Jacob Hurd sued for damages to his *Effie,* Judd directed three compatriots on the Rock Island Bridge Company's defense team. The lead attorney saved the choicest assignments for himself. He gave the opening address and then guided the best defense witness, the bridge operator Seth Gurney, through the pivotal opening testimony. Judd planned to take a back seat only when Abraham Lincoln presented the closing argument, reemphasizing Gurney's opening testimony.

Judd had belatedly recruited Lincoln for this purpose two months before the trial. The Windy City leader calculated that after he had pounded on jurymen's eardrums, his fellow Chicagoans would welcome a fresh Springfield voice. Judd especially liked Lincoln's voice for summing up a case "forcibly and convincingly." Moreover, Lincoln's rustic "personality will appeal to any judge or jury hereabouts."[9]

Months before the new recruit arrived in Chicago, the Judd team embraced its obvious strategy. The attorneys knew that their opponents would urge that after the drawbridge opened, the opening had remained so obstructed—so beset by savage winds and currents in so narrow and awkwardly placed a passage—that not even the *Effie*'s able captain could steam through unscathed. Norman Judd's team would have to counter that a decently competent river pilot could have outfoxed every alleged obstruction.

Before the trial, Lincoln only contributed his recent research at the bridge. He had proved, he claimed, that slow river currents in the drawbridge opening hardly sufficed to savage a mighty steamboat. Lincoln added little during trial testimony, for Judd usually consigned him to observe, in preparation for the closing address. And then, as the impatient Lincoln's starring moment neared, Norman Judd, thinking he had already won the case, moved that the presiding judge dispense with both sides' closing arguments!

6

Lincoln's likely reaction: Not again! The prospect of his undelivered closing address littering an ashcan recalled his most wounding court comeuppance. Two years earlier, after the McCormick Harvesting Machine Company sued Rockford, Illinois's John Manny and Company for allegedly copying McCormick patents, Manny's legal team had recruited Lincoln. The court's decision had the potential to transform the reaper industry and American patent law. Abraham Lincoln had apparently reached the big time.[10]

The excited Illinoisan had hurried to Rockford, eager to examine the Manny reaper. He had then sent his partners a legal brief, calling this reaper no harvester clone. His exhilaration, however, had blinded him to glaring clues that his invitation had been revoked. After signing him up, Manny's defenders had never written, not even to answer his inquiries—not even to inform him of the trial's changed date and its new Cincinnati location.

After discovering the revised schedule and locale in a newspaper, Lincoln had headed for the adventure. Upon arrival in Cincinnati, he had suffered a painful awakening. Manny's lawyers had recruited him only as a local resource for the expected Saloon Building trial under an Illinois judge. But after Ohio's U.S. Supreme Court Justice John McLean had assumed jurisdiction and moved the trial to his state, Lincoln's Illinois contacts became irrelevant.

When Lincoln appeared in Cincinnati, Manny's lawyers had barely said hello. Upon leaving, they had never said good-bye. In between, they had barred him from their high-powered work and from their high-society social-izing. Their brethren included Edwin Stanton, Pittsburgh's patent expert. Stanton had allegedly questioned whether the Illinoisan most resembled a long-legged giraffe or a long-armed gorilla. The snobby Stanton had con-cluded that nothing useful could be expected from a provincial with trousers too short, blue umbrella too gauche, and speech too common.

Lincoln had clinched the case for his ostracism by twanging that the law-yers should go out for dinner "in a gang." The sophisticates disdained any "gang" and therefore this supposed boor. Only years later would a mortified Stanton, having become Lincoln's admiring secretary of war, realize who had been the boor.

Lincoln had fled home immediately after the trial. Manny's lawyers had mailed back his brief, never opened. Now, two years later, Norman Judd sought to scotch his closing address in the *Hurd* case. Unlike Stanton, Judd admired Lincoln's fresh frontier speech. Still, yet another lead attorney now attempted to relegate the provincial's effort to yet another ashcan.

Judd's attempt, like Stanton's scorn, illuminated an important fact about Lin-coln's impressively rising career as a practicing attorney. He never quite reached the top. He always had to scramble for tiny retainers, spend six months a year on the dusty Circuit, occasionally push for a verdict he disliked, and beware humil-iations in his most important cases. Had he instead become Illinois's acknowl-edged lead attorney, in the manner of, say, Massachusetts's Daniel Webster, he might have later been less nervous when he first assumed the presidency.

7

In September 1857, Norman Judd's motion to dispense with closing arguments in the *Hurd* case distressed Lincoln for only a moment. U.S. Supreme Court Justice McLean, again presiding over an important Lincoln railroad case, ruled that jurors should hear both sides' closing arguments in such an criti-cal affair. McLean's decision benefited posterity as much as Lincoln. Among surviving documents on Lincoln's legal career, the *Hurd* closing address alone captures his voice, in speeches to judge and jury.

As Lincoln commenced his *Hurd* closing address, he deplored boatmen who had "kicked" railroads "with contempt . . . in this court." The insults recalled equally contemptuous "shouting and ringing of bells" on the river as the railroad "bridge . . . burned" and "fell." Steamboat enthusiasts, urged Lincoln, must instead cheer unimpeded rails "from east to west," when no riv-ers provide connections. Trains' nontraditional transportation has admirably built up "new communities with rapidity never before seen."

For their part, continued Lincoln, railroad enthusiasts must esteem the traditional unimpeded river travel between north and south—between "where it never freezes" and "where it never thaws." The court must help both transportation behemoths to "live and let live" and cease all "this trouble about the bridge." This was Lincoln's best Lyceum Address stuff, featuring rational courts saving serene republics from irrational disputes.

Provocative trouble would cease, Lincoln conceded, if train tracks could ride on "a suspension bridge, . . . high enough" above steamship chimneys, or in a "tunnel, low enough" below the river. But such utopian solutions would require "immense expense." A drawbridge without killing obstructions remained the only affordable peacemaker. To rescue the peacemaker, Lincoln meant to strip away allegations of the bridge's murderous obstructions.

Earlier, when watching the trial proceeding, Lincoln had symbolically previewed how his closing address would prevail. He had whittled away, Stephen Logan style, at a stick with his penknife. When his turn finally came, his closing address used Norman Judd's first witness's evidence to prune down allegations of the open drawbridge's obstructions.

Seth Gurney, the bridge's caretaker, had presented statistics from his logbook, showing that during the drawbridge's first seventeen days, ending with the *Effie*'s crash, twenty vessels had hit the bridge. In contrast, during the fourteen months since the bridge repair, 958 boats had passed through, with only seven accidents. "As the boat men get cool," Lincoln exulted, "the accidents get less. We may soon expect . . . that there will be no accidents at all."[11]

No accidents at all! Here the pruning tactic reached its climax, leaving Lincoln's opponents in argumentative trouble. Even if only 7 out of 958 ships had been damaged since the *Effie* disaster, protested Jacob Hurd's defenders, obstructions obviously still threatened. But did one accident in every 136.5 passages demonstrate intolerable menaces?

Only three of the twelve *Hurd* jurors thought so. The hung jury left Jacob Hurd with zero recompense, unless he cared to try again in this railroad-crazed environment. He did not.

When others dared the same suit, the U.S. Supreme Court demonstrated the wisdom of Jacob Hurd's retreat. In January 1863, Associate Justice John Caton ruled for the majority that if the Rock Island Bridge's opponents' court argument prevailed, "no lawful bridge could be built across the Mississippi, anywhere." No railroad bridges would mean no "great facilities for commerce," whenever "great rivers had to be crossed."[12]

No taste for containing Illinois's railroad bonanza—that court bias, throughout Lincoln's trio of important railroad cases, ensured iron horses' rescue of the state from its prerailroad plight. Whether protecting Lincoln's local railroad's best route to the Mississippi (*Barret*), or sustaining the Central's retirement of Illinois's crippling System debt (*McLean County*), or approving a railroad drawbridge over the Mississippi (*Hurd*), Illinois courts, with Lincoln's help, had promoted the state's booming participation in the Union's newly nationalized commercial economy.

Lincoln here turned his day job into the assignment he most coveted. He craved success as contributor to the Founders' national Union. The show in the Saloon Building met his prayers. Using his long-standing nationalistic Whiggery, deployed this time to help judges affirm a law crucial for a national economy, he had multiplied the Union's benefits to his newly important state. With a southern menace to political Union developing as fast as Illinois's blessings from economic Union, Abraham Lincoln's time had come to return to elective politics.

12

The Peoria Address and
the Strategy of Defense

❧

The May 1854 Kansas-Nebraska Act turned Abraham Lincoln's booming legal career into a secondary pursuit. The reborn politician, at last dismissing silence on slavery while still deploring antislavery radicalism, would spend eight and a half years seeking (and defining) the dead center of northern antislavery opinion. With a choice parable, he would illuminate a moderate's slow progress. He resembled, he would declare, a trapeze performer, creeping atop a high wire stretched over mortal danger.

1

A celebrated event at a favorite place enhanced that image. At 5:00 PM on June 30, 1859, Jean-François Gravelet, known as the Great Blondin, began his first crossing above Niagara Falls. Blondin crept along a taut hemp rope, two inches wide, 1,300 feet long, and 160 feet above the roaring falls. Spectators accomplished nothing, Abraham Lincoln warned, by shouting "lean a little more to the North" or "to the South." Better to "hold" their "breath" until Blondin was "safe over."

With the parable, Lincoln hushed visitors who demanded haste toward abolition. Like Blondin, he struggled to convey "an immense weight" of "untold treasures . . . safe across." The Union's unharmed passage demanded inching ahead. A rushed misstep could lose everything dear.[1]

In the same spirit in 1852, Abraham Lincoln had finally dared to speak his first several hundred antislavery words, before resuming his wordlessness for a final twenty-seven months. Henry Clay wisely perceived, emphasized Lincoln in a July 6, 1852, eulogy of his hero, that slavery could not be "at *once* eradicated, without producing a greater evil, even to the cause of liberty itself." The Great Compromiser denounced "those who would shiver . . . the Union . . . and even burn the last copy of the Bible," lest "slavery" continue "a single hour."[2]

Still, Henry Clay "cherished" the "moral fitness . . . of returning" Africa's "children. . . . Every succeeding year," Lincoln cheered, has strengthened the "hope." The "consummation" will be "glorious" if "coming generations of our countrymen" remove "slavery . . . so gradually that neither races nor individuals shall have suffered." Meanwhile, "a captive people" shall slowly be restored to "their long-lost Father land, with bright prospects."[3]

No Lincoln utterance more inspires modern shudders. Nothing better illuminates the American mid-nineteenth-century center. No other New World enslaved nation cherished the African colonization fantasy. Americans widely considered relocating huge racial groups neither impossible (after all, they beckoned millions of white Europeans across the Atlantic) nor immoral (after all, they removed hundreds of thousands of Native Americans from "unwinnable" competition with "superior" whites). By becoming the only sitting American president who sent a shipload of blacks to an overseas colony, Lincoln epitomized the ocean between his generation and posterity.

Lincoln challenged his era's conventional view of colonization by requiring blacks' consent to departure. He also modified Jeffersonian colonization by permitting emancipation without removal. Still, his Clay eulogy signaled his lasting hope that blacks' consent to depart might some distant day encourage whites' consent to emancipate.[4]

Lincoln's Clay eulogy added his unhappy concern, two years before the Kansas-Nebraska Act, that the Founding Fathers' (and his) great hope, whites' conversion to abolition, seemed to be ebbing. The eulogist compared Henry Clay's prayers for slavery's eventual disappearance with a "few, but an increasing number of men" who, "for the sake of perpetuating slavery, . . . ridicule . . . 'all men are created free and equal.'"[5] Lincoln approved long delays in terminating slavery, with or without African colonization. But he shuddered at backsliding from the revolutionary generation's hope for slaveholders' eventual consent to abolition.

Two years later, Lincoln's nemesis became the national guide to backsliding. For two previous decades, Lincoln had nursed jealous distaste for Stephen A. Douglas. When "we were both young," the continual loser remembered, "we were both ambitious." Where my "race of ambition has been a failure—a flat failure," his "has been" a "splendid success." Lincoln could "affect no contempt" for his "high eminence." But "the oppressed" have not "shared" his "elevation." If I could rise to Douglas's "eminence," with the afflicted alongside, he soared, I would "wear the richest crown that ever pressed a monarch's brow."[6]

Illinois's current crown prince, complained Lincoln, plays the lord over vassals. The Little Giant displayed a "continual assumption of superiority," supposedly belonging to "his elevated position." In contrast, my lowly stations have "done nothing to make any human being remember" that I "had lived."[7] And then U.S. Senator Douglas drove the Kansas-Nebraska Act through Congress, intensifying Lincoln's scorn.

Douglas's May 1854 law pronounced "inoperative and void" a critical portion of the Founding Fathers' 1820 Missouri Compromise. The segment had barred slavery from Louisiana Purchase territories that sprawled westward from Missouri, about six hundred miles to the Rockies, and northward, approximately eight hundred miles to the Canadian border. The some half-million virgin square miles exceeded all U.S. free labor states combined, minus California.

Douglas's replacement legislation decreed that after Congress opened this largely northern geographic zone for settlement, the South's Peculiar Institution could enter. After the territorial phase, slaveholders could achieve a slave state by rallying a majority for a constitution supporting bondage. Or a Yankee majority could create a free labor state by voting against slavery. Douglas famously called territorial residents' final decision "Popular Sovereignty."

The words proclaimed that each territory's populace would have ultimate sovereignty over whether slavery lived or died in their area. Local folks' decree, Douglas continually declared, was no one else's business, in or out of Congress. Or, to rephrase his Popular Sovereignty orthodoxy, slaveholders, previously barred from entering a vast largely northern virgin wilderness, could now come and perhaps conquer, and it would be no Yankee's business unless he, too, migrated to the area. Douglas's dictum turned Lincoln's twenty-year silence about slavery into a howl. Their colliding voices brought civil war far closer.

The Missouri Compromise's Founding Fathers had inadvertently invited this crisis. By barring slaveholding settlers from Louisiana Purchase territories north of 36°30′, the legislation had apparently forever settled the sprawl's slavery controversies. Yet everyone stood banned until Congress established territorial government and invited settlement.

For a decade before the Kansas-Nebraska Act, Stephen A. Douglas, as chairman of U.S. House and then Senate committees on the territories, had sought legislation that invited settlement while saying nothing about slaveholding settlers. Saying nothing said everything. Silence perpetuated the Missouri Compromise edict that no slaves could enter when others strode inside.

If Douglas wanted to welcome Yankee migrants, southerners had insisted for a decade, he had to repeal the Missouri Compromise's ban on slaveholding migrants. Northern outrage at gutting the Missouri Compromise, Douglas answered, could fatally divide the Union. "No ruthless hand," he declared in 1849, "would ever be reckless enough to disturb" such "a sacred thing." In 1854, weeks before his was the reckless hand, he added that "no man was so wild as to think of repealing the Missouri Compromise."[8]

On the last day of the 1853 congressional session, the not-yet-wild man almost avoided reckless repeal. Northern senators voted 17–4 to open Kansas and Nebraska territories for settlement, while silently retaining the Missouri Compromise ban on slaveholding settlers. Douglas needed four southern senators' concurrence to pass the bill. He could only persuade two.

In January 1854, Douglas tried a final time for a Kansas-Nebraska Law without Missouri Compromise repeal. But his climactic attempt collided with Missouri U.S. senator Davy Atchison's thunder against proscribing his slaveholding constituents from neighboring Kansas. When "Bourbon Dave" ranted, fellow southern Democrats heeded, especially southern congressmen who shared Atchison's Washington boardinghouse, the so-called F Street Mess.[9]

Missouri's Atchison warned F Street messmates that no honorable slaveholder could abide being barred from the Missouri Compromise zone like some leper. That southern sense of honor had for a decade helped deter the frustrated Douglas from opening Louisiana Purchase gates. Then, in 1854, Atchison added a warning about slavery's weakness in Missouri that rallied all three tiers of southerners behind his defensive zeal. The Border South senator hoped to shore up the very northern South vulnerability that the 1849 Lincoln, in his District of Columbia emancipation proposal, had hoped to expose.

In Atchison's Border South tier of vulnerable states (Delaware, Maryland, Kentucky, and Missouri), slaves comprised only one-eighth of the population.

A fifth of Border South blacks were free. Most counties were almost lily-white. Little sugar, cotton, or rice was grown. Agitation against slavery never altogether ceased.

In contrast, the seven states of the most southern South (South Carolina, Florida, Georgia, Alabama, Mississippi, Louisiana, and Texas) enslaved almost half their peoples and 98.5 percent of their blacks. The so-called Lower South or Deep South tier of states grew almost all Dixie's cotton, sugar, and rice. This home base of the committed slavocracy suffered relatively few lily-white counties and scarce antislavery heretics.

During the first half of the nineteenth century, these differences between the Border South and the Lower South widened. Slave sales slowly drained the institution from the more northern to the more southern South. When the more northern, more exposed proslavery worriers cried for help, the more southern, more consolidated slavocracy answered the summons.

When the Lower South aggressively leapt, the four states of the so-called Middle South usually gingerly followed. Southerners in the middle from Virginia, North Carolina, and Tennessee to Arkansas, with around a third of their population enslaved, could sound a little too Yankee for avid southerners' comfort. But the Middle South's slightly watered-down version of southern creeds was not as diluted as the Border South's.

In 1854, Davy Atchison feared that a purely nonslaveholding Kansas population, situated on Missouri's western border, could be fatal to his state's especially vulnerable southern sentiments. All other Border South states had only one free-soil neighbor. Missouri already had two: Illinois to the east and Iowa to the north.

In 1850, only Delaware had a lower slave percentage than Missouri's 12.8 percent (declining to 9.7 percent in 1860). Among the Border South's relatively few black belts, Missouri's was the least black with slaves. A large part of this most diluted southern plantation regime was also the most exposed. At the state's westward extreme, Missouri slaveholders lined the Missouri River, potentially in the gun sights of future Kansas settlers across the river.

The uncomfortable slaveholder situation generated an unsettled political situation. Only Missouri had an antislavery sometime-congressman: Frank Blair Jr. Leading Blair's state political party strode Atchison's opponent for U.S. Senate reelection, the famous Thomas Hart Benton. Benton urged "neutralism" on slavery. He would forget about bondage and agitate about everything else.

If Missouri accepted Benton's neutrality as southern pabulum, Davy Atchison conceived, his section was doomed. Yankee settlers would mass on Kansas's side of the Missouri River, reach over the border, and influence the huge majority of nonslaveholders (plus nearby blacks) against bondage. The unrest within a thrice-surrounded Missouri, Atchison told sympathetic F Street messmates, would soon emancipate his state, reducing the fifteen slave states to fourteen. Then slavery could not long endure in the other three Border South states—Kentucky, Maryland, and Delaware.

In contrast, if Congress repealed the Missouri Compromise ban, promised the senator, he would personally lead his state's border ruffians through the opened Missouri Compromise gates on their western border. Then proslavery Missourians would make Kansas the sixteenth slave state—and a stabilizing neighbor for all borderland slaveholders. By ripping asunder one of northerners' most esteemed laws, lest democratic siege overwhelm despotism in Dixie's exposed borderland provinces, Atchison brought the political requirements of democratic and despotic social systems to a more lethal conflict than even gag rules had invited.

5

At the beginning of 1854, Atchison's F Street messmates, all Democrats from farther South, rallied a swarm of southerners behind the Missourian. The sharper southern insistence narrowed Douglas's options. He could repeal the Missouri Compromise ban on slaveholding settlers. Then he could secure enough southern votes to open Kansas and Nebraska for settlement. Or he could keep the gates closed against everyone.

Douglas disdained a shuttered white men's territorial future. He had long dedicated his chairmanship of the U.S. Senate's committees on territories to unshackling white America's supposed Manifest Destiny. He would include all the Western Hemisphere in the white men's democratic republic. Feeling trapped by southerners' escalating insistence, the Little Giant reluctantly went for repealing the Missouri Compromise's exclusion of blacks. He would thus welcome all whites to America's vast northwestern terrain—and potentially their slaves too.

Douglas pushed his bill through his own senatorial chamber rather easily. The House of Representatives proved more difficult. On the House's final May 30 vote, over 85 percent of southerners cheered aye, and over 66 percent of northerners screeched nay. But half of Douglas's fellow northern Democrats sided with grateful southerners to pass the bill, 113–100.

Douglas knew his law would raise a "hell of a storm." He had tried to spare his republic the tumult. Yet he claimed a victory for settlers' control of their own affairs. The triumph, he asserted, would save the Union. His ten-year-long travail had shown, he thought, that decisions about territorial slavery should be made out in the countryside, not in Congress (where North and South would tear the republic apart).

Now, he bragged, each territory's residents would decide their own affairs. National busybodies, he hoped, would now hush about far-off folks' institutions—indeed should not care if some distant community voted slavery up or down. If everyone vowed to care only about slavery in their state or territory, national controversies would end, and Union would endure.

Care not about slavery, unless it affects your neighborhood! With that injunction as much as with his law, Stephen A. Douglas bid to be *the* American statesman. By opposing that injunction as well as the law, Abraham Lincoln rose toward *the* national debate of the midcentury.

6

Abraham Lincoln called Douglas's law an appalling retreat from the Founding Fathers. The Founders, he cheered, had based public sentiment on "all men are created equal" and "the consent of the governed." In the Founders' era, public opinion had slowly consented to emancipation in northern states and to congressional bans on slavery's expansion in territories west of the settled North. In contrast, Douglas now urged that congressmen and their constituents should not care whether settlers expanded slavery into northern spaces where the Founders had banned the institution.

Douglas's Don't Care-ism had become law, Lincoln explained, because the foe, like most northern Democrats, cared too little about the principles of 1776 to defy southern Democrats. By amorally siding with the South, northern Democrats gained too much patronage to side with the Founders. Only a revival of the Founders' seminal American idea could halt slavery's expansion *northward*.

"Whoever can change public opinion," Lincoln would tell Chicagoans in 1856, "can change the government." With command of "public sentiment," he would add two years later, "nothing can fail; *against* it, nothing can succeed." Consequently, "whoever moulds public sentiment goes deeper than he who enacts statutes or pronounces judicial decisions." The ideologue makes statutes and decisions "possible" or "impossible."[10]

Lincoln's master principle minimized most antislavery allies' omnipresent free-soil argument. In that "anti–Slave Power" logic, Republicans attacked slaveholders' antirepublican power over whites—over *them*. The U.S. Constitution's three-fifths clause added three-fifths of slaves to each state's white population when apportioning the House of Representatives. This three-fifths arithmetic gave southerners additional presidential electors as well as additional congressmen, since each state received one member of the Electoral College per member of Congress. This double violation of one (white) man, one vote gave one southern white man more proportionate power in two branches of the federal republic than one northern white man—and all because the Slave Power harbored antirepublican slaves.

Lincoln developed anti–Slave Power logic only once—indeed used the term only three times. As usual, when at his best as a politician no less than as a lawyer, he whittled away everything less crucial. His spare arithmetic stressed that despite the South's extra antirepublican power, the North possessed sufficient power to win, if Yankees remained true to the Founders' principles. So complaints about Slave Power were a distraction and appeals to the Founders' ideology of the essence.

The Kansas-Nebraska fiasco, urged this ideologue, proved that southern power only won, even with extra Slave Power, after a self-serving demagogue corrupted northern public opinion. If northerners passionately supported the Declaration of Independence's principles, Douglas's Don't Care-ism would tumble, allowing ideological power to whip Slave Power. Thus commenced Lincoln's version of the free-soil chant. Through 1860, it would rarely miss a beat.

7

In his 1852 eulogy on Henry Clay, Lincoln had sounded the alarm against southern proslavery writers who doubted that even white men were created equal. Such previously rare southern extremism escalated into a literary phenomenon in the same year that the Kansas-Nebraska Act became a political phenomenon. Lincoln subscribed to the *Richmond Enquirer.* The prominent newspaper occasionally published George Fitzhugh's essays.

In 1854, the Virginian collected his pieces in *Sociology for the South.* The book called the Declaration a self-evident lie for all races in all sections. "Men are not born physically, morally, or intellectually equal," claimed Fitzhugh, whether their skins are black or white. "Some were born with saddles on their back, and others booted and spurred to ride them,—and the riding does them good." Or, as the Virginian put it more benevolently, those of either race, when born "weak in mind or body, . . . have a natural right to guardians," alias "masters," born "to command and protect."

We have built slavery, concluded the Virginia reactionary, on superiors' "right and necessary" protection of inferiors. Yankees have instead erected free labor on the "exuberantly . . . fallacious" illusion that no man is inferior and needs protection. "One set of ideas," soared Fitzhugh, "will govern and control . . . the civilized world. Slavery will everywhere be abolished, or everywhere be re-instituted."[11]

Lincoln may have derived his later "house divided" conception from Fitzhugh's concluding flight. More surely, Illinois's mainstream politician took Fitzhugh's far-out appeal more seriously than did southern mainstreamers. Most white southerners urged the racist orthodoxy that all blacks should be enslaved, not Fitzhugh's color-blind heresy that some whites also needed a master. The South's majority, its nonslaveholders, scorned white slavery—*their* enslavement. Fitzhugh's extremism became too extreme even for Fitzhugh, who backed away from color-blind slavery on several pages of *Sociology*.

Lincoln still noted that the respectable *Richmond Enquirer* published the Virginian's work without protest against his heresy. The extremist's attack on American republican orthodoxy also seemed echoed in mainstream southern defenses. Proslavery cries had routed antislavery stirrings in Henry Clay's Kentucky. Davy Atchison had called in southern troops, then northern Democrats against Missouri whites who faltered on protecting slavery.

Slavery's spread into hitherto free-soil northern territories now seemed more likely than the institution's waning in Atchison's state. Where were the Founders' old presumptions, Lincoln despaired, that public opinion, Declaration of Independence style, would block southern advances in the North and someday undermine slavery in the northern South? Assuredly not in glaring 1854 opinions, whether Atchison sought to rout Missouri antislavery, or Douglas disdained caring about slavery, or Fitzhugh called "all men are created equal" a lie.

Lincoln's forebodings saturated his magnificent private letter to Kentucky's George Robertson in August 1855. Robertson had served his state as legislator, Speaker of the House, congressman, and Appeals Court chief justice. Judge Robertson, remembered Lincoln, had once indicated "belief that" slavery "was, at some time, to have an end."

"But I think that there is no peaceful extinction of slavery in prospect," Lincoln wrote Robertson. Our corroded public opinion makes us "not what we have been." We once called "'all men are created equal' a self evident truth." Now, "we call the same maxim 'a self evident lie.'"

Our revolutionaries, continued Lincoln, "adopted . . . emancipation" in "nearly half the states. . . . Not a single state has done the like since. So far as peaceful, voluntary emancipation is concerned," our slaves' "terrible . . . condition" is as "fixed and hopeless . . . as that of the lost souls of the finally impenitent." The Russian "Autocrat . . . will resign his crown, and proclaim his subjects free republicans sooner than will our American masters voluntarily give up their slaves."[12]

Lincoln equally feared that northern nonmasters would continue to stray from their ideology (and thus their power to block slavery's advances into northern territories). In his reconstruction of how the Little Giant had prevailed among Illinois Democrats, Lincoln wrote Joshua Speed that after "Douglas introduced the Nebraska bill," Democrats in our state legislature caucused. "No more" than "three" legislators favored Douglas's bill.

But "in a day or two," Douglas ordered up state "resolutions . . . approving the bill." Douglas's resolutions subsequently "passed" our legislature "by large majorities!!!" This atrocity, concluded the distressed Illinoisan, shows that when southerners unite, they "can, directly and indirectly, bribe enough of our men to carry the day" as "a *Democratic Party necessity.*"[13]

The Declaration of Independence, Lincoln conceived, had once routed such crass practicalities. "The Fourth of July has not quite dwindled away," he sarcastically told Judge Robertson in that seminal August 1855 letter. The Fourth remains, after all, "a great day—*for burning fire-crackers!!!*" Without the guidance of our ancient national ideology, he asked Robertson, can we "continue together *permanently—forever* half slave, and half free?" The problem "is too mighty for me. May God, in his mercy, superintend the solution."

For total fatalists, such deference to an all-powerful superintendent signaled retreat to helpless observing. For Lincoln, greater evidence of immoral forces beyond his control inspired greater striving to make whatever slight difference he could. He conceived that statesmen must recognize unalterable aspects of a situation, not to surrender to the fates but to locate places to brush the currents. In the face of rotting public opinion and a slide toward a house undivided Fitzhugh's way, the Illinoisan vowed to breathe whatever renewed life he could into the fading and only hope: Americans' belief in the foundations of their Declaration of Independence.

8

Abraham Lincoln spent four months after the Kansas-Nebraska law's passage preparing to orate for the first time on slavery and the Declaration. He saw Mary and the urchins even less than usual that 1854 summer. Instead of haunting distant law courts, he anchored in the State Library, a mile from home.

The Little Giant had participated in fifteen years of congressional slavery controversies. Former congressman Lincoln had personally observed only two years of the Washington turmoil. By studying documents on slavery from

Jefferson's time to his own, Lincoln bid to know more of this history than Douglas had witnessed.

He was as if again the would-be surveyor teaching himself geometry, sprawled alone on the New Salem grass. He was also as if again the novice lawyer, studying murky briefs to catch up with Stephen A. Logan's legal sophistication. When early fall 1854 breezes finally cooled Springfield's humid heat, the oft-times self-learner was ready, this time not to spar with obscure prairie lawyers but to combat Illinois's political colossus.

He first had to trap his foe. His ploy had perhaps never been seen before in American politics—certainly had never before been executed as successfully. He would follow the senator everywhere in central Illinois, as if part of the celebrity's very skin, badgering him to debate a supposed lesser. By continually rejecting the challenge, Douglas would look like a frightened luminary. If the prey relented, the pest might demonstrate that Illinois now had two national political stars.

On September 26, 1854, Douglas arrived in Bloomington for his initial large fall rally. Some five thousand folk crammed the little central Illinois village to hear him. The multitude included Lincoln, who challenged Douglas to a joint discussion of the Kansas-Nebraska Act.

Bloomington might seem an inauspicious place for such an auspicious beginning. The farmers' town arose some thirty miles from Peoria's splendid position on the Illinois River. No rivers visited Bloomington—not even the less-than-splendid Sangamon. But railroads had brought a new day. In the 1850s, Bloomington's population exploded almost 350 percent, as settlers poured into the area to seize agrarian opportunities.

Educational opportunities followed. Illinois Wesleyan University commenced in 1850. Illinois State University started in 1857, two miles up the road. David Davis and the Adlai Stevensons lived here. This would-be Athens of the Illinois prairies, Lincoln thought, would be an ideal place to debate Douglas.

Douglas demurred. That fall, he called Lincoln "the most difficult and dangerous opponent that I have ever met."[14] The Little Giant preferred to speak alone, to his own audience. He challenged the intruder to find his own listeners.

Lincoln preferred to teach Douglas's audience about their hero's folly. He attended the famous senator's long afternoon lecture in Bloomington. The uninvited spectator ostentatiously took copious notes. Then he announced, before Douglas's crowd dispersed, that he would answer that evening. By refusing to debate officially, Douglas suffered an unofficial debate, with the pest emitting the last word.

When Douglas arrived in Springfield eight days later to address more thousands at the state fair, Lincoln haunted the fairgrounds, demanding a debate.

The Little Giant again declined. Torrential rains forced Douglas indoors, to orate in a crammed House of Representatives chamber.

While Douglas spoke for hours, Lincoln paced the corridor outside the second-floor chamber. When Douglas's multitude streamed out, Lincoln, commanding the stairwell, announced that he would answer on the morrow. If Douglas cared to attend, promised the harasser, the senator could interrupt with questions.

Douglas came, dressed to the nines, and stationed himself in the center of the chamber's front row. Lincoln stripped to his shirtsleeves, everyman's garb. The contrast made Douglas seem the aristocratic bully as he peppered the commoner with questions. The favorite had lowered himself to the challenger's level. Oratorical talents could now determine the victor.

When Douglas arrived in Peoria twelve days later, Lincoln demanded a prearranged joint debate. This time, Douglas caved. The two agreed that Douglas would speak first, as long as he liked. Then Lincoln would answer, and Douglas could retort.

This time no rains came. They met the afternoon of October 16, 1854, in Peoria's Court House Square, packed with standing spectators. When Douglas finished in the late afternoon, Lincoln shrewdly told everyone to go home, sit, and dine. He would address the refreshed at 7:00 PM.

As darkness fell, Lincoln pitched into his oration. Barrels of burning tar provided some light. Houses around the square flickered with more. The well-fed crowd willingly stood in the semi-darkness for three hours. With Lincoln's prepared text imminently headed for the newspapers, word would fly past Illinois that the great Douglas had been bearded into an epic match with an obscure equal, over the destiny of public opinion in a torn Northland.

This gem of political scheming illustrated an important Lincoln gift—a talent sometimes disrespected in latter-day heroes. A genius for manipulation ranks low on the modern totem pole of political virtues. Yet masters of democratic politics must possess the supposedly unsavory capacity. Lincoln, perhaps democracy's greatest master, stood second to no one in deploying supposedly dark manipulation to attain the brightest republican forum: open debate in the fresh air.

By blowing slight leverage up to standing astride Stephen A. Douglas at Peoria, Lincoln brought back memories of his manipulative jewel a decade earlier, only eleven miles from Peoria. At the 1843 Whigs' Seventh Congressional District's convention, assembled at Pekin, he had been third in delegates' affections, behind both John Hardin and Ned Baker. But he had manipulated acceptance of a fragile "turn about is fair play" principle, alias the "Pekin Agreement," that Hardin and Baker did not much like. Lincoln thus had jimmied himself into the front of the Whig line four years hence, for a term in Congress after Hardin and Baker had their turn. Now in 1854, this upstart had jimmied himself into equal time with the far more powerful Douglas in a historic oratorical confrontation.

By putting off Lincoln so long, the champion had made the challenger's emergence more imposing. At preliminary nondebate encounters with Douglas in Bloomington and Springfield, Lincoln had rehearsed his major points before a national audience saw a word. After the rehearsals, Lincoln stood primed in Peoria for a nationally observed coming-out party.

He could not know the irony of Peoria as his place to come out nationally. Three decades after the Civil War, the town would become the vaudeville era's testing ground for whether comics and singers were ready for national tours. In the twentieth century, the famous Illinois comedian Jack Benny would help popularize the phenomenon's motto. Benny's "Will it play in Peoria?" would become the make-or-break question for many American performers.

9

Abraham Lincoln's Peoria performance featured his first sustained public exploration of slavery. The speech, one of his longest and most rambling, proved that terseness served him better. But he could not have been more successfully terse in Peoria about why he loathed the Peculiar Institution. He hated Douglas's injunction not to care about someone else's slavery, he emphasized, "because of the monstrous injustice of slavery itself. I hate it because it deprives our republican example of its just influence in the world." I hate it because "it forces so many good men amongst ourselves into an open war with . . . the Declaration of Independence."

The Kansas-Nebraska disaster, diagnosed Lincoln, occurred because "little by little," as "steadily as man's march to the grave, we have been giving up the OLD for the NEW faith." The Fathers began "by declaring that all men are created equal." Therefore, their Missouri Compromise barred slavery from Kansas-Nebraska. Now we say white settlers can allow some men to enslave others, and it is no one else's business. Hence we repeal the Missouri Compromise.

Lincoln would "let no one be deceived. The spirit of seventy-six and the spirit of Nebraska are utter antagonisms." Nebraska and slavery were founded in man's "selfishness." Opposition to enslaved Kansas-Nebraska must be founded in man's "justice." To save temporary peace, you can "repeal the

Missouri Compromise—repeal all compromise—repeal the Declaration of Independence." But you "can not repeal human nature. . . . The abundance of man's heart" will always mark "slavery extension" as "wrong; and out of the abundance of his heart, his mouth will continue to speak."

Peaceful silence, climaxed Lincoln, demands that we "return" slavery "to the position our Fathers gave it. Let us re-adopt the Declaration of Independence." Let us make previously free northern soil free again. Let "lovers of liberty everywhere join in the great and good work." Then "we shall not only have saved the Union." We shall have made it "forever worthy of the saving," and "millions . . . the world over shall rise up and call us blessed."[15]

10

The Peoria Address matched this magnificent rhetoric for the highest American ideals with a splendid call for the lowliest human virtue. Lincoln saw humility as elegance's natural twin. The slaveholder, he believed, might still eventually be converted to antislavery, assuming humble conversion appeals. Abolitionists' oft-times holier-than-thou posture, however, wrecked the possibility.

At Peoria, Lincoln detailed slaveholder thoughts that still seemed open to humble persuasion. Even proslavery stalwarts, noted Lincoln, despised slave traders. They abhorred the African slave trade. Their fellow southerners had freed almost a quarter-million blacks. Those tentative southern beginnings indicated a frail spirit that could over many years be nurtured—with the right nurturing.

His conception of proper nurturing harkened back to his 1842 Temperance Address. Successful temperance persuaders, he had contended, must renounce arrogant denunciations of those they would persuade. Yankee persuaders of southerners must follow suit, he had hinted in that single veiled sentence.

Twelve years later, Lincoln elaborated on the few words. Slaveholders, he had urged at Bloomington a month before the Peoria confrontation, are "neither better nor worse than we of the North." Southerners, he added in Peoria, "are just what we would be in their situation." Even in my nonslavery situation, "I should not know" how to emancipate immediately, even if "all earthly power were given to me." He saw "hope . . . in the long run," for freeing "all the slaves," and sending "them to Liberia." But "sudden execution is impossible." He would not "judge" our southern "brethren" tardy for preferring "gradual emancipation."[16]

His Peoria Address lamented the southern system largely because of its antirepublican features. He stressed that "all men are created equal" and that "no man is good enough to govern another man, *without that other's consent*. I say this is the leading principle—the sheet anchor of American republicanism."[17]

Only once, three years later, would he add the conventional Yankee lambasting, not at all humble, of slaveholders' other supposed sins. That exceptional moment aside, the stinging lash would never be found in Lincoln's words, or the smashed black family, or the master as rapist, or the driver as brute. Although famous for colorful stories to make a theoretical point, he told no tales about plantation atrocities. Such slams would only anger the slaveholders, possibly toward disunion, surely away from eventual consent to abolition.

He also refused to insult southern masters as doomed anti-Christians. His heavily evangelical Peoria audience heard not a syllable on Jesus and tyranny, or on the Golden Rule and enslavement, or on bondage and the Ten Commandments. Lincoln instead deployed rich New Testament metaphors without discussing controversial interpretations. He would later seek the same humble magic with the imagery in his House Divided Address.

At Peoria, he chose a famous biblical image for republican purposes, without a word about biblical purposes. "Our republican robe is soiled," he warned, "and trailed in the dust. . . . Let us turn and wash it white, in the spirit, if not the blood, of the Revolution."[18] Nothing here cited Revelation 7:14, or the holy text's words about "robes washed white in the blood of the Lamb," or Christian commentators' arguments about how red blood could wash robes lily-white.

By avoiding textual disputations, Lincoln appealed to Christians' glory in the biblical spirit. Yankee evangelicals considered his symbolic language an indication that he was theirs, even if his words were not precisely the Word's. Lincoln hoped that southern Christians would equally respond to nondoctrinal arguments about slavery's violations, if those who decried the violations came off as no holier than the violators.

11

His sole slide into arrogance at Peoria provided the classic exception that proved the rule. "I cannot but hate," Lincoln screeched, with Douglas standing right there, this man's "*declared* indifference, but . . . *real zeal* for the spread of slavery."[19] That holier-than-thou exaggeration distorted Douglas's "zeal." Although the Little Giant zealously preached against caring about other people's slavery, he had no zeal to spread the evil.

The righteous slur recalled the earlier Lincoln's almost duel with James Shields and his brawl with the Grigsbys. The latter-day Lincoln's rages usually remained buttoned up inside. In politics (as opposed to in his home!), only Douglas now could make the buttons momentarily slip.

Had Douglas chosen to resent the passing insult, the pair's clash of ideals might have degenerated into slugfests in the mud. But Douglas could be a magnanimous opponent, as he would demonstrate by holding his conqueror's top hat at the foe's First Inaugural. The supreme Democratic Party senator chose to ignore the Peoria exaggeration. The imminently supreme Republican toned it down ever after. He then came on as Honest Abe, self-made commoner in shirtsleeves, stripped down to arguing with a fellow republican about the Declaration of Independence's imperatives.

12

Lincoln curtailed his antislavery solutions even more severely than his blasts at Douglas. The Peoria orator had had more than enough of pursuing the unreachable. His unrestrained quest for the System and unrelieved rant at Mr. Polk's war had set his career back a decade and a half. He had watched extreme abolitionists' pursuit of immediate antislavery crash and burn against both northerners' distaste for blacks and their shudder at civil war. His own attempt at consenting manumission in Washington, DC, had perished within a week.

At Peoria, the moderate took only a single antislavery step. Lincoln urged "the distinction between" touching "the EXISTING institution" and reversing the recent "EXTENSION of it." He said nothing about slavery's "ultimate extinction" in southern states. Nor would he touch "ultimate extinction" for another four years (and then only very briefly and gingerly, just the way he had barely brushed slavery beyond the District back in 1849). Nor would he yet touch the possible annexations of the likes of enslaved Cuba. If we annex enslaved lands, Lincoln temporized in Peoria "we will, as hitherto, try to manage them somehow. 'Sufficient unto the day is the evil thereof.'"[20]

What if such avoidance threatened the Union? "Much as I hate slavery," Lincoln ducked, "I would consent to the extension of it rather than see the Union dissolved, just as I would consent to any GREAT evil, to avoid a GREATER one."[21] That plea echoed Lincoln's language when he backed away from Texas struggles, lest agitation savage Union. Might he retreat from opposing his horror, slavery's expansion *northward,* if the stand threatened the nation's survival?

Unanswered questions most threatened Lincoln's political health at Peoria when he fleetingly stumbled onto free blacks' rights. Tyranny over slaves, began his momentary wobble, stood in "total violation" of "the consent of the governed." Therefore all nonslaves must have "an equal voice in" government over them.[22] All free men, his listeners knew, included free blacks.

No Lincoln affirmation plays better in modern-day America. None played worse in mid-nineteenth-century Peoria. A year earlier, Illinois had approved a one-hundred-dollar fine for a free black who entered the state. If a newcomer could not afford the hundred dollars (about $2,650 in early twenty-first-century coin), she/he would be auctioned into indentured servitude.

Peoria folk mostly savored that latest black code and frowned at Lincoln's passing intimation that free blacks should vote. The Peoria orator immediately displayed his important skill at reversing scarce oratorical blunders. Few talents better served a comer almost exclusively dependent on spontaneous oratory, plus determined to hew to the center of a politically treacherous road, plus occasionally susceptible to leaving his more radical secret prayers visible.

With his next sentence after declaring that nonslaves must have an "equal" voice, Lincoln reminded his audience that he had just disclaimed making freed blacks "politically and social our equals. My own feeling will not admit of this," and "the great mass of white people will not" allow it. "Justice" is not the "question." No "universal feeling, whether well or ill-founded, can . . . be safely disregarded."[23]

At Peoria, Lincoln squared "all men are created equal" with white Americans' "universal feeling of black inequality" by reiterating that he combated "only the EXTENSION of a bad thing" to an area where it has "never yet been. . . . Where" slavery "already exists, we must of necessity, manage as we best can." Our opposition to Kansas-Nebraska, he reemphasized, only concerns "the carrying of slavery into NEW COUNTRIES."[24]

13

Posterity has not properly appreciated the importance of this Lincoln's line in the sand. In Peoria and for the next four years, Lincoln's antislavery position stressed sparing unenslaved territories from bondage, with no consistent insistence on barring slavery from *all* territories and no program for freeing slave states (aside from hoping southerners would slowly consent to the good work). This conservative tack, perfect for initially approaching a dangerously radical subject in a nation leery of extremism, fit racist central Illinois perfectly.

Border North Yankees primarily loathed the Kansas-Nebraska Act for opening *northern* geographic zones to the South's catastrophe. At Peoria, Lincoln offered his constituents the Declaration of Independence principles to slam the Founders' gates back closed against the other section's malignity. Instead of a strategy of attack, marching inside the South to abolish slavery, he formulated a strategy of defense, blocking slavery's expansion from areas where the atrocity had never been. He would drive slaveholders back from repudiating the Founders, back from competing with northern yeoman for the North's best lands, back from bringing waves of lower-class blacks into Yankee realms, back from infecting open northern debate with southern repressions of free speech. He would defend our ancestors, our acres, our Declaration, our democracy from infidels gathering outside.

Defend said it all. The Founders' wall of defense, Lincoln emphasized, had been breached. The Fathers' antislavery sentiment had been diluted. The revolutionary generation's constriction of slavery had been punctured. Restore the wall, revive the Fathers, recapture the ideology, and the republic would recover. Previously uncontaminated areas, where slavery had never been, would fill exclusively with white free settlers. Previously infected areas would incrementally liberate themselves. Over many decades, the Founders' wish for universal consent to freedom would prevail.

A popular maxim holds that offense is the best defense. That principle would have impelled northerners to preserve their domain by assaulting southern areas. Antislavery radicals such as William Lloyd Garrison always cherished the wisdom.

Antislavery moderates such as Abraham Lincoln long deplored the folly, not least as a political loser. Abolitionist assaults inside the South seemed to most northerners a shuddering prospect, auguring civil war in the nation and black equality in the North. Containing southern assaults on northern treasures was another matter. The future Great Emancipator, to repeat the crucial point, would hew to his Peoria strategy of defense, with only the slowest movement toward "ultimate extinction" in the South, until civil war stalemates made that Founding Fathers' conservatism seem the loser, including of Union.

Civil war would come not just because an aggressively defensive South, in the style of Davy Atchison, crusaded to control northern dominions, lest vulnerable southern neighbors become infected. Armed collision also would come because an aggressively defensive North, in the style of Abraham Lincoln, demanded increasing blockades against southern threats to Yankee geographic domains and to Union. Two colliding mainstream defensive thrusts, gathering relentless force in 1854, would take seven more explosive years to propel their protagonists to bullets rather than ballots. Only after civil war required more than strategies of defense would the Yankee mainstream—and Abraham Lincoln—turn toward invasive efforts to abolish slavery.

14

Lincoln's monumental life was all about becoming. He had a long way to travel from Peoria. His rookie defensive program trailed far behind Radical Republicans' coercive strategies, more popular in the Upper North. Yet this Border North mainstreamer's eloquent assault on Douglas's Don't Care-ism, his insistence on caring that slavery was a crime against the Declaration, and his agitation to keep the travesty out of where it had never been—all this updated conservatism advanced light years past twenty years of silence. After going too far for comfort in 1849, Abraham Lincoln recommenced in 1854 where he would end in 1865, as an evolving connoisseur of how to revive and lead the incrementally moving dead center of northern antislavery inclinations.

13

The 1855 Setback

❧❦

Three weeks after his October 16, 1854, Peoria Address and a dozen years after he limped from the Illinois House of Representatives, Abraham Lincoln won election to his former state legislative seat, with his largest majority ever. It was the first and not the last prewar time that great speeches questing office, not great performances in office, fueled his recovery. But the reborn legislator now had no effective political party. In his Clay eulogy, Lincoln had called that weapon indispensable.

1

The November 1854 election dulled both Illinois parties' weapons. Democrats lost their traditional sway over the state. Whigs lost their traditional reason to rule.

Illinois Whigs' battle cry, national resources must boost local development, now seemed less relevant. Federal promotion of Illinois railroads had worked its infrastructure magic. Whigs had lost their pre–Civil War National Bank. Manufacturers of harvesters, Illinois's key industrialists, needed no tariff protection. Their light shipping costs, when supplying neighboring farmers, undercut European manufacturers' heavy overseas freight expense.

In 1854, Whigs' diatribes against the Democracy shifted from economics to morals. On ethical subjects, ex-Whigs sprayed in several directions, including nativism, temperance, and colliding forms of antislavery.[1]

Years before the Kansas-Nebraska Act reignited antislavery, nativists had railed at the some 3 million German and Irish newcomers to America between 1840 and 1860. From 1850 to 1860, around a quarter-million foreign-born strangers settled in Illinois. Non-natives rose from an eighth to a fifth of the state's population. Newcomers especially cherished the Democratic Party, Catholic churches, and ethnic saloons.

Nativists usually called their anti-immigrant coalition the American Party (sometimes nicknamed the Know-Nothing Party). Non-natives must be Americanized, insisted the American Party, before exercising American privileges. American schools must educate non-native children. American governments must not support parochial schools. American polls must bar immigrants for twenty-one years.

Temperance enthusiasts added that liquor must not further pollute for-eigners. Illinois crusades against drunkards climaxed a year after the Kansas-Nebraska Act. Then a state referendum to ban liquor received 44 percent of the vote. Chicago Germans responded with their Lager Beer Riot, parading for their brew.

In post–Kansas-Nebraska Act Illinois as everywhere in the North, furors over slavery's expansion overshadowed riots about suds. The most conservative antislavery agitators, including Lincoln, would do no more than repeal Doug-las's new law, resurrect the Missouri Compromise, and ban slavery from pre-viously free territories. More radical antislavery moralists would ban *all* slave territories, previously free or not. They would bar slave states from admission into the Union. They would abolish slavery and/or the slave trade in Washing-ton, DC. They would democratize and/or scotch the Fugitive Slave Law. At the climax of their radicalizing campaigns, they would perfect a strangling cordon around U.S. slave states and choke the "curse" toward "ultimate extinction."[2]

Geographic locations, akin to the divide between Border, Middle, and Lower Souths, weighed heavily on whether antislavery northerners demanded more than keeping free territories free. The tier of Yankee states above the Border South, stretching westward from New Jersey on the Atlan-tic through Pennsylvania, Ohio, Indiana, Illinois, and Iowa, is here called the Border North. In these six Yankee states closest to the South, Douglas's initial opponents usually did not link banning slavery from previously free terri-tory to barring slavery from all territories, much less to securing bondage's "ultimate extinction" in states. These early warriors usually called their new party the Anti-Nebraska Party rather than the Republican Party (although they bowed to "Republican" nomenclature mostly during and always after the presidential election of 1856).

Their "Anti-*Nebraska* Party" name may seem strange in a movement ini-tially focused on saving Kansas from slavery. But "Anti-Kansas" seemed too confined. These moderates feared slavery would contaminate previously free soil not only in the relatively small Kansas terrain, west of the Border South's Missouri, but also in the huge Nebraska expanse, west of all northern states except California and Oregon. (Those two Yankee states comprised their own geographically separate world, far west of both Border North and Upper North states.)

By emphasizing that slavery threatened to spread northward no less than southward, Anti-Nebraska crusaders displayed a conservative bent, with nothing said about invading southern worlds. In 1858, Lincoln would bring the movement to preserve Yankee free soil to climax. He would campaign against Stephen A. Douglas's supposed desire for a post–*Dred Scott* Supreme Court decree, spreading slavery to northern *states* no less than territories.

The tier of Yankee states north of the Border North, here called the Upper North, ran from New England (Maine, New Hampshire, Vermont, Rhode Island, Connecticut, and Massachusetts) westward through New York to Michigan and Wisconsin (plus, after 1858, Minnesota). Upper North states harbored more Radical Republicans, although still only a minority, who favored crusading southward after a victorious Anti-Nebraska preliminary. Radicals' preferred name, Republicans, announced their intention to have at slavery's antirepublican infections beyond Kansas, Nebraska, and all currently free territories. The most radical Republicans aimed to purge slavery from the District, from southern enslaved territories, and from enslaved applicants for American annexation (or bar such annexations). Radical Republicans linked these preliminaries to imposing "ultimate extinction" of bondage on southern states.

Here as everywhere, understanding the U.S. collision between divided sections demands seeing the nation's divisions as more than "North versus South." Just as the "South" comprised different Lower, Middle, and Border Souths (with most of the Border South tending toward the Yankee side in the Civil War), so far east of California and Oregon, the "North" comprised Border and Upper Norths (with most of the Border North initially seeking only to preserve their own gates against slavery). The entire nation was a five-tiered affair, with passion for attacking bondage in southern states increasing as one moved northward and with most whites in the great borderlands, North and South, shuddering at more extreme folk above and below.

Borderland Illinois's geographic divisions mirrored the North's geographic collisions. In southern Illinois, southern migrants predominated, vestiges of slavery continued deep into the 1840s, Democrats usually ruled, and interest in imposing antislavery on territories south of Kansas-Nebraska ran low. In northern Illinois, by contrast, northern migrants predominated, nothing like slavery survived, ex-Whigs more often ruled, and extending antislavery below

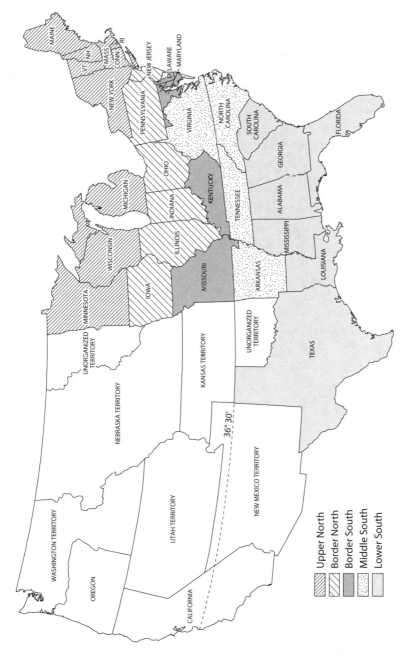

The five-layered Union

Upper North
Border North
Border South
Middle South
Lower South

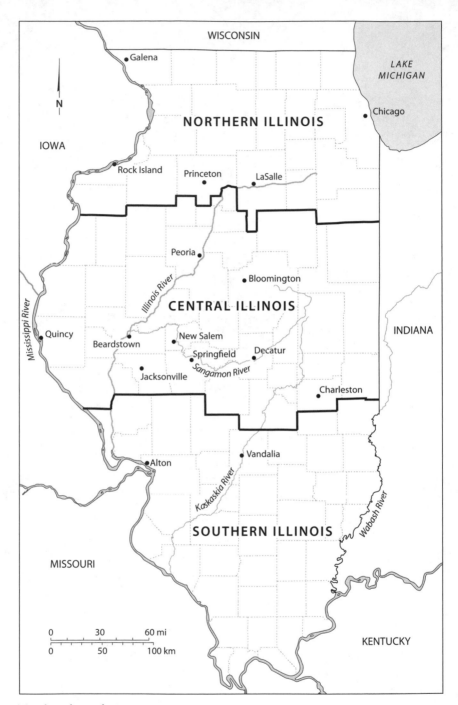

The three-layered state

Kansas-Nebraska awakened more interest. Between Illinois's north/south poles lay Abraham Lincoln's central Illinois, a mixed world seeking middle ground between spirits above and below.

Everywhere in Illinois as everywhere above the South, varieties of antislavery positions, compounded by various nativist and temperance insistences, raised the tough question, Where could a vital center be found capable of rallying enough moralists for a post-Whig majority?

2

For almost four years after the Kansas-Nebraska Act, Abraham Lincoln clung to his Peoria Address answer. Lincoln sought a moderate antislavery party, entirely focused on reversing Kansas-Nebraska. He would crusade only to ban slavery from previously free territories. He would say nothing about forcing "ultimate extinction" in slaveholding states (although he would occasionally echo the Founding Fathers' hope that slaveholders would eventually consent to emancipation). He would not agitate for or against nativism, temperance, or any antislavery advance beyond repealing the Kansas-Nebraska Act, lest his fragile coalition divide on lesser issues. Or, to put his initial antislavery program in the context of his life cycle, he had moved from twenty years of silence about slavery to speaking in favor of only the most contained antislavery proposal, despite loathing the institution as much as did William Lloyd Garrison.

He had trouble hushing himself about nativism. He could not abide disenfranchising immigrants. "How can anyone who abhors the oppression of negroes," he privately asked, "favor . . . degrading . . . white people?" We suffer "pretty rapid . . . degeneracy. . . . We began by declaring that '*all men are created equal.*'" Now we argue that "all men are created equal, *except negroes.* Next we will announce" that "all men are created equal, except negroes, and *foreigners* and *Catholics.*" In that case, Lincoln wrote, he would "prefer emigrating to some country where they make no pretense of loving liberty—to Russia, for instance, where despotism can be taken pure," with no "hypocrasy."[3]

Lincoln saw no hypocrisy in keeping his antinativist insistence private. Far-out extremists, he frowned, scream unproductive hatreds. Mainstream politicians, he cheered, repress counterproductive screeches. Railing against nativists will repel his "old political and personal friends" who espouse both nativism and antislavery. Without these nativists, he warned, we would lack "sufficient material to successfully combat the Nebraska democracy."[4]

By maintaining silence about nonslavery issues, Lincoln would consolidate everyone who hated the Kansas-Nebraska Act. So, too, by ignoring slavery issues beyond keeping free territories liberated, this party architect would concentrate all antislavery attention on Douglas's 1854 folly. Our *only* question, he emphasized, is *"shall slavery be allowed to extend into U.S. territories, now legally free. . . . That is the naked issue, and the whole of it."*[5] His preferred title for a new alliance, the *"Anti-Nebraska Party,"* said it all. Because radicals wished more corrections of blasted republicanism, they preferred the *"Republican Party"* nomenclature.

At the beginning of 1855, Lincoln drafted state legislative resolutions. His never-enacted proposals would have instructed Illinois congressmen to recapture pre–Kansas-Nebraska antislavery blessings, period. Our men in Congress, he wrote, should reverse Douglas's repeal of the Missouri Compromise. They should allow no portion of Kansas or Nebraska to come "into this Union as a slave-state." They should never again permit slavery into a territory "where it does not now legally exist." That wording, unchanged from the Peoria Address, again abstained from attacking slavery in states and territories already enslaved, whether now held or potentially annexed.[6]

Abraham Lincoln was here again the shrewd lawyer, eliminating extraneous reasons to oppose his core argument. He was also the repudiator of his former System overreach, determined never again to drive reform further than a possible majority's limits. Exploring horizons beyond keeping free territory liberated, he feared, would repel too many Border North conservative racists, alarmed that too much antislavery would bring on civil war and racial equality.

True to his refreshed conservatism, Lincoln would cling to his crippled Whig Party as long as it might become his moderate antislavery vehicle. Even if Whigs perished, he would join a new party on his grounds alone. His caution ironically compelled a larger gamble than his System spree. If an Illinois majority would coalesce more around antislavery than keeping free territory free, and/or more moral pursuits than antislavery, others would seize the richest political opportunity of his lifetime. But if he had carved everything extraneous from the only post-Whig moral position that could capture a Border North majority, he might lead a triumphant Illinois—and eventually national—moderate antislavery party.

3

The day after Peoria, Lincoln ducked Illinois's most radical antislavery faction. These spirits, a small minority based in northern Illinois, hoped that the state's new antislavery orator would join what they called the "Illinois Republican Convention." Their convention would convene in Lincoln's hometown, twenty-four hours after his nearby Peoria heroics. On October

17, the insistent moderate instead snuck out of Springfield before sunrise, ostensibly chasing legal business.

He need not have absconded. He had yet to learn that his Border North state could force more extreme Illinois "Republicans" to trim their sails. Radicals in the Springfield convention quickly retreated from broader "Republican" intentions, to proclaim only narrower "Anti-Nebraska" objectives.

A martyred brother's blood had taught the meeting's leader, the Reverend Owen Lovejoy, to temper boldness. In 1837 in Alton, Illinois, Owen had watched a proslavery mob murder his beloved older brother Elijah. The killers had silenced one of Illinois's most extreme abolitionists, an editor who had dared publish his incendiary newspaper across the river from outraged Missouri slaveholders.

The younger brother subsequently pitched his own antislavery tent north of Alton, indeed north of central Illinois. The Maine native settled in a northern Illinois town with a Yankee name, Princeton. There, Owen Lovejoy's Congregational Church members welcomed his liberal dogmas, imbibed at Maine's Bowdoin College.[7]

The Bowdoin evangelical chose his antislavery language as carefully as he selected his northern Illinois locale. He conceded that the black man "is degraded.... He is often vicious, I grant it.—He is often ignorant, repulsive; I do not deny it." But while a black's "germ of immortal existence" lies "buried" under "rubbish, . . . defaced, crippled, and confined," he remains "a man," a "divine miniature," and you "had better" remove your "foot from his . . . neck."

My small faction, Owen Lovejoy lamented, cannot stop all whites from abusing all blacks. If he had "the power," he said, he "would abolish serfdom in Russia," bondage in North America, and slavery in "Brazil." But Americans do have the "constitutional . . . power," he argued, "to prohibit slavery" in all "territories of the United States," not just in Kansas and Nebraska, and they have the "sacred obligation" to their "country," their "world," and their "God to do it."[8]

At their mid-October 1854 Springfield "Republican" convention, Lovejoy and mates initially declared "our unalterable opposition to any more slave States or Territories." That declaration advanced beyond Lincoln's outer limit: no enslavement of previously free territory. But on second thought, Lovejoy and compatriots retreated, Lincoln style, from the constitutionally to the politically possible. Their final resolutions erased their "unalterable opposition to any more slave States" and fudged on no "more slave . . . Territories."[9]

Delegates, hoping that the fudge might tempt Lincoln, appointed him to their "Republican State Central Committee." Lincoln declined. "I suppose my opposition to the principle of slavery is as strong as" any Republican's, he wrote to Ichabod Codding, Lovejoy's coleader and another *northern* Illinois preacher from New England. But Lincoln "also supposed" that Illinois radicals would find the "*extent*" of my territorial remedies "not at all satisfactory."[10]

Three days later, the *Chicago Free West,* the Lovejoy-Codding faction's newspaper in northern Illinois, confirmed Lincoln's supposition. The radical sheet condemned "Lincoln or any" trimmer who "would not pledge" opposition to "any more slave states." While Lovejoy's fanciers had erased that demand from their final convention resolutions, they, too, doubted that Lincoln would always serve them, "when the slavery question" beyond Kansas and Nebraska came up.

4

Their doubts hung over Lincoln's bid to soar from failing in the U.S. House of Representatives to flourishing in the U.S. Senate. Early in 1855, newly elected legislators would decide whether to reelect U.S. Senator James Shields, Douglas's right hand in Kansas-Nebraska transactions. That little Irishman had earlier been Lincoln's antagonist on the dueling grounds. If the new Illinois legislature elected Shields or some other Douglas Democrat, Illinois's Anti-Nebraska revolt against the Little Giant would be weakened. But if legislators selected an Anti-Nebraska candidate, Douglas's reign over Illinois would be crippled.

Lincoln meant to be prime crippler. As Henry Clay's admirer, governing in the Senate had always been his ambition. As Stephen Douglas's despiser, overturning the Little Giant had never seemed more plausible. Lincoln believed that his antislavery program, whittled down to reversing the Kansas-Nebraska Act, could best secure the necessary almost unanimity among Illinois's anti-Douglas factions. If all legislative opponents of Kansas-Nebraska united on the same senatorial candidate, the state would hand Douglas and his policies a historic defeat. But if as few as five Anti-Nebraska men flaked away over other issues, the Douglas faction could prevail again.

Lincoln sacrificed his recent comeback in the legislative election for the chance to ride his platform to the U.S. Senate. Since conventional wisdom dictated that no seated legislator should secure the legislature's U.S. senatorial nod, he resigned his legislative seat before his first session. He then wrote tirelessly around the state, serving as a one-man campaign machine for his senatorial candidacy. A Whig may "be elected," he wrote to a fellow Whig, "and I want the chance to be the man. . . . See whether you can do better than to go for me."[11]

Although he wrote several dozen similar letters, his sole voice could not dispel his largest obstacle: Lovejoy's faction's suspicions. So he shrewdly begged northern Illinois's two most prominent Anti-Nebraska congressmen, Elihu Washburne and Jesse Norton, to plead for him.[12] With equal shrewdness, he gave the two congressmen all the credit when more northern, more radical Anti-Nebraska men fell into line. "Through the untiring efforts of friends," chiefly "yourself and Washburne," he wrote Norton, "I finally surmounted the difficulty with the extreme Anti-Slavery men and got all their votes, Lovejoy included."[13] During his political no less than economic rises, this not entirely "self-made" man knew when others had to make his way.

Still, he had mostly helped himself. His historic Peoria Address had lifted him into the first rank nationally of Anti-Nebraska men, and his immediate senatorial campaign for himself seized the advantage locally. After Springfield's favorite moderate lined up commitments from most Anti-Nebraska legislators, the Lovejoy faction had nowhere else to go to form an anti-Douglas majority.

Illinois's little band of more radical antislavery men had foretold that they would reluctantly compromise, to avoid isolation. Their October convention had retreated from their preferences, in order to attract the necessary Anti-Nebraska moderates. Their belated and begrudging commitment to Lincoln's candidacy marked the first and not the last time that this fast-improving middle-of-the-road tactician, no longer the extremist who went all out for the System, had co-opted the antislavery thunder on his left.

5

Lincoln still needed one more Anti-Nebraska faction to vault into the U.S. Senate. He required the legislature's five ex-Democrats. These deserters of the Democracy, having quit their party in protest against Douglas's law, preferred their fellow Anti-Nebraska ex-Democrat, Lyman Trumbull. Their candidate, however, no Lincoln as a charmer or strategist or orator, would command only a ninth of Lincoln's tally on the legislature's first senatorial vote. How then could this ultimately mediocre senator have become Illinois's first antislavery selection for a blockbuster national position—and over the future Great Emancipator?

An explanation starts with a revealing surprise. In 1855, Lyman Trumbull possessed better antislavery credentials than the latter-day presidential emancipator. Lincoln came late to the antislavery mission. In contrast, Trumbull accomplished important early emancipation spadework, in a predominantly Yankee state still slightly enslaved until 1848.

Despite the 1787 Northwest Ordinance's antislavery provisions, it will be remembered, some five thousand Illinois blacks remained in bondage. Most of these unfortunates, comprising the so-called "French slaves" of colonial French settlers, had been left out of an ordinance that emancipated no Illinois black born before 1787 or (supposedly) their issue. Meanwhile, black so-called "indentured servants" would (supposedly) be freed after an agreed-upon term of service. Yet whites held most of the cards when interpreting such agreements (often unwritten) after a servitude contract (supposedly) expired.

Illinois courts settled disputes over these "supposedlys." Attorneys for "French" slaves urged that the ordinance freed children born after 1787 to enslaved parents. Meanwhile, lawyers for indentured servants argued that serviles' agreements to indentures had been coerced or had expired.

Lyman Trumbull usually accepted these cases, often won them, and charged no fee. Trumbull came to this calling from its American hotbed. The native New Englander looked like a consecrated Puritan—slim, stern, humorless, with stark gold glasses lining his square, tough face. His father was of Connecticut's ruling Trumbulls. His mother was of Massachusetts's inspiring Mathers.

The offspring of this charmed Yankee partnership, unlike most Upper North migrants to the Border North, saw his greatest chance for puritan mission in the *southern* part of his new state. There, Illinois slaves lived. There, as blacks' unpaid lawyer in slavery disputes, Trumbull could serve his conscience. Then as whites' paid attorney on nonslavery matters, he could support his family.[14]

After much success with blacks' indentured servitude cases, Trumbull hit the proverbial jackpot as Illinois courtroom liberator. In the crucial 1845 case of *Jarrot v. Jarrot,* he convinced the Illinois Supreme Court that children of "French" slaves, if born after 1787, should have been freed under the Northwest Ordinance. Three years later, a new state constitution finished Trumbull's *Jarrot* work by freeing all Illinois slaves.

In Illinois's 1854 popular elections, Trumbull parlayed his *Jarrot* notoriety into a difficult southern Illinois vault to Congress. By avoiding the nativist issue, in Lincoln's manner, Trumbull rallied southern Illinois's concentration of antislavery Germans, partially offsetting the region's many white southerners. In the same 1854 election, central Illinois's Lincoln won merely a state legislative seat, in an easier (for an antislavery man) district.

Throughout the 1840s, Lincoln had rarely fought for blacks in courts (and likely never for free). At the climax of Illinois's judicial emancipations, when Trumbull (for free) triumphed with *Jarrot,* Lincoln pled (expecting a nice retainer) that Robert Matson's fugitives should be reenslaved. Which antislavery man more deserved to oust that Douglas fancier, Little Jimmy Shields, from Illinois's second U.S. Senate seat?

Lyman Trumbull's credentials nourished the legislature's five Anti-Nebraska ex-Democrats' answer. These legislative titans had not rebelled against Douglas in order to be shoved undeservedly into an impotent corner of an ex-Whig-dominated Anti-Nebraska Party. To make their point that they must count, especially when their candidate arguably possessed the better antislavery case, they meant to stand firm against Abraham Lincoln.

6

At 3:00 PM on February 8, 1855, both branches of the Illinois legislature met in the Hall of Representatives to elect a U.S. senator. The scene awakened memories of a past Lincoln confrontation. In 1843, Mary Todd and Julia Jayne, then maidens in Springfield and intimate friends, had carried on Abraham Lincoln's ridicule of Jimmy Shields in the notorious "Rebecca" letters. The ladies' contribution to the farce had eased Abraham Lincoln and Mary Todd toward marriage vows and had provoked Shields toward the dueling grounds. Within months, Abraham and Mary had married, with Julia as the bride's attendant. Subsequently, the maid of honor had married Lyman Trumbull. Now Julia Jayne Trumbull and Mary Todd Lincoln sat together in the House gallery, watching their husbands duel each other and Jimmy Shields for a U.S. Senate seat.

On the first ballot, with 51 votes out of 100 apparently necessary to win, Lincoln received 45 selections (all Anti-Nebraska ex-Whigs), compared to Trumbull's 5 (all Anti-Nebraska ex-Democrats), Shields's 41 (all Douglas Democrats), and 9 scattered choices/abstentions.[15] The five Anti-Nebraska Democrats included John M. Palmer, the state senate's most powerful Democrat, and Norman Judd, Chicago's most powerful railroad lawyer (and soon Lincoln's superior in the *Rock Island Bridge* case). These ex-Democrats saw no reason why Lincoln should prevail over Trumbull in the state legislature's first pivotal antislavery election.

As more Anti-Nebraska legislators also wondered (and feared that Trumbull's anti-Lincoln supporters would elevate a Douglas crony), Lincoln's support shrunk and Trumbull's swelled. At the turning point, Douglas Democrats shifted from damaged goods (to wit Shields) to a seductive alternative, Governor Joel Mattson. The governor, although a Democrat, had never registered an opinion on Kansas-Nebraska. He now hinted that he would hedge on the Democrats' notorious law. His compromised words came from a Democratic Party charmer (until his massive corruptions became public knowledge years later).

Governor Mattson received forty-four votes on the legislature's seventh ballot for U.S. senator. After two more ballots, Mattson's support crept to forty-seven, two votes short of victory (since one or more of the one hundred legislators consistently abstained). Meanwhile, Lincoln's tally dwindled to fifteen, and Trumbull's shot to thirty-five.

A reluctant Lincoln saw his duty. He suspected Mattson's corruptions, deplored the governor's trimming, and guessed that this self-serving partisan would become Douglas's senatorial lackey. Lincoln thus ordered Stephen Logan, his floor manager, to switch his votes to Lyman Trumbull. On the tenth ballot, Trumbull won with fifty-one votes, four more than Governor Mattson.

The most outraged observer, Mary Todd Lincoln, blamed Julia Trumbull for crushing both Lincolns' ambitions. If she had been Julia, Mary stormed, she would have insisted that Lyman recognize that in a democracy, forty-five Lincoln men should rule five Turnbull men. Lincoln's wife vowed never to speak to her maid of honor again.

Her unrelieved bitterness about unoffending Julia mortified her politic husband, the least distressed loser in the family. Lincoln knew that he (and not poor Julia!) had allowed a loose end to doom his campaign. He had removed such extraneous, divisive matters as temperance, nativism, no new slave states, and slavery's "ultimate extinction" from his crusade against only "no slavery in previously free territories." But he had done nothing to eliminate festering Whig-Democratic antagonisms; and his candidacy had increased the old, now irrelevant friction.

Lincoln possessed unrivaled capacity to learn from failure and mend the error, for the next time around. Incredibly, after all he had been and would be through, he never lost faith (correctly!) that a next time would come. By belatedly crowning Trumbull, Lincoln began to shave away Anti-Nebraska Democrats' hostility to ex-Whigs' leadership in their shared new antislavery party.

Lincoln also toned down his advocacy of Whig economics. He knew that Anti-Nebraska ex-Democrats remained Jacksonians on financial matters. So he became (temporarily) as nondisruptive about economic Whiggery as about nativism.

His latest move from weakness to strength recalled his "turnabout is fair play" ploy at his district's 1843 Whig convention. After falling behind John Hardin and Ned Baker for congressional nomination, Lincoln had secured vague pledges that winners would give way to losers every two years. Four years later, this Pekin Agreement had eased Lincoln's way to Congress. So, too, three years after anointing Trumbull, this ever-shrewd loser would crusade to unseat Douglas, with Palmer, Judd, and Trumbull's support.

Lincoln's 1855 empowerment of Trumbull was hardly the choice that "anyone" would have made. Many, including Logan, believed that five

Anti-Nebraska ex-Democrats, if Lincoln had held firm, would have eventually caved in to forty-five Anti-Nebraska ex-Whigs. Abraham Lincoln calculated otherwise.

He knew that the critical five believed both that Trumbull possessed the better claim and that Anti-Nebraska ex-Whigs would ultimately fold. To this coldly detached analysis, rare in a fiery competitor, Lincoln added an even rarer realization. He saw that historical currents beyond his control narrowed his choices.

But by choosing effectively among the slight alternatives history offered, instead of ineffectively choosing a more desired impossibility, a sage could nudge the currents. That was a wise semi-fatalist's route to recovery. A potentially bitter loser had instead taken a hard look at why he had lost and blamed himself. The vanquished dreamer had thereby increased his chances that the next time, the victors would boost him to triumph.

14

The Lost/Found Speech

⊰⊱

After his early February 1855 setback in the Illinois U.S. Senate race, Abraham Lincoln's political schedule mercifully relented. The May 1854 Kansas-Nebraska Act had led to his massive summer research, then his triumphant October Peoria Address, then his failed quest for James Shields's U.S. Senate seat. Subsequently, politics turned quiet for almost a year, until tumultuous 1856 happenings.

1

The political hiatus gained Lincoln time for practicing law and indulging his second crop of sons. Willie and Tad were four and two years old. Lincoln had learned the hard way to savor fleeting moments. He had been away during much of Bobby's childhood. Eddie's death, a month before the boy turned four, had shown how swiftly such interludes vanish. Lincoln meant to seize perhaps his last chance.

He often took his tykes beyond residential confinement, to Mary's delight. Her two latest hellions had turned the tiny bungalow into a jammed space. Her best answer, blowing off the roof, remained a painful year distant in 1855. Father's temporary answer, taking their urchins to his office, brought lads' cries of delight and Mother's heaves of relief.

Billy Herndon suffered the consequences. Lincoln's style of fathering, like his style of almost everything, reversed Tom Lincoln. Or, as Billy saw it, Lincoln's reversal of his father's grim parenting sometimes meant nonparenting. At the office, when devouring political newspapers, Abraham seemed oblivious as Willie and Tad charged around, heaving ink bottles, scattering books, doodling on briefs, and pulling Uncle Billy's legs.

Mercy for the sorely tried junior partner only came when the newspaper reader snapped back into awareness. Then Father would wrap offspring in bear hugs, roll over the floors of Lincoln & Herndon, relish their crawling over his long legs, and guffaw at their jabbering. It was not unlike Lincoln on the Circuit, huddled in a chair on the sidelines, then suddenly returning to the storytelling. It was also not unlike Lincoln amid political turmoil, abstracted from action to ponder perhaps inevitabilities, then roaring back into decision making when he saw a slim chance to matter. But aside from this consistent double life, dwelling in the situation and beyond it too, who would have believed that the noncontroller of Willie and Tad was a tightly controlled political architect?

2

Political rebuilding called again as 1855 faded. Douglas supporters had claimed that Popular Sovereignty would peaceably establish a free labor Kansas. Few slaveholders, they had argued, would come to so northern a territory, not when the prime alternative, Texas and Arkansas's tropical climate and proslavery laws, boosted the Peculiar Institution. After many northern free laborers and few slaveholders settled in Kansas, went most northern Democrats' expectation, the Popular Sovereignty majority would reject the South's peculiarity. What magic, this statecraft! Popular Sovereignty would abolish slavery in Kansas without insulting southerners or provoking disunion.

In his Peoria Address, Lincoln had dismissed the alleged magic, in one of his most important words, as a *"lullaby."* He had conceded that slaveholders would never descend on Kansas en masse. Instead, a few diehards would arrive first and establish slavery before the masses arrived. Then "the difficulty of its removal will carry the vote in its favor." To bring slaves "in the incipient stages of settlement is the precise stake" that Davy Atchison and his slaveholding Missourians, poised across the Missouri River from Kansas, "played for and won in this Nebraska measure."[1]

The early Kansas tale played out according to Lincoln's script. Neighboring Kansas Territory, Davy Atchison reminded fellow western Missouri slaveholders, displays a Border South "latitude, climate, and soil." Neighbors "must have the same institutions." If Missourians fail to enslave Kansas, our state "must have free institutions."

Atchison urged Missourians who "reside within one day's journey" of Kansas to swarm temporarily over the border on the first territorial Election

Day and "vote in favor of your institutions."[2] Heeding "Bourbon Dave's" summons, on March 30, 1855, 4,698 Missourians, mostly one-day Kansans, overwhelmed the 1,210 permanent Kansans during voting for the first territorial legislature.

The elected Kansas legislators, convening on July 2, 1855, barred antislavery men from holding office or serving on juries. The solons enacted the death penalty for aiding fugitive slaves. They mandated two years of imprisonment for criticizing slavery. They required castration for a slave cohabiting with a white woman. So much for the "*lullaby*" that Popular Sovereignty would prevent slaveholders from enslaving a previously free northerly territory!

When Lincoln read newspaper reports of Kansas travail, his youngsters had to tug harder for his attention. Father sensed his political vacation ebbing, nativists' distracting issue fading, and the Whig Party expiring. With dismay about Kansas's undemocratic procedures abounding, an Anti-Nebraska Party, seeking only restored liberty in the previously free territory, might pave Lincoln's latest road back from defeat.

3

A year after the Trumbull setback, Lincoln fastened on the ideal moment to depart political hibernation. The first multistate Republican conclave was gathering in Pittsburgh. Owen Lovejoy and fellow Illinois radicals traveled toward the assemblage, hoping that a wider geographic movement would give them the leverage to overcome narrower Border North numbers. Instead of fighting them in Pittsburgh, Lincoln decided to crash an Anti-Nebraska newspaper editors' conclave in Decatur. With immoderate "Republicans" out of state, he liked his chances of swaying important opinion makers toward a moderate Anti-Nebraska crusade.[3]

The scribes' conference commenced on George Washington's birthday, February 22, 1856. By supposed "coincidence," the Springfield party-crasher "happened" to have business in Decatur that day. His latest "coincidence" recalled that "by chance" he had had early appointments out of town when Lovejoy and friends convened their October 17, 1855, "Republican" convention, blocks from his Springfield house. Canny politicians do amass "coincidences."

This time, a legitimate coincidence played into Lincoln's hands. As a twenty-one-year-old new Illinoisan, he had suffered Decatur's Winter of the Deep Snow. As editors assembled a quarter century later, another blizzard kept half the would-be travelers at home.

The shivering dozen who braved the snow comprised the perfectly sized assemblage for Lincoln's intimate persuasion and self-mocking whoppers. As the seemingly misplaced noneditor among distinguished editors, Lincoln told the sparse attendees, he felt like the man who crossed paths with a gorgeous lady. Upon scanning him from head to toe, the lovely princess blurted out that she never saw an uglier man. How can I help that, the poor fellow asked? Well, she replied, "you might stay at home."

Chuckling editors replied with delight that he had come. Mid-nineteenth-century American editors and politicians often became partners to devise a party's platform and spread the party's word. After candidates amassed governmental offices, editors stockpiled governmental printing contracts.[4]

The rapprochement required concurring partners. At the Decatur sessions, Lincoln's advice fit editors' observations. All agreed that at this divisive moment, they must seek only Lincoln's one reform, if they wished to rally Border North majorities. Editors' final resolutions married radicals' limitless repugnance of slavery to moderates' limited antislavery program, in the manner of the Peoria Address.

Their phrasing affirmed that "the spirit of liberty, as set forth originally in the Declaration of Independence, . . . recognizes freedom as the rule, and slavery as the exception." Still, the editors' declaration assaulted only a single violation of "all men are created equal." Their resolves insisted only on reestablishing the Missouri Compromise, thus restoring Kansas and Nebraska to exclusively free soil. Otherwise, their words supported the Fugitive Slave Law and never mentioned Washington, DC, emancipation, abolition in enslaved territories, or annexation of enslaved countries. As for "directly or indirectly" interfering with slavery "in the states where it exists," we "disclaim" any such "thought or purpose," and "we mean what we say, with full regard to the letter and spirit."

The Decatur Resolutions urged Illinoisans "to unite" upon this limited agenda, "without regard to difference of opinion upon any other issue" (read the old Whig/Democratic economic divisions, nativism, temperance, or further antislavery steps). "All who concur" that barring slavery from previously free territories must transcend all other concerns, the editors resolved, should meet in Bloomington on May 29 to form a statewide "Anti-Nebraska Party."

At the editors' farewell banquet, Lincoln toasted the Decatur Resolutions. In response, the scribes toasted Lincoln's future campaigns, whether for governor or U.S. senator. His answer asserted preference for the Senate and demonstrated his well-learned lesson from his first try for the prize. He asked his new friends to favor Congressman William Bissell, Lyman Trumbull's fellow Anti-Nebraska ex-Democrat, for governor, instead of any ex-Whig. Former partisan affiliations, Lincoln warned, must never again divide moderately antislavery colleagues.

Lincoln stopped short of promising to attend the May 29 Illinois State Anti-Nebraska Convention. He hid his intentions until early May, when he accepted Sangamon County's nomination as a delegate to Bloomington. Despite this judicious delay, Lincoln had known, back on George Washington's birthday, that his farewell to the Whigs and emergence as a new party chief had commenced in Decatur, where his Illinois adventures had begun in the frightening snow a quarter century earlier.

4

During the week before the Bloomington convention, national uproar over Missouri Compromise repeal escalated.[5] On May 21, 1856, Missouri's border ruffians invaded Free-Soilers' Lawrence, Kansas, headquarters. Proslavery marauders smashed houses, looted stores, incinerated the Free State Hotel, and sacked two newspaper offices.

The next day, South Carolina's Congressman Preston Brooks invaded the U.S. Senate chamber. Brooks brutalized Massachusetts's free-soil champion, U.S. Senator Charles Sumner, with a gutta cane. Sumner could not return to freedom's chamber for three years. Two days after Brooks savaged congressional free speech, New England's John Brown began his Kansas slaughters. "God's Angry Man" first earned his nickname by leading a massacre of five proslavery men in Pottawatomie.

After Preston Brooks had assaulted free speech in democracy's chamber and John Brown had annihilated peaceable debate on Kansas's prairies, blackmailing southerners piled on threats to majority rule in democracy's Union. Slaveholding extremists warned that if Kansas sought admission into the Union as a slave state and even if most Kansans opposed slavery, Congress must approve the Kansas minority's application to become a slave state. Otherwise, secession would ensue. Furthermore, if a Republican sought the presidency to outlaw slavery in national territories, northern majorities must defeat the incendiary or lose the Union.

The 1856 southern threats posed two perils to majority rule. Lincoln abhorred them both. The minority might depart after losing an election. Or losers, threatening to depart, might blackmail the winners into dropping the winning issue. Either way, majority victory in an election would be empty, and the Founders' City on the Hill would descend into minority tyranny.

As Abraham Lincoln descended on Bloomington, defending majority rule in national Union against blackmailing secessionists seemed as newly necessary as defending previously free soil against Kansas enslavement. The newly doubled strategy of defense dramatically changed Lincoln's statecraft.

The Peoria Address had contained little about a threatened Union. Slave-holders had seemed only to endanger previously free territories.

Now look! Threats to break up the Union had become rampant. Secessionists displayed grave doubts that a republic containing irreconcilable social systems would be their safest home. These extremists coveted smaller republics, with each former part concurring on cultural fundamentals and political objectives.

Lincoln had never given credence to small-is-best republicanism. As he emphasized in the Lyceum Address, he conceived that his generation had a sacred obligation to save the Founders' Union. That creation had featured a large national state, dedicated to spreading liberty and prosperity to self-made men in far-flung parts. Black slavery violated the ideal. Lincoln's solution, however, was not to wreck a great experiment but to save the Union, then use it, over many decades, to ease the defect away, with the consent of the slaveholders.

Lincoln had lately been part of two efforts to prove the utility of such unionism. In 1850, with its massive land grant for the Illinois Central Railroad, the central government had reached into backwater Illinois, bringing national resources and prosperity to otherwise stagnant citizens. In the same way, Congressman Lincoln had sought to reach into Washington, DC's environs with his 1849 antislavery resolutions, dreaming that federal funds would encourage white consent to black freedom, even beyond the District. Now, his generation's obligation to the Fathers required not secession, shivering the Union so that one part's minority dictatorship would withstand the other part's majority opinion, but victory over disunionists and blackmailers, so that peaceable agreement to universal freedom might some distant day prevail.

5

Lincoln assigned himself two imperatives at the Bloomington convention. He must convince his new party that the moderate Decatur Resolutions, with their emphasis on no slavery in previously free territories, must alone define antislavery platforms and establish candidates. Then he must arouse his folk against secessionists and their blackmail.

The party architect achieved the first necessity more easily than he expected. After dropping off his bag at Judge David Davis's elegant Bloomington residence, Lincoln sped to the town's meeting place, dingy Major's Hall. At this convention locale, he expected preconvention arm-twisting to be mandatory. Undecided delegates, he thought, would have to be persuaded to embrace the Decatur editors' limited antislavery program.

He found few wobblers to persuade. The decision to attend the convention (or not!) sifted out dissenters. Decatur moderates looked certain to claim a majority in Major's Hall. More radical Republicans usually decided not to come fight them in their building.

With moderate antislavery delegates commanding Major's Hall, Lincoln, chairman of the convention's nominating committee, shepherded a balanced ticket toward unopposed acceptance. At the top of the state ticket, Lincoln presented U.S. Congressman William Bissell, ex-Democrat and his surprise choice for governor in Decatur. Balancing Bissell came southern Illinois's favorite ex-Whig, Jesse Dubois, for state auditor. Francis Hoffman, a German American residing in northern Illinois, won nomination for lieutenant governor, balanced by Oziah Hatch, sometime Know-Nothing from central Illinois and the convention's choice for secretary of state. And so it went throughout nomination of a centrist slate, destined to sweep Douglas Democrats from statewide Illinois office in the November 1856 elections.

The platform committee, without Lincoln's participation, produced a document as congenial to Lincoln as the Decatur Resolutions and the Bloomington ticket. The Anti-Nebraska Party, declared the manifesto, favored "foregoing all former differences of opinion," except no "extension of slavery into territories heretofore free." A "legal guaranty against slavery," stolen from Kansas and Nebraska settlers, must be restored and never again torn from a hitherto free territory.[6]

With the (self-named) "Illinois Anti-Nebraska Party" in Lincoln's proverbial hip pocket, the moderate approved when the state conclave invited the more radical Owen Lovejoy to present an oration and serve as a delegate to the (self-named) "National Republican Convention," meeting in Philadelphia three weeks hence. Courtesy to a misguided loser cost the winners nothing and might yield support later. The elated Abraham Lincoln did not miss a trick on this victorious day.

6

After the single-day Illinois state convention adopted its candidates and platform, time abounded for speeches designed to fire up campaigners. Lincoln's hour and a half address at twilight, transpiring after Owen Lovejoy's half-hour speech, featured his fieriest moment ever. That perfectly remembered instant fits poorly with the oration's current title: The Lost Speech.

To put the misleading title in perspective, almost all Lincoln's speeches between the Peoria Address and the election of 1856 were "lost." Stenographers seldom replicated every oratorical word until 1857. Earlier, newspaper reporters occasionally recorded a few paragraphs. More often, they printed bits and pieces, between elephantine partisan comments.

Nor did listeners usually take copious notes on oratorical fragments and later reconstruct the whole. At the so-called Lost Speech, Billy Herndon remembered, "I attempted . . . to take notes . . . for about fifteen minutes." Then "I threw pen and paper away and lived only in the inspiration of the hour."[7]

Nor did inspiring orators often read from a prepared text, later published. Mid-nineteenth-century campaign oratory usually featured spontaneity. Lincoln used only a single note card for his so-called Lost Speech. After his outburst, a supporter or two claimed that he had sometimes waxed too hot. Fury should cool, they suggested, or icy critics would ridicule feverish exaggerations. So Lincoln and everyone else allowed almost all the so-called Lost Speech to vanish into the Bloomington twilight.

The thousands of words lost make the twelve key words perpetuated all the more striking. The surviving words transmitted what posterity calls an "aha" moment. Lincoln had come to this convention not only to dedicate the movement to no slavery in previously free territories, his sole strategy of defense in Decatur, but also to defend the Union against secessionists and their blackmailing, the fresh danger to majority rule that had lately surfaced.

His plea for his newly paired defensive crusade started with relaxed humor. He disclaimed shouldering rifles now, to march against secessionists. We should instead mass at the 1856 polls and shoot "paper ballots at them."

With silent pantomime, the orator transitioned from paper ballots to grave warning. Lincoln usually spoke without exaggerated gestures. This time, his sudden gestures without words arrested attention. He slowly bent his knees. He more slowly rose from a deep crouch. He stretched to his full six-foot, four-inch height. He elevated higher on tiptoes. He flung his long arms skyward, clenched his huge fists, and screamed at "SOUTHERN DISUNIONISTS, We won't go out of the Union, and you SHAN'T."[8]

Major's Hall fell deathly silent. Then bedlam. Men shrieked. Sound soared. Flung hats spiraled higher. The provoker stood frozen, a gigantic statue with gray eyes flashing and tousled hair flying, as tears moistened hard frontier faces.

With this surviving relic of an era of lost speeches, Lincoln had found— the only proper word—*found* the prime road to the Yankee heart. That is why the recovered pivotal fragment deserves to be rechristened the Lost/ Found Speech. Defending Union—that cause enflamed northern white men who cared little or nothing about abolishing slavery. Danger to Union—that stoked determination to push Kansas's thieves back, lest slaveholders abscond with everything dear. Passion for Union—that made up for necessities to ignore nativism, temperance, and old Whig economic issues. Conserving the

Union's majority rule from minority blackmail—that matched the conservative drive to save previously free terrain from slaveholders' bondage.

Lincoln here connected his past travails to his future heroism. Union boosted economically stagnant Illinois and its previously struggling self-made man. Union (and not emancipation) would long be an embattled president's crucial word. We will defend white men's economic opportunity in previously free territories, Lincoln reemphasized on May 29, 1856, and we will equally defend majority rule in perpetual Union. This brilliant mainstream politician, after securing proper candidates and platform words, had mated his new party to a twinned strategy of defense, in a dramatic instant that must never again be lost.

15

The *Dred Scott* Case
and the Kansas Finale

Three weeks after Abraham Lincoln's Lost/Found Speech climaxed the Illinois State Anti-Nebraska Convention, the National Republican Convention nominated California's John C. Fremont for the presidency. To win the November 1856 election, Fremont would need almost the entire North, to offset Democrats' almost entire South. The Californian would likely sweep the Upper North, where Republicans ran strongest and Radical Republicans rose highest. But could he secure the Border North?

1

A Border North vice-presidential candidate might help. New Jersey, far eastward in the Yankee battleground region, rallied behind its ex–U.S. senator William Dayton. Partly because he championed jury trials for alleged runaways, Dayton had lost his Senate seat. But before the eastern Border North martyr triumphed as vice-presidential nominee at the 1856 convention, western Border North delegates swarmed for Abraham Lincoln.

Illinois state legislators John M. Palmer, Norman Judd, and William Archer led the last-minute Lincoln surge. Their candidate, isolated back in Illinois, here collected another dividend from switching his supporters to Lyman Trumbull during the Illinois 1855 U.S. Senate election. Palmer and Judd, then grateful Trumbull partisans, had become passionate Lincoln boosters. Once again, this largely self-made man had attracted necessary assistance. Critical others would again boost the absent presidential candidate at the 1860 National Republican Convention.

Lincoln's 1856 helpers started too late to threaten Dayton. Yet 110 delegates (66 percent from the Border North) voted for the surprise alternative. While Dayton more than doubled Lincoln's tally, the Illinoisan more than doubled the third-place finisher's ballots.[1] The Illinoisan's strong second place served future notice.

An oft-noticed similarity, exactly a century later, highlights Lincoln's 1856 forewarning. In 1956, John F. Kennedy, then a little-known Massachusetts U.S. senator, would seek to snatch the Democratic Party's vice-presidential nomination from the respected favorite, Tennessee's U.S. Senator Estes Kefauver. Kennedy would do unexpectedly well in the convention's roll call vote (and even better than Lincoln a century earlier) before succumbing to Kefauver's head start.

In 1960 as in 1860, the loser for the vice-presidential nomination, four years earlier, would ascend to a famous presidency. Both presidential winners would suffer assassination. Both presidents' succeeding vice presidents would be named Johnson. Neither Johnson would approach his predecessor's popularity. In 1856, Lincoln rose toward quite the comparison.

2

Two weeks after his national boost, Lincoln suffered another local setback. In the late 1840s, Maine's Leonard Swett had migrated to Illinois.[2] Judge David Davis had introduced Swett to Lincoln amid a pillow fight, emblematic of why the tense Springfield attorney loved easy Circuit society.[3] As the Civil War approached, Lincoln and Swett remained among the last Circuit comrades who pled regularly before Judge Davis.

In mid-1856, Swett, an Anti-Nebraska moderate, sought Illinois's Third Congressional District seat, with Lincoln and Davis's blessings. But the congressional district's center of gravity lay north of Davis-Lincoln's central Illinois. Worse, northern Illinois's favorite, Owen Lovejoy, coveted the prize. On July 2, 1856, the Third District's Anti-Nebraska Convention nominated Lovejoy over Swett.

"It turned me blind," Lincoln raged, "when I first heard Swett was beaten."[4] Swett's friends vowed revenge. They meant to support an Anti-Nebraska moderate against Lovejoy, Anti-Nebraska radical, on Election Day. Lincoln preferred to honor impersonal realities. Splitting Anti-Nebraska ballots would elect a Democrat. Defying Lovejoy would forfeit radicals' energy.

I have just been touring Lovejoy's strongholds, Lincoln wrote David Davis five days after Swett's loss. The people's "great enthusiasm for Lovejoy" and "their likely great disappointment, if he should now be torn from them" makes it "best to let the matter stand."[5] A fuming Davis eventually concurred.

Owen Lovejoy won election to Congress in November 1856. Half a decade later, he would become one of President Lincoln's favorite congressmen. Lincoln specialized in turning losses into gains. He accomplished the feat particularly swiftly during that week in July 1856, when Leonard Swett's loss turned Lincoln "blind"—and toward seeing how to broaden his coalition.

Abraham Lincoln, shrewd party builder, knew that after believers had secured a nominating convention, victors had to attract enough semi-believers to win the election. Lincoln knew where to find reluctant compromisers. He had to convince Radical Republicans to remain in the moderate-dominated party.

3

Lincoln also had to convince Know-Nothings that the Kansas emergency took temporary priority over their anti-immigration fancy. The 1856 chore exasperated Lincoln. As an "At Large" rather than a "District" candidate for Illinois's Electoral College slate, he bore responsibility to electioneer wherever the cause faltered. Unfortunately, nativists in central Illinois especially required his attention.

When the canvass began, Lincoln guessed that Democrats' presidential nominee, Pennsylvania's James Buchanan, would attract some 48 percent of Illinois voters, with Republicans' John C. Fremont interesting around 42 percent, and nativists' American Party nominee, ex-president Millard Fillmore, tempting the pivotal remainder. With "Fremont and Fillmore men united," Lincoln calculated, we would "have Mr. Buchanan in the hollow of our hand; but with us divided, as we now are, he has us."[6]

Conservative ex-Whigs had hold of Illinois's American Party. They feared that clashes over Kansas-Nebraska would devastate Union. They prayed that contests over immigration would overshadow turmoil over Kansas.

Lincoln lavished more than half of his 1856 campaign speeches on meager nativist audiences in central Illinois. To convince auditors, Lincoln first had to persuade superpatriots that the nation would survive a Republican's presidency. Nativists feared that the so-called Pathfinder of the West might explore an antislavery path inside the South, provoking southerners to find a proslavery path outside the Union. Their apprehensions soared because even former "Anti-Nebraska" folk now used the "Republican" name.

Lincoln denounced the "unmixed and unmitigated falsehood" that Republicans' Fremont would menace "domestic institutions of existing States."[7] The Illinoisan saw equal "humbug" in "talk about the dissolution of the Union."

Echoing his Lost/Found Speech, he warned southerners that "the Union . . . won't be dissolved," for "*we won't let you*. With the . . . army and navy and treasury . . . at our command, you *couldn't do it*."[8] After fair warning sweeps disunion from southern heads, he reassured nativists, debate will narrow to the only legitimate question: Shall slaveholders seize hitherto free territories?

As in his Peoria Address, Lincoln thought that the Declaration of Independence's egalitarian principles could rout slaveholders. But equal rights, nativists feared, might compel white foreigners' right to vote. Lincoln, secretly cheering that right, understood why arguments beyond the Declaration must rally Know-Nothings.

His troubled campaign for Fremont occasionally tested an economic alternative. In the land of liberty, began Lincoln's 1856 materialistic innovation, the wage earner who "labored for another last year, this year labors for himself. . . . Next year, he will hire others to labor for him." For free laborers to move upward, "free Territories" must be reserved for "free white people."[9]

That economic appeal, overwhelming in many Republican strongholds, carried too many egalitarian dangers for this difficult audience. By featuring the American gospel that "every man can make himself," Lincoln seemed to invite blacks to make themselves. By conceiving that nothing should inhibit poor whites' climb up the ladder, he appeared to invite penniless immigrants to flood the Prairie State. By calling free labor and slave labor irreconcilable economic systems, he seemed to invite civil war.

Other Republicans often argued that free labor and slave labor created irreconcilable systems, especially damaging to white pioneers who competed with richer slaveholders for the best land. Lincoln used this powerful materialistic polemic significantly less often than his fellows. Arguments based on irreconcilable differences, he feared, would repel northerners who feared civil war. In 1856, facing his especially fearful nativist audience, he tabled his economic argument swiftly. He would brave his materialistic foundation for free soil only once, and only for several sentences, in the 1858 Great Debates with Douglas. Not until 1859–60 would Lincoln press his economic breakthrough, and even then less often than most Republican luminaries.

The upshot back in 1856: Few listeners heard Lincoln's freshest appeal. One consequence during this least successful of all his oratorical tours: Dead audiences. Yet despite his frustrations with nativists, too obsessed with their anti-immigrant ferocity and their alarm about impending civil war to entertain his antislavery moderation, Lincoln never criticized their (he thought) abomination.

His long-winning, ultimately losing Republican rival William H. Seward would pay dearly for lacking that caution. In 1856, the New Yorker expressed withering contempt for his Know-Nothing critics. When the American Party tumbled four years later, nativists would return the favor. They would support Lincoln rather than Seward when the Republican National Convention chose a presidential nominee. Lincoln's 1856 discretion, of no help during that awkward campaign, would help bring triumph in 1860.

4

The November 1856 election results vindicated the discouraged campaigner's preelection prediction. James Buchanan won a southern landslide, including all southern states except Maryland (where Millard Fillmore secured his only southern Electoral College votes). Fremont secured a compensating northern landslide only in the Upper North. The Pathfinder from California lost his own state, plus Oregon, plus every Border North state except Iowa and Ohio. The Republican collected only 39 percent of Border North popular ballots, too far behind Buchanan's 48 percent after the American Party snatched 13 percent of the votes.

Illinois exemplified how the American Party cost Republicans the Border North. Southern Illinois mustered only 23 percent for Fremont, compared to northern Illinois's 74 percent. Central Illinois, deciding between the extremes, gave an insufficient 37 percent to the Pathfinder. Too many potential central Illinois Republicans preferred the American Party's presidential nominee, Millard Fillmore.

Illinois's simultaneous governor's race underlined nativists' importance as swing voters. For governor, the American Party ran Buckner Morris, Chicago's mayor in the late 1830s and fading ever since. Democrats countered with William Richardson and Republicans with William Bissell, both rising Illinois congressmen.

Half the Illinois nativists preferred to choose between the two comers rather than haplessly back the drooping Morris. Five out of every six nativists who deserted Morris voted for the Republicans' Bissell over the Democrats' Richardson. The net result of nativists' selective defection: Republicans won Illinois's governorship by two points despite losing the state's presidential electors.

If we can convince nativists to drop their distracting cause, Lincoln had correctly predicted, they will help Fremont to victory. But after Lincoln's failed campaign efforts, how *would* Republicans persuade nativists that southerners endangered the republic more than foreigners?

The easiest answer: Let the South's galloping menace do the persuading. Two days after James Buchanan's presidential term started, the southern-dominated U.S. Supreme Court shockingly issued the so-called *Dred Scott* decision. Then as 1857 ended, southerners jarringly almost turned scarcely enslaved Kansas territory into a slave state.

Instead of invading the South, Abraham Lincoln had cautioned, we must repel southern invasions. His 1854 Peoria Address had roused Yankees to rout slaveholders' incursions into previously free territory. His 1856 Lost/Found Speech had awakened defense of the Union against blackmailing disunionists. The following two southern attacks, at both ends of poor Buchanan's first presidential year, vindicated Lincoln's strategy of defense in spades.

The Pennsylvanian's very first presidential moments indicated trouble ahead. His March 4, 1857, Inaugural Address maintained that an imminent Supreme Court decision, declaring he knew not what, would forever settle slavery questions in the territories. Just before Buchanan professed ignorance about how the Court would decide this *Dred Scott* case, he conspicuously whispered with Chief Justice Roger B. Taney on the inauguration stand. Forty-eight hours later, Taney announced the Court's infamous decision.

Spectators jammed Taney's cramped basement courtroom to hear his verdict. The wizened Marylander stood wrapped in a cloak like a mummy. With his almost eighty-year-old voice fading into whispers, the nation's aging antique, alias head justice, decreed that the Dred Scott black family, having been emancipated because taken to congressionally liberated territory, must be reenslaved. Congress, argued Taney, had no constitutional right to bar slavery from U.S. territories anywhere, and "anywhere" included where the Scotts had lived.

Blacks, reasoned Taney, "had no rights which the white man was bound to respect." Property, including property in humans, must never be confiscated without due process of law. Or to put the Court's decree in the way ruinous to Abraham Lincoln and all Republicans, no future Congress could constitutionally bar slavery from any national territory.

Taney's *Dred Scott* logic potentially devastated not only the Republican Party but also Lincoln's Lyceum Address. Twenty years previously, the Illinoisan had urged that supreme judges, after hearing pleas from supreme lawyers, would save calm and rationality among a potentially irrational populace. Now an apparently runaway Supreme Court made judges the problem rather than the panacea.

Almost alone among antislavery spirits, Lincoln had paid little heed to a supposed "Great Slave Power Conspiracy" to defeat northern majority rule. He had always believed that a Yankee majority, once raised to awareness of the Founders' ideological imperatives, could protect itself against any minority at the ballot box. But could citizens rout an irrational Supreme Court that never faced voters' verdict? The question helped drive Lincoln to most Republicans' conclusion. He concurred that the president and the justices had conspired to produce the *Dred Scott* decree—and that secret conspiring had scarcely begun.

6

President James Buchanan's postures on Inauguration Day had first provoked Republicans' incredulity. By whispering with the chief justice on the inauguration stage and still claiming to know nothing about Taney's intentions, Buchanan had aroused distrust. Thereafter, suspicions consumed Lincoln and most Republicans that at very least, President-elect Buchanan had perverted the separation of powers between executive and judicial branches.

That suspicion was demonstrably accurate. During the weeks before his presidency, the Pennsylvanian had secretly heard that while the Court, dominated by southerners, would keep the Scotts in chains, the judicial rationale remained uncertain. The Court could declare that the Scotts' late temporary residence in emancipated Missouri Compromise territories had not freed the family, for Congress had no constitutional right to emancipate slaves in U.S. territories. Or the Court could decree that the Scotts remained human property for less provocative reasons.

James Buchanan more feared continual provocations over territorial slavery than furor over one decision. For a decade, many national leaders had begged the Court to sweep the disruptive territorial issue out of Congress. The moment for the magic broom had arrived, the president-elect decided.

He thus wrote Associate Supreme Court Justice Robert Grier, his fellow Pennsylvania northern Democrat, urging that the *Scott* verdict definitively announce whether congressional territorial emancipation was constitutional. During the Court's secret *Dred Scott* deliberations, Robert Grier and another northern Democrat, responding to the imminent president's summons, signaled their willingness to accept the southern majority's logic. They would sign off on barring congressional edicts against territorial slavery. Then the previously wavering southern Court majority leapt to its historic decision.

The *Dred Scott* decision might not have required Buchanan's intervention. The five southern and two northern Democrats might have concurred on the verdict, even if the president had minded his own business. But the president-elect assuredly encouraged the Court's Union-threatening disaster.

Equally clearly, Buchanan's inaugural ceremony feint of ignorance about the imminent decision sustained widespread suspicions of a cover-up. Clearest of all, what little Abraham Lincoln could see from distant Illinois nurtured his conviction that conspiracies must be uncovered or slavery would blacken every *northern* inch.[10]

7

One hundred days after the decision, Stephen A. Douglas delivered a different verdict on *Dred Scott* happenings. Two weeks later still, an angry Lincoln replied. This exchange in the summer of 1857 elicited some of Lincoln's most revealing prewar arguments. The underappreciated debate may also have initiated his imminent belief that Douglas, like Taney, had become an arch conspirator against northern liberty.

The confrontation commenced in the usual Lincoln-Douglas fashion. On June 12, 1857, Lincoln came to hear the Little Giant's Springfield speech and to invite Douglas's audience to hear his reply. This time, Douglas's unusually ferocious insults led Lincoln to an unusual delay in replying. For two weeks, he struggled to find his customarily civil way to answer.

Douglas blasted Republicans for "violent resistance to the final decision of the highest judicial tribunal on earth."[11] The Little Giant also denounced the "Republican or abolition party's" insistence that our Founding Fathers "planted . . . this glorious republic" on "the perfect equality of the races." Instead, Douglas insisted, the Declaration of Independence limited equality to white Englishmen, whether living "on this continent" or "residing in Great Britain."

Our '76ers, praised Douglas, based their racially selective equality on "the purity of the white race." They insisted on the "great natural law" that racial "amalgamation" yields "degrading, demoralizing disease and death." In contrast, Republicans foster the unnatural abomination that blacks deserve "equality with white men at the polls, in the jury box, . . . and in the domestic circle."

On June 26, when the seething Lincoln finally cooled off enough to reply with at least some of his customary moderation, he still responded with his all-time most impolitic insult. Lincoln scorned the "counterfeit logic which concludes that because I do not want a black woman for a *slave,* I must necessarily want her for a *wife.*" Spewing commonplace abolitionist pornographic slurs for the only time, Lincoln claimed the *Dred Scott* case "affords a strong test" as to whether "Republicans or" Democrats most favor "amalgamation." Douglas, Lincoln claimed, was "delighted" when the Supreme Court doomed the Scotts' two daughters to perpetual enslavement, "subject to the forced concubinage of their masters, and liable to become the mothers of mulattoes in spite of themselves." These "very" circumstances, charged Lincoln, produce "all the mixing of blood in the nation."[12]

With that vilification of the master class, Lincoln risked his tactic for "ultimate extinction." Lincoln's constant bottom line before 1863, that slaveholders must consent to abolition, barred insulting those he must persuade. When Lincoln for this first and only time indulged in radical abolitionists' scurrilous language, he betrayed the fact that Douglas's oratorical knife had cut to the quick.

After his one-time-only pornographic fling, the agitated Lincoln charged more civilly that Douglas left slaves crushed under "all the powers of earth.... Mammon is after" the defenseless black. "Ambition . . . and philosophy follows," and "Theology" piles on. "They have closed the heavy iron doors" of "his prison . . . with a lock" requiring "a hundred keys." Key holders, "scattered to a hundred . . . distant places," research "what invention" will "complete . . . the impossibility of his escape."[13]

Lincoln called Douglas the arch researcher, seeking new ways to lock up the Declaration for whites' exclusive use. When Douglas finds "Republicans insisting that the Declaration of Independence includes ALL men, blacks as well as whites," the Little Giant answers that we want "to vote, and eat, and sleep, and marry with negroes!" Knowing "nearly all" whites' "natural disgust" for "an indiscriminate amalgamation of the white and black races," Douglas plasters that "odium" on all who say blacks and whites are in the slightest equal, and on all who seek "the slightest restraints on the spread of slavery," and on all who endorse "the slightest human recognition of the negro."[14]

Lincoln repeated his frequent endorsement of mid-nineteenth-century Americans' standard remedy. He called "only" separating "the races" the "perfect preventative of amalgamation." He hoped African colonization might whiten North and South. He conceded that putting an ocean between the races would be "difficult. But when 'there is a will, there is a way.'"

My party's way, continued Douglas's foe, better promotes "a hearty will . . . for colonization." We declare "the negro is a man; that his bondage is cruelly wrong; and that the field of his oppression ought not to be enlarged." Douglas's party instead denies a black's "manhood," dwarfs "to insignificance the wrong of his bondage," and cheers "the indefinite outspreading of his bondage."[15]

I would never whip up what Douglas calls "violent resistance" to the Court, added the now calmer Lincoln. Republicans consider "the Dred Scott decision . . . erroneous. We know the Court . . . has often over-ruled its own decision." We shall try "to have it over-rule this" one.[16]

Again, as the Founders' admirer, I would never declare "*all* men equal *in all respects*," whether "In color, size, intellect, moral development, or social capacity." Nor did 1776ers ever assert "the obvious untruth that all" Americans already enjoy total "equality." Nor were the Founders "about to confer" absolute equality on everyone. Instead they perpetuated an egalitarian goal, "familiar to all and revered by all" although "never perfectly attained." They prayed only that "all men are created equal" would be "constantly spreading and deepening its influence, and augmenting the happiness and value of life to all people of all colors everywhere."[17]

That lovely expression commenced Lincoln's new take on racial equality, safer for a moderate. He here turned the Founders' egalitarian goal into a safely remote target, allowing no creeping backward and requiring only inching forward. But where should the Founders' heirs *now* draw the line between racial equality and inequality? The question had troubled Lincoln since that fleeting moment in Peoria, when he had leaped all the way to full racial equality and then, feeling his audience's shudder, had instantly retreated.

He here originated a symbol that might ease racist voters toward "all men are created equal." He urged nothing like blacks' full equality but only their "natural right to eat the bread" they earn with their "own hands." At least in that way, they are "my equal and the equal of all others." At least in that humble way, he had no need to add, whites need not fear black equality.[18]

In the Lincoln-Douglas Debates and until the eve of civil war, Lincoln would wield his new "bread" gambit whenever white racism threatened to derail his pleas to include blacks *somewhat* in "all men are created equal." His "bread" originality always exuded homely rustic charm, amid frontier folk who cherished the labor of growing grains and the pleasure of consuming them.

Less fortunately for Lincoln, blacks' right to eat bread provided no answer to the proslavery argument. Southerners bragged that their slavery system alone guaranteed food on the table. No one, added proslavery apostles, guaranteed that unemployed Yankees could eat.

The brag that slavery alone fulfilled humans' right to food became central to slaveholders' defense. Their position was not just empty rhetoric. Whether because of their paternalistic promises to fellow humans or because starving their investment would be idiotic, slaveholders did almost always provide humble food akin to bread.

Unemployed Yankee proletariats also did sometimes starve. That northern problem would later become much more widespread, as wage labor multiplied in cities during the maturation of the Industrial Revolution. Lincoln's bread argument illustrated his major limitation as an economic theorist. He never came to terms with the free labor system's own drawbacks.

His June 1857 oration nevertheless shrewdly answered Douglas with as much racial equality as the Border North mainstream could tolerate. His revulsion for Douglas's ideal, locking up blacks in a demeaning prison, coming atop his revulsion for Taney's principle, "no rights which the white man was bound to respect," had left him searching, for two long weeks, for a morally legitimate and politically viable answer.

When he finally responded, he had to pull himself clear from an un-Lincoln-like bog of pornography that he would never inhabit again. He had then hardly climbed to posterity's egalitarian heights. Still, with his bread analogy, he rose high enough to talk about partial racial equality with a new cogency and a fresh elegance, to people frightened to go there at all. He thereby brought practical, moderate antislavery to an early—and revealingly limited—climax.

8

Lincoln once again resided distant from the action when affairs in Kansas headed toward 1857's second, post–*Dred Scott* illumination of southerners' galloping menace. Northerners' surges to Kansas had swiftly turned slavery's advocates, initially in control of the territory, into an overwhelmed minority and their slaves into a speck. In late 1857, seventeen thousand whites peopled Kansas. The proslavery crowd barely numbered six thousand. Slaves totaled maybe two hundred.

Proslavery Kansans' only hope—immediate entrance into the Union before the numbers became still more forbidding—faced daunting obstacles. According to the Democracy's Popular Sovereignty dogma, settlers' decision on slavery must accompany their application for statehood. No Kansas majority would approve slavery. No congressional majority would approve an enslaved state's application without a settlers' vote for bondage. Only a pretense of a referendum on slavery could sneak largely free labor Kansas into the Union as the sixteenth slave state.

The so-called Lecompton Convention, meeting in Lecompton, Kansas, in September–October 1857, almost delivered enough of a pretense. Proslavery delegates allowed Kansans to decide on slavery—sort of. Citizens, decreed the convention, could not vote on the whole Lecompton Constitution, which prohibited emancipation for seven years. Voters could, however, reject a separate Article 7, prohibiting new slaves from being imported before the seven-year moratorium on abolition expired.

Proslavery settlers argued that this ploy allowed virtual Popular Sovereignty. By voting against new slaves, the institution's enemies could make bondsmen so scarce (again, only circa two hundred blacks!) that slavery would be almost nonexistent until it could be polished off, seven years hence. Antislavery settlers retorted that they wanted the abomination removed *now*, thereby ending slaveholders' shenanigans. Four days before Christmas, 95 percent of antislavery citizens boycotted the Lecompton referendum on solely Article 7. As a result, Kansans' right to import more slaves passed, 6,266–567.

Four days into the New Year, 80 percent of proslavery Kansans boycotted antislavery Kansans' extralegal referendum on the entire Lecompton Constitution. The constitution lost, 10,793–1,162. Combining the two votes, a whopping 63 percent of Kansas's voters rejected the Lecompton Constitution. Still, Kansas applied for admission to the Union with at least seven years of slavery.

9

In Congress, almost all southerners insisted that slightly enslaved Kansas be admitted to the Union. The Buchanan administration and most northern Democrats nervously concurred. Every Republican angrily opposed. The critical voice, however, echoed from the Yankee who had most given southerners their 1854 Kansas opportunity.

After some stalling, Stephen A. Douglas decided that a Lecompton referendum on solely Article 7 defied his Popular Sovereignty rules too outrageously. He demanded that the constitution be returned to Kansans for a fair vote on the whole document. Douglas's stand enraged most of his southern supporters, who managed to secure the Lecompton Constitution's approval in his own U.S. Senate, 33–25.

Yet the senator helped convince twenty-two of fifty-three House Democrats to stand with six stray southerners and all ninety-two Republicans against a Kansas state on Lecompton terms. On April 1, the House coalition voted 120–112 to return the Lecompton Constitution to the prairies. Proslavery Kansans' defeat outraged most southerners, partially fractured the Democracy, and elated House Republicans, who supplied 77 percent of the lower chamber's anti-Lecompton surge.

10

In Springfield, Lincoln shunned celebrations. The largely Republican congressional victory, Lincoln anguished, because partly Douglas's triumph, might devastate his own 1858 campaign to unseat the Little Giant. Republicans might celebrate their anti-Lecompton alliance with Douglas by allying with the longtime enemy again. If Illinois Republicans chose the greatest Illinois Democrat as *their* nominee in the upcoming U.S. senatorial election, Lincoln's senatorial ambitions would be thwarted for at least four more painful years.

Shades of the Illinoisan suffering that long on the political sidelines after John J. Hardin and Ned Baker swept by him for the Whig congressional nomination in 1843. Rather than succumb passively, Lincoln plotted a historic struggle to drive a Douglas nomination out of Republicans' heads. He would warn that an expanding national conspiracy directed a swollen national crisis, with the Little Giant presiding as chief conspirator—and seeking slavery in Illinois!

16

The Great Debates

❧❦❧

As 1858 commenced, some eastern Republicans, massing around Horace Greeley's *New York Tribune,* urged Illinois counterparts to support Stephen A. Douglas's Senate reelection. The Little Giant, they reasoned, had helped foil southern expansionists' bid to make Kansas an enslaved state. "Douglas's abuse of us," Billy Herndon stormed back, "has been so slanderous, dirty . . . and *continuous* that we cannot soon forgive and *can never forget*."[1] Lincoln gloomed that "if the *Tribune* continues to din" Douglas's praises "into the ears of its five or ten thousand republican readers in Illinois," we cannot hope "that all will stand firm."[2]

1

Republicans' questionable firmness recalled Douglas's previous absconding with Lincoln's supporters. In the 1840s, Lincoln had championed national aid for Illinois's underdeveloped infrastructure. But in 1850, Douglas, usually a state's rights opponent of nationalistic flings, had secured the Illinois Central's congressional land boon. After watching economic bonanza boost his rival, Lincoln might now have to watch Illinois Republicans help reelect the tormentor.

Douglas had dominated Illinois for two decades, after John Todd Stuart (at a bitten thumb's expense) had momentarily squeaked by the Democrat to Congress. Since Douglas would control southern Illinois, Lincoln's chance of unseating the senator would depend on adding contested central Illinois to Republican-dominated northern Illinois. In 1856, Lincoln's central Illinois campaign for Fremont had fared badly. A year later, Douglas had fared brilliantly in the congressional Lecompton showdown, collaborating with Republicans.

If you can't beat them, declares a commonplace refrain, join them. As some Republicans rephrased the conventionality, joining Douglas to beat southern expansionists in Congress might be easier than defeating the giant in Illinois. Furthermore, Douglas's pet panacea, Popular Sovereignty, just might keep slavery out of northern territories, since white majorities in nontropical climes might always prefer free labor.

For four years, Lincoln had excoriated that *"lullaby."* He had rightly prophesized that Popular Sovereignty would give early slaveholding settlers a head start in a territory. Then it could be the very devil to root them out. Lincoln now charged that Douglas only temporarily collaborated with Republicans. The manipulator would supposedly rejoin Roger B. Taney, fellow racist Democrat, whenever political winds shifted.

Lincoln conceived a double way to stop his nemesis's reelection to the senate. He would argue that the Little Giant secretly conspired with Taney to spread slavery to northern states. Then he would echo a little of Radical Republicans' chant that barring slavery's expansion would ultimately lead to its extinction.

Stopping the supposedly impending enslavement of the North could triple Lincoln's defensive strategies. Beyond repelling slavery from previously free territories and deterring blackmailing disunionists' threats, he would now repulse imminent conspiracies to plaster bondage on northern states. To finalize his triumph, he would suggest some vague, slow, safe "ultimate extinction" of slavery.

The new departures, however, together created a wild fling of the dice. Accusing Douglas of proslavery conspiring might make the accuser seem a demagogue. Calling for some "ultimate extinction" might make the moderate seem a radical. The System had taught Lincoln to shun desperate ploys. Then again, he had never been so desperate about stopping Douglas.

2

Abraham Lincoln had also never been more sincere—or more controversial—than when damning Stephen A. Douglas and Roger B. Taney as co-conspirators to nationalize slavery. Before Lincoln's rants, few credited a Douglas-Taney judicial conspiracy to condemn the whole North to slavery, much less that the supposed villains had planned the Supreme Court's endgame before the *Scott* decision. How did Lincoln come to believe this (as posterity knows) serious distortion?

Perhaps Douglas's ugly racism in his June 1857 oration, reminiscent of Taney's loathsome language about blacks in the *Scott* decision, started to distend Lincoln's suspicions. Or perhaps when Douglas suddenly appeared in some eyes as Mr. Republican, Lincoln's conspiratorial frame of mind, already encompassing James Buchanan, ballooned to cover the Little Giant too. At any rate, as 1858 started, the Illinoisan gave every indication of honestly believing that the Douglas-Taney conspiracy, with or without President Buchanan's subsequent help, threatened to enslave the North.

Lincoln saw Taney's courtroom as a hatching ground for northern slavery. Emphasizing the U.S. Constitution's protection of property, *Dred Scott's* judges had banned territorial emancipation. Taney's crew would next decree, so Lincoln conceived, that the Constitution's property guarantees equally barred state emancipation. After a Douglas education in not caring about slavery, Lincoln warned, the northern public would accept the follow-up decree.

Ever more northern Republicans, Lincoln despaired, seemed at the mercy of Douglas's "stupendous humbug." They could not see that this arch snake in the prairie grass was "the most dangerous enemy of liberty, because the most insidious"; that he "will tell a lie to ten thousand people one day, even though he knows he may have to deny it to five thousand the next"; that he "never lets the logic of principle displace the logic of success."[3] Doubting Yankees must be taught that their amoral colossus would gladly ride a proslavery conspiracy to the nation's Executive Mansion.

Lincoln conceded, in a candid August 1858 draft of a speech, that "personal ambition" sharpened his suspicions. But he believed that those with sharpened sight must help the blind to see. He especially must stop Douglas from "bringing all men to indorse all court decisions," and all to "care not whether slavery be voted down or voted up," and all to believe that "negroes are not men," and all to conclude that slavery poses "no moral question." Then no "barrier will be left against" the Supreme Court making "slavery . . . lawful everywhere."

A "Supreme Court decision," Lincoln warned, once "acquiesced in by the people effects the whole object." Douglas prepares Yankees for acquiescence. QED! Can I prove that Douglas conspires for northern acceptance of Taney's next enslaving abomination? Well, is "*one* word of his opposed to" making slavery national? Are not "many" words "strongly favoring it?" Can "any means" be "so well adapted to reach the end?"

This "evidence," Lincoln climaxed, while "circumstantial only," seems "inconsistent with every hypothesis save . . . a powerful plot to make slavery universal and perpetual in this nation."[4] A campaign for Douglas's U.S. Senate seat, he thought, if largely based on exposing the Douglas-Taney conspiracy, could safely add a *brief* prediction (and *prediction* only). The senatorial aspirant meant to prophesize that decades after Republicans routed the conspiracy, southerners themselves would safely fashion "ultimate extinction."

As to *how* currently intransigent slaveholders would someday see their way clear to voluntary manumission, and with what if any northern contribution, the predictor planned to offer no clue. He equally planned, and would religiously live up to the plan for four more convulsed years after 1858, that "ultimate extinction" must always depend on the South's consent and never on the North's coercion. He had insisted on that condition during (and ever since) his sole previous "ultimate emancipation" gambit, that instantly dropped 1849 DC voluntary emancipation plan. While the House Divided Address, and especially its conspiracy charge, changed much about the process of becoming Lincoln, his thinking about the noncoercive process of southern consent to "ultimate extinction" had not changed a whit.

3

True to his zest for political theater, Lincoln aspired to announce his new departures in a dramatic performance. He hoped for another "aha" moment, akin to his glory at the 1856 Bloomington Anti-Nebraska Convention. That time, his Lost/Found Speech, emphasizing that the South "SHAN'T . . . go out of the Union," had electrified only his immediate audience. This time, he would instantly publish his explosive alarm about imminent conspiracy (and his vague prediction about "ultimate extinction"). Publication would ensure that this time, his historic words would endure, long after his listeners scattered.

The inauguration of a memorable senatorial campaign seemed the perfect occasion to warn the populace of a momentous plot. The Founding Fathers, distrusting popular elections, had decreed that state legislators must select senators (just as the Electoral College must elect presidents). But Abraham Lincoln, modernizer of Federalist/Whig elitism, hoped that two statewide parties' nominating conventions would present voters for state legislators with two finalists for U.S. senator. Then, when citizens voted (directly) for their party's state legislators, they would also be voting (indirectly) for their party's nominee for U.S. senator. If this novel tactic anointed him Republicans' senatorial nominee, Lincoln planned to celebrate with a state convention acceptance speech as historic as his nomination.

The performance followed this unprecedented script. On June 16, Lincoln walked six blocks from his Springfield house on Eighth and Jackson, scene of Mary's roof raising, to the State Capitol, locale of his System debacles. Some 1,200 convention delegates cheered his arrival.

The Republican conclave swiftly anointed him its "first and only choice for United States Senator." That evening at 8:00 PM in a jammed, sweltering House of Representatives chamber, Lincoln's acceptance speech, ever after entitled the House Divided Address, centered on precluding a supposedly malign chief justice and an allegedly foul U.S. senator from conspiring to spread slavery throughout a staggering republic.

4

Short speeches served Lincoln best. Only his two greatest presidential orations, the Gettysburg Address and the Second Inaugural, would be slimmer than his 3,173-word, circa thirty-minute warning to this nominating convention. His introduction, destined to become an American classic and the oration's only widely remembered fragment, exemplified brevity's power. It contained some sixty fewer words than the eventual Gettysburg Address.

"In *my* opinion," famously began the heart of the introduction,

> "A house divided against itself cannot stand."
>
> I believe this government cannot endure, permanently half *slave* and half *free*.
>
> I do not expect the Union to be *dissolved*—I do not expect the house to *fall*—but I *do* expect it will cease to be divided.
>
> It will become *all* one thing, or *all* the other.
>
> Either the *opponents* of slavery, will arrest the further spread of it, and place it where the public mind shall rest in the belief that it is in course of ultimate extinction; or its *advocates* will push it forward, till it shall become alike lawful in *all* the States, *old* as well as *new*—*North* as well as *South*.
>
> Have we no *tendency* to the latter condition?[5]

To minimize "ultimate extinction," Lincoln turned the then-unfamiliar words into a fleeting prediction rather than a dense program. After slavery's "opponents . . . arrest" the institution's "further spread," his introduction prophesized, "the public mind" (not the public government) "shall rest" (not act!) "in the belief" (not on a program to ensure!) that slavery "is in course of ultimate extinction" (and only "in course," with the arrival time indistinct).

After the barest hint of "ultimate extinction," Lincoln's introduction came down hard on the third leg of his now tripled strategy of defense. He would now defend against not only enslavement of previously unenslaved territory and assaults on perpetual Union but also against slavery's "further spread" to "*all* the States." The wordsmith closed the introduction with a giveaway transition sentence: "Have we no *tendency* to the latter condition?"

Those eight words bridged a canyon. On one side of the transition sentence stood the speech's minuscule "ultimate extinction" prediction, encased in the oration's slim introduction (a tenth of the whole although a thousand times more remembered). On the other side of the transition sentence, the oration's nine times longer, almost forgotten main argument pounded away at the supposed Douglas-Taney plot to nationalize slavery (while adding nothing about "ultimate extinction").

Missing that verbal bridge multiplies misunderstandings. For example, Springfield's Lincoln Museum displays, chiseled into its vestibule walls, the House Divided Address's entire introduction—except the signature last sentence. The museum's exhibit equally omits Lincoln's nightmare that Taney's Supreme Court would force slavery on the North. Resurrecting those eight transitory words underlines why the tag line for the 1858 orator must be warrior against slavery's imminent nationalization—and not yet (indeed not for five more years) ready to force slavery's "ultimate extinction." No single sentence better illuminates why the tale of becoming Lincoln must wander and waver, before a coercive emancipator strikes.

5

"We can not absolutely *know*," Lincoln conceded after the transition sentence, that the road from the Kansas-Nebraska Act through the *Dred Scott* decision and on toward northern states' enslavement proves "preconcert . . . from the beginning." Yet "different workmen—Stephen, Franklin, Roger, and James for instance," while working "at different times and places," have produced "timbers" with all "tendons and mortises . . . fitting" suspiciously "exactly." So we "find it impossible to not *believe*" that Douglas, Pierce, Taney, and Buchanan "all worked upon a common *plan* or *draft*, drawn up before the first lick was struck."[6]

All the conspiracy's licks, continued Lincoln, aimed at perfecting "*squatter sovereignty*," alias the perversion that "if any *one* man" enslaves "*another*, . . . no *third* man shall be allowed to object." Throughout the design, Douglas would educate "*Northern* public opinion to not *care* whether slavery is voted *down* or voted *up*."[7]

Moving as Douglas amorally commanded, congressional Democrats had repealed the Missouri Compromise's ban on slaveholders. Moving as Buchanan conspiratorially directed, Supreme Court judges had ruled that Congress must allow territorial slavery. "Put *that* and *that* together" and "ere long," plotters might secure "another Supreme Court" ruling, "declaring" that no "*state*" can "exclude slavery." Then "we *shall lie* down pleasantly dreaming that the people of *Missouri* are on the verge of making their State *free;* and we shall *awake* to the *reality,* instead, that the *Supreme* Court has made *Illinois* a *slave* State."[8]

"*How* can we best" educate public opinion to deter this disaster? Some Republicans, Lincoln noted, call Douglas their "*aptest* instrument. . . . They remind us that he is a very *great man,*" while "the largest of *us* are very small ones."

Yet "'a *living dog* is better than a *dead lion.*' Judge Douglas, if not a *dead* lion," is "*caged* and *toothless . . . for this work.* How can he oppose" slavery's "advances" into the North? "He don't *care* anything about it. His avowed *mission is impressing* the 'public heart' to *care* nothing about it."[9] Since Douglas's heart "is not *now* with us" and "does not *promise* to *ever* be," concluded Lincoln, we must choose "undoubted friends—those whose hands are free, whose hearts are in the work—who *do care* for the result." Our caring hearts then shall make free white laborers' "victory . . . sure to come."[10]

6

HEARTS! In an age of evangelical revivalism, the House Divided orator became romantic revivalist. Just as preachers in packed revival tents wrenched sinners' wandering hearts from Satan toward Christ, so Lincoln in the jammed secular convention tugged citizens' wavering sentiments from Douglas's Don't Care-ism to caring about slavery's iniquity.

The secular sacredness inspired that title: The House Divided. Three New Testament tales featured these words of Jesus to the Pharisees (Matthew 12:25, Mark 3:25, and Luke 11:17). The House Divided Address copied the holy vocabulary only once—in the introduction, without explanation. Lincoln had earlier deployed the words at least three times, fully explained. Yet in prior uses, he had not seemed a revivalist. Here the exhorter's plea for converted hearts seemed spiritually saturated with biblical houses divided.

The gospel title eased northern evangelicals' doubt about Lincoln. Did Christian urgency, they had wondered, impel Lincoln's moral flights? Lincoln's lack of church membership, his sparse church attendance, and his inconsistent fatalism had not announced an orthodox believer. His introduction, however, featured holy imagery, and he soared in evangelical estimations.

"Ultimate extinction," his introduction's two other inspiring words, likewise uttered a single time without explanation, also eased doubts, this time among antislavery zealots. They had wondered whether Lincoln's stress on containing slavery would ever liberate slaves. He had never before publicly emitted "ultimate extinction." Now the two words predicted that stopping slavery's expansion would (somehow) start its extinction.

Radical Republicans still held Lincoln at arm's length. They craved explanations of how and when his save-the-North-first strategy would weaken the South's institution, and how and when the killing blow might come. But extremists' suspicions had eased, especially among reforming romantics.

Romantics' increased estimation of Lincoln illuminated one of his most important changes. The forty-eight-year-old Lincoln's House Divided Address seemed more than two decades removed from the twenty-nine-year-old's Lyceum Address. He had then seemed an eighteenth-century Age of Reason holdover, deploying courts' legal rationality to control mob passions. He now seemed a nineteenth-century Age of Romanticism convert, rousing popular passions to override judicial error. The horror of the *Dred Scott* decision had finalized quite the change.

Style served substance in this romantic oration. Vivid symbols alerted slumbering hearts. The House Divided augured smashed Union. Supreme Court plots foretold northern slavery. Christian republicans must unmask a conspiratorial Judas. Then a misty dream of "ultimate extinction" might replace the vivid nightmare of Illinois's imminent enslavement.

7

Yet the oration's romantic style also displayed the genre's defects. The appeal to hearts sacrificed rational heft. Why can't this divided house, Douglas would ask, survive contentions, like most houses? Is it plausible that Taney would nationalize slavery? And how, when, and where would "ultimate extinction" prevail? The thinness of the House Divided Address, when proclaiming these oratorical flights, handed Douglas an advantage before the Great Debates even commenced.

A less romantic stylist would have provided thick evidence that conspiracies to nationalize slavery existed, that a second enslaving *Dred Scott* decision loomed, and that "ultimate extinction" would take off from stopping Douglas. Dense proof was necessary because even antislavery luminaries seldom shared Lincoln's premonitions of northern enslavement. Lincoln's party allies usually stormed at a supposed "Great Slave Power Conspiracy," plotting to overwhelm Congress. Compatriots far less often spotted Supreme Court plotters, scheming to enslave states.

William H. Seward's famous 1858 Irrepressible Conflict speech, for example, while much like the House Divided utterance, included nothing about conspiratorial plots or enslaving courts. Seward was more accurate. Douglas and Taney hardly conspired to foist slavery on northern states.

Lincoln would soon soften charges that Douglas led the conspiracy. Instead, the Republican would turn the Little Giant into plotters' dupe. As for alleged judicial plotters, Lincoln never divined what had secretly happened between President-elect Buchanan and the Court during *Dred Scott* deliberations (a "plot" intended to save the Union!). He also never guessed that Buchanan's plotting with the Supreme Court had swiftly ended or that Douglas had no involvement with *Dred Scott*'s southern judges (who had their doubts about slavery and their conviction that state's rights formulas must keep federal hands off the Peculiar Institution).

Fortunately for Lincoln's historic reputation, he would squelch his conspiracy notions after 1858 and become a coercive emancipator after 1862. Or, to give the statesman his due, no one better spotted his own errors and kept moving on.

8

A second *Dred Scott* decision, nationalizing slavery, today seems as far-fetched as a Douglas-Taney conspiracy. Roger B. Taney, southern state's rights Unionist, would have had to flip into anti-Taney to slap down his salvation for Union: a state's sole power over its labor institutions. A state, the chief justice had affirmed in *Groves v. Slaughter* (1841), "exclusively . . . has a right to decide for itself whether" to "allow" slaves "within its limits."[11]

Taney and mates had for decades been moderate southern Democrats. Most still echoed Andrew Jackson's famous toast: "Our Federal Union, It Must Be Preserved." Most harbored severe doubts about slavery (especially Taney, who had freed his slaves and remained glad of it). These state's rights judges' line in the sand, Taney's *Groves v. Slaughter*, protected each state's total control over its labor system. Such southern Unionists scarcely threatened to annihilate *Groves v. Slaughter* in the name of everywhere enslaving the national republic (and thereby enormously threatening the Union).

Lincoln's 1838 Lyceum Address had prayed that sober judges, helped by wise opposing attorneys, would counter popular hysterias. In his 1847 *Matson* case, an enlightened circuit court had indeed precluded riots over fugitive slaves. In the *Dred Scott* case, however, a misguided Supreme Court had discredited the panacea. Instead of counting on a rational legal system to control wild popular passions, Lincoln now thought that an aroused populace must stymie bigoted judges. His move from legalistic salvation to romantic rescue aimed to save his North from Douglas's moral indifference run free, lest Taney ran amok, lest black slavery ran rampant throughout the North. But how far had Lincoln's defensive stride from rationalism to romanticism taken him toward that Promised Land, "ultimate extinction"?

9

Perilously far, Stephen A. Douglas meant to demonstrate. Lincoln had claimed that the Union could not remain divided (without saying why); and that "ultimate extinction" would come (without detailing how or when); and that a killing conspiracy operated (without supplying proof); and that the Court would enslave the North (without demonstrating plausibility). Soon enough, Douglas would warn, these flimsy evasions will drop away, and that pregnant "All," in *All* Men Are Created Equal, would spawn not only fractured Union but also racial amalgamation.

Before the House Divided Address, Lincoln had tested his oration before some dozen friends. He had never before so rehearsed. When Lincoln read the words "house divided" and "ultimate extinction," only Billy Herndon gushed that "the speech . . . will make you president." All others attacked the seeming radicalism as sure "to drive away a good many voters" or "ahead of its time" or a "d—d fool utterance."[12]

A week after the speech, John L. Scripps, Lincoln's Chicago friend and newspaper editor, pinpointed the problem. Our doubters fear "we are not sufficiently conservative," Scripps warned Lincoln. They read "ultimate extinction" as a Republican "pledge . . . to make war upon the institution in the States."[13]

Lincoln shot back a plea that he had never believed or asserted that "any power outside of the slave states" could "constitutionally or rightfully interfere with . . . slavery where it already exists." He had only *predicted* that slavery, once barred from expanding into "new territories" and "free states, will then be in course of ultimate extinction." But this reply to Scripps, like his House Divided Address, never explained how "ultimate extinction" would proceed—and without provoking disunion.[14]

10

When the 1858 senatorial campaign began, Douglas rejected joint debates about "ultimate extinction" or about any issue. If he campaigned apart, the Little Giant knew, his speeches would outdraw the challenger's. If they appeared together, he would have his "hands full" with "the best stump-speaker . . . in the West."[15]

The best western stump speaker, deploying his best anti-Douglas tactic, trapped the Little Giant. Wherever the Democrat went, the Republican followed, listening to Douglas and then responding. That routine commenced in two (of Illinois's nine) congressional districts, starting in Chicago on July 9–10 and recurring in Springfield on July 17. These brilliant, widely published exchanges should be considered part of the Lincoln-Douglas Debates (as should the bitter June 1857 exchange in Springfield).

After the Chicago/Springfield 1858 unofficial debates, both disputants desired changes. Douglas wanted relief from Lincoln's always having the last word. Lincoln wanted release from Douglas's always choosing the first subject. The Little Giant also wished respite from his foe's hounding his every step.

On July 31, they finalized a revised version of the Chicago/Springfield theatrics. They would stage one open-air debate in each of Illinois's seven other congressional districts. They would take turns going first for an hour, with the rival responding for an hour and a half and the initial speaker closing for half an hour. Joint debates would transpire in Ottawa and Freeport in late August, in Jonesboro and Charleston in mid-September, and in Galesburg, Quincy, and Alton in early October.

Otherwise, they would campaign solo. Each traveler eventually covered near five thousand miles in one hundred days. Both concentrated on almost dead-even central Illinois. Their individual campaigning brought this showdown up close and personal to hundreds of crossroads, beyond the debate extravaganzas.

To share the confrontation's peak excitement, thousands journeyed to joint debate sites on horses, trains, boats, wagons, or aching feet. Upon arrival, sojourners usually found standing room only, limited food, and scarce shelter. But they relished bands blaring, cannon booming, and parades marching. Then they savored oratorical duels between Illinois's two supreme politicians at a supreme American moment. Few listeners minded being squeezed together for three hours, with a shattering national crisis demanding that they help arbitrate.

Douglas, a foot shorter, inches rounder, and thousands richer, usually rode his private railroad car to the debate town's outskirts, He then sometimes drove two or four prancing horses to the outdoor forensic duels. His bride Adele, less than half his age, usually adorned his carriage. His sky-blue jacket with its shiny brass buttons gleamed atop his white ruffled shirt. His deep, booming voice signaled a commander's assurance. He sounded and

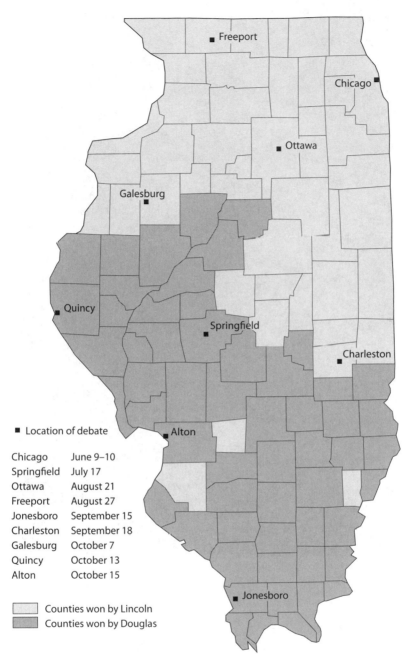

Freeport

Chicago

Ottawa

Galesburg

Quincy

Springfield

Charleston

■ Location of debate

Chicago	June 9–10
Springfield	July 17
Ottawa	August 21
Freeport	August 27
Jonesboro	September 15
Charleston	September 18
Galesburg	October 7
Quincy	October 13
Alton	October 15

Alton

Jonesboro

Counties won by Lincoln
Counties won by Douglas

Lincoln-Douglas geography

Stephen Douglas

looked like a titan who had come to the frontier with educational credentials beyond most Illinoisans, then transcended other seekers politically, passed rival entrepreneurs financially, and now ached to teach the upstart to defer to his betters.

The challenger, far taller, lankier, and poorer, sounded and looked like a scrambler who had arrived in central Illinois with a mere speck of blab school education. Dusty shoes encased his flat feet. His fraying suit failed to approach his ankles or his fists. His deliberately unbrushed hair epitomized

Abraham Lincoln, ca. 1860

everyman's appearance. His sorry green umbrella threatened to snare an ear if opened. His thin tenor voice cracked when he strained for effect. Usually he accompanied scruffy spectators on primitive trains, with his matronly wife, twice Adele's age, back home.

While Lincoln's appearance bespoke past economic struggle, his words showcased continued political deprivation. The seeker, nine years removed from any office, lamented that Senator Douglas "is of world wide renown." He seems "a certainty, at no distant day, to be the President." His "round, jolly, fruitful face" exudes prospects of "postoffices, landoffices, marshalships, and cabinet appointments, . . . sprouting out in wonderful exuberance" and beckoning "greedy hands."

In comparison, noted Lincoln, I have held scant positions. "Nobody has ever expected me to be President. . . . In my poor, lean, lank, face, nobody has ever seen . . . any [patronage] cabbages . . . sprouting."[16] If this apparently over-matched loser could even come close to the superstar, poor initial impressions could send him doubly soaring.

As it turned out, neither debater soared invincibly. Specious claims, unanswered points, and irrelevant exaggerations abounded. But few complained then, and none should now. The disappointing sparring can be easily skimmed. The arresting phrases illuminate a national house precariously standing, with a titan and a comer both straining to shore it up.

11

In the Great Debates as in his House Divided Address, Lincoln emphasized vivid alarms about Illinois's imminent enslavement, not fuzzy possibilities of slavery's "ultimate extinction." He again shuddered most at Douglas and Taney's supposed conspiracy "to . . . nationalize slavery." But Douglas usually scorned to debate that "infamous lie." No man "claiming any degree of intelligence or decency," the Little Giant roared, "ever dreamed" that a "ridiculous . . . court" would bar a state from prohibiting "slavery within her own limits!" He would not allow Lincoln's "utterly reckless and unscrupulous . . . moral treason" to distract him "from showing up" ultimate extinction, that "revolutionary principle."[17]

This debate strategy thrived, for the Douglas-Taney conspiracy could seem far-fetched and "ultimate extinction" alarming. During Lincoln's previous tiptoes down the antislavery high wire, he had combined killing hands on slavery, an inch inside northern terrain, with hands altogether off, an inch inside southern states. His slight House Divided recalibration, although devoid of timetables, programs, and probabilities, nudged antislavery south of the Mason-Dixon Line. Douglas pounced on the exposed morsel.

Lincoln at first sought refuge in parsing words. I meant "ultimate extinction," he protested, as "a prediction only, . . . a foolish one perhaps." Can't Douglas distinguish between a *purpose* . . . and an *expectation?* I have often expressed an expectation to die, but I have never expressed a *wish* to die."[18]

Douglas would no more discuss this quibble than allow the Great Debates to focus on fancied conspiracies. He instead relentlessly accused his foe of fostering explosions over an "ultimate extinction" inferno. Lincoln usually changed the subject instead of answering the accusation. He wished to debate the horror of slavery, not the mysteries of "ultimate extinction."

"I have always hated slavery, I think, as much as any Abolitionist," Lincoln declared.[19] "The real issue" between "Judge Douglas and myself," he soared, "will continue" long after "our poor tongues . . . shall be silent." In the "eternal struggle between . . . right and wrong," whether involving the "common right of humanity" or "the divine right of kings," commoners' enemies ever say "You work and toil and earn bread and I'll eat it." Whether the monstrosity pollutes the "mouth of a king," living "by the fruits of" his subjects' "labor," or befouls the tongues of "one race, . . . as an apology for enslaving another race, it is the same tyrannical principle."[20]

Since Douglas will not call tyranny wrong, charged Lincoln, our senator will help spread the abomination. Since we admit no "right to do wrong," we will prevent the crime from enlarging. Quarantining the wrong from infecting "new countries where it has not already existed" is "the peaceful way, the old-fashioned way," our "Fathers'" way toward moral triumph.[21]

By teaching "that the negro has no share," however "humble, . . . in the Declaration of Independence," Lincoln climaxed, Douglas and his Democrats muzzle "cannon that thunders" July Fourth's "annual joyous return." They blow "out the moral lights around us." They prepare "the public mind . . . for making the institution of slavery perpetual and national."[22] At a time when "all this quibbling about" the inferiority of "this man and the other man—this race and . . . that other . . . race" portends such disaster, let us "unite as one people throughout this land," once again "declaring that all men are created equal."[23]

12

Douglas answered that he could only legitimately care whether his state harbors the institution. "Wisely," we "prohibited it in Illinois forever." No Illinoisan "would be more strenuous in his opposition to the introduction of slavery" here "than I would." But by settling "it for ourselves, we exhausted all our power over that subject. . . . Each and every other State" must "decide . . . the same question . . . for itself."[24]

My foe's meddling in other states, continued Douglas, will poison Union. Lincoln "tells you that this Republic cannot endure permanently divided into slave and free states." He tells you "not" to "be content with regulating your own affairs and minding your own business." You must "invade the Southern States, abolish slavery there, and" make all "the States all one thing." This "inevitable and irresistible result of Mr. Lincoln's House Divided invites a warfare between the North and South, to be carried on with ruthless vengeance."[25]

More criminally still, warned Douglas, my detractor thinks he joins the Founders in considering "the negro . . . his brother." But like the Fathers, I call the Negro no "kin of mine." Like the Founders, I oppose "negro equality, . . . Indian equality," and "Coolies . . . equality."

The Founders' racial inequality, continued Douglas, promises eternal white men's Union. Lincoln's racial equality instead promises emancipation, civil war, and negroes flowing into Illinois, covering "our prairies until in midday they will look dark and black as night." Then we will suffer "Cuffee elevated to the bench, . . . marrying any woman he may select," and "amalgamation, demoralization, and degradation."[26]

13

"Negro equality! Fudge!" exploded Lincoln privately.[27] But Douglas endlessly smeared Lincoln with that fudge, and the Republican had difficulty changing the subject. One alternative was to replace debates on racial equality with contentions about free white laborers' opportunity, once black slavery had been thankfully barred from virgin lands.

Opportunity for all white men, however, had its own slippery slope— that nativist problem. As in 1856, Lincoln skidded when he touched the otherwise promising topic. "Irrespective of . . . right or wrong in enslaving a negro," he wished free white laborers could monopolize "new soil and better their condition." Then the full dimensions of his wish escaped. He wished "an outlet for *free white people everywhere*," so that "Hans, and Baptistes, and Patricks . . . from all the world may find new homes and better their conditions."[28]

The 1858 Lincoln, sensing counterproductive impacts on swing nativist voters as soon as he uttered the words, instantly scotched white men's opportunity as well as that of "Hans, Baptiste, and Patrick." A safer debate alternative was to mock Douglas's racial smears. Anyone who "argues me" from "all men are created" to "perfect social and political equality with the negro," Lincoln exclaimed, uses "a specious and fantastic arrangement of words" to "prove a horse-chestnut to be a chestnut horse."[29] He followed with a telling biblical illustration, deepening his June 1857 argument that equality, racial or otherwise, was a distant goal, not a present necessity.

"As your Father in heaven is perfect," Lincoln read from "the Lord's" command, "be ye also perfect." Our "Savior," went his commentary on the reading, expected no "human creature to . . . be" as "perfect" as "the Father in heaven." Instead, He established a "standard," to determine which lesser mortal has "attained the highest degree of moral perfection." So I say, "let all men are created equal . . . be as nearly reached as we can." Let us rise whenever possible in the Republican direction of universal human freedom. Let us never sink in the Douglas direction of "one universal slave nation."[30]

Lincoln conceded that political necessity required his uncompromising direction to include compromised racism. He agreed "with Judge Douglas" that the black "is not my equal in many respects—certainly not in color, *perhaps* not in moral and intellectual endowment" (emphasis mine). Lincoln hoped African colonization would put an ocean between unequal races. "While they do remain together," however, the "white race" must monopolize "the superior position."

He would not make "voters or jurors of negroes," or qualify "them to hold office," or permit marriages "of white people with negroes," or favor turning a negro into "a citizen. . . . But in the right to eat the bread, without the leave of anybody else, which his own hand earns, he *is my equal and the equal of Judge Douglas, and the equal of every living man.*"[31]

That climax, repeating his June 1857 presumption that slaveholders did not even supply slaves their daily bread, again underestimated southern masters' paternalistic code and self-interest. In 1858, however, racist Illinoisans cared little about his shaky bread argument and much about his provocative *perhaps,* as in blacks are "not my . . . equal, perhaps . . . in moral and intellectual endowment." That "perhaps," standing out from Lincoln's one hundred–plus racist words, epitomized why some racists suspected he kept preference for racial equality hidden, just as Douglas claimed.

14

The relentless Douglas meant to uncover other Lincoln evasions. The Little Giant knew that the Republican had previously opposed only slavery's expansion to hitherto unenslaved territories. More radical Republicans promised to prohibit slavery in *all* U.S. territories. They would also bar new slave states from the Union and prohibit U.S. acquisitions of enslaved terrain. They would abolish slavery and the slave trade in Washington, DC, prohibit the interstate slave trade, and repeal the Fugitive Slave Law on their way to forcible imposition of "ultimate extinction."

By pounding queries at Lincoln about these Radical Republican initiatives, Douglas sought to reveal that the foe secretly stood provocative miles beyond his former safety zone: barring slavery only from previously free terrain. Lincoln's answers wavered on barring slavery from *"all"* territories. Almost every time he addressed the query in 1858, he stressed his old conservative formula: banning slavery only from territory "where it had not already gone." But once, very prominently at Freeport, he espoused his party's crusading motto: prohibiting "slavery in all the United States Territories."[32]

Lincoln more consistently rejected advanced Republicans' other proposals.[33] He opposed "unconditional repeal of the fugitive slave law" and "prohibition of the slave-trade between the states." While he would be "exceedingly glad to see slavery abolished in the District of Columbia," under the right conditions, he would not now seek that blessing.

More provocatively, while Lincoln "would be exceedingly sorry" to consider "admission of any more slave States," he "did not now, nor ever did stand pledged" never "to admit them." The Republican moderate sought to minimize that divergence from his party's radical wing. Territories with little or no slavery, he blithely speculated, would improbably generate a slave state's application for Union membership.

Douglas dismissed that "*lullaby*" argument. New Mexico Territory, while containing few slaves, might apply to enter the Union as an enslaved state. A few initial territorial slaveholders might eventually forge a slave state, as Lincoln's anti-"*lullaby*" screech had warned about Kansas. So, too, Texas had congressional permission to turn itself into up to four more states (and some of those new slave states might have few slaves). And so, too, an annexed heavily populated slave nation, such as Cuba, would qualify to enter the Union immediately, just like Texas, having spent no time with slavery weakening or ending under a territorial antislavery decree.

The Cuban possibility gave potential importance to another startling 1858 Lincoln break from most Republicans. He refused to pledge against "acquisition of any new territory unless slavery is first prohibited therein." He would instead judge a proposed annexation of a slave nation on whether "I might think such acquisition would or would not aggravate the slavery question among ourselves."[34] If southerners' insistence on an acquisition exceeded northerners' concern about appeasing the demand, Lincoln's formula might compel appeasement.

These 1858 wobbles, reminiscent of Peoria evasions in 1854, illuminated a Lincoln who still did not publicly oppose *all* expansions of slavery. By perhaps allowing annexation of enslaved tropical territory, plus by perhaps permitting enslaved annexations to become states, this very moderate Republican left freedom's gates a speck open to the hemisphere's southward enslavers (so long as they did not push northward!). After speeding too far, too fast on the System and on DC emancipation, this seeker had learned to move as slowly on outlawing *all* slavery expansions as on stressing "ultimate extinction."

Douglas still pressed to know how that radical-sounding "ultimate extinction" fit with his opponent's supposedly *moderate* Republicanism. Lincoln seldom answered. He would only *predict* that once we "arrest the further spread" of slavery, bondage "*would be* in the course of ultimate extinction, and the public mind *would*," as in the Founders' time, so "believe." We could then leave the "institution . . . alone for a hundred years, if it should live so long," while those "in the States where it exists" mull how it should go "out of existence in the way best for both the black and the white races."[35]

This mouthful from a someday Great Emancipator startles even more than gates slightly ajar for enslaved Cuba. Even more surprisingly, the nonimminent emancipator gave no clues about how contained southerners would ultimately abolish slavery, even in a hundred years. And how might those watching from the North someday help?

Lincoln refused to speculate about such endgames, lest he lose the middle game. He stood, he thought, at the slavery controversy's crossroads, where history would take "one turn or the other." If "Douglas and his friends have their way" at the turning point, they will "plant slavery over all the States." But if we command the critical juncture, we can limit the abomination "forever" to "the old States where it now exists." Then constrained southerners can choose "the peaceful way" toward "ultimate extinction," in their own world and in their own way and in "God's own good time."[36] The bottom line: While Lincoln dared the words "ultimate extinction" for the first time and quite often in the last half of 1858, he still emitted no endgame strategy beyond letting the contained South voluntarily chose its own tactics. Then, in 1859–60 as in 1854–57, no mention of "ultimate extinction" can be found in the Lincoln remains.

The Great Debates were as barren of effective ways to salvage the republic as of ways to end slavery. Both Lincoln and Douglas cared mightily about rescuing the Union. Neither creditably saw how to do it.

Douglas's solution, that Yanks must stop caring about other folks' slavery, sought the impossibility, as Lincoln argued, "of caring nothing about *the very thing that everybody does care the most about*."[37] Lincoln's solution, that slaveholders must accept walls against slavery's expansion, exuded the miscalculation, as Douglas warned, that slaveholders would abide being "driven to the wall."[38] With neither debater charting a viable path past slavery extension issues to permanent Union, their confrontation illuminated a nation all too close to dissolving.

In the public's November 2 balloting directly for state legislators and indirectly for a U.S. senator, northern Illinoisans, as usual, overwhelmingly selected Republican legislators while southern Illinoisans, as usual, overwhelmingly chose Democrats.[39] Central Illinoisans, as usual the arbitrators, narrowly favored enough state legislators to reelect Douglas, 54–46. In Lincoln's own bit of central Illinois, Sangamon County voted 53 percent for a pro-Douglas legislator.

Likely a speck too many conservative neighbors still wondered, after all Douglas's pounding, if Abraham Lincoln was moderate enough. The Little Giant was relentless; Lincoln held some precarious positions; and central Illinois swing voters were skittish. On that ultimate middle ground, neither Lincoln nor Douglas had safe margins in enough counties.

Lincoln could have easily lost dozens of central Illinoisans over "Hans, Baptiste, and Patrick," and more dozens over stopping racial equality at the "bread" line, and more dozens on the vagary of "ultimate extinction," and more dozens on misty tropical annexation positions, and more dozens on far-out conspiracy accusations. Despite his artful juggling of loaded issues, Abraham Lincoln needed to face fewer of them. Then he could have taken fuller advantage of his masterly assault on Douglas's moral evasions.

While rightly claiming "some" enduring "marks" for "liberty," the Republican despaired that I will "now sink out of view, and shall be forgotten."[40] Yet 467 more Lincoln votes, scattered as needed in five central Illinois counties, would have elected enough legislators to retire America's leading U.S. senator. The Republican's almost victory, plus his rare talent for regrouping after defeats, augured yet another comeback.

17

The Cunning Revisions

⬥⫥⬥

During his campaign tour in the early fall of 1859, Abraham Lincoln cunningly revised his Great Debates points. His capacity to face and correct his missteps had fueled all his comebacks. But he never sought recovery more ingeniously than when editing his Great Debates positions. Only ten months after his epic loss, he smoothed his rocky campaign trail toward the Senate into a gliding path toward the presidency.

1

His quest for the presidency, so soon after falling short for the Senate, may seem audacious, even for a comeback specialist. Yet a promising fact buoyed Lincoln's latest rebound. Stephen A. Douglas's ballots, though sufficient to win Illinois's 1858 U.S. Senate race, would have lost the state in a presidential contest.

Thanks to the state legislature's undemocratic apportionment, Lincoln's 54 percent of 1858 Prairie State voters had secured only 46 percent of the legislators, selectors of U.S. senators. But Lincoln's plurality of popular votes would have swept Illinois's democratically apportioned Electoral College representatives, selectors of presidents. By winning the 1860 Republican presidential nomination and then repeating his 1858 Illinois popular support, Lincoln could begin to reverse Republicans' fatal loss of the 1856 Border North. Could any other nominee match that prospect?

Lincoln had intensified the query by weakening Douglas in the South. In the Great Debates' famous Freeport Question, Lincoln had asked how Popular Sovereignty majorities could control slavery's territorial fate, after Taney's

Dred Scott blockade ruled territorial abolition unconstitutional. In his Freeport Reply, Douglas had answered that however the Supreme Court upheld territorial slavery, the institution "can not exist a day or an hour anywhere" without local police regulations, such as fugitive slave laws. Lincoln has heard that "answer," Douglas exaggerated, "a hundred times from every stump in Illinois."[1]

The Freeport Question amplified Douglas's reply a thousand times. Detesting what they now more clearly heard, proslavery men demanded that the Democracy's 1860 platform require congressional proslavery territorial regulations when necessary to stymie antislavery local police. Douglas would not accept that rejection of local whites' decisions. Most southern Democrats would not accept his defiance of slaveholders' territorial necessities. By fracturing the Democracy, the Freeport Question could clear a Republican nominee's path to the presidency.

2

Lincoln prayed that a widely distributed compendium of the Lincoln-Douglas Debates would multiply his support for Republicans' 1860 nomination. The compendium project stalled over a year. The delay stretched beyond a classic Illinois political interregnum, with nothing scheduled until Congress met at the end of 1859.

During the fallow summer months, Lincoln wrote shrewd private letters to Republican leaders, urging campaigns only for the party's essence. Simplify, simplify simplify, again ran the Illinoisan's unconventional formula for uniting a political coalition. Lincoln again distrusted the conventional partisan strategy: Give everyone a little something. Instead, he believed, everyone should hush about everything but the one crucial area of agreement.

"In every locality," Lincoln instructed Indiana's Congressman (and future U.S. House Speaker) Schuyler Colfax, we must "look beyond our noses." We must say "*nothing* on points where" Republicans probably "shall" "disagree. . . . Massachusetts Republicans" must cease nativist-style "tilting against foreigners," lest they "ruin us in the whole North-West. New Hampshire and Ohio" Republicans must "forbear tilting against the Fugitive Slave Law," lest they "utterly overwhelm us in Illinois." And if Ohio Republicans, Lincoln warned Ohio governor Salmon P. Chase, even "*introduced*" their recent state convention platform "plank," entitled "A repeal of the atrocious Fugitive Slave Law," at "the next Republican National Convention," they "will explode" the conclave.[2]

Despite the warning against their governor's pet anti-fugitive-slave-law strategy, Ohio Republicans invited Lincoln to come help win their October

1859 state canvass. The Illinoisan's ensuing September 16–October 1 speaking tour started with Ohio's Columbus, Dayton, and Cincinnati, continued at Indianapolis, and ended at Wisconsin's Milwaukee, Beloit, and Janesville. Without announcing any such motive, Lincoln had begun America's first multistate oratorical campaign for a presidential nomination.

His triumph in Cincinnati, where he delivered his best speech to his largest audience, seemed especially presidential. He starred in the city where the *McCormick Reaper* case attorneys had snubbed him four years earlier. Talking partly to men from the Bluegrass State who crossed the Ohio to hear their fellow native Kentuckian, Lincoln mixed heavy-handed demands with lighthearted familiarity. We intend "to beat you" on slavery's expansion to territories, declared the Republican, but "in no way to interfere with your institution" inside your state. "We mean to remember that you are as good as we" are and "have as good hearts . . . as we claim to have. . . . We mean to marry your girls when we have a chance—the white ones I mean—and I have the honor to inform you that I once did have a chance."[3]

He chose not to say that he twice did have the chance. Mary Owens's former fancier, alias Mary Todd's eventual husband, had heard that some Kentuckians meant to split the nation at the Ohio River. After "you have divided the Union because we would not do right with you," he puzzled, why will you be "better off" when we lack "obligations to do anything for you?" "After you . . . split the Ohio," will you "push your half" of the river "off a piece" from "us outrageous fellows?" Or will you "build . . . a wall" halfway across the river, keeping "that moveable property of yours" from coming "hither?" Or "will you make war . . . and kill us all?" True, "you are as gallant and as brave as" we are. But "there are" fewer "of you [Loud cheering]."[4]

During his tour's less humorous moments, the Illinois Republican continued to stress his previous main thrust: that the "Republican Party's . . . underlying principle . . . is hatred . . . of Slavery . . . in all its aspects, moral, social, and political." We see "great danger of the institution" being "made alike lawful in all the states." We will deter that northern disaster in "every *legitimate, Constitutional* way. With Slavery in the [southern] States," we have "nothing to do. But when it attempts to overleap its present limits, and fasten itself upon free territory," we mean to "force it back."[5]

To force slaveholders back from expansion into neighboring Yankee areas, Lincoln continued to emphasize, Republicans must force northern public opinion back from Douglas. Lincoln found it "almost impossible . . . to speak of politics without" denouncing Douglas.[6] The foe would not call slavery "*wrong.*" His amorality inflicts a "gradual and steady debauching" on Yankee "public opinion"; and "public opinion in this country is everything." Unless northerners passionately consider slavery wrong, they will allow early territorial settlers in northern areas to import a little of the institution.

That speck of despotism, as irremovable as "the Canada Thistle," will cost "succeeding" settlers "infinite difficulty and a long struggle" to dig it out. Witness Kansas, where a bit of early slavery had to be uprooted at the risk of "civil war." Worse, only morally aroused northerners will deter Roger B. Taney or a southern successor from slaveholders' logical next step: a second *Dred Scott* decision, wiping out state emancipation laws. That decree, however now delayed, will unleash a "flood of slavery . . . over the free States. . . . We shall be" as "helpless" as "sheep."

In 1859, however, unlike in 1858, Lincoln conceded that southern imperialists will not yet "sound the bugle" for slavery's nationalization. "That day" had to be postponed.[7] After the 1858 election, Taney and fellow southerners know that Douglas has as yet only half-debauched Yankee public opinion. He has "merely . . . *soaked*" our beliefs . . . like wood for ox-bows . . . preparatory to the bending." But when Douglas's amorality sufficiently softens our morals, judicial disaster will "be tolled in through the gap of Douglasism."

3

With such vivid new frontier images as intractable Canadian thistles and tractable ox-bows, Lincoln enhanced the conservative side of his old anti-extension message. His September 1859 orations simultaneously trimmed his 1858 stance's slightly radical side. Lincoln's recalibration started with omitting both his 1858 overblown accusation of an imminent Douglas-Taney conspiracy and his underexplained mention of the institution's "ultimate extinction." Moreover, "all men are created equal" became scarcer in 1859 emphases.

With those revisions, Lincoln saved himself from arguing around the fact that black equality could not be immediately achieved. Nor did he now have to repeat his misconception that free men alone receive daily bread. Nor did he have to explain how and when slavery's containment would yield its "ultimate extinction." Nor was he compelled to make an *immediate* Douglas-Taney conspiratorial strike plausible.

Looking back at the Great Debates, he saw that his accusations of immediate conspiracy, emphasized so heavily in the House Divided Address and in his 1858 campaign, had not prevailed. Douglas mocked or ignored the possible red herring too easily. Lincoln also recognized that deploring the Little Giant's Don't Care-ism hardly required claiming that a conspiracy *verged* on striking. So Douglas and Taney as *immediate* producers of a second *Dred Scott* decision disappeared from Lincoln's rhetoric. Still, the Douglas target, grotesquely spreading amorality as prelude for an *eventual* strike, remained front and center.

"Ultimate extinction," introduced more gingerly and infrequently than "conspiracy" back in 1858, was altogether dropped in 1859–60. Lincoln could not win the presidency in 1860 as a Great Emancipator, and he knew it. He had to hew exclusively to slavery's nonextension into *territories* and omit all mention of abolition in *states*.

Meanwhile, a gift from Douglas helped lighten Lincoln's struggles with "equality." Speaking in Memphis on November 29, 1858, the Little Giant declared that on Louisiana sugar plantations, whites considered the slavery question "not . . . between the white man and the negro but between *the negro and the crocodile*." A visitor, responding to this viewpoint, would side with the Negro over the crocodile and "go for the white man" over "the negro."[8]

Douglas did *not* say that *he* preferred to compare Negroes with crocodiles. But Lincoln took Douglas's foul language that way and raced to the (political) bank with the ugliness. Douglas climaxed his linguistic horrors, alleged the Republican in September 1859, by debasing Negroes "from the condition of a man . . . to that of a brute."[9] By insisting that Negroes are men, not crocodiles, Lincoln could hammer Douglas without as often risking "all men are created equal."

By treading more lightly on "all men are created equal," turning silent on "ultimate extinction," and dropping *instant* conspiracy, a more convincing Republican could more easily go for total nonexpansion of slavery. At Peoria and in the Great Debates, Lincoln had waffled on most Republicans' uncompromising call for zero territorial slavery expansion, anywhere. His own previous position, no slavery in previously free territories, could have allowed both new slave states and annexed slave territories far to the South. During his 1859 Border North swing, however, Lincoln closed his tropical loopholes. He, too, was now pledged to no slavery expansion, everywhere in present or future Union.

Lincoln's readjusted conservatism came accompanied with a richer foundation for nonextension. For three years, the moderate had only fleetingly dared a view of irrepressible economic antagonism between northern and southern cultures. On this speaking tour, he more often added a freshly refined materialistic dimension to his moral case against slavery's expansion.

The North-South debate, according to this clarified version of Lincoln economics, erroneously posits only "two ways" to produce labor. Capitalists could supposedly either "hire" consenting men "to labor" or "buy the men and drive them to it." Sectional disagreement thus focuses on whether workers "are better off" as "slaves" or as "hired laborers."

Yet hired employees include no "more than one eighth of" northern laborers. Nor is any "permanent class of hired laborers amongst us." To comparatively few wage laborers and almost no enslaved laborers, we have added a third class—by far our largest class—men who work their own land without help or with only temporary aid from hired laborers. Our temporary hirelings, in turn, usually save to "buy" their own "land" or "shops" and then to hire their own temporary laborers.

Our employee "of yesterday labors on his own account to-day and will hire others to labor for him tomorrow." Instead of a slave labor culture or a wage labor civilization, Yankees enjoy an "advancement" society, a largely free entrepreneur economy, beyond permanent labor for others in any capacity.[10]

With one natural illustration, this alluring abstraction could become Lincoln's supreme plea for the presidency. But painful memories almost always prevented him from using his own life to illustrate white bottom-dwellers' upward possibilities, if slaves were kept out of a free-soil world. When his friend John L. Scripps asked for a campaign autobiography, Lincoln offered only bare facts about his early climb. "He seemed to be painfully impressed with the extreme poverty of his early surroundings," noted Scripps.

Lincoln claimed "the utter absence of all romantic and heroic elements" in his youth. He decried the "great . . . folly" of making "anything out of my early life." One sentence in Gray's "Elegy" said it all, according to the man who suffered through it: "'The short and simple annals of the poor.' That's my life, and that's all you or anyone else can make of it."[11]

Only once on the 1859 campaign trail did Lincoln fleetingly seek to make more of it. He then briefly noted that he "had been a hired man twenty-eight years ago." He had hardly considered himself "worse off than a slave. . . . He was now working for himself." Fellow northern laborers, if "industrious, and, sober and honest," will "accumulate capital" and can "hire others people to labor," who themselves can "become an employer." That is "the true, genuine principle."[12]

This scarce campaign moment indicated the true principle's electioneering potential, if wrapped around his own life. But never again in 1859 and only once in early 1860 did Lincoln escape his shudder about his preadvancement past enough to pose as advancement's poster child. Instead he celebrated risen poor men with unrelieved impersonality. He would need 1860 help to become opportunity's Rail-splitter.

4

Latter-day fanciers of the Great Emancipator will wince less that he skirted his own opportunity tale than that he celebrated only *whites'* chances. They may also find disappointing opportunism in his 1859 retreats both from mentioning "ultimate extinction" and from emphasizing "all men are created equal." They may even consider his twisting of Douglas's ugly mirth about crocodiles to be crass campaigning.

Yet disappointment about Lincoln's shrewd expediency hinders appreciation of his empowering flexibility. The antebellum North, and especially the Border North's central Illinois, was no hotbed of antislavery idealism. The more southerly tier of Yankee states contained fewer Radical Republicans than the Upper North and more racist bigots, intolerant nativists, and frightened Unionists. A Border North politician, when appealing for antislavery, had to watch his slightest step, especially when the winds shifted.

The breezes had turned since early 1858. Previously, widening territorial antislavery to include "ultimate extinction" in states had seemed necessary to deter Border North Republicans from Douglas. In contrast, narrowing agitation to include only slavery's containment now seemed mandatory, to lure ex-Whig conservatives toward Republicanism. By stepping slightly backward, Lincoln regained his balance for steps slightly forward—and for grasping the dead center of northern opinion.

His slightly revised stance yielded the confidence to insist on shuttering *all* slave expansion, lest southern imperialists seek enslaved Cuba. He also acquired the nerve to publicize a skillfully redrawn portrait of three, not two American labor systems. So, too, by seizing advantage of Douglas's crocodile folly, plus by scotching his own folly about an *imminent* Douglas-Taney conspiracy, plus by not even breathing the words "ultimate extinction," plus by easing off difficult nuances about equality, he forged a simpler, more instantly persuasive, more purely conservative anti-extension argument, perfect for rallying moderates toward his (unannounced!) presidential campaign. If "increasingly brilliant partisan" seems dubious praise, how else could an oft-defeated commoner in the stubbornly moderate Border North have gathered the choicest reins for magnificent achievement?

5

During 1859's last three months, the national slavery controversy reignited. On October 11, Ohio Republicans scored a milestone victory, electing the governor and almost two-thirds of state legislators. Five days after Republicans' Ohio breakthrough, Connecticut's John Brown broke into western Virginia's Harpers Ferry federal arsenal.

Brown's blunders doomed his promised slave revolt. After failing to alert slaves that he had arrived, the revolutionary trapped his eighteen invaders in

Harpers Ferry's engine house. No black came to wield his slim gang's thousand pikes. Instead U.S. Marines, led by (who else!) Robert E. Lee, sped in on October 18. Lee's men killed half the insurrectionists (including two of Brown's sons) and captured the badly wounded chief. On December 2, Virginia hung the unrepentant revolutionary.

Three days after the hanging, Missouri's John Clark initiated a two-month-long House of Representatives crisis. Congressman Clark condemned Hinton R. Helper's book of the previous year, *The Impending Crisis of the South.* The North Carolinian's volume argued that a slave society provided scarce opportunities for nonslaveholding whites. Helper urged raggedy southern yeomen to vote down the slaveholders and expel the slaves.

Missouri's Clark warned that most Republican congressmen had endorsed a so-called *Compendium,* containing most of Helper's book. Some Upper North Republicans had printed one hundred thousand cheap copies of this *Compendium,* designed to bring native-son antislavery flooding into the South. Hinton Helper's southern writings, hoped these northern Republicans, might arouse native nonslaveholders' revolt against slaveholding aristocrats.[13] No "outside agitators" this time! Insiders would do in the slaveholders, with outsiders financing only the most northern South's own reformers.

John Clark, damning this formula, warned that Helper's North Carolina ideas, when boosted by northern Republicans' dollars, could undermine slaveholders' exposed northernmost realm. Clark sounded like his fellow Missourian Davy Atchison in 1854, warning that antislavery settlers in neighboring Kansas must be deterred from bringing democratic agitation inside a Border South despotic realm. For the second time in five years, a northern South leader had grown concerned about his least consolidated slaveholder system, with Yankee foes approaching the gates. Like Atchison, Clark had initiated an extended congressional imbroglio, intended to close off southern discourse from northern contamination.

Clark moved that the House declare no Republican endorser of the Helper campaign "fit to be Speaker." The Republican majority still sought, throughout forty-three ballots, to raise a Helper endorser, Ohio's John Sherman, to the Speaker's chair. Sherman, then more famous than his brother, the future Civil War general William Tecumseh Sherman, had endorsed the *Compendium* without reading it. But Republicans' loyalty to the uninformed endorser prolonged the intensifying deadlock.

By January 1860, congressmen from both sections toted pistols and bowie knives to chambers. Meanwhile, South Carolina's governor secretly conspired to send an army to Washington, in case bullets should replace ballots.

On February 1, however, the House's forty-fourth ballot peaceably raised a Republican nonendorser of Helper to the Speaker's chair.

Although Helper usually insisted on nonviolent reform, his book gained Washington notoriety simultaneously with Brown's violent invasion. The late 1859 pairing augured two unrelated southern lower-class internal resistances, black and white, violent and nonviolent, to upper-class rule. Even if Helper hewed to peaceful reform, southerners doubted that his antislavery diatribe, within earshot of slaves, would inspire only peaceable resistance.

As usual, dictators at home could tolerate only racially sanitized democracy—republicanism for whites only, with discussions of blacks silenced. During the Helper controversy, a southern-led Senate inquiry acquitted Republicans of furthering John Brown's violent outsider intervention. But peacefully donating to Helper's nonviolent insider cause—that was another matter, as most Republican congressmen's endorsement declared. If northern Republicans financially boosted southern Republicans' writings, thus opening slaveholders' closed society a little more to southern natives' antislavery heresy, an irrevocable clash between democratic debate and despotic control could be looming.

6

Abraham Lincoln echoed almost all Republicans' dismay at John Brown. Speaking in Kansas in early December 1859, he "sympathized with . . . Brown's hatred of slavery." Still, "Brown's insurrectionary attempt" remained "treason." Not even "great courage, rare unselfishness," and opposition to "a great evil" could justify "violence." Thus "if we should constitutionally elect a President and therefore you undertake to destroy the Union, it will be our duty to deal with you as old John Brown has been dealt with."[14]

In revealing contrast, Lincoln remained tight-lipped about Helper's nonviolent reform. Illinois's favorite Republican had always emphasized that outsiders should stop only slavery's expansion into territories, leaving insiders to decide slavery's fate in slave states. Now Hinton R. Helper sought to arouse fellow southern insiders with a message akin to Lincoln's new economic appeal, and Republicans financed the spread of the northern message southward. The result: Congress paralyzed for almost two months.

Might Lincoln have secretly been contemplating some such northern encouragement of southern heretics, during his silence about how to secure "ultimate extinction"? Might he later finance the South's own reeducation, using presidential resources? Answers began to emerge only after the lately defeated Illinoisan rode his improved campaign appeal toward Washington redemption.

18

The Cooper Union Address

Two weeks after Abraham Lincoln's oratorical tour consolidated his Border North base, he received a golden opportunity to add Upper North support. A telegram, dated October 12, 1859, from New York's James A. Briggs, offered him two hundred dollars to "speak in Mr. Beechers church Brooklyn on or about" November 29.[1] Henry Ward Beecher, Harriet Beecher Stowe's famous brother, preached at Brooklyn's huge Plymouth Church. Briggs wrote Lincoln on behalf of several Plymouth Church worshippers.

1

The would-be New York hosts commanded the Young Men's Central Republican Union, the ultimate sponsor of Lincoln's forthcoming oration. Despite their title, the Young Men included such middle-aged souls as Horace Greeley, editor of the *New York Tribune*, and William Cullen Bryant, poet and editor of the *New York Evening Post*. These Big City opinion makers wished to identify the best Republican alternative presidential candidate, if New York's favorite, U.S. Senator William H. Seward, should trip over his supposed radicalism.

Salmon P. Chase, flashing his practical deficiencies, declined an invitation similar to Lincoln's. The Illinoisan, demonstrating his practical acumen, changed the invitational terms. Eastern sophisticates, the prairie orator understood, would sniff at a midwestern stump harangue. A frontiersman would need a massively researched, meticulously worded text, exuding no hint of country bumpkin. Perfecting that assignment would take months, especially since Billy Herndon would beg help with Springfield legal drudgery.

Lincoln sought to delay his Big City lecture until well into 1860. After some tugging and hauling, he agreed to speak on February 27, three months after the originally suggested November 29 date, still for the originally proffered two hundred dollars (about $5,300 in twenty-first-century cash).[2] The Illinoisan ultimately would speak three weeks after the U.S. House of Representatives tamed its Helper brawls and with the Republican National Convention assembling in under twelve weeks.[3]

2

While preparing for his late February appointment, Lincoln piled legal papers higher and deeper atop Billy Herndon's groaning desk. The senior partner now cared only for the State Library's musty political documents. Almost daily for many hours, the huge man sat with his elbow bent ninety degrees on the library table, his thumb under his chin, a finger around his nose, and the hand's three other fingers clenched in a belligerent's fist. He had long since graduated from blabbing elementary texts on the prairie grass. As in his months of research for the Peoria Address, he had become the cultivated scholar in advanced libraries, as unaffected a frontiersman as ever but as learned in his specialty as New York City sophisticates.

He focused his latest research on (what else?) exposing Stephen A. Douglas's latest supposed nonsense. Upon reading Douglas's newest thrust, a long article on Popular Sovereignty in *Harper's New Monthly Magazine* in September 1859, Lincoln had invaded a colleague's office, crying: "This will never do. He puts the moral element out of the question. It won't stay out."[4] Months of research, Lincoln hoped, would facilitate pouring the moral element back in. He meant to demonstrate that among signers of the Constitution who had served in Congress, most had voted to prohibit territorial slavery.

On George Washington's birthday, February 22, 1860, exactly four years after the 1856 Decatur Editors' Convention, the sometimes scholar packed his hard-won demonstration in Mary Lincoln's trunk. He boarded a train heading vaguely toward his latest guest appearance, hoping to match his impact on Illinois newspaper scribes. His train journey exemplified recent American progress. In 1850, a trip from Illinois to the Big City had consumed around two weeks. In 1860, iron horses pulled the System's old advocate to his rendezvous in three days.

Lincoln had championed national infrastructure to enable isolated midwesterners' economic climb. National transportation also enabled his political climb. The busy lawyer might have declined the Young Men's invitation if round-trip transportation had still demanded almost a month.

Subsequently, another Republican president-elect might have traveled to Washington.

While traveling toward his historic rendezvous in a quarter of the old time, Lincoln hardly experienced railroad utopia. While birds soared some 800 miles from Springfield to New York, Lincoln's conveyance meandered 1,200 miles. Missing connective tracks required the Illinoisan to haul Mary's trunk to different trains five times, thrice in the middle of the night. After the transfers, trains' hard benches made sleep fitful. After a final transfer in Jersey City to the ferry over the Hudson River, the exhausted Lincoln arrived in Manhattan eleven hours late and two days before his lecture. He conducted his first interview while lying on a sofa.

Exhaustion intensified. He had alarmingly noticed, when scanning the latest *New York Tribune,* that his lecture had been moved from Brooklyn's religious Mecca to New York City's secular palace, the Great Hall in Cooper Union. Fearing that his carefully wrought speech would fail in the new setting, Lincoln spent most of the next forty-eight hours desperately rewriting.

He sporadically paused to roam widely from his then-famous hotel, the Astor House on West Broadway (located just north of the latter-day World Trade Center's habitats). He attended a Beecher sermon in Brooklyn, posed for Matthew Brady's famous cameras, purchased a luxurious top hat, and accepted a plush lunch invitation. En route to the feast, however, he pleaded that he must return to his revisions this moment, lest his lecture proved disastrous.

As the hour of his address approached, the apprehensive orator reluctantly stopped revising and found his tailored suit, purchased in Springfield for the occasion. The extravagance cost half his lecture fee, one hundred dollars. The splurge revealingly differed from his acquisition of his first suit, a rough homespun affair for his legislative debut, using sixty borrowed dollars. He had come a long way.

After donning the suit, rumpled from tossing in Mary's trunk, the aspirant dashed out of Astor House into a swirling snowstorm, his hair still unbrushed. He headed some three miles north and east to Cooper Union, praying that his emergency lecture revisions had saved a rich opportunity.

3

His nervousness yielded an ironic boost toward triumph—a wretched start. Lincoln had made a political living out of appearing overmatched, then rising to the occasion. The contrast between his audience's dim expectations at the onset and his surpassing performance at the climax made him seem the more overwhelming. He never seemed to metamorphose more astonishingly from country hick to national seer than in Cooper Union.

It was the right stage for an underestimated self-made man. Peter Cooper, founder, builder, and financial angel of Cooper Union, embodied Horatio Alger–style heroics. After rising from rough beginnings and scant formal education, the multimillionaire industrialist had developed the first American steam locomotive (the *Tom Thumb*), the first transatlantic telegraph cables (the forerunner of AT&T), and the first gelatin emporium (the initial producer of Jell-O). For his climactic accomplishment, a Mecca to give impoverished youngsters a free practical education in "arts, engineering, and architectures," Peter Cooper had lately finished Cooper Union's massive Lower East Side red brick building on Seventh Street, between Third and Fourth Avenues.

Cooper Union's Great Hall, consuming the basement, held 1,800 red leather chairs. The basement's sixteen thick columns intruded between spectators. Its dozen mirrors reflected its twenty-seven ceiling chandeliers, each with six gas burners. The eerily lit room, permitting unusually good night vision, contrasted with the columns' obstructions, impeding inside views. So, too, speakers' voices collided with hissing gas, yielding strange acoustics. This Great Hall, dedicated to promoting Peter Cooper's self-help mission, initially unnerved a self-helper from the provinces, eager to seize his unsettling Big City opportunity.

At 8:00 PM on February 27, the evening's chairman, the *Post*'s William Cullen Bryant, welcomed the rookie to the podium. "Mr. Cheerman," began Abraham Lincoln. His Kentucky-Indiana accent saturated his usual high-pitched beginning squeak. His mussed suit drooped on his huge frame. His frock coat ballooned out in back, as if covering a trailing rural conveyance. A pant cuff stuck two inches above a shoe. He stood rigidly, fearing that his collar might fly up, as had embarrassingly occurred at Brady's photographic studio.

If Lincoln had been at his confident best, he would have sped his first five hundred comparatively boring words into fifty striking sounds. Instead the uneasy stranger climaxed his initial dragged-out monotone by losing his place in the manuscript. He fell silent for interminable seconds, pawing contrary pages back in order.

Perhaps his rarest natural gift rescued him. He could simultaneously act and detach himself from the action—observe himself dispassionately while passionately striving. This time, watching himself flailing, he perhaps remembered that he had always delivered stunning speeches on huge occasions. He perhaps recalled that he had never prepared so superbly. He perhaps rejoiced that his sleepy beginning had ended and his fireworks could begin.

For whatever reason(s), the stumbler suddenly saw his way clear. His eyes, accustomed to outdoor speeches in sustained sunshine, adjusted to flickering gaslights. An Illinois friend, stationed in the rear, signaled that his midwestern twang had cut through eastern lamps' hissing. He began to orate in his normal tenor tones, shaking his head as usual to punctuate his best points. The audience, sensing his relaxation, leaned forward. The orator, feeling his opportunity, pitched into a transfixing performance.[5]

4

Lincoln began as so often with a Douglas quotation. The Little Giant had declared that "our Fathers . . . understood . . . better than we do now" whether the Constitution allowed congressional bars against slavery's spread. So what was the Founders' better-than-our understanding about slavery's territorial expansion, asked Lincoln?

To answer, the Illinoisan had explored the thirty-nine original constitutional signers' subsequent congressional votes on territorial slavery. For half an hour, as Lincoln presented his findings about six congressional roll calls, listeners counted Founders' votes with him, amid rising excitement. They came to his conclusion before he announced the good news: At least twenty-three of the thirty-nine Constitution signers had voted at least once in Congress to ban the "wrong" from territories!

The audience erupted. No eastern sophisticate had provided such scholarly proof of Republicanism's anti-extension origins. Then the frontier's haunter of libraries shocked them again. *"Enough!"* Lincoln shouted. With that one-word transition sentence, halfway through his speech, he invited them to ascend from quantitative to qualitative proofs of Republican sublimity.

Enough! came perfectly timed. The front half of his speech, all hard quantification, would have tediously cluttered the second half's prose poetry. More of his statistics also might have given listeners too much time to think about missing numbers. Some of the Founders' votes indeed indicated that Congress could constitutionally bar slavery's expansion. But many of their other votes demonstrated that they considered Popular Sovereignty equally constitutional and often wiser.

Lincoln also played loosely with his fraction of statistics. Two of his six congressional votes banned the few recently imported Africans from U.S. territories. That noncontroversial issue was irrelevant to whether the many long-since "Americanized" slaves could enter national territories. Scrubbing the two votes on scarce lately imported Africans would have reduced Lincoln's twenty-three right-voting Fathers to nineteen (of thirty-nine)—a minority!

The first half of the Cooper Union Address thus displayed a clever statistician, so long as you didn't thinking too hard about the cleverness. Yet if his partial truth could win no historical prizes, he had no such objective. He wished to establish cultivated credentials and then sprint toward cosmopolitan triumph. With *"Enough!"* his glorious sprint began.

5

The performance solidified and then swept past his Lost/Found Speech's "aha" moment. Blackmailing southerners, Lincoln warned the Cooper Union faithful, threaten to "destroy the government, unless" they alone can "construe and enforce the Constitution." Slaveholders will "rule or ruin." If we elect "a Republican President," and they "destroy the Union," they will blame "the great crime" on us, for not electing their candidate. "That is cool! A highway man holds a pistol to my ear and mutters through his teeth, deliver" your cash "or I shall kill you, and then you will be a murderer!"[6]

To justify blackmail, Lincoln continued, secessionists call us dangerously sectional, citing our exclusively northern voters. But by their criterion, we shall soon no longer "be sectional." We will "get votes in" their southern "section this very year," he boasted (alluding to Hinton R. Helper!).[7]

Southern blackmailers, continued Lincoln, call themselves "eminently conservative" and us "revolutionary, destructive, or something of the sort." But we conservatively insist only that slavery, as the founding *"fathers marked it,"* be again deemed *"an evil not to be extended, but to be tolerated and protected"* wherever it now exists. Southerners "reject, and scout, and spit upon that old policy."

Then they disagree on revolutionary substitutes. Some favor "reviving the" African slave trade. Others seek a territorial "Congressional Slave Code." Some urge Congress or the Supreme Court to forbid territorial abolition. Others laud "the 'gur-reat pur-rinciple' that 'if one man would enslave another, no third man should object, fantastically called 'Popular Sovereignty.'" But none "can show a precedent or an advocate" when our Founding Fathers "originated . . . our government."[8]

Again, southerners charge that Republican supposed revolutionaries "stir up insurrections," citing "Harper's Ferry! John Brown!!" Their indictment fails. "John Brown was no Republican" and Harpers Ferry witnessed no "slave insurrection." Instead, "white" non-Republicans attempted "to get up a slave revolt" and "the slaves refused to participate."[9]

Here as always, emphasized Lincoln, we have vainly tried to persuade southerners that we will "let them alone" inside their states. We only oppose their expansion beyond their borders and inside ours. "What will" ever "convince them?" Only this: We must "cease to call slavery *wrong,* and join them in calling it *right*," with "*acts* as well as in *words*." We must swallow all *words* that deem slavery "wrong," whether "in politics, in presses, in pulpits, or in private." Then we must repeal all *acts* that indict slavery.

They will probably retort, "'Let us alone, *do* nothing to us, and *say* what you please.'" But "we do let them alone." They will "accuse us of" plotting "until we cease" our most important way of "saying." Northern blacks, having been freed, announce slavery's "wrong" more emphatically than "all other sayings." After "all those other sayings shall have been silenced," and "the overthrow of" the North's own emancipation shall "be demanded," we will have "nothing . . . left to resist" their ultimate "demand": abolition repealed, free blacks reenslaved, and slavery nationalized.

Some peacemakers would have us relax, Lincoln scoffed, because southerners "have not demanded" slavery's nationalization "just yet." But eventually, slaveholders "can voluntarily stop nowhere short of this consummation. Holding as they do that slavery is morally right, . . . they cannot cease to demand" that "all words, acts, laws, and, constitutions against it" must be "swept away. If it is right, we cannot justly object to" making it universal. "If it is wrong, they can not justly insist upon its extension. . . . The whole controversy" depends upon "their thinking it right, and our thinking it wrong."[10]

Lincoln reiterated that we must let the "wrong . . . alone where it is. . . . But can we . . . allow it to spread into the National Territories and to overrun us here in these Free States? If our sense of duty forbids this, then let us stand by our duty." Let us resist blackmailers who seek to coerce us into "a policy of 'don't care,'" when "all true men do care." Let us withstand "Disunionists" who try to command "true Union men to yield." Let us remember that "divine rule" forbids allowing "sinners" to prevail. "LET US HAVE FAITH THAT RIGHT MAKES MIGHT, AND IN THAT FAITH, LET US, TO THE END, DARE TO DO OUR DUTY."[11]

Rising auditors offered three thunderous cheers. A *New York Tribune* journalist, observing the excitement, termed Lincoln "the greatest man since St Paul." Both Horace Greeley and William Cullen Bryant called this political oration the "best" they had "ever . . . heard," with Greeley adding that he had "heard some of Webster's grandest."[12]

It was assuredly Lincoln's grandest development of moderate antislavery. In Cooper Hall, he said not a word to encourage abolishing slavery in the South. Every phrase fastened on defending the North's manumitted blacks, previously free territories, majority rule, and republican Union. Even a more radical Salmon P. Chase fancier, such as James A. Briggs, rallied to this strategy of defense, even if he meant later to proceed past a merely defensive triumph.

Briggs, having initiated the speech, finalized the celebration. Mailing the two-hundred-dollar speaker's fee to Lincoln, he wished that it could be "$200,000" ($5.3 million in early twenty-first-century cash!), "for you are worthy of it."[13]

Lincoln valued his other reward a million times more. The Border North's favorite had made himself a formidable second choice in the Upper North, after the vulnerable Seward, for the Republican presidential nomination. No oration equally transformed American presidential nominations until William Jennings Bryan's 1896 Cross of Gold Speech.

6

The triumphant orator next assumed less cosmic duties. His family scene had improved after his wife raised their Eighth and Jackson roof. With her thirst for space somewhat satisfied, her grief over Eddie's death ebbing, and her joy over Eddie's two replacements booming, Mary Todd Lincoln had become a more congenial spouse.

Her husband spent more time in his less troubled home. Abraham especially relished romps with Willie and Tad, nine and seven years old in early 1860. The lads, no longer toddlers and not yet teens, exemplified the middle years of growing up, when many adults find offspring most delightful. The lads' squeals cascaded when Father entered the house. The giant, rolling on the floor with them, squealed louder.

The elder son was again odd male out. Sixteen-year-old Bob had rarely experienced preteen home frolic. His distracted father had then been excruciatingly rising, while his stormy mother had often been forbiddingly unsettled.

Of late, Father's youthful hardships had begun to affect Bob's trajectory. Some self-made men, remembering their travail as productively toughening, want their male offspring to benefit from the same challenges. Others, Lincoln especially, want their sons spared the agony. Abraham splurged on Springfield's best private education for Bob, in the hope that the son of a blab school "graduate" would more easily rise with an Ivy League diploma.

Bob spent three years at Springfield Academy, then four years down the road at Illinois State University's prep school, where desultory studying yielded a "B" average. Father and son, coveting American education's supposedly highest boost, dreamed of a Harvard degree. So in August 1859, Bob traveled to Cambridge, Massachusetts, for entrance exams.

Predictably, Harvard turned him down. Equally predictably, both Lincoln males scorned failure. Harvard's president suggested a redemptive year at Phillips Exeter Academy in Exeter, New Hampshire, the eastern elite's favorite stepping-stone to Cambridge. The mortified son and frustrated father came to an understanding. Abraham would foot Exeter's bills if Bob would try hard to conquer the exhausting program, designed to reverse a Harvard rejection. The day after Father finished at Cooper Union, he took the train up to Exeter, anxious to see if his son was fulfilling the expensive bargain.

He delightedly found that the latest Lincoln to fall was rising brilliantly, with good grades, galloping confidence, and splendid grace. The wild difference in the preparations of father and son was nourishing a second coming of the family's ascendency. If haughty eastern Exeter and grubby western blabbing seemed impossible to reconcile as mounting blocks, both fostered determination to rise above humiliation, the passion Robert most imbibed from Abraham. Difficult studies were steeling the provincial son to overcome, just as rural illiteracy had goaded the father. The road ahead for the finishing school aspirant would be less agonizing than for the blab-prepared climber.

Their two paths never crossed more intimately than before or after those several charmed New Hampshire days, the son seeking Harvard and business triumph, the father questing the presidency and political immortality. Bob Lincoln's journey would lead to the presidency of the Pullman Car Company, then to retirement at his fabulous Vermont estate, Hildene. There Americans can visit, experiencing how the Lincolns, having landed and prospered in seventeenth-century New England, came back east from western adventures, the son as lord of a spectacular manor after the father had helped save opportunity's nation.[14]

7

For two weeks after Cooper Union, Lincoln mixed quality time with Bob and eleven orations, scattered through Massachusetts, New Hampshire, Rhode Island, and Connecticut. Writing to Mary, Abraham lamented his New England "difficulty." His listeners, he gloomed, had read his Cooper Union Address, and he had nothing to add.[15]

He erred. His Yankee auditors loved the second coming of his Cooper Union brilliance. Moreover, two of his latest novelties, anticipated in his late Border North speeches but unheard in New York City, spiced his repetitions.

During his Border North tour, "Canada Thistles," his analogy for a slight but lethal territorial introduction of slavery, had newly illuminated how just a bit of a thick-rooted organism becomes excruciating to eradicate. He had also used freshly soaked ox-bows as an analogy for bending the rigid, illustrating how Douglas's amoralism would allegedly bend northern opinion someday to accept slavery's nationalization.

In Connecticut's Hartford, the midwestern frontiersman climaxed such vivid illustrations with *snakes,* illuminating a moderate's distinction between containing and assaulting slavery. Suppose, said the veteran of Indiana reptiles slithering in forest underbrush, "I find a rattlesnake" on a slaveless "prairie." When "I . . . kill him, everybody would . . . say I did right. But suppose the snake was in a bed where children were sleeping." My "strike . . . might hurt the children or . . . exasperate the snake," who "might bite the children. . . . Slavery is like this. We dare not strike at it where it is." Nor can we tolerate snakes entering a slaveless area where offspring will be sleeping. "New Territories are the newly made bed" where "our children are to go." The Republican Party insists "upon keeping" rattlesnakes "out of the bed."[16]

On another occasion, "snakes" bailed Lincoln out of momentary New England trouble. In New Haven, he fleetingly affirmed that "a black man," like "every man," is "entitled" to "better" his "condition."[17] The racially impolitic affirmation marked the latest rare time when Lincoln's guard slipped, displaying his secret wish for more racial equality than a moderate dared espouse. It was also the only prewar time he returned, for a split second, to the racial radicalism of his fleeting Peoria sentence, calling for black voting.

The momentary slips indicated where he might stand if practical politics shifted. But as always before 1864–65, the politician instantly shoved such political indiscretion back under cover. Lincoln reverted to instructing New England whites that you must not "be degraded, nor have your family corrupted by forced rivalry with negro slaves. I want you to have a clean bed, and no snakes in it!"[18]

8

In another New England variation on Cooper Union theatrics, Lincoln lifted his most promising 1859 oratorical advance during his Border North lecture tour, his opportunity argument, to higher ground. Other Free-Soilers made more use of the economic argument that black slaves' presence undermined free whites' chances. But upon hearing about the recent strike of Massachusetts's shoemakers, Lincoln leapt to affirm *"a system of labor"* where a laborer "CAN *strike*" or "quit." While Republicans propose no "war upon capital, we do wish to allow the humblest man an equal chance to get rich." In "free society when one starts poor," a lowly fellow can "be a hired laborer this year," then "work for himself," then "hire men to work for him! That is the true system."

Lincoln fleetingly enhanced the true system by using his own rise, in one memorable sentence, to illustrate the wonder. He was "not ashamed to confess," he claimed, "that twenty-five years ago I was a hired laborer, mauling rails." I worked "upon a flat-boat," he momentarily bragged, like "any poor man's son!"[19]

But he *was* ashamed, or that inappropriate word would not have slipped momentarily out. Nor would he have used this materialistic argument for only a single sentence, in 1860 as in 1859. As much as he desired the presidency, the shame of his impoverished years left him unable to maximize this political advertisement for Abraham Lincoln, folk-hero exploiter of lower-class opportunity. Unembarrassed others would have to portray the raggedy white mauling rails, when the not-totally-self-helper returned from his triumphant Upper North tour.

19

The Presidential Election
and the Fruits of Revision

After Cooper Union and New England, Lincoln's oratory no longer could boost his 1860 presidential campaign. Traditions discouraged presidential candidates from speaking at national conventions and orating on campaign trails. America's self-made man needed assistance as he approached the finish line.

1

The first helpmate contributed before custom muffled Lincoln—and without the candidate's encouragement. On December 21, 1859, the Republican National Central Committee met in New York City's Astor House to select the national convention's May 1860 locale. Cleveland, Philadelphia, St. Louis, and New York, each with a favorite son for the presidency, bid for the conclave.

Norman Judd, Illinois's committeeman, suggested a "neutral" alternative. Since Illinois has no declared Republican presidential candidate, Judd dissimulated, my booming Chicago can welcome all delegates equally. After the Chicagoan spoke, Chicago won by one vote, Judd's.

Norman Judd's fakery fell slightly short of a lie. Two months before Cooper Union, most national committeemen and most Americans considered Lincoln a noncandidate. When the convention convened in May, Lincoln might remain a noncandidate, the Windy City a neutral site, and Chicagoans seeking only conventioneers' dollars. But if Lincoln became a candidate, the Chicago locale might tilt the nomination his way.

Lincoln, inexperienced in convention manipulation, dismissed this craftiness. He wrote Judd before the National Committee's meeting that "some of our friends . . . attach more importance to getting the National convention into our State than . . . I do."[1] Judd still fashioned a Christmas present for his uncomprehending patron.

2

Four and a half months after Christmas, another campaign operative's surprise gift—and another weird boon from Lincoln's perspective—initiated the Illinoisan's official presidential pursuit. On May 9, 1860, the state's Republican convention, meeting in Decatur, selected Illinois delegates to the national convention. His state's conclave, Lincoln hoped, would announce his presidential candidacy amid unanimous support.

Decatur appropriately staged this latest Lincoln beginning. Here thirty years before, the Tom Lincolns had disembarked from the Sangamon River and shivered through The Winter of the Deep Snow. Here Abraham had helped his father and John Hanks, his mother's cousin, raise the migrants' log cabin and rail fence. Here a quarter century later, Lincoln had been a "surprise" visitor to that auspicious 1856 editors' meeting. The gathering had called the state's Anti-Nebraska Party into convention, seeking antislavery moderation.

In 1860, a Republican comer championed Decatur's climactic initiation. Richard J. Oglesby, fifteen years younger than Lincoln, would win three post–Civil War terms as governor and one as U.S. senator.[2] Two decades earlier, the then unknown Oglesby had self-indulgently wondered if he and Lincoln might be destiny's twins. Both self-helpers, born in Kentucky, early migrated to Illinois, settling first near Decatur. Both enjoyed little formal schooling and endured much proletarian labor.

Both aspirants inched beyond the lower class in Illinois lawyer/Whig circles. As a fifteen-year-old political junkie, Oglesby first observed Lincoln in Whigs' 1840 "Tippecanoe and Tyler Too Campaign" for William Henry Harrison. The teenager cherished Lincoln's celebration of Harrison's rise from log-cabin origins.

In 1860, Oglesby plotted a similar celebration of Lincoln's early rise. Oglesby had learned, from his own travails, why shame darkened many self-helpers' recollections. The inhibition, he suspected, caused his melancholy older hero's silence about early struggles up from the mud.

As director of arrangements at Illinois's 1860 State Republican Convention, Oglesby meant to advertise Lincoln's self-help persona. Before the Decatur conclave, Oglesby gave John Hanks a carriage ride to Tom Lincoln's old homestead. Here Hanks identified some thirty-year-old fence rails as "for sure" among those he and Abe had "mauled" (a common frontier word for hacking logs into fence posts). After the wily Oglesby refined the vocabulary, the mauler became the Rail-splitter. After Hanks loaded several supposedly identified rails on board, Oglesby drove back to Decatur, convinced that he transported mauled keys to the presidency.

Three thousand Illinois state conventioneers and spectators crammed into Decatur's temporary so-called Wigwam on May 9. Oglesby, presiding, asked Lincoln to come forward. With no room to stride, Lincoln reluctantly accepted a wild ride above the crowd. Burly frontiersmen conveyed his huge frame upward and onward, amid roars with each advance.

After fanciers plunked a disheveled Lincoln on stage, Oglesby asked celebrants to squeeze room for two guests to march forward. In paraded John Hanks and the local carpenter, Isaac Jennings. The pair carried two fence rails that Hanks had authenticated, framing a banner declaring:

ABE LINCOLN
The Rail Candidate of the People for 1860 . . .
From A Lot of 3,000
MADE BY
Abe Lincoln and John Hanks
In 1830 . . . [3]

The crowd's responsive screams seemed to lift this wigwam's canvas roof. The "Rail Candidate," still uneasy about being celebrated as an ex-mauler (and never overjoyed to be called Abe), allowed that he might have split these relics. But from this moment forward, his image shot past his diffidence.

Within hours, the state's conclave unanimously nominated the rechristened Rail-splitter for president. Within days, Illinoisans' demand for "Lincoln Rails" became omnivorous. Within weeks, the Rail-splitter moniker lifted Lincoln as much as the Old Hickory label had elevated Andrew Jackson. The Free-Soil leader, having stressed economic arguments for Republicanism less than many others, had become the crusade's supreme materialistic symbol.

Few seeming ironies are less ironic than this spectacle, featuring America's champion self-helper helped to his supreme self-help image. Perhaps no one rises solely by her/his own efforts. Assuredly, Lincoln was not that sport. He had received retrieval of his surveying tools from "Uncle Jimmy" Short, avenues toward the law from Bowling Green and John Todd Stuart, free shelter from Joshua Speed, free board from Bill Butler, legal training from Stephen Logan, uplift for the state economy from the national government, and the Chicago convention locale from Norman Judd. Now Dick Oglesby contributed the Rail-splitter bonanza. Imminently, David Davis would add convention tactics and so-called Wide-Awakes would pile on campaign parades. Lincoln-style ascension meant one's own tortuous steps—plus capacity to attract collaborators.

3

In contrast to boosters' last-minute concoction of the Rail-splitter title, Lincoln had long since alone secured his "Honest Abe" moniker. The older label boosted him higher than ever amid one new 1860 circumstance. While insistences on containing slavery and perpetuating Union predominated during Lincoln's presidential election, Republicans also stressed the Democracy's supposed corruption.

Republican assaults on the Franklin Pierce/James Buchanan administrations' alleged slime, increasingly shrill during the 1850s, peaked in 1860, when the U.S. House of Representatives appointed a committee to investigate governmental corruption. Pennsylvania's Honest John Covode chaired this so-called Covode Committee. Honest John's committee uncovered too little corruption to recommend Republicans' hope, President Buchanan's impeachment.

But investigators' eight-hundred-page report highlighted public printing contracts used to buy votes, post office funds disappeared into postmasters' pockets, public lands sold beneath value to valued friends, and plunder of the national treasury deployed to finance campaigns. Throw the thieves out, chorused Republicans, or politicos will destroy a reeking republic.

The Covode Committee's dissenting Democrat's retort: Republicans do it too. The rejoinder the more compelled Republicans to nominate a candidate above the stench. Honest Abe seemed supremely beyond the Washington swamp.

Lincoln's reputation as a breath of fresh air had commenced with his torment over breaking his word to marry Mary Todd. When he subsequently honored his broken promise, local gossips whispered that only undying commitment to unhappy pledges could explain the groom's folly. More fairly, provincial wags conceived that only unyielding honesty could explain Lincoln's determination to repay every cent of his "national debt." No matter that his oft-times inebriated business partner, William Berry, had created much of the burden or that the likes of Denton Offutt commonly fled the sheriff. Honest Abe had promised to repay the loan. Promises demand delivery.

In his political no less than personal life, Lincoln delivered consistently honest performances. The contrast with Illinois's governor, Joel Mattson, came to underline Lincoln's scrupulousness. In 1855, the Democrat, when seemingly incorruptible, had almost defeated Lincoln and Lyman Trumbull for the U.S. Senate. But Mattson left the governorship in the late 1850s as a disgraced crook, caught helping himself to $250,000 in Illinois and Michigan Canal script.

Throughout slavery extension controversies, Honest Abe called slavery above all else *wrong*. He nevertheless emphasized that he was no better than southerners. If he had remained in Kentucky, he too might have tolerated the sin. Even if he acquired invincible power, he would remain unsure how to eliminate the curse.

But allowing a republican atrocity to spread—there he drew the ethical line. American politics has rarely seen such rectitude without self-righteousness, such soaring without haughtiness, and such devotion to converting others without disdain for the fallen. Honest Abe could never become Joel Mattson!

Lincoln chose campaign leaders equally above suspicion. His chief partisan, Circuit Judge David Davis, had no background in national wirepulling and no aspiration for that circus. Lincoln's favorite Illinois judge dreamed instead of scrupulously serving a higher court (and President Lincoln would place him on the nation's highest bench). Davis's chief campaign lieutenant, State Senator Norman Judd, aspired largely for higher state office. After Judd whiffed in the Illinois governor's race, President Lincoln would consolingly appoint him U.S. minister to Prussia.

Davis and Judd little resembled the opportunists that Lincoln's chief opponent, William H. Seward, unleashed to rally conventioneers. Thurlow Weed, notorious party boss and wielder of government favors, led Seward's charge. Weed's most recent triumph bore an infamous title: The New York City Gridiron Fraud. The Gridiron extravaganza involved not footballs but railroads. After donating lush contributions to Republican coffers, profiteers had received plush legislative charters to run iron rails throughout the metropolis's grid. As Weed, so-called "Wizard of the Lobby," defended the trade-off, New York needed well-financed Republicans as much as well-connected streets.

Lobbyists' Wizard contrasted with David Davis, incorruptible judge. The difference, along with Honest Abe's well-earned title, gave Lincoln an advantage over Weed's man, Seward, on the corruption issue. The issue gave Lincoln an even larger advantage over Pennsylvania's favorite son, Simon Cameron, a Weed-like winker at enriching graft.

Illinois Republicans' favorite never mentioned malfeasances in office. Lincoln's reputation did the speaking. Honest Abe talked almost exclusively against those twin abominations: spreading slavery and smashing Union.

Avoiding a subject even better served Lincoln on another secondary issue: nativism. Back in 1856, nativists had formed the national American Party, bent on barring new immigrants from voting for twenty-one years. After the American Party waned, ex–Know-Nothings still distrusted America's new European millions. Former American Party voters also still resented previous assaults on their characters. Their grudges still focused on their old bitter Republican antagonist, William H. Seward.

Abraham Lincoln, in contrast, had mostly hidden his disgust with nativists. Only in one 1858 sentence had he orally welcomed "Hans, Baptiste, and Patrick" to become rising Americans. Only in one 1859 public letter had he scorned the inconsistency of "commiserating" with "the oppressed . . . negro" and then oppressing "*white men . . . born*" abroad.[4]

But with one shrewd gesture, he furthered his old insistence that haters of slaveholder expansion, blackmail, and disunion must bury loathing of each other on other issues. Illinois delegates to the Republican National Convention, he instructed, should include both Orville Browning, once a mild apostle of nativist repression, and Gustave Koerner, always a passionate promoter of immigrant rights.[5] Meanwhile, Seward (and Edward Bates) gave no such signal of embalming past furies about nativism. No way would Honest Abe permit nativist distractions or Gridiron venalities to waylay Republican mission.

5

Beyond corruption and nativism, Lincoln needed to be the clearer *moderate* antislavery man. Some conceived that Lincoln's passing House Divided/"ultimate extinction" utterances in 1858 matched Seward's two apparently radical outbursts, celebrating an "Irrepressible Conflict" between North and South and an antislavery "Higher Law than the Constitution." Recognizing his exposure, Lincoln had begun muting "ultimate extinction" almost as soon as he uttered the words. Within months, he had removed the provocation entirely.

Silence, however, does not advertise a retreat. Even in the early twenty-first century, few realize how quickly and completely the 1859–60 Lincoln backpedaled from "ultimate extinction." His voiceless pullback came only in the easily missed form of what he no longer said and had never explained. In May 1860, realizing the need to illuminate his distance from Seward, Lincoln scribbled a last-minute note to his convention lobbyists. He pleaded that while "I agree with Seward in his 'Irrepressible Conflict'" speech, I do not endorse his "Higher Law doctrine."[6]

These hurried, worried words said too little to derail Seward unless Lincoln's campaign team massively advertised them at the convention. The Illinoisan would not himself pursue his party's leader the way he hounded the Democrats' Douglas. He anticipated what Ronald Reagan would later call "the 11th Commandment: Thou shall not speak ill of other Republicans." Lincoln also gratefully remembered that back in 1848, Seward had instructed him that successful northern politicians must renounce silence on slavery.

With Lincoln as silent on Seward as he had once been on slavery, most delegates, when en route to the convention, considered a more experienced veteran of Washington's slavery wars the better alternative to the New Yorker. Edward Bates of Missouri, Simon Cameron of Pennsylvania, Chase of Ohio, or even the seventy-five-year-old U.S. Supreme Court Justice John McLean, dissenter on the Court's *Dred Scott* decision and judge in the *Rock Island Bridge* case, all had champions. As the Chicago convention began on May 16, few suspected that Lincoln, having spent only two unsuccessful years in the national capital twelve years a-gone, would swiftly rout Seward and all other Washington grizzled veterans.

6

Chicago's inventiveness along with Circuit-mates' pleas underlined the fresh alternative. When delegates arrived at the nouveau city's hastily constructed convention arena, they marveled that the sprawl, accommodating twelve thousand folk, had been built in less than five weeks for fewer than six thousand dollars. Equally surprising, this momentarily largest U.S. public indoor arena, essentially a temporary overgrown pine-plank barn sporting a canvas roof, displayed some of opera houses' sight lines and acoustics.[7]

"Wigwam," the old word connoting Native Americans' dwellings, now also indicated North American whites' new convention halls (even if these "wigwams" resembled Native American houses only in the canvas roof!). Under the Chicago Wigwam's canvas, delegates dominated the ground floor, except for spectators' standing-room-only areas. Luckier onlookers sat in second-floor galleries, lining three sides of the arena. From the hall's fourth wall, featuring the stage and rostrum, the canvas roof slanted upward, pitching orations outward.

The design gave ground-floor observers, able to see little and sit seldom, a compensating clear hearing. The seated audience in second-floor galleries could hear equally well and better see a riot of colors. Every male gallery spectator had to bring a female. The ladies dressed to the nines.

Indoors, the convention's colorfully inventive scene thus illustrated what midwestern rethinking could accomplish. Outdoors, the Wigwam's neighborhood raised the lesson literally toward the sky. Delegates' overgrown barn sat on the downtown edge of the great bend in the Chicago River, where the drive now called Wacker intersects with the street then and now called Lake. Kitty-corner across the river now thrives the Merchandise Mart, that low-slung, rectangular exception to towering skyscrapers, downtown Chicago's latter-day commanders.

Back in 1860, the Wigwam's locale starred Chicagoans' latest fling at tempting fate. The city's Great Lakes watery connections had always promised extravagant profits. But the low-lying water table had also delivered lethal epidemics. While the Native American word that inspired the name "Chicago" remains in dispute—perhaps "Chicagou" or "Chicagoua" or "Shi-kaakwa" or?—all possibilities connoted the skunky smell arising from the habitat's skunkweed; and Native Americans marveled that the stench failed to deter white men from coming and settling and sickening.

For two decades, whites' gamble on the miasma had paid off. The soaking bog, with 150 inhabitants in 1833, became home to almost one hundred thousand fortune hunters by 1854. At midcentury, after the city's connections between midwestern lakes and western rivers had yielded booming but not quite record growth, entrepreneurs and the national government had doubled down on progress. Ten railroads barreled into the metropolis from east and west by 1860. Landed innovation joined watery experiments to propel urban expansion rates beyond New York City's.

Unrivaled harvester factories followed, then sprawling lumberyards, then the Chicago Board of Trade's unmatched pit for turning mountains of grain into piles of cash. These 1850s engines of materialism helped finance emblems of culture—the Chicago Historical Society, Northwestern University, the first University of Chicago, Lake Forest and Wheaton Colleges, and McVicker's Theatre (with its Athenian front and costing eighty-five thousand dollars). Visitors filled fifty luxury hotels, all walking distance from the nation's largest railroad station. The leading new hostelry, the all-brick, five-story, 240-room Tremont House, rivaled New York City's Astor House. As the saying goes, the sky seemed the limit for a swamp town grown immense.

The limit lay underfoot. In 1854, disturbed wetlands retaliated. Downtown, sharing the water level of the Chicago River and Lake Michigan, proved difficult to drain of metropolitan wastes. While a cholera epidemic killed 5 percent of Chicagoans, survivors sunk into contaminated mud with every sloshing step. A street sign, pointing downward, called the slush the fastest route to China.

In 1855, desperate city councilmen decided to remove downtown streets, install a raised sewer system pointing down toward the Chicago River, pave over the saving drain, and hope that property owners would lift their structures to streets' four-to-eight-feet-higher grade. The gamble would fail if capitalists balked at the cost and moved elsewhere, leaving empty sanitized streets above abandoned dilapidation. But most entrepreneurs, as city councilmen had predicted, chose to elevate their profitable downtown structures rather than risk unproved Chicago locales.

To save their buildings, capitalists enlisted a mechanical army, composed of five-foot-tall screw jacks.[8] When operators rotated these machines' handle a quarter turn, the leverage lifted ten tons an inch. Line up these bulky monsters and their bulging operators every several yards on all sides of even the city's largest structure, rotate handles simultaneously, and an urban behemoth creeps skyward, with folks inside feeling no tremor. The five stories Briggs House (Hotel) received its painless screw jack boost in 1857; the equally immense Matteson House two years later; and the palatial Tremont House in 1861.

At first, entrepreneurs paid no heed to neighbors' plans. With screw jacks applied irregularly, shared sidewalks became a riot of stairs. Pedestrians took several strides forward, then several steps up, then forward again, then down, then forward. They shopped in a steeplejack course miscast as an invitation to spend.

Starting in early April 1860, several shopkeepers cooperated with neighbors. In the breakthrough example that preconvention month, six thousand laborers gave a quarter turn to six thousand screw jacks every time their boss blew a whistle. The machines simultaneously lifted an entire city block of structures to the same street grade, first on one side of Lake Street and then on the other. By the first of May, with Republican conventioneers due in fifteen days, the entire block and all its commercial emporiums, including a double marble bank, had been raised exactly the same four feet, eight inches. Outside the shops, Lake Street's straight sidewalks invitingly contrasted with downtown ups and downs.

Chicago capitalists would spend years seeking to raise all downtown streets to Lake Street's level. They would not entirely succeed until the Chicago Fire of 1871 leveled downtown, inviting replacement structures to be rebuilt on the same grade. Subsequently, Chicagoans would not transcend their worst sanitation threat until they reversed the Chicago River's flow at the end of the century. That follow-up miracle relieved Lake Michigan from the contamination that the lifted sewer system spawned. But the screw jack revolution, in its 1860 Lake Street climax, began establishing a level, dry footprint for Chicago's signature skyscrapers.

Republican conventioneers, arriving days after the Lake Street breakthrough, had to stroll only three blocks from the Wigwam to see the phenomenon. A further tour of downtown revealed urbanites and their screw jacks everywhere lifting their habitat out of a quagmire. Theirs was that new world, America, remaking a community's destiny, just when that new symbol, the Rail-splitter, sought a newcomer's breakthrough. Then was a stale old-timer really the best choice to lead a nouveau western nation past its lethal slavery crisis?

7

The towering Rail-splitter exuded similarities to screw jack behemoths. Both epitomized the Midwest's determination to rise, whatever forbidding odds must be overcome. Both sought not to revolutionize but to save. If screw jacks could lift an entire city block beyond contaminated wastes, perhaps a shrewd giant could hoist the North beyond slavery's contaminating spread—and with an antislavery strategy more consistently cautious than rival remedies.

With Lincoln back in Springfield, as custom dictated, the Rail-splitter's convention operatives, with David Davis in the lead, lobbied for their candidate. Bates, Cameron, Chase, and McLean fielded only skeletal support teams. Thurlow Weed deployed well-trained, well-financed professionals. But the Wizard's experienced campaigners, experts at disciplined conquests, had never faced such amateurish hijinks as David Davis's.

During the most revealing incident, a thousand Seward pros paraded around downtown behind a lavishly costumed brass band, singing "Oh, Isn't He a Darling." Meanwhile, some dozen Lincoln novices scrambled around the Wigwam, buttonholing delegates and pounding arguments into the only ears that mattered. When Seward's parade reached the Wigwam, New Yorkers discovered doors locked, the arena jammed, and their tickets superseded by Honest Abe loyalists' counterfeit ducats.

Seward delegates shoved inside. They found that Illinois convention planners had located their seats distant from undecided states' delegates. Screaming at these deciders could not help. Lincoln men had enlisted leather-lunged bawlers, notorious for being heard all the way across Lake Michigan, to scream for the prairie favorite.

Amateurs' dirty tricks mattered less than their honest appeal, generated from their peculiar base. Lincoln's convention lobbyists, mostly country lawyers, gathered semi-annually for three months, to share Judge Davis's Circuit. The lawyers cherished the absentee from the Lincolns' rebuilt house. Their hero, long in prestige and height but short on pretense, was just one of the fellows. When Davis asked them to search out wavering delegates and spin colorful tales of their eccentric commoner, they relished the assignment. They were the first of the devoted volunteers who would transform American electioneering. Those who followed rarely knew their favorite as well.

For a quarter century, Lincoln had been inadvertently feeding Circuit intimates material to highlight his personal qualities. He was their most hilarious after-hours companion, with his frontier tales and smelly jokes, and the most morose, with his shrinks into a corner to gloom. He was their best Fives (street handball) player when he could swat the orbit with long arms and their worst when he had to pursue the projectile atop flat feet. He was their most passionate compatriot when he exploded at Douglas, and their least sensual when he shunned liquor and cigars.

Davis's team assured delegates over and over again, per Lincoln's last-minute instructions, that their eccentric Circuit-mate renounced Seward-style Higher Law. Their compatriot considered no law higher than the Constitution. Federally imposed emancipation inside the South, he believed, would shatter Union. He had told New Hampshire citizens two months earlier that "wrong as we think slavery to be, we should let it alone in the States where it exists, because its extirpation would occasion greater wrongs." Yet "true Union men" must never "yield" to disunionists' blackmail, lest slavery "spread over the National Territories and over-run us in the Free States."[9]

Besides detailing Lincoln's limited and defensive insistences, plus warning about Seward's allegedly unlimited and assaulting Higher Law, Lincoln's team deployed their Rail-splitter's *second*-love plan. "I am not the *first* choice of a very great many," Lincoln had admitted. "Our policy, then, is to" offend "no . . . others," leaving "them in a mood to come to us, if . . . compelled to give up their first love."[10] It was like offending no slaveholders, leaving them in a mood to consent to antislavery, many years hence.

8

On May 18, the convention's third day, the first presidential nomination roll call reaffirmed that first love did not suffice.[11] With a two-thirds majority required for nomination, William H. Seward received 173.5 ballots. He needed 59.5 more votes to triumph. Lincoln garnered 102 votes, 71.5 fewer than Seward but more than twice anyone else's tally.

The first ballot's second-place finisher enjoyed better second-love prospects. In the Border North, Lincoln won all Illinois and Indiana first-ballot votes and tied Seward with 2 from Iowa. The three other Border North states together cast 95 votes for favorite sons (Ohio's Salmon Chase, Pennsylvania's

Simon Cameron, and New Jersey's William Dayton). Only 3.5 Border North delegates voted for Seward—a minuscule foundation for catching Lincoln in Lincoln's region.

In contrast, Lincoln's 19 first-ballot votes from New England laid a solid future foundation in Seward's Upper North. On the convention's second ballot, the Upper North's Vermont and the Border North's Pennsylvania together switched 54 votes from their favorite sons to Lincoln. That boon, plus 3 more votes from Border North Iowa (where Lincoln now had a majority), plus a scattered sprinkle of other new support lifted Lincoln to 181 votes, only 3.5 behind Seward.

On the third ballot, Chase and Dayton released their Border North delegations. Sixty-three percent of Ohio and New Jersey delegates joined fresh dribbles from elsewhere to lift Lincoln within 1.5 votes of victory. The Rail-splitter led Seward 231.5–180 overall, 142.5–7 in the Border North, 42–21 in New England, and 42–22 in the South.

Seward led Lincoln 140–42 in northern delegates beyond the Border North. But that 77 percent strength did not compensate for Lincoln's 95 percent sweep of the Border North and Seward's shortfall in New England, whose delegates voted 66 percent for Lincoln. The Illinoisan's trip up North after Cooper Union, designed primarily to check up on Bob, had yielded double pleasure.

With Lincoln partisans begging for the clinching 1.5 votes after the convention's third ballot, the smallpox-scarred, verbally challenged chairman of the Ohio delegation, David Cartter, rose to stammer that his Border North state had four more votes for Lincoln. Wild cheers inside the Wigwam echoed cannon blasts outside. After telegraph wires silently sped the tidings to Springfield, Lincoln announced that "I must go home," for "a little . . . woman there . . . is more interested in this matter than I am." A celebrant cheered the only way that Mary may have been *more* interested: "We'll give you a larger house on the fourth of next March."[12]

9

Lincoln's victory, achieved with only three ballots in less than two hours, came startlingly fast. Preconvention speculation had underestimated the Rail-splitter's charisma, Chicago's freshness, David Davis's campaigners, and the Upper North/Border North split. The early guesses that someone other than Lincoln would triumph had also paid too little attention to Chase's greater radicalism on fugitive slave laws, Seward's *supposedly* greater tendency toward emancipation, the New Yorker's assuredly greater tendency to bait nativists, and Cameron's omnivorous hunger for spoils. After the choice narrowed to Lincoln vs. Seward, the Upper North's favorite's *apparently* more radical antislavery and assuredly more bitter antinativism weighted the scales disastrously against him on the Rail-splitter's Border North terrain.

Appearances deceived. Seward harbored as compromising a version of antislavery, and Lincoln concealed as uncompromising a loathing of nativism. But delegates voted on what they could see. In addition to looking more moderate on slavery and less ferocious about nativism, Honest Abe seemed the better enemy of Gridiron corruptions.

The myth persists that Lincoln's triumph also hinged on David Davis's corrupt convention bargains. In the largest alleged example, Davis supposedly guaranteed Pennsylvania's Simon Cameron a cabinet position in exchange for the Quaker State's second-ballot switch to Lincoln—this despite the Rail-splitter's warning to *"make no contracts that will bind me."*[13] In fact, Davis bound only himself. He promised only to lobby Lincoln on Cameron's behalf.

The Pennsylvanian sought better assurances from Seward's team. But New Yorkers, doubtful that Simon Cameron could deliver enough Border North votes, offered nothing. Cameron then procrastinated about approaching Bates or Chase or Dayton, fearing that none of them could stop Lincoln. After delaying and delaying Pennsylvania's convention votes, Cameron was reduced to hoping that David Davis would secure something from Lincoln. The unsavory sideshow reaffirms the central point. The showdown between Lincoln's solider Border North and Seward's shakier Upper North dominated this convention; and the attractive Rail-splitter seemed the better bet to reverse Republicans' killing 1856 Border North loss.

10

A surprising group, *southern* Republicans, largely supported the future Great Emancipator on the final tally. Except for six Texans, the South's eighty-eight Republican delegates (19 percent of the convention) represented Dixie's most northern states. Over half of the Border South Republicans voted for Lincoln on the third ballot. Had these forty-three southerners selected anyone else (say, the borderlands' Edward Bates), Lincoln would have fallen well short of a third-ballot two-thirds majority.

American vice-presidential nominations usually seek to broaden their party's base. Lincoln's 110 first-ballot votes for second place on Republicans' 1856 ticket (and Border North New Jersey's William Dayton's triumph for that vice-presidential nomination) had served accurate notice that future

Border North politicians might defeat Upper North Republicans. So when Kentucky's Cassius Clay, Henry Clay's cousin, garnered 101.5 votes on the first roll-call ballot for Republicans' 1860 vice-presidential nominee (only 8.5 votes fewer than Lincoln's vice-presidential support in 1856), partisan imaginations soared.[14] Might this southern heretic have signaled that the almost entirely northern party could become a national movement, with Border South no less than Border North supporters added to Republicans' Upper North hegemony? What a promising replacement for national Whiggery that previously underwhelming Yankee Republican opposition to the Democracy would then become! Abraham Lincoln, hopeful professional politician, spotted the first signs more carefully than most.

Cassius Clay, Republicans' 1860 emblem of Border South potential, had gone north for college, to Yale.[15] Enchanted by the Connecticut scene, he had gone home to free his slaves and to trumpet New England's free labor way for his state. At his aptly named *White* Hall estate, the equally well-named Lion of *White* Hall had schemed to turn Kentucky's blacks as scarce as Connecticut's. Too many supposed racial inferiors, Clay thought, turned lush Kentucky poorer than rocky New England. Remove blacks, enslaved or free, and whites' opportunities would soar.

Kentucky legislators would achieve the windfall cost free, Clay predicted, if they emancipated slaves at age twenty-one. Before black youths became eligible for freedom, Cassius Clay projected, masters would sell the serviles to Deep South buyers. With blacks gone, rich land purchasers and poor white yeoman would rush in to develop their race's new Mecca.

Kentucky slaveholders preferred their old Mecca. They smashed the Lion's antislavery press, overwhelmed his campaign for governor, and sent him scurrying for reinforcements. The quest landed him in the Republican camp in the late 1850s. This other Clay hoped that his state's tiny Republican Party, once fortified with a Republican national administration's Kentucky patronage, could slowly become formidable challengers of the ruling class.

Cassius Clay's hopes received further notice when he and Missouri's Frank Blair Jr. successfully orated as invited guests before New York City Republicans in Cooper Union, earlier in February 1860 than Abraham Lincoln appeared. But would a President-elect Lincoln make the 1860 convention's second choice for vice president his first choice to receive Kentucky largesse (or make sometime congressman Blair his first choice for Missouri patronage)? If so, could Clay's (or Blair's) reinforced heretics, over many years, rally their Border South states' huge nonslaveholding majority against the slaveholders? The questions hung fire, with the politic Lincoln hinting at no answers before the November election.

11

Although a long shot for the nomination in early May, the nominated Lincoln became odds-on favorite for the presidency in late June. Lincoln's prospects soared when firestorms at two National Democratic Conventions, April 23–May 3 and June 18–23, incinerated the Democracy.

Lincoln had helped cause his opponents' conflagration. During the 1858 Great Debates, he had asked how a territorial majority could emancipate, per Douglas's Popular Sovereignty formulas, after Roger B. Taney had declared territorial emancipation unconstitutional. Douglas had answered that a territorial legislature could emancipate by doing nothing to protect slavery. Southerners had retorted that if territorial legislatures did nothing, Congress must protect Taney's decree and their possessions.

Douglas scorned that annihilation of local sovereignty. When the Charleston Democratic Convention voted on whether to add congressional protections of slave territories to its platform, the Little Giant's northern partisans defeated the southern minority. Then most southern delegates exited America's only surviving national party. The second Democratic Convention in Baltimore failed to bridge the division.

Southern Democrats subsequently selected Kentucky's John Breckinridge (Buchanan's vice president) to run for the presidency. Northern Democrats countered with Douglas. A week before the Republican Convention nominated Lincoln, a new Constitutional Union Party boosted Tennessee's U.S. Senator John Bell, to protect "The Constitution, . . . The Union, and The Laws" (somehow!). By July, the two southerners contended for their minority section's favor, while the two Illinoisans skirmished for their majority section's support.

12

Illinoisans witnessed Lincoln versus Douglas yet again, this time to lead the nation rather than the state. Three decades earlier, upon arrival in midwestern backwaters, both would have called such a climax hallucinatory. But Douglas had championed the federal government's Illinois Central Railroad land grant, a success epitomizing Lincoln's Whig nationalism. This rare mutually applauded law had swiftly made Illinois a star in the nation's transportation revolution, then a titan in national markets, then a magnet for migrants, whether American or European.

After their state's economic takeoff, Illinois's two luminaries had soared in national politics. When the two former bottom-dwellers contested the nation's highest office, both treasured one gem beyond national land for the Illinois Central. The nation itself, Illinois's ladder to the top and theirs too, must be preserved.

The latest (and last) Lincoln-Douglas showdown lacked that formerly omnipresent element: debates. Previously, the Rail-splitter had chased confrontations with the front-running Douglas. Now, with the National Democracy a relic and its Little Giant reeling, Lincoln preferred presidential candidates' tradition: No campaigning.

With Republicans owning the Upper North and southerners angry with Popular Sovereignty's champion, only the Border North could reverse Douglas's plunge. This battleground tier of six states possessed 82 electoral votes, 54 percent of the 152 votes required for Electoral College victory. If Douglas could capture three Border North states, he could deny Republicans an Electoral College majority. Then the U.S. House of Representatives would choose between the top three Electoral College candidates, with each state's delegation possessing one vote. Lincoln figured to struggle in that arena, for fifteen southern states would wield almost as much leverage as eighteen northern states.

Lincoln considered more Great Debates no way to minimize the risk. He knew that in his Border North base, the Democracy's split had weakened Douglas, while the American Party's collapse had strengthened Republicans. He also believed that his freshly revised anti–slavery-extension, antidisunion message, with its politically salutary absence of *imminent* conspiracy and "ultimate extinction," needed no further elaboration. So he remained in Springfield, charming visitors with everything except Republican oratory.

His best campaigners paraded rather than orated. So-called Wide-Awake young men, wearing shiny black military capes and waving flaming torches atop mauled rails, nightly marched in cities large and small, celebrating the Rail-splitter. On October 9, when three Border North states chose Republican local candidates, Douglas in effect conceded. The patriot turned southward, vainly seeking to preclude a secessionist response to Lincoln's imminent victory.

13

On November 6, Lincoln polled only 39.9 percent of the nation's popular votes and 2 percent of southern ballots.[16] But with his 54.1 percent of northern voters, he amassed 98.4 percent of the majority section's 60.4 percent of Electoral College representatives. He thus secured twenty-eight more northern electors than national victory required.

Those figures miss the critical difference between two Norths. In the Upper North, Lincoln won every Electoral College representative and a landslide 60.2 percent of popular votes. In the Border North, the Rail-splitter won almost as complete an Electoral College victory, securing every representative except three of New Jersey's seven. Yet Lincoln's share of Border North popular votes declined from overwhelming (56.3 percent in Pennsylvania and 54.6 percent in Iowa) to reasonably safe (52.3 percent in Ohio), to precarious (51.1 percent in Indiana and 50.7 in Illinois), to inadequate (48.1 percent in New Jersey). The Rail-splitter barely won central Illinois and lost his own Sangamon County (as he had in 1858 and would in 1864).

If 0.6 percent of his Illinois and Indiana supporters had voted for Douglas, Lincoln would have lost twenty-four Electoral College votes. That Border North reversal, if coupled with even more minuscule desertions in California and Oregon, would have left Lincoln three votes short of Electoral College triumph. Or to put this close call more dramatically, if one in a thousand of his voters nationally, scattered in the right places in Illinois, Indiana, California, and Oregon, had switched to an opponent, only an elusive House of Representatives majority could have elected the Rail-splitter president. At the 1860 Republican Convention, many delegates had feared that an apparently more radical candidate than Lincoln would lose the more moderate Border North and thus the presidency. The battleground area's election results vindicated that prescience.

The figures also reaffirmed the importance of Lincoln's rare capacity to regroup after defeats. His slight loss in Illinois's 1858 U.S. Senate ballots, after adopting precarious positions especially on immediate conspiracy and "ultimate extinction," generated his politic revisions in 1859, which in turn helped generate his slight victory in close 1860 presidential races. Never before had this comeback specialist rebounded quite so fast or skillfully (which, in view of his previous rebounds, is saying a mouthful). A prime lesson of his prewar plummets and recoveries: Be willing to face your own shortcomings, painfully, boldly, and quickly.

14

In Middle and Lower Souths, Republicans won only 1,887 votes. But in the four Border South states, Lincoln secured 24,508 ballots, 5.8 percent of the tally. The Rail-splitter's share of these least slaveholding southern states' votes ranged from disappointing (0.9 percent in Kentucky) to light (2.5 percent in Maryland) to promising (10.3 percent in Missouri) to impressive (23.7 percent in Delaware).

Dismay about the South's supposedly perished antislavery sentiments had haunted Lincoln's marvelous 1855 letter to George Robertson. He had then, before, and ever after seen that the house divided could be reunited peacefully only if southerners incrementally consented to emancipation. Might Border South Republicanism now be gradually nurtured toward that eventual consent? As Lincoln had indicated in the Great Debates, he could wait a hundred years for that national antislavery salvation.

15

Abraham Lincoln had long waited (although not that long!) for mastery of the northern dead center. At first he had tripped over reforming too much (as with the System and with DC emancipation). Then he had stumbled over changing too little (as with avoiding slavery altogether and condoning Texas Annexation). Then he had experimented too dangerously (as with unsubstantiated charges of an immediate Douglas conspiracy and unexplained visions of "ultimate extinction").

But at just the right moment, he had trimmed his appeal to perfect duplication of mainstream antislavery's defensive sweet spot. His climactic strategy of defense included banning slavery's expansion everywhere, seeing a conspiracy to nationalize slavery as a distant rather than tomorrow's threat, turning mute on "ultimate extinction," and waxing ferocious against minority blackmail and disunion. A half decade after the Kansas-Nebraska Act, his halting steps toward the sweet spot, reminiscent of the Great Blondin inching along a high wire atop Niagara Falls, had finally reached the other side.

He remained a very long step short of triumphant statecraft. No man had previously become president so much because of what he said, so little because of what he did. Nor has any other president lost so many pre-presidential bids for office. This inexperienced officeholder would have to overcome staggers as president-elect and as inaugurated president before he could inch toward becoming America's greatest president.

20

The Erratic Interregnum

During the four-month interregnum between Abraham Lincoln's November 6 election and his March 4 inauguration, the experienced campaigner advanced his familiar moderate antislavery positions. In contrast, the inexperienced administrator stumbled around unfamiliar disunion situations. The trouble, obvious in his uneven First Inaugural Address, would continue during his first six weeks in the Executive Mansion, making his presidential beginning as erratic as his interregnum.[1]

1

Ever since shamefully (in their own eyes) retreating from defiance of the federal protective tariff in the 1832–33 Nullification Crisis, South Carolina's aristocratic republicans had monopolized the only state that might force a disunion crisis on everyone else.[2] With their towering property qualifications for state office, their most-malapportioned American state legislature, their abhorrence of national parties and "mobocracy," and the South's highest percentage of slaves, South Carolina patriarchs meant to preserve their vow: Our aristocratic minority will block fanatical majorities. As a prominent Carolina state legislator exclaimed when asked what his constituents thought, "Think! They will think nothing about it. They expect me to think for them *here.*"[3]

Southern gentlemen in less enslaved states preferred to think for themselves. In 1832–33, Carolina's patriarchs ordered up a national government where one tiny state (theirs!) could nullify congressional laws. But the implacable U.S. president, the South's own Andrew Jackson, and the American mainstream (including the South's) defied the edict.

Again in 1850–52, when South Carolinians sought disunion, every other southern state preferred Union. According to Carolinians' nullification/secession theory, one state could legitimately strike for freedom and force everyone else to reconsider. But Carolina aristocrats, uneasy that southern white majorities might again reject their command, again retreated.[4]

In October 1860, Governor William Gist, bewaring yet another South Carolina loss of nerve, initiated a secret correspondence. Gist sought clandestine reassurances that after Lincoln's election, some Lower South states would follow if his state plunged. His correspondents included one Upper South governor and all Lower South chief executives except Texas's Unionist governor, Sam Houston.[5]

Governors' replies, mostly counseling against separate state secessions, usually urged a southern convention to plan southern states' united strategy. South Carolina's advance guard scoffed that all southern states would never agree to anything, much less disunion. After summoning the courage to go it alone at last, South Carolinians unanimously seceded on December 20, 1860. Now, prayed those proud to have finally done it, reluctant states will have to depart.

Alas, enough states might not join the precipitous state unless federal repression changed the issue. Before South Carolina's secession, Lower South debate had centered on whether Abraham Lincoln would immediately menace slavery. After Carolina's strike, the southern issue swerved to whether Dixie's whites would tolerate Lincoln's "coercion" of a seceded state. No legitimate democratic government, many southerners insisted, could murder citizens who had withdrawn their consent to be governed. The slavery issue had started the secession train rolling. The Union issue could turn disunion into a runaway express.

2

Fearing that disaster, lame-duck president James Buchanan preferred to mull options rather than deploy firepower. In less than a week, however, a subordinate aborted procrastination. U.S. Major Robert Anderson, once Lincoln's Black Hawk War commander, now commanded eighty-five exposed soldiers in frail Fort Moultrie, perched on Charleston harbor's outer edge. On December 26, Anderson ordered his men, under cover of night, into unoccupied Fort Sumter, as massive as the rock it crowns at the harbor's Atlantic Ocean entrance.

In Washington, South Carolina's envoys demanded that Buchanan order Major Anderson back to feeble Fort Moultrie or out of their new nation. Northerners insisted instead that Buchanan must reinforce Anderson's brave initiative. By evacuating Sumter, President Buchanan might seem to concede that no republican government can legitimately coerce citizens who withdraw their consent to be governed. By instead reinforcing Anderson, the president would appear to claim that no election losers could legitimately withdraw from winners' governance.

Buchanan wavered for five days. Then rumors spread that the president would imminently dispatch ship(s) to fortify Robert Anderson's command. South Carolina's envoys, come to Washington to arrange U.S. capitulation to secession, telegraphed the South Carolina secession convention, warning that coercers approached.[6]

The southern revolution's founding fathers immediately sprayed secret telegrams around the only third of the South that they thought might adequately respond, meaning the disproportionately enslaved Lower South. South Carolina titans claimed that federal ships would imminently reinforce all Lower South forts, not just Charleston's Fort Sumter. You must seize your state's federal installations, ran the South Carolina call to arms, before overwhelming Yankee suppression descends (even before any state votes on whether to join South Carolina).

On January 9, Buchanan's reinforcing ship, the *Star of the West,* penetrated Charleston's inner harbor and steamed toward Fort Sumter, bearing two hundred soldiers, one hundred rifles, and ninety days' rations. When several rebel cannonballs splashed close by, the *Star* retreated. These potential first shots of a civil war accelerated Lower South secession.

Before secessionists' captures of Union arsenals and forts commenced in early January 1861, southern voters and secession convention delegates had debated whether Lincoln's menace to slavery required disunion. Posterity never will know whether that issue alone would have propelled all the most enslaved states to join South Carolina. We do know, however, that rebellion spread unstoppably in the most tropical South, after Buchanan dispatched the *Star of the West* and South Carolina revolutionaries secretly warned (erroneously) that other coercers steamed toward the blackest black belts.

Lower South secessionists' early January hauls included seventy-five thousand rifles, every federal arsenal below the Upper South, and all Lower South fortresses except Fort Sumter in Charleston harbor, Fort Pickens in Pensacola (Florida) harbor, and the less important Forts Taylor and Jefferson in the Florida Keys. Amid the military frenzy, Mississippi started trans–South Carolina departures from the Union on January 9. The Texas secession convention completed the Lower South's exodus on February 1.

In mid-February, with the bottom dropped out of the old Union, seven former parts of the United States of America, convening in Montgomery,

Alabama, formed the Confederate States of America. In contrast, the eight Upper South states, containing two-thirds of southern voters, paused to await further developments. In late January, James Buchanan also paused. The lame-duck president accepted informal truces, maintaining the status quo at the four remaining federal-held forts inside the Confederacy. After March 4, Abraham Lincoln would have to resolve his besieged forts' precarious situations.

3

Two months before Lincoln left Springfield, congressmen debated middle ground on slavery issues. On December 18, Kentucky's U.S. Senator John J. Crittenden, occupying Henry Clay's old seat and seeking to emulate the Great Compromiser, introduced several slavery compromises. Only Critten-den's "hereafter acquired" proposal bore potential to abort secession.

This key proposition would divide the western United States at latitude 36°30', where the old Missouri Compromise line ran westward from Missouri's southern border to the Pacific. Crittenden proposed that in U.S. territories now held *and hereafter acquired,* slavery would be banned north and protected south of the line. Among U.S. territories now held, nothing would change. Slavery already existed south of 36°30', while free labor monopolized terrain north of the line.

Territories "hereafter acquired," however, might transform events. A dozen Caribbean and South American prizes, situated in steamy climes below 36°30', were either already enslaved or ripe for enslavement. With these tropical acquisitions, including heavily enslaved Cuba and Brazil, the Slave Power could master the U.S. republic.

That new possibility inside the Union might lure Lower South states to reconsider their recent thrusts outside. (South Carolina was not reconsidering under any circumstances!) Meanwhile, potential U.S. acquisitions above 36°30' required no Crittenden Compromise to remain free soil. Crittenden's line thus offered southerners a possible vastly expanded tropical kingdom and northerners nothing beyond continued Union.

For a few northern Republicans, continued Union sufficed. The party's minority of compromisers speculated that 36°30' might bring the Lower South back and/or retain the Upper South. These Republicans' pliability yielded Lincoln's only intervention against Crittenden's sundry proposals. Lincoln could tolerate, reluctantly, some Crittenden proposals. He could approve admitting barely enslaved New Mexico to the Union as the last slave state, judiciously revising the Fugitive Slave Law, or initiating a constitutional amendment barring Congress from emancipating slave states.

But he could not abide 36°30'. Crittenden's proposed line would cancel Lincoln's late conversion to halting slave expansion everywhere. Earlier, the Illinoisan had opposed only slavery's spread to previously free, largely northward territory. For years, that priority had left him soft on the nation's possible expansion southward, to acquire the likes of enslaved Cuba. In the mid-1840s, he had winked at Texas Annexation. In his 1854 Peoria Address, he had waffled on annexation of enslaved tropical nations. During the 1858 Lincoln-Douglas Debates, he had declined to "stand pledged" against tropical annexations.

During the year before the Cooper Union Address, however, the skillful reviser of his own rhetoric had turned against that softness with a convert's hardness. He had insisted on barring slavery from all U.S. territory. Meanwhile, he had silenced his brief, tardy, and vague speculations about "ultimate extinction" in enslaved states. With that new trade-off, he had won the Republican nomination and the presidency.

Now, John J. Crittenden's compromise would sabotage Lincoln's climactic free-soil position while perhaps helping to turn vast tropical Western Hemisphere nations into Union slave states. Equally intolerable to the president-elect, surrendering nonexpansion would make minority blackmail, not majority decision, democracy's arbitrator. As Lincoln had declared in the Lost/Found Speech and at Cooper Union, minority's blackmail of majorities, no less than minority secession from election results, would demolish majority rule.

Five weeks after his election, Lincoln wrote two Illinois Republican congressmen, warning them (and through them, all Republican congressmen) against "compromise of any sort" on "the *extension* of slavery. The instant you" relent, "they have us under again; and all our labor is lost, and sooner or later must be done over." We must "hold" as "firm as . . . a chain of steel" on slavery's expansion, for "the tug has to come & better now than later."[7]

Writing a Pennsylvania congressman, Lincoln added that "we have just" won offices by carrying "an election on principles fairly stated. . . . Now we are told . . . the government shall be broken up, unless we surrender" our winning principles "to those we have beaten, before we take the offices." That majority "surrender" will be "the end of us and of the government. . . . A year will not pass" before southerners will blackmail us "to take Cuba," if we want them "to stay in the Union." By now surrendering "all we have contended for," he added to an important Indiana Republican, we would suffer Douglas's rebirth, Taney's resurgence, "filibustering" to acquire and then turn "all" land "South of us" into "slave states," and "an early Supreme court decision," outlawing abolition in states.[8]

While most congressional Republicans already opposed slavery's expansion below 36°30', their president-elect's added outrage reduced the slight possibilities of "hereafter acquired" to none. The decisiveness illuminated a cardinal Lincoln characteristic. "I am slow to learn," to repeat one of the Railsplitter's most self-revealing quotations, "and slow to forget that which I have learned. My mind is like a piece of steel, very hard to scratch any thing on it and almost impossible after you get it there to rub it out."[9]

He had been slow to decide against U.S. expansion to slaveholding tropics. But once he belatedly saw his way clear to banning slavery's spread everywhere in the national domain, whether in terrain now held or hereafter acquired, he would allow nothing to rub out his conversion—and certainly not minority blackmail. Nothing was superficial about this crisis, except the desperate compromises that floundered against newly won, now fiercely protected convictions.

4

In this uncongenial atmosphere for peaceable settlements, a single Crittenden constitutional amendment won congressional approval.[10] This first version of a Congress-approved Thirteenth Amendment, ultimately ratified by only six states, sought another direction than the subsequent 1865 fully ratified Thirteenth (abolishing slavery). Because the final Thirteenth later crowned Lincoln as the Great Emancipator, he might seem a weird advocate of the first version, decreeing that *Congress* could never emancipate slave states.

Yet Lincoln had reiterated several dozen times that Congress had no authority to end slavery inside *states*. Each state alone, he had consistently maintained, must decide about its own labor systems. Republican Party proponents of the first Thirteenth answered that the measure just might delay, limit, or even abort disunion.

Lincoln doubted that prayer. But he saw no drawback in trying other folks' chimera, even if only to disprove the fantasy. So on December 20, 1860, the day of South Carolina's secession, the president-elect sent word through Weed to Seward in Washington that he favored the amendment. On December 26, Seward wrote back, declaring that he had received Weed's message and had introduced the perpetual bar to *congressional* emancipation.[11]

There Lincoln's involvement with the proposed constitutional amendment stalled for eight weeks. Not the president-elect but Crittenden, Seward, Charles Francis Adams, and especially Ohio's Republican congressman Tom Corwin sustained this so-called Corwin Amendment. Then, days before his inauguration, Lincoln apparently twisted the arm of at least one Yankee congressman. Thanks in part to the twisted arm(s), the amendment passed its last congressional hurdle at 2:00 AM inauguration morning, with not a vote to spare. The proposed Thirteenth would next be sent to the states for possible ratification.

Eleven hours after congressional passage, in a last-minute insertion to his First Inaugural Address, Lincoln declared that I "have not seen" the "amendment" that just "passed Congress." But he understood "the effect" to be that "*the federal government* shall never interfere with the domestic institutions of the States" (emphasis mine). He had "no objection" to making that already "implied constitutional law . . . express, and irrevocable."[12]

In his haste to applaud the last-minute congressional vote, Lincoln mistakenly expanded "Congress" to "the federal government," in regard to who "shall never interfere with" a state's slavery. He occasionally committed such verbal errors when rushed, as when he momentarily approved free black voting at Peoria. This latest misstatement, like that faux pas, could have theoretically made a difference, including to Lincoln's own imminent form of "federal interference."

The misspeak in his Inaugural Address aside, Lincoln's actions bespoke his real intentions. The extremist southern crowd, watching what he did rather than what he uttered, paid no attention to what he inaccurately announced. They instead paid alarmed attention to the "federal interference" he had inaugurated, which had nothing to do with Congress or Thirteenth Amendments. Lincoln's immediate menace to slavery, as his South Carolina foes saw it, involved using federal resources to help the most antislavery southern politicians *persuade* their least enslaved Border South tier of states to emancipate gradually—and he was already openly exploring that experiment.

5

For six post–Kansas-Nebraska years, Lincoln had deployed only defensive strategies, seeking to contain slavery's expansion and stymie disunion. But after he had been elected, the president-elect dared a new version of his aborted 1849 District antislavery tactic. He would reach inside the South to stimulate agreement to "ultimate extinction." He again wanted no part of forced abolition and thereby, he thought, assured civil war. He wished only peaceable emancipation, with slaveholders consenting and Union perpetuated.

In 1849, Congressman Lincoln had suggested using federal funds to lure District citizens toward voluntary consent to liberate their people (including their slaves outside the District). Similarly in 1861, President-elect Lincoln placed his faith in federal patronage positions to help entice Border South emancipation.

Envisioning and deploring that strategy, North Carolina's Congressman John A. Gilmer wrote Lincoln on December 10, 1860, asking in part whether the president's patronage "appointments to office." in southern states "would . . . attempt to . . . impair the institution of slavery." On December 15, Lincoln responded that "as to the use of patronage in the slave states, where there are few or no Republicans, I do not expect to inquire for the politics of the appointee." Or to remove the veil, he *did* plan to inquire about a potential southern appointee's politics, where more than a few Republicans thrived.[13]

We do not know whether North Carolina's Gilmer saw beneath the veil. We also do not know whether secessionists saw beneath Lincoln's Inaugural Address version of the veil. In the March 4 speech, the new president pledged that if "hostility to the United States in any interior locality shall be so great and so universal as to prevent competent resident citizens from holding the Federal offices," he would not "force obnoxious strangers among the people for that purpose." Or to remove his latest veil, he *did* plan to give federal offices to resident nonstrangers who opposed slavery, in southern places where opposition to slavery seemed promising.[14]

Lincoln hoped his appointments would swell Republicanism in slave-holding quarters where his party had somewhat commenced (i.e., only in the Border South). Cassius Clay, late second-place finisher for the Republican vice-presidential nomination, had advocated this strategy. According to this other important Kentucky Clay, northern Republicans needed only to appoint southern Republicans to offices inside vulnerable Border South states. Then empowered natives would eventually spread antislavery opinions inside the least southern South.

With two out of his seven cabinet nominations, the inaugurated president commenced, with no veils this time, his/Clay's attempted empowerment of Border South dissenters. Missouri, home of Attorney General Edward Bates and a slave population under 10 percent, had voted 10 percent for the Railsplitter. Maryland, home of Postmaster General Montgomery Blair, contained as many manumitted blacks as slaves. Montgomery Blair's brother, Frank Blair Jr., the South's only antislavery congressman, had been Missouri's prime antislavery thorn in Davy Atchison's side.

Four years after helping to provoke Atchison into the Kansas-Nebraska Act, Blair Jr. had traveled to Illinois to support Lincoln's campaign against Douglas. Two years further on, he had traveled to Cooper Union days before Lincoln. Blair had there urged that freed blacks should be colonized in Latin America, partly to ease Border South opposition to emancipation.

With Bates and a Blair on his cabinet team, America's new Border North president hoped to help further his party's message in Border South outposts. Southern Republican postmasters, customhouse officials, and marshals, Lincoln prayed, would double as antislavery persuaders. Postmasters, especially well positioned for the work, might remove censorship from southern mails and thus sprinkle some antislavery appeals inside slaveholders' homes.

Lincoln rejected making Cassius Clay, the Republican National Convention's prophet of the patronage strategy, a third Border South cabinet member. He instead appointed Clay ambassador to far-off Russia. Kentucky, compared to Missouri and Maryland, held less Republican potential. Lincoln's Border South patronage policy sought *practical* antislavery. Unleashing the erratic Lion to make Washington trouble would serve no practical purpose.

By elevating native southerners who had some support within their least enslaved southern states, Lincoln sought progress without invasions. No Republican, his patronage system announced, would hold federal office in the southernmost South. The northern president would hand salaried positions (and thereby perhaps stronger voices) only to native Republicans in the northernmost South. Then many years of Border South's natives' own democratic debates could determine whether the least southern South would eventually consent to emancipation.

Perhaps Lincoln had secretly plotted this maneuver during his fleeting 1858 months of mentioning, then dropping, "ultimate extinction." Perhaps also Cassius Clay's 1860 vice-presidential candidacy had rekindled the patronage possibility. But assuredly the incoming president's prayer for bolstered Republicanism in southern fringes now floated in the open air.

6

Thereby poisoned "mobocratic" air, thought South Carolina reactionaries. In their state, only heavily propertied squires could hold office. Lincoln's "wild" republicanism would instead allow scruffy demagogues to rouse poor white and vengeful slaves inside infected hinterlands. John Townsend, rich disunionist, entitled his pivotal 1860 Charleston pamphlet THE SOUTH ALONE *should govern* THE SOUTH, *and* AFRICAN SLAVERY *should be controlled . . .* ONLY *. . . by* THOSE *. . . friendly to it.* We must not "wait in the Union a single day," warned Townsend, while Lincoln is "organizing his cabinet and distributing his offices," using the federal treasury "to bribe fanatics amongst us."[15]

The *Charleston Mercury* warned that our "most immediate danger" threatened lightly enslaved "Frontier [Border South] States." Throughout our upper hinterlands, cautioned southern fire-eaters' major newspaper, democratic agitation will swell slave runaways and expand slave insubordination. With "the tenure of slave property . . . weakened," more blacks "will be sent down" river "for sale." Then "the Frontier States" will "enter *on the policy of making themselves Free States.*" An "Abolition Party in the South," hoping to whiten Dixie and to

John Townsend, hair perfectly coiffed, prepared to urge fellow South Carolina aristocrats to sever "mobocratic" America and squash Border South contamination

rally slaveless whites, will make "the contest for slavery ... no longer ... between the North and South" but "in the South, between the people of the South."[16]

South Carolina's latest "No Way" recalled the state's extremists' initiation of silenced congressional slavery discussions in gag rule times. The same concern about too much democracy for slaveholders' health had later stimulated Davy Atchison's appeal for partial repeal of the Missouri Compromise. "Bourbon Dave" had meant to preclude a free labor Kansas neighbor's open democratic politics from unsealing Missouri's shakily closed society.

So too in 1859, Missouri's Congressman John Clark had summoned southern colleagues to deny the House of Representatives' Speaker's chair to Republicans who approved circulating Hinton R. Helper's *Impending Crisis* inside the South. Now, disunion's advance guard meant to stop Lincoln's federal patronage from encouraging Border South dissent. For the third time in seven years, open discussions, endemic to the world's most democratic political system,

Lincoln, hair deliberately unbrushed, prepared to rally fellow commoners to save democratic Union and seek Border South conversions

rubbed against closed discussion, endemic to the world's most powerful slavery regime, helping to thrust the republic into yet another national crisis.

Lincoln might have at least temporarily defused that crisis. On December 15, in his answer to North Carolina congressman John Gilmer, the president-elect could theoretically have announced that he would appoint *no* southern Republican to office, *anywhere.* That soothing message, received in the South right before the South Carolina secession convention, just might have defused an 1861 secession crisis.

But the tiny possibility could not deter the president-elect's gargantuan reasons to reject that appeasement. By successfully threatening to depart the republic unless the winners handed office to the losers, Lincoln believed, minority blackmailers would destroy majoritarian democracy. By giving patronage to allies so they might build an opposition party in the losers' lair, Lincoln hoped, the southern wing of a newly national Republican Party might constrict slavery over many years (Lincoln's accepted time frame) where slavery was weakest (the president-elect's test site).

In Great Debates times, it will be recalled, Lincoln had lamented that Douglas's "round, jolly, fruitful face" exuded "postoffices, landoffices, marshalships, and cabinet appointments," while "my poor, lean, lank, face" offered no patronage "cabbages . . . sprouting." In his 1855 Robertson letter, Lincoln had lamented the decline of southern antislavery sentiments. Now an antislavery movement showed signs of perking up in the Border South, and he had the "cabbages" to nurture the proponents.

According to the president-elect's Whiggish conception of a far-flung national republic, the federal government should help make local initiatives plausible. The Illinois Central Railroad epitomized that glory. So, too, national patronage, Lincoln hoped, might gradually help swell popular agreement to a spottily enslaved state's citizens' own dawning antislavery idea.

His model statesmen had incrementally begun emancipation's gradual evolution. The Founding Fathers had started cleansing the nation of slavery, hoping that reeking sores could be slowly cured. They had turned a nationwide curse into a sectional evil by pursuing change with great patience. It had taken fifty-one years after 1776 to emancipate New York and twenty years after that to remove Illinois's version of the calamity. If the Upper South could be voluntarily disinfected at the same turtle pace and then the Lower South, all without a civil war, Lincoln could approve long delays.

But the Founders' good work, the president believed, must resume. Tragically, he had lamented to George Robertson in 1855, the Fathers' gradual antislavery approach had disappeared. He had been elected president five years later, just when faint signs of southern antislavery sentiment reappeared. He would do what he could to fan the feeble sparks, using his offices in southern provinces to encourage southern natives to make consent to antislavery a Border South possibility.

This persuasive approach might seem the least dangerous Republican antislavery strategy conceivable. Lincoln's appointments assuredly threatened a lesser and slower peril than coercive Radical Republicans' hopes to expunge the Fugitive Slave Law, or to arouse slave runaways, or to abolish bondage inside the South's federal forts, or to light a "ring of fire" around slave states. But no such radical propositions could carry the 1860 Border North or thus the presidential election. Lincoln's more conservative proposal was as far north as a Yankee majority would go, to begin an "ultimate extinction" process inside the South.

South Carolinians thought Lincoln's heresy went perilously far. In the face of the Rail-splitter's Whiggish conception of vast national republics, stimulating incremental transformations of backwater provinces, South Carolina aristocrats the more cherished small republics, with distant governments doing little and no heretical agitators deploying national resources to stimulate local dissent. By daring secession, South Carolina separatists hoped to escape Lincoln's persuasive republic. By using patronage, Lincoln hoped to strengthen antislavery persuasion where southerners might be most amenable.

Both these climactic antagonists had unusual leverage. South Carolina reactionaries could ignite a secession movement that could spread like wildfire, in the Lower South, if bullets flew. Lincoln could encourage a Border South Republican discourse that could alarm Carolina toward the first disunion. South Carolina despots preferred showdowns on the battlefield to democratic challenges in their hinterlands. Abraham Lincoln preferred defying the secessionists to surrendering majority rule and local persuasion. That inflammatory situation comprised a key reason why a closed slave labor society and an open free labor society, sharing the same republic but not the same view of how political systems must serve social systems, careened toward trial by war.[17]

7

Lincoln managed the slavery issue with aplomb during the interregnum, for his experience with the subject and theory about patronage helped him hit this ground running. Issues surrounding the Union's forts, however, unsettled a fledgling crisis manager, especially inexperienced with armies and administration. It was like standing at the unfamiliar Cooper Union rostrum, fumbling through an oration's first pages while summoning the confidence to triumph.

Not since mourning an adored mother and a beloved sister, plus suffering a grim father in Indiana's snake-ridden wilderness, had the melancholy Lincoln so wondered whether his talents could further his fortunes. His worried uncertainty studded his last correspondence from Springfield with uncharacteristic words: *"Strictly confidential," "For your own eye only," "Private," "Very Confidential," "Private & confidential."*[18] As he departed for Washington on February 11, 1861, a day before his fifty-second birthday, Lincoln confessed to Springfield neighbors that with his "strange, chequered past" crowding "upon my mind," he faced "a task more difficult than that which devolved upon General Washington. . . . Let us all pray that the God of our fathers may not forsake us now."[19]

During his trip to the inauguration, the anxious novice aspired to sell himself and his cause to worried citizens. He could have traveled 781 miles from his old home to his new in three days by transferring between the four fastest trains and foregoing public appearances. He chose instead to transfer between eighteen trains over a meandering 1,904 miles in twelve days, with incessant pauses to greet the folk.

The great orator thus subjected himself to his most frustrating oratorical tour since the 1856 Fremont campaign. A different version of the same problem invited his frustration. He again could not give folk what they came to hear. Four years earlier, his heavily Know-Nothing auditors had wished to hear his feelings about nativism's place in a Republican regime. He had not been able to tell them what he really thought without emptying the room.

Now, his listeners most wished to hear how he could save the Union without firing incriminating first shots. He could not tell his constituents because he wondered himself. Throughout his dawdling railroad journey, he waxed firm on refusing to tolerate disunion. He waned irresolute, however, on how to stop secession without pulling the first trigger.

He usually proclaimed that he ought not yet proclaim a plan. He would never reach Washington before Inauguration Day, March 4, he often claimed, if he had to explain his strategy incessantly en route. Prudence dictated announcing his intention just once, after studying all angles, on Inauguration Day.

With his second-most constant theme, he insisted that "there really is no crisis . . . except an *artificial one*, . . . gotten up . . . by designing politicians." Nothing is "going wrong. . . . Nobody is suffering anything." Leave the "artificial crisis . . . alone and it will go down of itself."[20]

But what if this hardly artificial confrontation would not go down by itself? In Philadelphia's Independence Hall on George Washington's birthday, Lincoln claimed that "no blood" will be "shed, unless it is forced upon the Government. The Government will not use force unless force is used against it." "Prolonged applause" erupted, accompanied with the cry, "that's the proper sentiment."[21]

A strategy of defense against southern aggression had indeed been Lincoln's proper sentiment ever since he announced it in the 1854 Peoria Address. Instead of attacking slavery inside the South, he had defended Kansas-Nebraska territory where slavery had never been, defended majority rule in Union against minority blackmail and disunion, and defended northern states' free soil against the alleged Douglas-Taney conspiracy to nationalize the South's Peculiar Institution. Now if the Confederacy fired obvious first shots against Union forts, many Unionists in the most northern South would leap behind his latest defense of *their* treasure too: their nation, undivided.

In late December, Lincoln had told a New York congressman that "if Mr. B surrenders the forts, I think they must be retaken."[22] Yet before Mr. B's watch ended, rebels had seized all but four forts, everywhere in the Confederacy.

Retaking so much governmental property would require multiple invasions, starting with the Lincoln administration's multiple first shots. That hail of invasive bullets might turn too many southerners, still clinging to Union, against a war starting with headline-making assaults on fellow Southrons.

To win the public relations game over who fired first shots, the new administration could try to maneuver rebels into blasting one of the four remaining Union forts on Confederate terrain. But what if the rebels refused to be maneuvered—just sat and waited until Union soldiers inside forts were starved out? That end game without incriminating shots looked likely at the most symbolically important Union-retained Lower South fortress, Fort Sumter in Charleston harbor.

During the interregnum, an exasperated Lincoln sometimes wondered whether retaking one of the Union's several dozen lost forts might be easier than tricking rebels into firing first at a retained fortress. Thinking out loud, he asked an Indianapolis crowd whether a government that "insists upon holding its own forts, *or retaking those forts which belong to it*," would be any more or less coercive? (emphasis mine).[23] He thus ignored the appearance of how combat commences. *Holding* a fort against a Confederate barrage could look like a defense. *Retaking* forts long since seized, after invading Confederate states, would look like an aggression.

The president-elect's Indianapolis speech also advertised his need to regrasp a secret of his prewar antislavery triumphs. He must never self-righteously ridicule the despots, in the manner of holier-than-thou abolitionists, or he would never win their consent. Yet in what Lincoln's Indiana partisans considered a corking bawdy joke, he likened secessionists' concept of Union to a "free-love arrangement," to be left whenever "passionate attraction" fades.

In place of a ridiculer's condescending tone, Lincoln needed his prewar modest affirmation that he was no better than wavering southerners and hardly had all the answers. Otherwise he would never woo southern Unionists who might otherwise join insulted brothers outside the Union, especially if *his* soldiers traveled far to spew many insulting first shots.

8

Lincoln's missing humble tone on matters military contrasted with three enchanted presentations on this otherwise discouraging interregnum trip. During the train travel, his wife usually remained unseen. Once, however, as he talked to Lancaster County, Pennsylvania, folk from the back of his car, he famously pulled Mary astride. He had "come out," he had been telling constituents, "to see them and let them see him, *in which he thought he had the best of the bargain!*" To clinch his case that he was the worst of the bargain, the ungainly giant "brought . . . out" his tiny better half. Look at "the long and the short of it," he urged. "Loud . . . laughter" and "enthusiastic cheers" erupted "as the train moved off."[24]

In another famous example of his populist instinct, the newly bewhiskered president-elect dove into a Westfield, New York, crowd, searching for eleven-year-old Grace Bedell. His youthful admirer had lately written him that if you "let your whiskers grow, . . . you would look a great deal better, for your face is so thin. All the ladies like whiskers and they would tease their husbands to vote for you and then you would be president."

In Westfield, Lincoln, sporting his new whiskers, apologized for still looking worse than the ladies. He then begged to thank the lass who had tried to remedy his predicament. "A small boy, mounted on a post . . . cried out 'There she is, Mr. LINCOLN.'" The president-elect "reached her" as she "was blushing all over her fair face, . . . and gave her several hearty kisses," amid "yells of delight from the excited crowd."[25]

The same exceptional public grace, rooted in the equality that Lincoln considered an American essence, inspired his greatest bit of a speech on this troubled trip. Lincoln had long been keeping his disdain for Know-Nothings under almost as careful disguise as his prayers for blacks' emancipation and for the same reason—he must condition the promptings of his heart with the practicality of his policies. To stop slavery's expansion into hitherto free territories, he had needed votes both from antislavery immigrants (especially Germans) and from anti-immigrant nativists. Only occasionally had he briefly allowed his anti–Know-Nothing hatred out of hiding, as in that "Hans, Baptiste, and Patrick" 1858 outburst.

New practicalities now opened. After the election, swelling disunion had made nativism less important, including to the nativists. With the next national polling distant, a cautious Republican could dare some egalitarian truths. Abraham Lincoln could come down from his Know-Nothing fence.

He rhetorically celebrated dismounting on his birthday night, February 12, in Cincinnati. He started his ten-minute oratorical gem by calling whites born in other countries "no better than any other people, nor any worse." Every white man has the "duty to improve" his "own condition" and "to assist in ameliorating mankind." We ought not heap "up greater burdens" on "foreigners, . . . borne down by . . . tyranny . . . abroad, who desire to make this the land of their adoption." In our "extensive and new" and "less densely populated" country, our "government" should instead cut up "the wild lands into parcels, so that every poor man may have a home."[26]

9

If most Lincoln moments on this trip had been as beguiling as Abraham's introduction of "the long and the short of it," his hug of Grace, and his embrace of immigrants, he might have better refreshed his bond with worried constituents. Instead, those moments remained fleeting. The details of his fort strategy seemed the key to the immediate future. Here he seemed to stumble between wise waiting for all the facts and vulnerable irresolution about bewildering predicaments.

Lincoln signaled a tougher stance, but without specifics, three days before this tour was scheduled to end. Speaking to the New Jersey legislature in Trenton on February 21, he again refused to "detail . . . the course I shall . . . pursue" on Union forts until using "all the information and all the time at my command." For now, he could only say that no one "is more devoted to peace than I am" or "would do more to preserve it. But it may be necessary to put the foot down firmly," he exclaimed as he slowly lifted, then stomped a foot. His "audience broke out into cheers so long and loud" that he could not be heard "for some moments."[27]

Yet what successful action could match these applauded words? The elusive answer must not feature a glaring federal first strike that would infuriate wavering southerners. His foot must look to be stomping in defense, as obviously as in Peoria. But how—how in the world—could he create that illusion out of the sorry fort material he inherited from Buchanan?

10

After he received another flattering reception upon arrival in Philadelphia that February 21, Lincoln looked forward to tomorrow's agenda. He planned to raise the flag over Independence Hall and then address the Pennsylvania legislature in Harrisburg. But before he could retire, he heard distressing news. Locked in his Philadelphia hotel room with Norman Judd and Allan Pinkerton, the famed detective, Lincoln received warnings about an alleged conspiracy to massacre him in Baltimore, the day after next.

Pinkerton pointed out that after arriving in enslaved Baltimore on the train from Philadelphia, the president-elect would have to traverse a mile-long crowded street between two railroad depots, to transfer to the train for Washington. The detective had heard that toughs conspired to engulf the president-elect en route, then slit his throat. Pinkerton urged sneaking through "Mobcity" rather than parading down Baltimore's perilous avenue. The detective also wished to steal the president-elect off to Washington

The hats back on the right heads! Allan Pinkerton (*left*), master detective, wearing his "Kossuth" hat, and Abraham Lincoln, wearing his signature stovepipe hat, at Antietam battlefield, October 3, 1862

immediately. Only after arriving safely, counseled Pinkerton, should the endangered traveler send regrets about canceling his Pennsylvania agenda.

Lincoln winced at the probable widespread verdict. Auditors might think that today's raised boot in Trenton had camouflaged a coward, too inexperienced and frightened for tomorrow's storm. He dodged the coward label for a day by refusing to cancel the morrow's Pennsylvania appointments. But he agreed to be spirited away afterward. By traveling incognito the next night, he would duck appearing in Baltimore in broad daylight.

On February 22, after his last appointment in Harrisburg, he disappeared. No one paid attention when a drab train from Harrisburg arrived early at West Philadelphia's depot. Allan Pinkerton hustled Lincoln into a darkened carriage that aimlessly traversed the streets until the detective banged on the ceiling, signaling full speed ahead to the main Philadelphia station.

As the slightly stooped giant disembarked and crept toward the train to Baltimore, his defining appendages were absent. No tiny Mary graced his arm. Instead Kate Warne, Pinkerton's tough-looking twenty-three-year-old assistant and one of America's first female detectives, clutched his coat, thrown over his shoulders and hiding his huge fists. His usual rigid black stovepipe hat also remained hidden. Instead, his "Kossuth" hat seemed to announce someone else's head. After all, who can imagine Abraham Lincoln crowned with a soft gray short topping, featuring the round wide brim on one side pulled nattily down and a bright long feather gracing the opposite curve?

The widowed Madame Kate, playing a young sister guiding an aging brother, delivered the "invalid" to a private railroad car. The train pulled away from Philadelphia, unnoticed. It arrived at Baltimore's President Street Depot, unsuspected. Horses dragged Lincoln's car a mile through the dark and empty streets, undiscovered. At the Camden Street Depot, the imminent titan's conveyance was coupled to the train to Washington, undetected. At 6:00 AM, the president-elect arrived in his new "hometown." He immediately rode a hack to his preinaugural residence, Washington's Willard Hotel. He left Kate and the "Kossuth" hat forever behind. His inauguration, where he had promised to reveal plans about those confounded forts, loomed nine days ahead.

21

The Troubled Inaugural Address

❧❦❧

On March 4 at noon, the imminent president, upon emerging from the Willard Hotel, risked public view for the first time since departing from Allan Pinkerton. Winfield Scott's troops immediately surrounded his barouche and remained throughout the Inaugural Parade. With federal soldiers substituting a manly shield for Madame Kate's feminine wiles, the concealed president-elect wore his signature stovepipe hat instead of that quaint (on him) "Kossuth." But this time, Lincoln meant to become the protector rather than the protected. If his Inaugural Address saved the nation from secession, detectives and troops might no longer need to spare him from assassination.

1

Early in 1861, Clark Smith had given Lincoln time and space to draft the address. Smith, married to Mary Todd Lincoln's sister, Ann Todd Smith, had lent his brother-in-law the boon of time by chaperoning Mary and Bob Lincoln (now a Harvard freshman) during a late January 1861 New York City visit. Lincoln's wife had purchased extravagantly, assuming that her First Lady responsibilities and her husband's twenty-five-thousand-dollar annual presidential salary at last justified splurging. Her breakout in the Big City instead augured a rift in their relationship that would widen in the Executive Mansion.

Clark Smith's gift of space, bestowed before squiring Mary and Bob around Manhattan, released Lincoln from distracting visitors. Lincoln's distractions, beyond Mary's spending, would multiply in the presidential mansion. But in simpler Springfield's modest Yates & Smith, selling "Boots, Shoes," and "Fancy Dry Goods" on Capitol Square, Clark Smith prepared a top-floor cubbyhole for Lincoln, reached through Clark's private office. While Smith and his two wards spread their wings in New York City, Lincoln crammed his frame into a minuscule oasis and drafted his Inaugural Address.

2

As Lincoln wrote his draft, the seven Lower South states completed their revolution. The four Middle South states, with a third of the southern population, and the four Border South states, with another third of Dixie's people (and over half its industries), hung back. If southern Unionists retained control of the eight states, the Confederacy would be staggering. If all southern states seceded, Abraham Lincoln would be stricken. If the Middle South departed the Union but the Border South remained, a civil war could turn long and brutal.

With his Inaugural Address draft, the great orator sought to stall secession with language before guns escalated disunion with bloodshed.[1] He would eliminate, his words soothed, not slavery but only its extension. Rebels believe "slavery is *right,* and ought to be extended." We believe "it is *wrong,* and ought not to be extended." That is "the only dispute."

Minorities must obey a majority's nonextension decree, continued Lincoln's draft, until they win a subsequent election. "A constitutional majority is the only true sovereign of a free people. . . . Unanimity is impossible." Minority rule is "inadmissible." Rejecting majority rule ensures "anarchy or despotism."

Lincoln struggled with Confederates' retort: that a minority's right of revolution supersedes a majority's right to rule. Confederate president Jefferson Davis's Inaugural Address praised "the Declaration of Independence" for broadcasting an "inalienable" revolutionary "right." Confederates, Davis cheered, uphold democrats' supreme idea: "Governments rest on the consent of the governed." By deploying its right of revolution to withdraw its consent to be governed, a minority revokes a majority's right to rule.[2]

Abraham Lincoln cherished Davis's premises. In the 1847 U.S. Congress, the Illinoisan had lauded Texans' revolt against Mexico. In his suggested January 9, 1852, resolutions on Hungarian freedom, drafted in Springfield, he had reiterated "the right of any people . . . to throw off" their "government, and to establish such other . . . as they may choose."[3] Then how could the Rail-splitter deny southerners' natural right to choose another government?

To Lincoln's exasperation, his best answer could yield his worst result. No legitimate natural rights revolution, he thought, could seek to preserve an unnatural republican monstrosity. But neither his Inaugural Address draft nor any subsequent speech dared publicize this conviction. Many southern Unionists, Lincoln knew, opposed a disunion revolution only because they thought his menace to slavery dubious. By declaring a revolution to save slavery automatically "wicked," Lincoln could clear the Union of southerners.

Only once, in an unpublished and scotched draft of his message to Congress, July 4, 1861, did he stray even halfway down the politically forbidden path. There, his pen scratched that "the right of revolution" only becomes "a moral right when exercised for a morally justifiable cause." Otherwise, "revolution is no right but simply a wicked exercise of physical power."

Yet even in this suppressed exclamation, Lincoln omitted the clinching sentence: that a revolution to save unnatural slavery wickedly perverts natural rights. Recognizing that he verged on forbidden terrain if he meant to retain anyone south of Illinois, Lincoln eliminated the provocative preliminary sentences before sending Congress the July 4, 1861, message.[4]

By swallowing his supreme argument against slaveholders' right of revolution, Lincoln might seem a cowardly republican. But this Republican had often underplayed impractical moral revulsions, in order to achieve practical moral priorities. He had crawled toward barring slave extension southward. He had only tardily, briefly, and vaguely mentioned slavery's "ultimate extinction." He had only once expressed distaste for masters' sexual transgressions. He had usually bitten his lip about Know-Nothings' disenfranchisements. By hiding his conviction that enslavers, when revolting to preserve immoral slavery, automatically became immoral revolutionaries, the president-elect brought the biographical trend to revealing climax.

3

Lincoln's Inauguration Address draft fell back on his secondary (and more dubious) argument against secessionists' natural rights legitimacy. Before smashing a government, the Declaration of Independence had proclaimed, rightful rebels must face a mortal threat to lives, property, or sacred honor. But slaveholding rebels, according to Lincoln's draft, confronted no such peril. Disunionists allege, scoffed the president-elect, that Republicans *"avowed . . . to destroy"* slavery. But "to my knowledge," Lincoln's draft soared, "no . . . Republican . . . has ever avowed . . . any such purpose."

That *no* defied reality. Lincoln's southern federal appointments carried antislavery purposes. Equally assuredly, Radical Republicans hoped to ignite a "ring of fire" around slave states. Some hoped additionally to fan fires inside. They would inspire fugitive slaves and nonslaveholding heretics to rise against the master class. By pretending that *no* Republican desired such infernos, Lincoln would hardly convince southern Unionists.

His draft also offered nothing to ease southern Unionists' apprehension about civil war. Many southern enemies of secession would side with the rebels if the Union fired first shots. En route to Washington, the president-elect had repeatedly promised that his Inaugural Address would announce a peaceable strategy for retaining Charleston's Fort Sumter and Pensacola's Fort Pickens. But his speech's draft suggested no way he could avoid a choice between shattering the peace and abandoning the forts.

Worse, his draft suggested that *he* might order first shots. In early 1861 private letters, Lincoln had insisted that respectable governments must recapture stolen possessions. In Indianapolis, he had called reclaiming seized property as mandatory as preventing new seizures. His Inauguration Address draft accordingly announced that he would "*reclaim* . . . public property and places" (emphasis mine). His draft pledged "no invasion of any State . . . beyond what may be necessary for these" objectives.[5]

Some promise to limit invasion! *Reclaiming* federal property would require invading seven seceded states. Then who would seem the aggressor? The answer would likely mock the Inauguration Address draft's concluding sentence: "With *you,* and not with *me,* is the solemn question of 'Shall it be peace, or a sword?'"[6]

4

Statesmen often request commentary on troubled speeches' drafts. The prewar Lincoln, however, had vetted an oration only once before. Then he had changed nothing in his House Divided Address, despite allies' withering criticisms.

Before leaving Springfield, in contrast, a worried president-elect prepared for several prespeech appraisals of the Inaugural Address draft. In early February, Lincoln asked William Bailhache, publisher of Republicans' *Illinois Daily State Journal,* to make secret copies of the handwritten draft. Bailhache printed a dozen duplicates and then disassembled the type. The president-elect hid the documents in a black satchel, entrusted to son Bob when leaving Springfield.

Upon arrival in Indianapolis on February 11, Bob handed the satchel to a Bates Hotel clerk. He then trotted off to party while his father strode off to speak. Later that evening, the older Lincoln asked for the satchel. Harvard's new freshman shamefacedly confessed the handoff.

With "a look of stupefaction," reflecting "visions" of the unrevised "Inaugural in all the next morning's newspapers," the president-elect "forced his way through the crowded corridor" to the hotel office. Upon hearing that his satchel likely lay amid yonder "small mountain of carpetbags," Lincoln attacked the pile. He plunged his key into similar valises. The key worked. A half-dozen searches failed. Strangers' playing cards, whiskey flasks, and torn clothing tumbled from satchels, while onlookers tittered. Finally, gaslights flickered on the speech, shining like gold in sunlight to the relieved traveler.[7]

Consequences swiftly became indisputably golden. Lincoln had urgently searched partly because his Illinois friend, Orville Browning, headed home on the morrow. Lincoln coveted Browning's critique of the draft. Thanks to the frantic search, Lincoln handed the troubled document to the friendly critic before Browning's departure.

Five days later, Browning mailed Lincoln his only suggestion. The president-elect should expunge the pledge "to reclaim the public property and places which have fallen." He should pledge only "to hold" not yet fallen property and places. Browning agreed with Lincoln that fallen forts should be recaptured. You can, however, reclaim federal installations as "well, or even better, without announcing the purpose in your inaugural." Lincoln accepted the canny revision.[8]

Without Browning's or any other advisor's urging, Lincoln also wisely subtracted the draft's unsupportable premise that "*no*" Republican sought abolition. The president-elect instead urged that *he* sought no peril to slavery. *He* sought only to stop slavery's expansion.

Secessionists retorted that Radical Republicans would pressure Lincoln to move beyond nonextension. Moreover, Lincoln's own slightly forward march, featuring Republicans appointed to federal offices inside the South, sought a southern debate on the antidemocratic institution, within slaves' and nonslaveholders' hearing. That specter had helped provoke South Carolinians, trusting only a closed slaveholder society, to secede from Lincoln's open democracy before it was too late.

Many southerners conceived that South Carolinians exaggerated Lincoln's immediate menace. They preferred to wait and see what the supposedly dangerous Lincoln actually did. Still, at least half the Southrons who remained inside would leap outside if Republicans fired a civil war's first shot. Did Lincoln so intend, at Fort Sumter or Fort Pickens or elsewhere? If not, how would he enforce Union laws inside rebel-held terrain?

On March 4, 1861, Lincoln still had no answers. His final Inaugural Address embraced the best poor alternative. He accepted most of William H. Seward's many slight verbal suggestions to soften his evasion. Where Lincoln's first draft, for example, climactically stormed that

> With *you,* and not with *me,* is the solemn question of "shall it be peace, or a sword?"

Seward famously (and woodenly) suggested a soothing climax:

> The mystic chords which proceeding from so many battlefields and so many patriot graves [and] pass through all the hearts and all the hearths in this broad continent of ours will yet again harmonize in their ancient music when breathed upon by the guardian angel of the nation.[9]

Lincoln more famously (and more poetically) climactically lulled with:

> The mystic chords of memory, stretching from every battle-field and patriot grave, to every living heart and hearthstone, all over this broad land, will yet swell the chorus of the Union, when again touched, as surely they will be, by the better angels of our nature.[10]

In print, Lincoln's stylistic superiority overwhelms. But at the inauguration, jarring forebodings made lovely rhythms underwhelming. Apprehensive citizens, impatient to hear how their leader could squelch disunion without firing first shots, deplored his failure to provide his promised solution. Unless the inaugurated president solved the problem swiftly, the Union's remaining two-thirds of southerners might fatally dwindle.

Everything he had learned from past crises warned against seizing the offensive. No one excelled Lincoln at relying exclusively on strategies of defense. Yet how could he defend a fort without an offensive first shot if the enemy fired no shot—just sat and waited until his starving men departed? Only after six presidential weeks would he see how to bring the epic of becoming Lincoln to a proper prewar finale.

22

Forts Sumter and Pickens
and the Emergence of
an Impressive Administrator

❧⊰⊱❧

Since the Civil War's first shots savaged Charleston's Fort Sumter, Pensacola's Fort Pickens has faded in the important story of how the epic commenced. The oversimplification blurs Pickens's significance before March 28 and Lincoln's critical shift thereafter.[1] A day after his March 4 inauguration, the president adopted a fused strategy for both forts. On March 28, Lincoln's fusion, as he put it, *"fizzled."*

Within a week, the alarmed commander-in-chief and his advisors developed severed Pensacola and Charleston tactics. Within another week, their ingenious strategy of defense at Fort Sumter sought to turn an inevitable loss into a winner. The team built on strategies of defending against aggressive slaveholders that Lincoln had deployed since the 1854 Peoria Address. This time, the tactical finesse pinned the onus for starting the brothers' war on the Confederacy. As leader of the brilliant replanning, the inexperienced chief executive maximized others' contributions and added a decisive wrinkle, thereby emerging as an impressive administrator.

1

Both Forts Sumter and Pickens dominated islands inside important harbors. After secession, both empty shells provided havens for Union soldiers. The night of December 26, 1860, it will be remembered, six days after South Carolina seceded, U.S. Major Robert Anderson moved his eighty-five federal soldiers from paltry Fort Moultrie to massive Fort Sumter, guarding Charleston's Atlantic Ocean outlet.

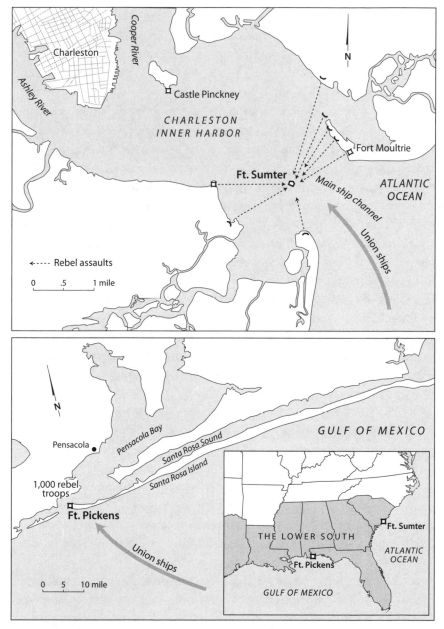

Charleston

Cooper River

Ashley River

Castle Pinckney

CHARLESTON
INNER HARBOR

Ft. Sumter

Fort Moultrie

ATLANTIC
OCEAN

Main ship channel

Union ships

N

←---- Rebel assaults

0   .5   1 mile

N

Pensacola

Pensacola Bay

Santa Rosa Sound

Santa Rosa Island

GULF OF MEXICO

1,000 rebel
troops

Ft. Pickens

Union ships

0   5   10 mile

THE LOWER SOUTH

Ft. Sumter

ATLANTIC
OCEAN

Ft. Pickens

GULF OF MEXICO

Forts Sumter and Pickens

Then on January 10, the day after Florida seceded, U.S. First Lieutenant Adam Slemmer transferred his eighty-two Union troops from vulnerable mainland barracks near Pensacola, Florida, to formidable Fort Pickens on Santa Rosa Island. The long, thin island stretched along narrow Pensacola Bay waters, separating the mainland from the Gulf of Mexico. Fort Pickens, on Santa Rosa Island's western tip, controlled Pensacola's Gulf outlet.

These two piles, the last major Union-held forts in the seven prewar Confederate states, differed in a critical way. Confederate batteries encircled Fort Sumter, repulsing Union resupply from all directions. Confederate armaments, in contrast, guarded only Fort Pickens's Pensacola side, inviting Union reinforcements from the Gulf of Mexico.

The consequence: the Union soon had to surrender the more vulnerable Charleston fortress while consolidating the more impregnable Pensacola bulwark. Fort Pickens, together with the Union's two lesser Gulf forts, Taylor and Jefferson in the Florida Keys, would protect Lincoln's Civil War fleet as it swept from the Atlantic via the Gulf, toward dominance of the Mississippi.

Before cannon pounded, however, both Pickens and Sumter counted symbolically more than militarily. The fortresses demonstrated that the Union still ruled some of the Confederacy's claimed terrain. Symbolically, Fort Sumter, threatening Charleston's first revolutionaries, loomed larger than Fort Pickens, menacing Florida's follow-up rebels. But during Lincoln's presidency's initial twenty-four days, the new chief executive hoped that an easily reinforced Fort Pickens would continue to enforce federal law, if Fort Sumter had to be surrendered. That trade-off might somewhat mollify the Upper South, still undecided about secession and cursing the thought that Lincoln's first shots might provoke war against southern brethren.

2

Federals' staying power in Fort Pickens, compared to their fragile hold on Fort Sumter, became glaring before President-elect Lincoln assumed the presidency. On January 9, 1861, on the one hand, Confederate cannon easily repulsed the Union's *Star of the West* from reinforcing Fort Sumter. In late January, on the other hand, federals' *Brooklyn,* carrying Captain Israel Vogdes's company of U.S. soldiers, steamed unimpeded toward Fort Pickens. Vogdes's warriors could double Fort Pickens's troops.[2]

On January 13–14, Pensacola rebels briefly jailed three U.S. messengers. Continued arrests and longer imprisonments could cripple communications between Fort Pickens and Washington. While trains sped couriers from Washington to Pensacola in three to four days, messengers risked city detention before catching a boat to the island fort. By sailing the Gulf route to or from Fort Pickens, in contrast, Washington's messengers could bypass Pensacola interference. Still, a one-way sea journey took over a week longer than landed travel.

In late January, Florida rebels desired to halt reinforcements more than delay communications. If the Union kept would-be reinforcing soldiers outside Fort Pickens, Confederate authorities proposed, Pensacola rebels would cease interfering with the area's federal troops, including their interchanges with Washington. On January 28, U.S. President James Buchanan accepted this informal "Truce of Fort Pickens." The terms left federals untouched inside Fort Pickens, potential reinforcing Union troops unimpeded aboard ships anchored nearby, and contacts with Washington unobstructed.[3]

Washington's first post-treaty messenger, speeding by train to Pensacola and by boat across Pensacola Bay, arrived at Fort Pickens before the *Brooklyn* lumbered in via the Gulf. War Department orders, commanding obedience to the new truce and delivered to Captain Israel Vogdes upon his February 6 arrival, kept his eighty-eight federal troops huddled aboard ship. But if Abraham Lincoln wished easy reinforcement of a symbolic fort within four days of inauguration, he could dispatch a train-borne messenger, traveling under the truce and bearing orders for Vogdes's troops to surge into Fort Pickens.

3

On Inauguration Day, Lincoln knew nothing about Israel Vogdes's possibilities at Pickens or about Robert Anderson's impossibilities at Sumter. Subsequent outgoing presidents sometimes briefed incoming presidents. James Buchanan shared nothing with Abraham Lincoln until March 4. Then the retiring chief executive whispered, "I think you will find the water of the right-hand well of the White House better than that at the left."[4] The president-elect did not chuckle.

The next morning, the War Department delivered Major Robert Anderson's dismal communiqué from Fort Sumter, received on Inauguration Day. The major reported that in six weeks, Fort Sumter troops would have no rations and no hope of resupply. That same March 5, the new commander-in-chief also heard that near Fort Pickens, enough U.S. troops to double the fortress's manpower hovered on the *Brooklyn,* awaiting a presidential order to step ashore.

Lincoln instantly envisioned compensation for Fort Sumter's likely surrender. Before Anderson departed Sumter, the Union could reinforce its other symbolic fort. Northern Republicans would cheer. Then, having acted against disunion at Fort Pickens, Lincoln could abandon Fort Sumter peacefully, claiming military necessity. Border and Middle South Unionists would applaud—and might not secede.

Before retiring on March 5, the new president *orally* commanded his highest-ranking general, Lieutenant-General Winfield Scott, to order Captain Israel Vogdes's company, still aboard the *Brooklyn,* to occupy Fort Pickens. Six days later, Lincoln learned that Scott had sent nothing to Vogdes.[5] The president, having seldom administered anything, had discovered that orders from the top sometimes disappear down below.

Having learned to avoid *oral* orders, the novice commander *wrote* to Winfield Scott on March 11, directing Captain Vogdes's company ashore. Lincoln left General Scott free to choose how to convey the command to Vogdes. The deferral allowed Scott's deteriorating faculties and dread of civil war to slow the order's transmission disastrously.

The seventy-four-year-old lieutenant-general had been a precocious brigadier-general at age twenty-seven, conqueror of Mexico City during the Mexican War, and Whig nominee for president in 1852. Now he was a physical wreck. An inch taller than the towering Lincoln and more than a hundred pounds heavier, Scott could no longer mount a horse or walk unaided on gout-ravaged feet. Acute dropsy, excruciating rheumatism, and dizzying vertigo further slowed thinking and movement.

Worse, Scott's memory had slipped. He evidently forgot that in mid-January, three federal envoys to Fort Pickens had been released only hours after their Pensacola arrest. Thereafter, "The Truce of Fort Pickens" had eliminated arrests, inviting three times faster Union communications via trains to and fro Pensacola.

Still worse for quickly ordering Vogdes into Fort Pickens, Scott, a Virginia Unionist, prayed that peace might soothe secessionists toward reunion. The lieutenant-general loathed the president's March 5 oral command to reinforce Fort Pickens, if he ever heard it (and perhaps Scott never did, whether because of deafness or bureaucratic snafus or convictions about proper strategy). When Lincoln *wrote* the follow-up order, the aged warrior obeyed with all deliberate slowness.

Neither Fort Pickens nor the *Brooklyn* could receive telegrams. A train traveler bearing commands from Washington to Pensacola, to repeat a key fact, arrived within four days. Travel by Gulf ship took around three times longer. Lincoln's two-fort strategy prioritized speed. Israel Vogdes had to reinforce Pickens before Robert Anderson starved in Sumter.

Winfield Scott instead prioritized peace. He sent the order to Vogdes slowly via the Gulf, guaranteeing that delivery would take at least eleven days.[6]

The general and his staff almost doubled the minimum. Scott's subordinate squandered a full day writing the message and two more days sending it. The War Department lost four more days by dispatching the order indirectly to Key West instead of nonstop to Pensacola. Lincoln's March 11 command reached Captain Vogdes only as April dawned, with Fort Sumter's troops almost out of rations. Because of subsequent delays, Vogdes's troops would enter Fort Pickens only after the first-shot drama climaxed at Fort Sumter.

4

Earlier in March, Lincoln had assumed that Fort Pickens's reinforcement (and thus symbolic cover for Fort Sumter's surrender) would swiftly occur. He thus turned his attention to patronage appointments. The swerve may seem counterproductive during a crisis. Lincoln differed. He considered party the producer of action, turning talk into legislation. He viewed patronage as the fuel of party, paying bills for a blessing. He envisioned appointments as levers of balance, smoothing factions into compatriots. He saw Republican patronage appointments in the Border South as his best presidential beginning, to achieve slavery's peaceful "ultimate extinction."

Eleven years earlier, as Zachary Taylor's presidential term began and Lincoln's congressional term expired, the Illinoisan had sought appointment as General Land Office commissioner. His undeserved (he thought) rejection had initiated five years of powerlessness. That ugly memory nourished his latter-day obsession with early-term presidential patronage.

Under Buchanan, Democrats had occupied 1,520 presidential-appointed offices. Lincoln dismissed 1,195. Others dismissed themselves by seceding with their states. Lincoln replaced each departed Democrat with a Republican. The Illinois Whig Party's state repairman of the early 1840s had morphed into the Republican Party's national engineer.[7]

In March 1861, Republican applicants crowded the Executive Mansion's East Room. Others lined up out the doors and down the path. A later sympathizer, noting Lincoln's tormented appearance, asked whether trouble afflicted the battlefield. "It isn't the war," Lincoln replied. "It is the post office in Brownsville, Missouri."[8]

5

During his first presidential month, Lincoln finished all-day patronage interviews around 9:00 PM. Dinner with Mary followed. Only later could he concentrate on his forts. For three weeks, he had the luxury of assuming that

Israel Vogdes, by reinforcing Fort Pickens, could ease public swallowing of Fort Sumter's surrender.

At a March 15 cabinet meeting, Lincoln's team unanimously approved his Pickens strategy. Sumter tactics invited more dispute. Secretary of State William H. Seward urged that surrendering Fort Sumter, whatever happened in Pensacola, might lure Confederates back to Union. The supposedly more radical contender for the Republican presidential nomination now appeared more compromising than the victorious moderate.

Only two cabinet members dissented from Seward's reasoning. The key dissenter, Postmaster Montgomery (Monty) Blair, age forty-seven, was the only cabinet member younger than the fifty-two-year-old president. The chief winced at older advisors' fuddy-duddy tones and fancied the Blairs. Monty's brother Frank Blair Junior, the only prewar southern Republican congressman, embodied Lincoln's hope that presidential patronage could strengthen a Border South antislavery party.

Frank Blair Senior (Monty and Frank Junior's father) stormed Lincoln's office on March 11. The elder Blair, formerly President Andrew Jackson's advisor, demanded that Lincoln tame Charleston rebels as decisively as Old Hickory had quenched 1832–33 nullifiers. Surrendering "Fort Sumter," the patriarch thundered, would compound "treason with treason." Later, conceding that accusing a president of treason may have been "impertinent," the antique asked Monty to make any necessary "apology."⁹

Lincoln wanted no apologies from the Blairs. He believed that the Border South clan made more sense than other advisors. At least the Blairs regretted Fort Sumter's likely fall; and a Blair in-law's proposal to save the fortress interested the president.

The proposer, former navy captain Gustavus Fox, had married a Levi Woodbury daughter, as had Monty Blair. The elder Woodbury and senior Blair had together served as President Jackson's advisors. Gus Fox, now a Massachusetts businessman, admired a Crimean War tactic. Before Lincoln's administration commenced, the ex-navy captain had visited Washington, championing the ploy's utility at Fort Sumter.¹⁰

Fox wished to transport reinforcing troops, provisions, and warships to a rendezvous point on the Atlantic, ten miles from Charleston harbor. Then under hopefully dark night skies, small steam tugboats might sneak reinforcements past Confederate batteries, guarding the harbor's entrance, and deliver the lifesavers to nearby Fort Sumter. If sneak attackers suffered premature discovery, Union ships might rescue the martyrs. On March 13, Monty Blair brought his brother-in-law to the White House to press the scheme.

Abraham Lincoln asked Fox to repeat the presentation at the March 15 cabinet meeting. From Lincoln's perspective, the cabinet too quickly rejected Gus Fox's gamble. The president conceded the scheme's risks. The turbulent Atlantic might deter ships' rendezvous, and a bright night might doom tugboats' sneak toward Fort Sumter.

Still, no alternative to Sumter's surrender surfaced, a devastating fact if Israel Vogdes's reinforcement at Fort Pickens failed. Lincoln would then have to invade other Confederate state(s) and assault ex-federal fort(s), with *his* first shots blazing. Southern Unionists continued to find such invasive aggression against southern brothers unacceptable.

On March 19, the increasingly worried president, hearing no news from Fort Pickens, asked Fox to visit Fort Sumter and reevaluate the tugboat plan. Lincoln also asked two friends to reexplore Charleston opinions. Lincoln suspected that when Seward urged that peace could lure rebels back, the misunderstanding exceeded any Fox miscalculation.

Gus Fox found what he wanted to find at Fort Sumter. At night on water's edge, he could barely hear a rowboat approaching. Meanwhile, Lincoln's two other traveling informants found only one Charleston whisper for reunion.

When the trio reported back to Lincoln, the president winced at his options. In March 24–27 meetings with Fox, Lincoln clarified that he still preferred Vogdes's reinforcement at Pickens to tugboat gambles at Sumter. But if Vogdes failed in Pensacola, Lincoln conceded, Fox's gambit in Charleston might have to be risked.

Fox answered that time for contingency planning narrowed. In two weeks, Fort Sumter troops would starve. Why not order the War and Navy Departments to prepare for Sumter's possible last-minute rescue? Concurring, Lincoln asked Fox to write "preliminary orders" for ships and equipment. He should deliver the provisional "memo" to the Executive Mansion and the departments before leaving for New York early on March 28.[11]

"Preliminary" rightly described Gus Fox's "preparations." Nothing had been decided. Yet the heightened alert nourished Lincoln's leap to a false conclusion that afternoon, ushering in the midpoint of the Sumter/Pickens drama.

6

A newspaper item, noticed in the Executive Mansion, apparently on March 28, stung the president into action. The newspaper reported that the *Brooklyn* steamed away from Pensacola, four hundred miles to Key West, to collect supplies. The news alarmed Lincoln. Captain Vogdes's men, he supposed, bobbed at sea on their ship, somewhere in the Gulf! Far-off warriors could hardly secure Fort Pickens's reinforcement before Fort Sumter's starvation.[12]

Winfield Scott, Lincoln hoped, could shed light on the apparent disaster. That evening, Mary would give her first state dinner. General Scott had accepted an invitation. In the late afternoon, Lincoln summoned the lieutenant-general "at once."[13]

Upon Scott's hurried arrival, Lincoln discerned that the general knew nothing about the *Brooklyn*'s journey to Key West. Nor did Scott know where the ship bearing the March 12 command, ordering Israel Vogdes into Pickens, might now be wandering. Nor did Scott wish Lincoln's command delivered. The nation's leading general advised his commander to evacuate Fort Sumter *and* Fort Pickens! Soothing news of Union troops' double departure, the Virginian claimed, might retain southern Unionists and regain departed rebels.

The president answered this "cold shock," as he put it, with a rare (for him) tirade. My "administration," roared the commander-in-chief, "would be broken up" without a "more decided policy." If General Scott could not carry out his superior's "views, some other person might!" The old hero, unaccustomed to a withering, limped away.[14]

That night at Mary's dinner, no guest discerned the bantering host's fury. Only after the feast did Abraham pull cabinet members aside. Lincoln whispered his discovery and urged teammates to convene at noon on the morrow, Good Friday.

That night, the chief executive could not sleep. The next lunchtime, Lincoln said little until all had spoken. Then he asked colleagues to write their thoughts, to inform his later reconsiderations. While he had usually been an oratorical lone ranger during familiar peacetime situations, he clearly wished his team's full participation in unfamiliar wartime decisions.

Past experiences with collaboration eased Lincoln's transition. His climb as a lawyer had mixed characteristically private studies with some aid, especially Stephen Logan's lessons. Then, as party architect, he had sometimes merged his usual solo planning with bids for support. His graceful surrender in 1855, to ex-Democrats' insistence on Lyman Trumbull for U.S. senator, had gathered champions of his 1856 vice-presidential bid. So, too, his humble self-mockery at the early 1856 Decatur Editors' Convention had collected journalistic voices for defending only previously unenslaved territories. Now the famous self-helper wished more assistance with more bewildering wartime puzzles.

As the Illinoisan listened to welcome advice, he preferred not to be called Mr. President. He fancied "Lincoln." He squirmed at the cabinet table as if at a country auction. One foot sprawled atop the table at a weird angle, then the other at a weirder angle, until both crashed, entwined like a pretzel.

The thud, like much about this oddly shaped giant, invited underestimation. A few wartime advisors would continually patronize the (they thought) oaf. But most early 1860s colleagues savored this midwesterner's rough-hewn equality, not in voting (after everyone exclaimed, he decided) but in shaping his verdict.

During the March 29, 1861, lunchtime meeting, all cabinet members supported Fort Pickens's reinforcement. In contrast, almost half the cabinet, led by William H. Seward, favored Fort Sumter's surrender rather than Gus Fox's tugboats. Only Gideon Welles urged an enhanced tugboat scheme.

Before tugboats approached Sumter, Welles suggested, rebels should be notified that incoming soldiers would be landed only if Confederates repulsed incoming provisions. After the warning, rebels might prefer allowing more rations to facing more troops. Still, Welles conceded that the notice had "little probability" of deterring rebels from mauling Fox's tugboats.[15]

Lincoln saw the greater probability. Welles's *non*-surprise attack would destroy any chance that tugboats could sneak past Confederate cannon. Worse, alerted rebels might merely scare off hapless tugboats with a few splashing cannonballs, repeating the *Star of the West*'s nonevidence about who commenced civil war. To transform a Welles-style notice with "little probability" of success into a game winner, a first-shot strategy with more bite had to be concocted.

7

While the president pondered improvement of Fox-Welles tactics, Seward campaigned against any version of Welles's memo. The secretary of state had secretly promised Confederates an imminent withdrawal from Sumter! Even had Seward never issued that promise, the first officer of the cabinet, lately a disappointed second for the Republican nomination, might have stormed at becoming second to Welles at the administration's first policy decision.

Lincoln meant to salvage the important Seward. As partisan of reinforcing Fort Pickens instead of Fort Sumter, the secretary of state could leave Winfield Scott's crawling Pensacola effort in the dust. On Good Friday afternoon, after the cabinet meeting, Lincoln summoned Seward. Did the secretary know any military leader, young, vigorous, and informed, who might rescue the Florida fortress? Seward did. Lincoln asked to see the fresh face immediately.

Seward swiftly reappeared with the U.S. Army Corp of Engineers' Captain Montgomery Meigs (Lincoln's future quartermaster general). "Monty"

Meigs, forty-four years old and a husky six-foot, two-inch presence, exuded the manly force that Seward knew Lincoln craved, after Winfield Scott. The captain could mount a horse, cheered the secretary, no less than engineer military and civic triumphs. Meigs's credits included building the Washington Aqueduct (conveying freshwater from Great Falls to the fetid city) and remodeling the Capitol Building (that unfinished backdrop for Lincoln's unfinished fort policy at the inaugural).[16]

Lincoln informed Meigs that the previous late afternoon, Scott had confessed disapproval of reinforcing Fort Pickens. The disapproving lieutenant-general, continued Lincoln's report of yesterday's earthquake, did not know whether troops ordered to reinforce Pickens had instead sailed toward Key West. Since his orders had apparently "fizzled out," the exasperated president inquired, "could Fort Pickens" still "be held?"

Of course, Meigs thundered, unless "the Navy" has "lost it already." To reinforce Pickens properly, added Seward, Lincoln should listen to this vigorous "young man" rather than "any old general." Lincoln promised to let them "know in a day or two."[17]

This monumental Good Friday had started horrendously, amid trepidation that Fort Sumter would fall before apparently far-off troops could reinforce Fort Pickens. The day had ended auspiciously, with possibilities that Seward (and Meigs) might salvage power in Pensacola, while Fox (and Welles) might save face at Sumter. Upon returning to family quarters, the commander-in-chief, having not slept the night before, suffered violent headaches. The next night, he "keeled over," and Mary had to put him in bed.

8

The Pickens situation was worse than the exhausted Lincoln imagined, although not for the reason he supposed. The newspaper rumor erred. Vogdes's troops were not aboard the *Brooklyn,* heading toward Key West. Vogdes had transferred them to the federal warship *Sabine,* anchored near Pensacola, before the *Brooklyn* departed. The War Department learned the happier truth in a Vogdes communiqué, received in early April.[18]

Since the erroneous newspaper report had triggered Lincoln's Good Friday uproar, one might think that false news here classically shaped ensuing real news. But accurate news about Pensacola swiftly became more important. On Easter morning (March 31), Major Erasmus Keyes, Winfield Scott's military secretary, told his superior that his research seemed to reveal an unsalvageable Fort Pickens.

Go tell William H. Seward, ordered Scott. Minutes later, Keyes informed the secretary of state that General Scott had ordered him to warn of difficulties at Fort Pickens. "I don't care about the difficulties," screeched Seward. Find Captain Meigs "and bring him here."

Scott's military secretary swiftly returned with the captain who had impressed Lincoln on Good Friday. Seward ordered Monty Meigs and Erasmus Keyes to present Lincoln with a detailed plan to save Fort Pickens at 3:00 PM that very Easter afternoon.

The two planners arrived early, thanks in part to Keyes's previous research. In preparation for advising Scott that morning, Keyes had discovered that rebels massed a thousand troops across Pensacola Bay from the fort. Adam Slemmer's eighty-two men inside Pickens, even if reinforced with Israel Vogdes's eighty-eight troops, would likely face slaughter if six times more rebel warriors crossed Pensacola Bay.

To rescue Fort Pickens, Keyes and Meigs advised the president, Vogdes's troops, if they ever landed, would require a nine-hundred-man additional reinforcement. Within three weeks, the two army officers promised, they would pour all necessary troops through Pickens's Gulf opening. The two warriors left the Executive Mansion bearing the president's oral orders to Winfield Scott: "I wish this thing done."[19]

For the second time in March, Fort Pickens had inspired that Lincoln anomaly, instant decision. The next day, Monday, April 1, the commander-in-chief ordered Scott to send daily written reports. He also commanded all hands to mass behind the Keyes-Meigs initiative.[20] On April 2, Lincoln sliced presidential patronage interviews to three hours daily.[21] By April 3, his departments helped prepare two packed vessels for departure to Pensacola. Seward supplied financing with his ten-thousand-dollar Secret Service slush fund. Keyes and Meigs amassed ships, supplies, and soldiers in New York City.[22]

Presidential indecision, however, still paralyzed dim hopes of Fort Sumter's rescue. Lincoln could no longer hope that triumph in Pensacola would compensate for surrender in Charleston. Vogdes's light brigade would be inadequate, if and when it landed at Fort Pickens; and the Keyes-Meigs heavy reinforcement would fill the Pensacola fortress only after starvation emptied Fort Sumter. Lincoln, always hating to be rushed, craved more hours to ponder his apparently only alternative: the shaky Fox-Welles tugboat tactic.

On March 30, the president ordered Fox in New York City to "make ready" without incurring "binding engagements."[23] As April dawned in the Big City, Meigs and Keyes thrived with written, binding orders to depart for Pickens at week's end. Gus Fox stumbled with oral, tentative orders to prepare to reinforce Sumter sometime. The Keyes-Meigs duo also used Seward's Secret Service slush fund, while Captain Fox had to beg loans from wary financiers.

On April 2, the stymied Fox returned to Washington for more discussions. More talk, however, yielded no more decisiveness. On April 3, Fox privately wrote that "my expedition is ordered to get ready but I doubt if we shall get off. Delay, indecision, obstacles." Thus "war will commence at Pensacola."[24]

9

The contrast between Lincoln's rush toward Pensacola and delay about Charleston helps explain Secretary of State Seward's bid to take over. On the one hand, Lincoln had turned Fort Pickens's reinforcement over to Seward, producing decisive progress. On the other hand, the president had hindered Gus Fox from producing a decisive flotilla—and still might order a crippled mission into Charleston harbor.

Seward calculated better prospects if the president gave him the same power over Sumter previously granted over Pickens. Then Fox's fiasco would be aborted. A needless war might be avoided. Reunion might be negotiated. The monumental stakes impelled the secretary of state to dare his infamous April 1 letter to the president.

After "a month's administration," the secretary of state began, we have no "policy. . . . Further delay" will "bring scandal on the Administration" and "danger upon the country."

Seward urged abandoning Fort Sumter, to cool the slavery issue. He favored reinforcing Fort Pickens, to emblazon the Union issue. He proposed showdowns with Europe's Latin American intruders, to fan U.S. nationalism. Either the president or a cabinet member, concluded Seward, could supply this decisiveness. The secretary of state sought neither "to evade nor assume" that "responsibility."[25]

A lesser president would have shouted down Seward, as Lincoln had roared down Winfield Scott. The Illinoisan instead shrugged, akin to his recent response to the elder Blair's screech about treason. Decades of adversity had hardened the Illinoisan's inner shell, arming as calculating an operator as ever distinguished between dangerous critics and paper tigers. Scott, after stunting policy, had scarce utility. Seward and the senior Blair, after merely sounding off, remained more useful. So the president sprayed fury on the general while brushing off Blair and Seward.

Bemusement saturated Lincoln's immediate letter back to Seward. Why did Fort Sumter represent a "slavery" policy and Fort Sumter a "Union" policy? Why did some Latin American obscurity, unmentioned until yester-day, demand confrontation today? Why wonder about his policy after his pledge "to hold, occupy, and possess" the government's "property and places?" And why volunteer to enforce my pledge, when "*I* must do it?"[26]

With that *I,* Lincoln perfectly climaxed a note that no historian saw for decades. Perhaps Seward never saw the scribble either. Lincoln may have answered verbally, for the note survives in his papers, not Seward's. Yet whether Lincoln responded with pen or voice, his private putdown epito-mized a canny executive's discreet hushing of valuable paper tigers.

10

Three days later, during the afternoon of April 4, Lincoln summoned Fox and finally ordered the captain to sail. The president also commanded his depart-ments to give Fox every assistance. Fox responded that the decision might be fatally late. Only a sketchy force might reach Charleston harbor before Robert Anderson's men starved.

"You will best fulfill your duty to your country," Lincoln shot back, "by making the *attempt*" (my emphasis).[27] The president had stalled for almost a week because he distrusted little tugboats, darkened skies, and turbulent seas. Now he thought he saw a wiser gamble.

Whatever the state of Fox's "attempt," envisioned Lincoln, the administra-tion would deliver a Gideon Welles–style notice, days earlier than the navy secretary had envisioned and bristling with a graver threat. Welles had pro-posed giving notice only right before reinforcing tugboats approached Fort Sumter. He had suggested warning only that soldiers as well as nourishment would be landed, unless the food was allowed ashore.

Instead, President Lincoln would serve notice days before Union rein-forcing vessels approached the Charleston environs. His initial warning would add that unless the rebels permitted the food landing, ships and sol-diers might remain in the neighborhood, and another warning might later be issued. After this initial warning, Lincoln would gamble, Confederates would either permit the initial food delivery or reduce the fort with obvious first blasts. Otherwise an altered military balance of power might threaten their queen city, after Union ships arrived and stayed.

Either rebel response, Lincoln projected, would permit a Union public relations coup. If Jefferson Davis allowed the food delivery, the fort would be saved peacefully, at least for now. If Confederates reduced the fort before Union vessels neared Charleston, rebels would blatantly advertise their first shot(s).

Lincoln did not want to think about a third alternative. Rebels might post-pone their answer until Fox's "attempt" appeared. Then Confederates could better judge whether a real menace intruded. If Confederates called the bluff and Fox brought too little, rebels could maul the "attempt" with trifling or no shots, then peaceably starve Robert Anderson into capitulation.

The gambling president would hardly master this situation, whatever happened (as his secretaries later bragged).[28] His feint would succeed only if rebels blasted the fort or authorized the food delivery before the U.S. Navy crashed the party. Yet the presidential sleight of hand offered better odds of winning the first-shot game than Fox's frail tugboats or Welles's lesser memo.

Towering administrators listen patiently, without airs that they already have the answers. Then they choose between suggestions, perhaps adding wrinkles that raise policy to a new level. Few additions at a critical moment have been more promising than Lincoln's bluff.

11

Fox sped back to New York City on April 5, finally armed with authorizations to sail for Sumter. The following day, while Fox at last flourished with New York suppliers, Meigs directed his first loaded steamship toward Fort Pick-ens. Erasmus Keyes remained behind, preparing a lesser steamer for departure in two days.

On April 6, the president learned that an aging military leader had again delayed his reinforcement command to Israel Vogdes. Not the seventy-four-year-old Winfield Scott but the sixty-one-year-old Captain Henry A. Adams this time stalled. In 1852–53, when Matthew Perry sailed toward Japan, this Henry Adams had been "Captain of the Fleet." In February–April 1861, Perry's former captain commanded that *Sabine,* anchored near Pensacola and bearing Vogdes's soldiers after the *Brooklyn* steamed to Key West.

On April 1, when the army's March 12 order to reinforce Pickens finally meandered into Israel Vogdes's hands, Vogdes asked the navy's Adams to transport the army's soldiers aboard the *Sabine* to Fort Pickens. Adams refused. A *navy* superior, the old salt claimed, must command a naval subor-dinate to obliterate "The Truce of Fort Pickens," perhaps starting a civil war. Like General Scott, the veteran Adams preferred to delay a rookie president's potentially war-provoking command.

Adams, fearing he may have overstepped a captain's bounds, dispatched a train-bound courier to Washington, asking for instructions. On April 6, upon receiving the query, Navy Secretary Gideon Welles sped the answer back. Captain Adams must deliver Vogdes's men to Fort Pickens at "the first favorable opportunity."[29]

Almost simultaneously on April 6, the administration dispatched two couriers, bearing Lincoln's notice to South Carolina authorities. The couriers had time to travel and Confederates time to decide before Fox's reinforcing ship(s) approached Charleston. Coincidently, on the same day that Welles reordered Vogdes into Fort Pickens, Meigs's major reinforcing vessel left for Pickens, Keyes readied the follow-up ship, Fox prepared for departure to Sumter, and couriers left for Charleston and Pensacola, bearing the administration's final prewar notices and commands.

12

Or was it a coincidence? Some latter-day commentators believe that the April 6 news of Vogdes's latest delay *caused* the president to dispatch the warning to Charleston rebels. After Washington heard about the newest screw-up, runs the theory, Lincoln had to rush Fox's scheme rather than dawdle again.

That theory underrates the Keyes-Meigs transforming information, delivered to the president on Easter afternoon. The commander-in-chief had then learned that Vogdes's reinforcement of fewer than a hundred men would be no match, whenever it finally landed, against Confederates' thousand-man buildup. Never again after Easter had Lincoln misconceived that Vogdes's trifling solders at Fort Pickens might overshadow disaster at Fort Sumter.

On April 4, Lincoln had finally decided that a bluff at Sumter might best extricate his Union from a morass. April 6 became the day not of decision but of action on a frenzied week of decisions, starting with false news but soon erupting from real news that Vogdes's undermanned company could hardly compensate for Fort Sumter surrender.

After arriving in Charleston on April 8, Lincoln's messengers recited the president's notice to South Carolina officials, who sped the warning to Confederate president Jefferson Davis. "An attempt will be made," ran Lincoln's rewording of Welles's memo, "to supply Fort-Sumpter with provisions only." Unless Confederates "resisted" that "attempt" or attacked "the Fort, . . . no effort to throw in men, arms, or ammunition will be made, without further notice."[30]

"Without further notice"! Welles's notice would have warned Confederates only of a food delivery. Lincoln added that approaching ships might stay and defend the fort. This classic bluff sought to induce rebels to play their cards, either authorizing additional rations or reducing the fort, before waiting to see whether Fox's "attempt" justified either reaction.

13

Between April 6, when the president dispatched his notice to Charleston, and April 9, when Gus Fox's vessels embarked for Fort Sumter, the tugboat fancier sought a formidable fleet. Fox hoped his brainchild (and his life!) would ride on more than Lincoln's feint. The ex-captain also still thought his strategy could prevail. In New York City, Fox leased three expensive tugboats and the former Collins Line's even more expensive black-and-red *Baltic*. After commercial misfortune, the luxury steamboat, meant for wealthy vacationers, now transported scruffy soldiers, frolicking in millionaires' mirrored Grand Saloon before suffering deadly battlefields.

Fox compensated for his splurge by begging free use of three minor naval vessels plus a floating colossus, the *SS Powhatan,* the most powerful U.S. warship. The ex-captain ordered all vessels to rendezvous ten miles from Charleston harbor on the morning of April 12, when starvation would begin in Fort Sumter.

<h2 style="text-align:center">14</h2>

While the *Baltic* steamed toward Charleston, Jefferson Davis's cabinet debated whether to assault Fort Sumter before Lincoln's ship(s) appeared. Davis favored immediate strike. Only Secretary of State Robert Toombs would wait.

While the rebels could not know how much Yankee sea force would be arriving, they knew that a fraction of northern battleships could overwhelm Charleston's meager portion of barely developed Confederate sea power. Better to savage Fort Sumter *now,* most rebel leaders thought, before intruding vessel(s) might double the trouble. If Lincoln had listened, he would have gloated, "I told you so."

A phenomenon Lincoln had not anticipated bolstered his bluff.[31] Jefferson Davis cared more about other cards. Davis and Lincoln equally saw the "advantage," as the Confederate president wrote, of manipulating the foe to pull the first trigger, thus infuriating "border states." But only Davis considered "that advantage . . . overbalanced by other considerations," especially relieving "our territory . . . of a foreign garrison." Rebel inability to clear vital ports could spawn doubts about the new nation, in Border South states and among European trade partners. For President Davis, certainty about ousting Yankees trumped niceties of who fired first.

On April 3, Davis had ordered his Pensacola commander, Braxton Bragg, to fire first shots, if an initial assault would bring certain victory at Fort Pickens.

After Bragg dithered uncertainly in Pensacola, Davis coveted a certain tri-umph in Charleston, secured before Yankee ship(s) caused more dithering.

Just before war started, Robert Anderson received a last chance. He must immediately surrender or suffer imminent bombardment. Anderson responded that he would yield in three days, unless Union ships delivered rations. Rebels knew that federal ships bearing food would beat the deadline, whatever else might be arriving. At 4:30 AM on April 12, the first Confederate blow slammed Fort Sumter.

Yankees began returning fire at 7:00 AM. The delayed response (and doz-ens more Confederate cannonballs before Union firepower answered) reem-phasized that rebels had fired first. As the light and sound show exploded over secessionists' first city, Charleston aristocrats on rooftops whooped delight. At 2:30 PM the next day, Robert Anderson surrendered.

The following day, Yankees in the ruined fortress reopened fire. Ander-son had permission for one hundred salutes to his flag before abandoning his post. On the forty-seventh round of symbolic blasts, Union troops killed two of their own—the Battle of Fort Sumter's only casualties. Yankees honored their flag with three more shots before eerie silence prevailed.

15

Two mornings earlier, an hour and a half before the initial Confederate bombardment, former captain Gustavus Fox, aboard the unarmed *Baltic,* had steamed on schedule to his flotilla's appointed rendezvous point, ten miles from Charleston. That April 12 morning, only Fox's least important ship joined the *Baltic.* Other expected vessels, including the three tugboats, arrived late, left early, suffered capture, never left wary owners, experienced crippling gales, or brought crippling orders. As for the mighty *Powhatan,* bureaucratic confusions (and an unconfused William H. Seward!) had directed the vessel to Fort Pickens. As Lincoln had gloomed, Fox's plan, unless augmented with an ominous revised version of Welles's notice, could lose in too many ways.

The *Powhatan* debacle showed that Lincoln had greater difficulty with petty snafus than with big strategy. When angry administrators pounded his carelessness about the *Powhatan*'s direction, Lincoln exceeded his record for apologies. Gus Fox meanwhile topped his record for exasperation. The for-mer captain fired countless signals into the Charleston evening sky, alerting the *Powhatan* that here I am!

The next day, only Fox cared where his scattered pieces might be bobbing. Even his entire fleet could not have reversed the second fatal day of Fort

Sumter's bombardment. Still, Fox sailed frantically around the harbor's out-skirts, begging help to bring his remnants to the rescue.

A sympathizer offered a little schooner, loaded with ice. If he had accepted the offer, Fox conceded, he would have "been knocked to pcs."[32] He would as certainly have been knocked to pieces if Confederates had waited to inspect his "attempt" before replying.

A day later, the ex-captain commenced safer duty. After friendly fire inside Fort Sumter felled two Anderson troops, Confederates delivered survivors to the peaceable *Baltic*. As Fox directed the pleasure ship home, exhausted troops and futile rescuers barely noticed their Grand Saloon.

16

One more same-day coincidence, akin to April 6 happenstances, momen-tarily reconnected Forts Sumter and Pickens's severed finales. On April 12, hours after rebels fired on Sumter, Navy Secretary Gideon Welles's order to land Vogdes at Fort Pickens arrived in the Pickens environs. That early eve-ning, Vogdes's little company swept into the Pensacola fort without incident, exactly a month after the War Department wrote Lincoln's initial reinforce-ment order.[33]

Equally without incident, Keyes-Meigs's nine-hundred-man buttress for Vogdes's eighty-eight souls landed in two waves within the week.[34] On April 16, the massive passenger ship *Atlantic,* sister of the *Baltic* in the ex-Collins Line, arrived with Montgomery Meigs and two-thirds of Union rescuers. On April 19, the smaller steamer *Illinois* completed the reinforcement. The added troops' control of Fort Pickens would endure. The resulting safer Gulf avenues for the Union's Mississippi River conquerors would speed Lincoln's navy and army toward slicing the Confederacy in half.

Lincoln seized a more important advantage from his best way to lose Sum-ter. He had maneuvered rebels toward looking like assaulters of Union, as many in the wavering Upper South saw the first shots at Fort Sumter. "You and I both anticipated," Lincoln victoriously wrote Fox, that "the attempt to provision Fort-Sumpter would" advance our "cause. . . . The result" justifies "our anticipation."[35] Our "plan," the president added to Orville H. Browning, "succeeded. They attacked Sumter," and its fall "did more service than it oth-erwise could."[36]

If Confederates had allowed federals' food to land or Fox had snuck nour-ishment past rebel batteries, the president would also have been pleased. But he had expected neither pleasure. He had thought that Confederates proba-bly would oust their foe from the fort. Yet by "losing" the right way, attracting pulverizing first shots (and then some!) by merely delivering bread to hungry men, Lincoln's climactic strategy of defense turned a lost fort into a winner. None of his prewar strategies of defense, whether deployed against enslaving previously unenslaved territories, or against surrender to despotic blackmailers, or against capitulation to a Supreme Court's supposed next *Dred Scott* decision, had so dramatically rallied his Union against the Slave Power.

17

The triumphant loss immediately paid a lush dividend. On April 15, Lincoln's hastily prepared proclamation called seventy-five thousand volunteers to answer rebels' first shot. Angry Border South Unionists swiftly helped oversubscribe the call.

Lincoln's haste, however, yielded a miscue. Volunteers' "first" assignment, his proclamation announced, will "probably be to re-possess . . . seized . . . forts."[37] Orville Browning and then Lincoln himself had deemed *re-possess* improper in the Inauguration Address draft.

After carelessly repeating, in his first important presidential proclamation, the misstep expunged from his first presidential address, Abraham Lincoln deployed his rare capacity to admit mistakes. He had meant to say, he pled, that volunteers must first protect Washington from capture. His corrected plea thrived. Three days after his first presidential triumph, he had fallen again and raised right back up again, with many Border Southerners helping him save *their* nation's capital.

18

On his slow road toward the triumphant loss of Fort Sumter, Lincoln's collaborators, with the exception of Winfield Scott, had found their leader modest, unassuming, and eager for counsel. Lincoln's first dividends had included the Seward-Meigs-Keyes leap beyond Vogdes on Fort Pickens and the Fox-Welles bypass of Scott on Fort Sumter. The president's crowning touch, bluffing secessionists toward first blasts at Sumter, completed his team's first presidential victory.

The councilors with most reason to deplore Lincoln offered his truest testimonies. William H. Seward, loser in 1860, had come to the 1861 cabinet with some jealous scorn for the inexperienced winner. Then Seward had badly stumbled before Lincoln, without a critical word, had swept past the New Yorker's indiscreet, empty promises to Confederates. After a puffed-up Seward had offered to take over from the alleged lightweight,

Lincoln had moved on as if the secretary's ego mattered too little to be punctured.

To Lincoln, inflated egos indeed did not matter, if egotists pitched in with the team. Seward, like most teammates, swiftly understood. "Executive skill and vigor are rare qualities," William H. Seward wrote his wife on June 5, 1861. While "the President . . . needs constant and assiduous cooperation," he "is the best of us."[38]

Among other teammates, Gus Fox had least reason to share Seward's revised opinion. Another Lincoln singular trait, endless pondering before decisions, had marooned Fox in perilous Charleston. Fox would have been a sorely threatened ex-captain if rebels had called Lincoln's bluff.

The tugboat fancier still pronounced the right nuanced conclusion: When Lincoln "had the time to listen to, and to weigh facts and arguments presented to him, his judgment was superior to his party associates."[39] The forgiving Fox, soon Gideon Welles's assistant secretary of the navy, joined Seward as their forgiving leader's soul mate during awful wartime nights. *There* thrived a superior administrator.

19

Was the chief's *moral* judgment equally superior when his bluff helped provoke rebels toward firing first shots, in a war that killed 750,000 Americans (more than all other U.S. wars put together)? A commonplace answer, that Jefferson Davis also preferred war to surrendering his nation, is right—and irrelevant. The question here is not whether Davis acted ethically but whether Lincoln's goad to action was morally legitimate.

Lincoln's bluff would raise fewer latter-day scruples if he had provoked war to liberate slaves. As combat began, however, the future Great Emancipator ridiculed the notion. "The excitement of the hour," he exclaimed three weeks after hostilities commenced, has "bewildered and dazzled . . . some of our northerners." They seem "inclined to think that the war is to result in the entire abolition of Slavery."[40]

He thought that dazzled radicals, despite their usual admirable devotion to rescuing blacks, as usual risked the rescuing agent. When cannon first roared and long afterward, the chief Republican presumed that winning the war, like winning elections, required inspiring the largely moderate majority that ruled a largely conservative Union. Only that Union, Lincoln believed, could combine the world's greatest political democracy with the world's widest economic opportunity. Only Union, he remembered, had saved underdeveloped Illinois from economic stagnation. Only Union, he prayed, could salvage immigrants from nativists' oppression. And only Union, he conceived, might someday shatter blacks' chains.

On July 4, 1861, the Declaration's eighty-fifth anniversary, the president wrote Congress that today's issue "embraces more than the fate of these United States. . . . The whole family of man" wonders "whether . . . a government of the people" and "by the same people" can endure "against its own domestic foes."[41] Rebels would smash the world's only "government whose leading object is to elevate the condition of men—to lift artificial weights from *all* shoulders—to clear the paths of laudable pursuit for *all*—to afford" to "*all* an unfettered start, and a fair chance" (emphasis mine).

To preclude racists who thundered "incendiary" and abolitionists who sneered "hypocrite," Lincoln added, as often before, that "necessity" demands "partial and temporary departures" from "*all.*" His clinging to Union, to effect all other American redemptions, reechoed that signature 1845 private letter, declaring that "free states' . . . paramount duty" to "Union . . . and perhaps to liberty itself (paradox though it may seem)" is "to let the slavery of the other states alone." Fifteen years later, Lincoln still knew that no white majority would find "paramount duty" in seeking blacks' "unfettered start and . . . fair chance." He must first save mankind's greatest temple of (white) economic and political freedom; and he still considered the (racially tainted) treasure alone worth war.

Yet he still hoped that someday the saved temple would "lift artificial weight from *all* shoulders." Four terrible years later, emancipation would lift the most crushing weight from blacks' shoulders, with 180,000 black troops among the heavy lifters. One hundred and fifty–plus years later, this scribbler cannot see how the lifting could have occurred as swiftly without saved Union—or how a nation without a moral leader as crafty as the bluffer could have as well endured its most frightful test.

EPILOGUE

(Slowly) Becoming
a Coercive Emancipator

✦⟐✦

A wartime epilogue deepens perspective on three troubled Lincoln peace-time forays: his uneven marriage, his crushed Whiggery, and his problematic fatalism. His presidential years also highlight his supreme prewar talent: his antislavery finesse. Few have better harnessed strategic brilliance to a moral cause in a resisting republic. As the wartime president brought his flair to climax, his prewar ascent with antislavery (and prewar floundering with Whiggery) became clearer—as did his domestic travail and perplexing fatalism.[1]

1

When courting in the early 1840s, Mary Todd fastened on Abraham Lincoln's political potential. Her political talk attracted her coveted politician. Yet her refined cultivation unsettled her awkward admirer.

Her relatives warned that political camaraderie poorly bridged social differences. The husband's meager household, they predicted, would exasperate the polished heiress. Lincoln, fearing them right, canceled their engagement. Mary, determined to prove them wrong, coaxed him back. Mary Todd Lincoln then mostly settled in, despite some domestic uproar, as the political comer's parsimonious wife.

She remained, however, a rich man's daughter. In the mid-1850s, she sold land gifted by her father to blow the roof off the Lincolns' one-and-a-half-story bungalow, then turn it into a handsome two-story residence. The pleased wife the more dreamed of decorating a grand presidential mansion, while her husband directed epic national events.

A First Family Executive Mansion album: Mary Lincoln entertaining (*top left*), Robert Lincoln visiting from Harvard, with top hat (*top right*), Abraham Lincoln reading to Tad (*bottom left*), Willie Lincoln in a photograph taken shortly before his death in 1862 (*bottom right*)

Even before entering the Executive Mansion, Mary Todd Lincoln began efforts to transform the tired dwelling into a resplendent treasure. She expected that the twenty-thousand-dollar congressional stipend for the mansion's renovation ($530,000 in early twenty-first-century lucre) would finance lush rooms. She further anticipated that the president's twenty-five-thousand-dollar annual salary would sustain sumptuous receptions.

During eleven Philadelphia and New York buying sprees, the First Lady chose luxurious gowns, rugs, draperies, wallpapers, furniture, and china. Her $3,195 Haughwout china featured an American eagle. Her substitute for family suppers, with M.L. replacing the eagle, cost $1,106.73. Her rugs included a $2,500 velvet extravagance, with pale green waves rippling. Her French wallpaper extracted $6,800. Her "Lincoln bed" has long outlasted her gold-fringed draperies.

She spent a third more than Congress appropriated. The disapproving president disdained those "*flub dubs* for that damned old house, when the soldiers can not have blankets."[2] The irked wife scrambled after funding.

Oregon's U.S. Senator Edward Dickinson Baker's funeral increased the couple's strain. Lincoln's friendly ex–Illinois Whig rival, the "Gray Eagle" with the pet bird, had introduced the president at the inaugural. Lincoln had named his second son Edward Baker Lincoln. When Senator Baker became an early Civil War casualty, slain at Ball's Bluff, October 21, 1861, Lincoln wept uncontrollably.

At the funeral, Mary defied her critics. Rather than the traditional black dress, she wore her new lilac affair, with matching gloves and hat. "I wonder if the women of Washington expect me to muffle myself up in mourning for every soldier killed," she muttered.[3]

Not division over flub dubs but eleven-year-old Willie Lincoln's 1862 death most afflicted the couple. Better Washington times featured chatter about politics and their surviving sons, Bob and Tad, during afternoon carriage rides. But inside the Civil War Executive Mansion, storms sometimes blew even harder than Mary's kin had predicted.

This relationship, to stay relatively stable, required a roof atop the wife's extravagances. After turmoil over extravagances and agony over Willie, Mary's plunge passed through Abraham's 1865 assassination, Tad's 1871 death (at age eighteen), a lunatic asylum, and Bob's alienation. The moral of her dive: Be careful what you wish for.

2

Before Abraham's careful antislavery statecraft, he squandered political capital with expensive ventures. His state's floundering "System" accelerated his political slide. National Whiggery's costly proposals intensified voters' apprehensions.

Andrew Jackson's Democracy won six of eight presidential elections from 1828 to 1856. Victors gutted Whigs' national bank, limited federal internal improvements, and quashed protective tariffs. Democrats, applauding a private economy without public interference, gloated that the Age of Jackson would outlast the nineteenth century.

Lincoln departed his dissolving Whig Party slowly. He never surrendered Whig conceptions. He stopped discussing Whigs' agenda only because politics required practicality. Then, early in the Civil War, when his deceased cause sprang back to life, he hurried back to its support, helping to bring the lately crushed program to long-lasting triumph.

Lincoln's mammoth wartime armies required massive transportation, banks, and taxes. The administration responded with elephantine aid to nationalistic development. Republicans' new national bank rained paper dollars on the nation, without gold or silver backing. The party's Legal Tender Act required lenders to accept greenbacks for repayment. Lincoln's administration piled on over $2.4 billion of bonds, backed only by promises to repay.

Paper promises augured Illinois Whigs' doom in "System" days. This time, however, booming taxes sustained mountainous bonds. Protective tariff rates swelled over a third. The first federal income tax peaked at 10 percent of earnings by war's end.

The paper cash financed the monster war and Lincoln's climactic boost to a nationalized economy. The administration's Pacific Railroad Acts of 1862 and 1864, plus federal land grants providing more acres than Texas contained, plus more than $30 million in federal bonds yielded a transcontinental railroad within eight years of his death. In 1873, trains sped from the Atlantic to the Pacific in three days (matching Lincoln's 1860 time between Springfield and Cooper Union). Several Mississippi River spans reemphasized the importance of the *Rock Island Bridge* case.

Thus did Whig economics, like Lincoln's career, rise from collapse in Illinois's 1840s to triumph during the Civil War. The Age of Lincoln had replaced the Age of Jackson.[4] The Republican Party, continuing Lincoln's federal stimuli for economic takeoff, would win fourteen of eighteen presidential elections between 1860 and 1928, more than doubling the length of Jacksonians' reign. Then the Great Depression made Lincoln's economics as outmoded as the Civil War had made Jackson's, leading to the Age of FDR. The moral of the story: Time your splurge correctly.

3

Posterity can string Lincoln's prewar political efforts, whether seeking spending splurges for Whigs or restrained antislavery for Republicans, on his dozens of extended speeches. Once inside the Executive Mansion, however,

Lincoln emerged for no public orations until his Gettysburg gem, November 19, 1863. After Gettysburg, he only occasionally addressed regiments and fairs until his magnificent Second Inaugural Address, March 4, 1865.

His two wartime verbal classics ended before audiences' admiration could swell. His 272 words at Gettysburg's National Cemetery took two minutes. His Second Inaugural's 701 words lasted under four minutes longer.

Yet Lincoln needed no more Gettysburg moments to reemphasize his concentrated case against slavery. One finger suffices to count the times he had indulged in others' sprawling reasons for denouncing the evil. Abolitionists and Radical Republicans routinely damned slaveholders for allegedly generating brothels, smashing families, and savaging Christianity. Lincoln preferred five abstract words: All Men Are Created Equal.

"Four score and seven years ago," the president began at Gettysburg, "our fathers brought forth . . . a new nation, conceived in liberty, and dedicated to the proposition that all men are created equal." After "a great civil war, testing whether . . . any nation so conceived and so dedicated can long endure," we must "highly resolve that" our "honored dead . . . shall not have died in vain—that this nation, under God, shall have a new birth of freedom—and that government of the people, by the people, and for the people shall not perish from the earth."[5]

The Gettysburg orator knew that in November 1863, eleven months after his Final Emancipation Proclamation, most slaves had experienced no "new birth of freedom." Nor had any freedmen yet enjoyed government *"by"* (black) people. He also knew that after former Harvard president Edward Everett's two-hour oration, studded with extravagant images, few Gettysburg listeners would remember his two minutes, urging one abstraction. But few now remember an Everett syllable, and schoolchildren memorize each Lincoln word. His climactic expression of his antislavery inspiration still presides during July Fourth fireworks, reaffirming government of, by, and for equal Americans.

4

The purely secular Gettysburg Address contrasts with Lincoln's highly religious March 4, 1865, Second Inaugural Address. Christian messages had saturated no earlier Lincoln oration. Still, some previous wordings (the House Divided Address, for example) had encouraged evangelicals to hope he would become theirs.

Then, during the war, the former Kentucky/Indiana farm boy who had mocked preachers and the Illinois adult who had shunned churches despondently attended Washington, DC's New York Avenue Presbyterian. As Ned

Baker's killing, then Willie Lincoln's death, then 750,000 soldiers' decimations brought unprecedented slaughter, the despairing president asked, ever more desperately asked, Why? Why must this horror continue? Why won't Jehovah decree *enough*?

"The Almighty has His own purposes," Lincoln's Second Inaugural Address answered. While sinners' "offenses" bring "woe unto the world," God "gives to both North and South, this terrible war, as the woe due to those by whom the offense" of "American Slavery . . . cometh."

Southerners deserved more woe, hinted the orator. He mocked slaveholders for asking "a just God's assistance in wringing their bread from the sweat of other men's faces." But while his refashioned bread analogy unbalanced the scales, Yankee culpability (including his own) newly weighed unbearably.

"Let us judge not," he winced, so "we are not judged." If "God wills" that *both* sections' punishment shall "continue, until all the wealth piled by the bonds-man's two hundred and fifty years of unrequited toil shall be sunk, and until every drop of blood drawn with the lash, shall be paid by another drawn with the sword," we should "discern" no "departure from" His "divine attributes." Instead, all who "read the same Bible and pray to the same God" and have suffered the same punishment for complicity in the same crimes should "bind up the nation's wounds," displaying "malice toward none" and "charity to all," so all may "cherish a just and a lasting peace."[6]

Lincoln never specified his own crimes and complicities. But his generalizations continued to spin around his Doctrine of Necessity. He still believed that internal "motives" and external forces determine human action. But he still insisted on man's moral responsibility to act honorably. He still pounced on scarce moments when slim choices might bring slight improvements. Yet he never explained how his obligation to choose moral advances could square with a fatalistic philosophy that denied choice.

When friend Joseph Gillespie raised the thorny question, it will be remembered, the great politician dismissed the great philosophic query as "a very unprofitable field of speculation."[7] Speculating about wartime free will versus determinism wasted as much precious time as prewar railing against Whigs' demise. Instead, Lincoln endlessly searched for the few moments when slight exceptions to man's helplessness seemed redemptive.

His inability to end the frightful war, however, forced an inconsistent fatalist to wonder about his guarded exceptions. Perhaps he had deluded himself about his possibilities *ever* to choose, just as he had deluded himself about possibilities of peaceable emancipation. Perhaps God deployed presidential failures as His means to extend punishments, just as He had perhaps used Lincoln's pre-1854 shunning of antislavery politics to swell the Slave Power.

While Lincoln had considered his motives honorable, his Doctrine of Necessity decreed man's dimmed ability to see. Adding an Angry God to his secular semi-fatalism the more turned man's plans into illusions. With the Second Inaugural, a humbled Christian sank to his knees, praying that Americans would be spared further punishment.

His plea for mercy, however, never turned his incomplete fatalism into total resignation. The more the wartime president suffered, the harder he studied what little he might accomplish. The more he deployed the specks he thought he saw, the less he thought of writing dense explications of determinism. Whatever this practical man's missing philosophic reconciliations, his exertions hardly indicated surrender to necessity.

5

Lincoln's prewar and wartime exploits both featured not only unexplained deviations from strict determinism but also careful deployments of antislavery finesse. Before the war, the master politician conceived that only very limited pursuit of "ultimate extinction" could keep Border and Upper North inside the same Republican Party. During the first half of the war, he believed that only turtle-slow emancipation might keep a third of the South and the North inside the same Union.

While Lincoln's efforts to nudge the prewar balance of power had concentrated on his adopted Border North, his wartime attempts centered on his native Border South. He realized that "to lose Kentucky is nearly the same as to lose the whole game. Kentucky gone, we cannot hold Missouri, nor, as I think, Maryland. Those all against us, and the job on our hands is too large for us."[8]

Kentucky, declaring its neutrality, had at first barred both antagonists from its terrain. Lincoln deplored neutrality almost as much as secession. Yet just as firing the first Civil War shot could lose wavering southern Unionists, so blundering into the first violation of Kentucky's neutrality could sacrifice the vacillating state. Lincoln kept his troops away.

During 1861's first eight months, sentiment for Union slowly increased inside "neutral" Kentucky as southern soldiers massed outside. Lincoln, continuing to allow theoretically unallowable neutrality, gambled that rebels would cross Kentucky's border first (repeating Fort Sumter's finale). The poker player again guessed right. On September 3, Confederate general Leonidas Polk swarmed into Kentucky. Then the state's leaders invited Yankee rescuers to enter. Angry Kentuckians helped federal invitees push Polk's army outside. Welcomed saviors remained inside.

Lincoln's variations on "first judiciously pause, then decisively pounce" continued elsewhere in wartime southern borderlands. In Maryland, federals successfully waited to jail secessionist legislators until Unionists verged on control. A sloppy version of waiting at least secured stalemate in Missouri. With Lincoln usually playing difficult cards shrewdly, the borderland's third of southern whites edged toward augmenting northern might.

6

Yankees' chance to supplement southern white troops with southern blacks drove a key prewar struggle toward wartime climax. Again combating Lincoln's antislavery gradualism, impatient Radical Republicans demanded that blacks be freed to augment his army. Radicals also insisted that runaway slaves should swell Union ranks and shrivel Confederate capacities.[9]

Lincoln answered that overly swift emancipation would repel whites faster than it would attract blacks. Northern Democrats and white borderites, while now marching for whites' Union, would drop their rifles, the president feared, rather than kill for blacks' liberty. The president would compel emancipation *if*—if extremists' remedy could strengthen rather than sabotage his main concern: saving the Union. As Lincoln wrote Horace Greeley in August 1862: Despite my "oft expressed *personal* wish that all men every where could be free," my "*official* duty . . . *is* to save the Union, and is *not* either to save or to destroy slavery. If I could save the Union without freeing *any* slave I would do it, and if I could save it by freeing *all* the slaves I would do it."[10]

Before the war, the same fear that forcible emancipation would shatter Union had compelled Lincoln's resistance to Radical Republicans. For six years after the Kansas-Nebraska Act, he had insisted only on slavery's nonextension in previously free territories. Only in the second half of 1858 had he vaguely suggested a link between ending slave expansion and starting bondage's "ultimate extinction"—a shadowy linkage he dropped before his 1859 campaign. Only in early 1861 had he come back to "ultimate extinction," limited as always before to seeking masters' consent and this time featuring Border South Republicans preaching voluntary reform from patronage posts.

On March 6, 1862, as Border South Republicans begged help with faltering persuading, Lincoln achieved a congressional resolution, offering "pecuniary aid" for "gradual abolishment."[11] He thereby revived the monetary boost to persuasion behind his 1849 District of Columbia proposal. National funds, again ran his hope, would lure slaveholders toward consent to manumission. In 1862, the president also convinced Congress to finance a $500,000 freedmen's colonization experiment near Haiti, renewing another of his prewar hopes to ease southerners toward agreement to black freedom.[12]

In the fall of 1862, with Border South whites still withholding their consent to emancipation and almost all free blacks refusing consent to colonize, Lincoln called both groups to Executive Mansion meetings. Time was evaporating, he warned Border South leaders, for compensated agreement to emancipate. Black equality, he told black leaders, required blacks to leave America. After that cringeworthy Lincoln moment, only some 450 blacks accepted federal free tickets to depart.

Before the ship left, Radical Republicans' pressure to emancipate intensified. Border South allegiance to Union tightened. Blacks' clamor to join the federal army heightened. Fugitive slaves multiplied. Confederate defiance continued. Union casualties became alarming. Coercive emancipation plus sable brigades might be necessary, as radicals insisted, to win the war and save the Union.

Still, Lincoln doubted that white racists would fight for black freedom, just as he had doubted that prewar Border North Republicans would vote for Radical Republicans. When Congress authorized a *final* presidential coercive emancipation proclamation, sixty days after July 17, 1862, Lincoln stalled with a *preliminary* proclamation on September 22, delaying an ultimate proclamation for another one hundred days, until January 1, 1863.

The Preliminary Emancipation Proclamation ushered in Lincoln's final, frantic, one hundred days of seeking consent to emancipation, thus precluding a Final Emancipation Proclamation's forced antislavery. He dispatched envoys to three Confederate states, promising that departed states could retain slavery if they elected U.S. congressmen before January 1. Adding more incentives on December 8, the president's annual message to Congress urged a constitutional amendment, offering seceded brethren compensation for abolition, financing of colonization, and reprieve from the imminent Final Emancipation Proclamation.[13]

To accept the offer, a seceded state needed only to return to the Union before January 1, 1863, and agree to emancipate before 1900! In 1858, Lincoln had accepted possibilities of a one-hundred-year wait for southern agreement to "ultimate extinction." He now endorsed a thirty-seven-year delay to gain the boon, ending only when the twentieth century began. The long holding pattern would start with a controversial constitutional amendment, secured in merely twenty-three days! For this final gasp of an expiring dream, the great orator deployed his most convulsed oratory since the 1838 Lyceum Address:

The aging of Abraham Lincoln:
Pre-congressional, 1846–47 (*top left*),
pre-presidential, August 12, 1860
(*top right*), pre–Second Inaugural,
February 5, 1865 (*right*)

"We cannot escape history. . . . We shall nobly save, or meanly lose, the last best hope of earth."

His friend Orville Browning had the right word for that finale—"hallucination."[14] Congress bothered with no words. The last words were Lincoln's. Eight days into 1863, the commander-in-chief privately exclaimed that "after . . . hostilities" commenced, "I struggled nearly a year and a half to get along without touching the 'institution.'" Then "I gave a hundred days fair notice." Secessionists "could have . . . wholly avoided" forced emancipation "by simply again becoming good citizens of the United

States. They chose to disregard" their opportunity. Now, "broken eggs can not be mended."[15]

Anger suffuses this key Lincoln letter as well as sadness, also saturating the later Second Inaugural and enduring in Augustus Saint-Gaudens's *Standing Lincoln*. His prayers for the Founding Fathers' incremental, consenting abolition had lasted during his seventeen years, 1837–54, of almost total silence on slavery, then through his seven years, 1854–61, of almost exclusively defensive strategies against further slaveholder advances, then through the first twenty months of bitter civil war.

The noncoercive emancipator's quarter century ended abruptly with the Final Emancipation Proclamation. From the proclamation's first day, January 1, 1863, to his last day, April 15, 1865, neither whites' extravagant praise for a forceful "Great Emancipator" nor freedmen's weeping thanks for a redeeming Messiah altogether obliterated his regret that a horrendous war had exploded a devout dream.

He knew now that his pacific vision had projected unacceptable costs, not least blacks' monster payment of yet another century in chains. But he could not forget all those deaths and that routed fantasy of peaceful progress with the consent of the tyrants. Photographs captured his turmoil as his lifelong melancholy deepened into exhausted lamentation, conditioning a hero's joyful relief. Transition moments do not come more convoluted than Lincoln's at the dawning of 1863.

But as so often, this signature Lincoln "defeat" led to remorse, reconsideration, regrouping, and redemption. As Saint-Gaudens emphasized, he stood tall even at the lowest points, aching to turn disappointment into triumph. He knew now that emancipation no less than Union demanded heavy-handed imposition. His army, for the first time including blacks, must compel antislavery everywhere his January 1, 1863, Final Emancipation Proclamation required—and immediately.

7

The Final Emancipation Proclamation omitted "All men are created equal." Few judges, on and off Taney's bench, conceived that presidents could constitutionally chase racial equality. Lincoln's proclamation had to be a strictly military order, seeking only to crush rebellion.

Warning contrary judges away with every syllable, the Final Emancipation Proclamation declared a "military necessity" for "suppressing . . . armed rebellion." The commander-in-chief's decree liberated slaves within seceded states, except in exempted conquered areas. The military, continued the command, must "maintain . . . freedom" of those emancipated and receive freedmen into U.S. "armed services." Exempted areas included Tennessee, fractions of other Confederate states, and (implicitly) the loyal Border South.[16]

The widespread exemptions foster the myth that the historic proclamation immediately liberated no one. The fallacy misses Lincoln's instant determination to move decisively. His army swiftly recruited blacks in conquered non-exempt areas, including Florida's southern tip, southernmost coastal South Carolina and Georgia, and much of eastern Arkansas.[17] Federal enlisters also immediately recruited northern and Border South free blacks. Lincoln's augmented army more easily drove into rebel bastions, where liberated bondsmen and fugitive slaves further swelled Union ranks.

On March 26, 1863, Lincoln, pleased with his (bounded) new war, sought to erase one boundary. He wrote Tennessee's military governor, Andrew Johnson, urging that "If you have at least *thought* of raising a negro military force, . . . please do not dismiss the thought."[18] After Governor Johnson abhorred the thought, the commander-in-chief issued an October 1863 military order, liberating borderland and Tennessee slaves who consented to join his army. Loyal masters received three hundred dollars per departed bondsman. In this variation on Lincolnian consent, blacks became the consenters, while masters received payments to hush.[19]

Lincoln also eased whites' objections by moving slowly in Kentucky. That Border South state contained the region's highest percentage of slaves and loudest protesters against the commander-in-chief's October 1863 supplemental decree. For nine months, Lincoln limited his Kentucky recruiters to enrolling only freed blacks or slaves with masters' permission to serve.

In June 1864, however, with most white Kentuckians relenting, his army welcomed the state's volunteering blacks, with or without masters' approval. The recruitment surge doubled Kentucky sable arms to almost 24,000, half of Border South slave volunteers. The president's patience with Kentucky masters, as with Kentucky "neutrals" earlier, had triumphed.[20]

Before the war ended, some 450,000 *southern* troops (including around 130,000 southern blacks) served in the Union army, compared to 900,000 southerners in Confederate armies. The Great Emancipator's final armed forces also included some 50,000 northern free blacks. His war had become the North plus the northern third of the South, including most of its blacks and whites, against only two-thirds of the white South, with many of its slaves fleeing toward invading armies.[21]

The finale reemphasized that the sectional conflict had never pitted a monolithic antislavery North against a monolithic proslavery South. Rather, a South more consolidated for eternal bondage toward its lower end challenged a North more determined on antislavery toward its upper end, with most Americans somewhere in between. The Border North and Border South dominated the middle ground.

Lincoln's slow prewar antislavery policies helped secure the Border North in a very close 1860 presidential election. His creeping wartime emancipation consolidated the also closely divided Border South. He had demonstrated, in peace and war, that a mainstream leader who dominates the great middle and keeps in touch with one extreme can become a historic reformer.

As events proved, secessionists had correctly perceived softness in their borderlands, just as Davy Atchison, back in Kansas times, had correctly worried about unconsolidated Missouri. Lincoln, son of the Border South and migrant to the Border North, had incrementally helped turn the middle ground into his terrain. When the middle decided, the extremes' tight war turned lopsided.

8

Lincoln's private thoughts no less than his public policy evolved. He never addressed innate racial equality, which he considered another abstruse waste of time. Whatever potential black newborns possessed, he had long suspected that slaves' experiences left many hapless, like "fish on a trot-line." Nine days before his Preliminary Emancipation Proclamation, the president told Chicagoans that if we armed the blacks, "I fear that in a few weeks, the arms would be in" rebels' "hands."[22] The day before his Final Emancipation Proclamation, he finalized his black colonization experiment near Haiti. Twenty-four hours later, his proclamation called black soldiers to serve not as frontline warriors but as back-line guards of conquered "garrisons" and "forts."[23]

By 1864, however, some ex-slaves admirably manned dangerous frontline positions. Some black patriots, acting like egalitarians should, demanded equal pay for equal performance. Some preferred no payment to inferior payments. These unpaid "extremists" served with equal zeal.

President Lincoln came to see that his sable warriors' freedom in peacetime might require more than a wartime military proclamation. The president helped collect the (barely sufficient) congressional votes for the Thirteenth Amendment on January 31, 1865. After Lincoln's death and near the end of 1865, sufficient states ratified freedom's decree.

It then seemed an eternity since late February–early March 1861, when the president-elect had similarly collected the final (barely sufficient) congressional votes to submit the original Thirteenth to the states. That never-ratified amendment would have banned *congressional* emancipation. The earlier Thirteenth provides a salutary beginning shock: An eventual Great Emancipator sought to bar a powerful emancipation weapon with his last pre-presidential effort! But the shock only superficially introduces Lincoln's transformation.

He had always thought *congressional* emancipation unconstitutional and, like all imposed abolition, likely to replace peaceful Union with immense bloodshed. He had instead sought masters' consent to emancipation, during his prewar "ultimate extinction" moments and well into wartime. But after two years of civil war, he sadly knew that emancipation must depend on Union bullets, not rebel agreement.

Wisely, he stalled on coercing the Border South until that least southern South managed begrudging concurrence. On January 31, 1865, borderland congressmen agreed, 19–5, to the final Thirteenth. Two months earlier, their states had all voted for the Great Emancipator's reelection. *Their* president's administration, no longer proposing black colonization, dispatched a ship to bring back failed colonizers.[24] As with his Second Inaugural Address, remorse eased a shaken victor's slow transformation.

9

Lincoln took only baby steps toward another new birth of freedom. Beyond emancipation loomed the logic that since all men are created equal, freedmen must become equal citizens. According to Lincoln's countervailing initial logic, slaves deserved not unlimited equality but the limited right to eat the bread made by their own hands. The formula, while up to Lincoln's standards in verbal finesse, neared the bottom in accuracy and moral power.

When he reconsidered black suffrage, he moved as cautiously as ever on racial reform. A year before the war ended, he wrote Michael Hahn, Louisiana's governor, "barely" suggesting "for your private consideration, whether some of the colored people" might be "let in as" citizens, "for instance the very intelligent, and especially those who have fought gallantly in our ranks. . . . But this is only a suggestion . . . to you alone."[25]

The tone here was all politic Lincoln: "barely" suggesting, "to you alone," that "some" *might* be "let in." From similar bare beginnings, Lincoln had inched toward a close presidential election, then toward a precarious emancipation. Would his hallmark, incremental advances, continue during a convulsed Reconstruction?

The question hung fire a year later, when Lincoln went public with his whisper to Governor Hahn. On April 11, 1865, two days after rebels' surrender at Appomattox, the president addressed Washington, DC, celebrants (and a few angry foes). He urged readmitting Louisiana to the Union, despite a state constitution with no provision for black voters. While he favored suffrage for "the very intelligent and" for "our . . . soldiers," we should "take" the document "and help to improve" it. The improvement, he hinted, might require "some new announcement."[26]

Amid the cheers, John Wilkes Booth, rabid southerner and renowned actor, wanted no new announcement. So "that is the last speech he will ever make."[27] Three days later, when the president attended a melodrama at Ford's Theatre, Booth imitated Brutus slaying Julius Caesar. The actor aimed his one-shot derringer at the president's head and fired.

It was Good Friday. Four years earlier on the sacred day, an anguished Lincoln had asked his cabinet, the day after his wife's first state dinner, how to replace "fizzled" plans for Forts Sumter/Pickens. During the next 1,478 days, his team crept toward triumph. Then the bullet struck.

The next morning, Secretary of War Edwin Stanton mourned at the bedside. During Cincinnati's Manny reaper trial, this Pittsburgh lawyer had had allegedly wondered which wild animal Lincoln most resembled. The latter-day president, forgiving the travesty, saw Stanton's potential. The chief executive's forbearance won the nation a great cabinet member. Lincoln had equally succeeded by forgiving Secretary of State Seward's prewar attempted quasi–coup d'état.

A winning president must provide forgiving atmospheres for helpful teammates. Secretary of War Stanton, who had needed the boon more than most, had given back all that he had. As Lincoln's life ebbed, Stanton delivered the right verdict: Now he belongs to the ages.

10

We cannot know whether Abraham Lincoln could have brought off his newest desire: a slowly improving Reconstruction, akin to slowly developing antislavery policy in prewar times and slowly developing emancipation in killing times. If successful, he would have demonstrated again that his was a centrist nation, especially on racist matters; and a reformer who slowly nudged the fates might triumph.

But he had lived to help demonstrate why civil war came and why both sections' internal geographic divisions critically mattered, why Yankees worshiped Union and why blacks' freedom evolved with great difficulty, why convulsive American reform mixed caution with progress and American achievers combined self-help with assistance, how America's first national market economy took off and how formerly mauled Whigs became its prophets. The important impersonal demonstrations came amid dizzying personal somersaults, propelled by much awesome statecraft and some deplorable conceptions. The epic tale, like the melancholic striver, will always illuminate the American mainstream's shortfall and glory.

Gratitudes

Three splendid educators set me on the trail that culminates with this volume. Sonia Salk Heller, my American history teacher at Chicago's Francis W. Parker High School, urged that political history must be based on social history in the largest sense. Arthur M. Schlesinger, Junior, director of my honors thesis at Harvard College, taught that history must be written for more than academics. Kenneth M. Stampp, director of my Ph.D. dissertation at the University of California, Berkeley, instructed that history for any audience must be based on rigorous research.

For forty-three years, I stretched to meet these standards while writing about the antebellum slaveholders. I then benefited from Guggenheim, NEH, and American Antiquarian Society Fellowships and from a fine circle of antebellum southern specialists, including Joel Williamson, Craig M. Simpson, Chaz Joiner, David Moltke-Hansen, George Rable, Gene Genovese, and Vernon Burton. When I followed Vernon's excellent lead by moving between southern and Lincoln studies ten years ago, I enjoyed the impressive circle of Lincoln scholars, expertly led by Harold Holzer and Frank Williams.

At the start of my fresh beginning, Bill Cooper invited me to test my Lincoln migration in the Walter Fleming Lectures in Southern History at Louisiana State University. He then superbly critiqued the result. My Lincoln foray progressed thanks to the University of Virginia's magnificent facilities for visiting scholars, including my multiyear fellowship at the Virginia Foundation for the Humanities, managed by Rob Vaughn and featuring the endlessly helpful Ann White Spencer; the opportunity to try out ideas in Miller Center lectures; the research aids at the Alderman Library, with its exemplary "LEO" service; and the helpful academic colleagues around the lovely Grounds, including Mike Holt, Erik Alexander, Bill Miller, Peter Onuf, Gary Gallagher, Ed Ayers, Liz Varon, Brian Balogh, Maurie McInnis, and Calvin Schermerhorn.

During prepublication revisions, Anne Goodyear helped with the analysis, Annette Spaldoni with the images, and Emily Freehling with the ornery computer. Appropriately, the University of Virginia Press is publishing this result of my Charlottesville years, with Ellen Satrom as managing editor, old friend Dick Holway as my acquisitions editor, and Susan Murray as copy editor—and all three the best I have ever experienced. Kate Mertes finished it off with expert indexing.

My wife and our two offspring all have history degrees. All have moved beyond my profession. All have taught me about unsuspected worlds. All have thus enhanced this book while expanding my life. I gratefully dedicate this climactic historical adventure to these best of all helpmates.

Notes

Introduction

1. *Standing Lincoln* is also often titled *Abraham Lincoln: The Man*—the sculptor's original title.
2. The Lincoln Forum (www.thelincolnforum.org) provides up-to-date news on Lincoln publications and events. For a nominal fee, one can join the forum, receive its publications, and attend its excellent annual meetings.

A pursuit of Lincoln well begins where I commenced: relishing the sights. Springfield offers the Lincoln home, grave, law office, the Abraham Lincoln Presidential Library and Museum, the Illinois Executive (governor's) Mansion, and the Old Capitol Building. The New Salem restoration and the Long Nine Museum flourish near Springfield. Chicago's Lincoln remnants feature Augustus Saint-Gaudens's *Standing Lincoln* and the Abraham Lincoln Bookstore. Lincoln highlights in Washington, DC, include the White House (usually called the Executive Mansion in Lincoln's day), the Capitol Building, a superb reproduction of Saint-Gaudens's Robert Shaw Memorial in the National Gallery, the Old Soldiers' Home in Bethesda (President Lincoln's summer dwelling), Ford's Theatre, and the Lincoln Memorial. Farther north thrive Cooper Union in New York City, the Augustus Saint-Gaudens National Historical Site in Cornish, New Hampshire, and Robert Lincoln's Hildene in Manchester, Vermont.

Sundry distinguished biographies offer perspective on Lincoln from cradle to grave. While some think newest is necessarily best, the oldest biographies benefit from authors' intimate experience with the protagonist. Late nineteenth-century beneficiaries of the advantage included Billy Herndon, Lincoln's last law partner, and John G. Nicolay and John Hay, his Executive Mansion secretaries. See Douglas L. Wilson and Rodney O. Davis's expert edition of *Herndon's Lincoln* (Urbana, IL, 2006); plus Nicolay and Hay, *Abraham Lincoln, A History*, 10 vols. (New York, 1890).

From the early to mid-twentieth century, the best Lincoln biographies included Carl Sandburg's colorful and impressionistic *Abraham Lincoln: The Prairie Years*, 2 vols. (New York, 1926), and his *Abraham Lincoln: The War Years*, 4 vols. (New York, 1939); J. G. Randall's sober and scholarly *Lincoln the President*, 4 vols. (New York, 1945–55); and Benjamin P. Thomas's excellent single-volume *Abraham Lincoln: A Biography* (New York, 1952). Two mid-twentieth-century semi-biographies present especially acute biographical insights: Richard Hofstadter, "Abraham Lincoln and the Self-Made Man," in *The American Political Tradition and the Men Who Made It,* by Hofstadter, 93–136 (New York, 1948); and Richard N. Current, *The Lincoln Nobody Knows* (New York, 1958).

In more recent times, the longest and densest biography is Michael Burlingame's encyclopedic *Abraham Lincoln: A Life,* 2 vols. (Baltimore, 2008). The shortest and nimblest is James M. McPherson's lithe *Abraham Lincoln* (New York, 2009). The most distinguished recent mid-sized biographies include Mark E. Neely Jr., *The Last Best Hope of Earth: Abraham Lincoln and the Promise of America* (Cambridge, MA, 1993); David Herbert Donald, *Lincoln* (New York, 1995); Allen C. Guelzo, *Abraham Lincoln: Redeemer President* (Grand Rapids, MI, 2001); Richard Carwardine, *Lincoln: A Life of Purpose and Power* (New York, 2006); Ronald C. White Jr., *A. Lincoln* (New York, 2009); and Eric Foner, *The Fiery Trial: Abraham Lincoln and American Slavery* (New York, 2011). The superb images in Phillip B. Kunhardt Jr. et al., *Lincoln: An Illustrated Biography* (New York, 1992), bring a Lincoln introduction to climax.

Prologue

1. Daniel W. Crofts, *Lincoln and the Politics of Slavery: The Other Thirteenth Amendment* (Chapel Hill, NC, 2016).
2. Roy P. Basler, ed., *The Collected Works of Abraham Lincoln,* 9 vols. (New Brunswick, NJ, 1953–55), 4:271; hereafter cited as *CW.*

1. The Rising Lincolns and the Kentucky Plummet

1. Useful publications on the first five generations of American Lincolns include Ida Tarbell, *In the Footsteps of the Lincolns* (New York, 1924); Waldo Lincoln, *History of the Lincoln Family . . .* (Worcester, MA, 1912); William E. Barton, *The Lineage of Lincoln* (Indianapolis, IN, 1929); Louis A. Warren, *Lincoln's Parentage and Childhood* (New York, 1926); and Kenneth J. Winkle, *The Young Eagle: The Rise of Abraham Lincoln* (Dallas, TX, 2001), esp. 1–9. One of the most suggestive Lincoln articles is Thomas L. Purvis, "The Making of a Myth, Abraham Lincoln's Family Background . . . ," *Journal of the Illinois Historical Society* 75 (1982): 149–60.
2. Tales of the Tom Lincoln family's time in Kentucky are well spun in Albert J. Beveridge, *Abraham Lincoln, 1809–1858,* 2 vols. (New York, 1928); and Ralph Lawrence Miller, *Lincoln and His World,* 4 vols. (Mechanicsburg, PA, 2006–8 [vols. 1–2]; Jefferson, NC, 2011–12 [vols. 3–4]).
3. *CW,* 4:24, 7:504–5, 5:12, 528.
4. John L. Scripps (editor of the *Chicago Tribune*) to William H. Herndon, June 2, 1865, in *Herndon's Informants: Letters, Interviews, and Statements about Abraham Lincoln,* ed. Douglas L. Wilson and Rodney O. Davis (Urbana, IL, 1992), 57; hereafter cited as *HI.* This superbly edited, colorful, full collection of the best after-the-fact-recollections somewhat makes up for the lack of more direct information about Lincoln's early life. It is *the* place to gain a feel for the man's

early history, albeit as remembered by others, as well as to understand how uncertain is a history based almost entirely on memories. *HI* also contains a superb index, making location of any subject easy. For the index on Kentucky, see 805. Wilson and Davis, eds., *Herndon's Lincoln* is very useful on Lincoln's boyhood years.

5. *HI*, 499.
6. R. Gerald McMurtry, "The Lincoln Migration from Kentucky to Indiana," *Indiana Magazine of History* 38 (1937): 385–421.

2. The Indiana Plunge

1. *CW*, 4:62.
2. Excellent materials on the Indiana years are in Beveridge, *Lincoln*, 1:38–99; Miller, *Lincoln*, 1:32–90; *HI*, index for Indiana on 805; Louis A. Warren, *Lincoln's Youth: Indiana Years, Seven to Twenty-One, 1816–30* (New York, 1959); and Brian R. Dirck, *Lincoln in Indiana* (Carbondale, IL, 2017).
3. *CW*, 1:386.
4. Burlingame, *Lincoln*, 1:11.
5. *HI*, 118.
6. *CW*, 6:16–17.
7. Ibid., 4:6.
8. Ibid., 1:379.
9. *HI*, 127, 152.

3. The Illinois Crash

1. *CW*, 4:61.
2. *HI*, 12.
3. F. B. Carpenter, *Six Months at the White House with Abraham Lincoln . . .* (New York, 1866), 97–98.
4. Gary A. O'Dell, "Denton Offutt of Kentucky: America's First Horse Whisperer?," *Register of the Kentucky Historical Society* 108 (2010): 173–211, esp. 191.
5. Good material on Abraham Lincoln's New Salem years, including his earliest crash and first recovery, are in Beveridge, *Lincoln*, 1:100–159; Miller, *Lincoln*, 1:91–221; Benjamin P. Thomas, *Lincoln's New Salem* (New York, 1954); and *HI*, index for New Salem on 805–6. John Mark Faragher's *Sugar Creek: Life on the Illinois Prairie* (New Haven, CT, 1986), illuminates a nearby prairie community with many similarities.
6. This quote and "winked out" in the next paragraph are from *CW*, 4:65.
7. This rough comparison of mid-nineteenth-century and early twenty-first-century statistics, like all such comparisons in this volume, is based on Robert Sahr's helpful tables at http://liberalarts.oregonstate.edu/spp/polisci/research/inflation-conversion-factors-convert-dollars-1774-estimated-2024-dollars-recent-year. At the bottom of the page click on Individual Year Conversion Factor Tables, then on pdf.
8. The Lincoln quotes in this paragraph and Herndon's "wrinkles" quote in the next paragraph are from Burlingame, *Lincoln*, 1:76.

4. The New Salem Recovery

1. *CW,* 1:5–9.
2. Don E. Fehrenbacher and Virginia Fehrenbacher, eds., *Recollected Words of Abraham Lincoln* (Stanford, CA, 1996), 146. The Fehrenbachers' large collection of recollections importantly supplements *HI,* this time with evaluations of many items' probability.
3. Paul M. Zall, *Abe Lincoln's Legacy of Laughter* (Knoxville, TN, 2007), 78. Lincoln's humor, while enticing and critical for understanding the man, has usually only survived in especially suspicious recollections. Zall's book earns more trust than most because it confesses errors in an earlier attempt, welcomes the Fehrenbachers' criticisms, substitutes more reliable texts, and presents the cull with sensible warnings. For further perspective, see Richard Carwardine, *Lincoln's Sense of Humor* (Carbondale, IL, 2017).
4. Zall, *Lincoln's Laughter,* 50.
5. Ibid., 57.
6. *HI,* 719.
7. Ibid., 396.
8. Ibid., 384–85.
9. Harry E. Pratt, "Lincoln in the Black Hawk War," *Bulletin of the Abraham Lincoln Association* 54 (1938): 3–14.
10. *HI,* 368.
11. *CW,* 4:64.
12. *HI,* 171.
13. Theodore Calvin Pease, ed., *Illinois Election Returns, 1828–1848* (Springfield, IL, 1923), 262.
14. Harry E. Pratt, *The Personal Finances of Abraham Lincoln* (Chicago, 1943), 17–19.
15. Wilson and Davis, eds., *Herndon's Lincoln,* 87.
16. Zall, *Lincoln's Laughter,* 37.
17. Ibid.
18. Pratt, *Lincoln's Finances,* 20–23. Pratt's research and mine permit only guesses at Lincoln's income from surveying.

5. The Rise and Fall of a State Legislator

1. Excellent volumes on Lincoln's legislative years include William L. Baringer, *Lincoln's Vandalia: A Pioneer Portrait* (New Brunswick, NJ, 1949); Miller, *Lincoln,* vol. 2; Paul Simon, *Lincoln's Preparation for Greatness: The Illinois Legislative Years* (Urbana, IL, 1971); and John H. Krenkel, *Illinois Internal Improvements, 1818–1848* (Cedar Rapids, IA, 1958). Gabor S. Boritt began the important process of connecting Lincoln's early state economic statecraft and the Rail-splitter's later national heroism in the brilliant *Lincoln and the Economics of the American Dream* (1978; Urbana, IL, 1994).
2. *HI,* 146.
3. Wilson and Davis, eds., *Herndon's Lincoln,* 231.
4. *HI,* 197.

5. *CW,* 2:220–21.

6. Richard K. Cralle, ed., *The Works of John C. Calhoun,* 6 vols. (New York, 1851–70), 2:190.

7. George Rogers Taylor, *The Transportation Revolution, 1815–1860* (New York, 1951) expertly supplies national perspective.

8. *HI,* 476; *CW,* 1:135.

9. Ibid., 1:32.

10. John M. Lamb, *A Corridor in History: The Illinois and Michigan Canal, 1836–1899* (Romeoville, IL, 1987), offers the best entry into Lamb's remarkable research on Illinois's attempt at its own "Erie Canal."

11. *HI,* 478–79, 588–89.

12. Pease, ed., *Illinois Election Returns,* 299.

13. Robert W. Johannsen, *Stephen A. Douglas* (New York, 1973), the best biography, details the Little Giant's Illinois start in chaps. 1–3.

14. Illinois *House Journal,* 1836–37, 36. This source is usually available for the antebellum years in openlibrary.org.

15. For details on the final law and its passage, see Krenkel, *Illinois Internal Improvements,* esp. 70n.

16. Robert W. Johannsen, ed., *The Letters of Stephen A. Douglas* (Urbana, IL, 1961), 67–68.

17. *CW,* 1:48.

18. Simon, *Lincoln's Legislative Years,* 183.

19. John Joseph Wallis, "What Caused the Crisis of 1839?," National Bureau of Historical Research Paper 133, April 2001, presents a splendid analysis of this crucial event in Illinois history.

20. Pease, ed., *Illinois Election Returns,* 321.

21. Burlingame, *Lincoln,* 1:143.

22. *CW,* 1:135–38.

23. Ibid., 1:148.

24. *CW,* 1:135, 196.

25. Ibid., 1:144.

26. Ibid., 1:243–44.

27. Pease, ed., *Illinois Election Returns,* 344.

6. The Rise and Limits of a Pre-1850s Lawyer

1. *HI,* 450. A lucky posterity can choose between three easily accessible, early twenty-first-century manuscript presentations:

   (*a*) in a three-DVD set: *The Law Practice of Abraham Lincoln: Complete Documentary Edition* (2000);

   (*b*) on the Internet: papersofabrahamlincoln.org: The Law Practice of Abraham Lincoln: Second Edition (2002); and

   (*c*) in print: Daniel W. Stowell et al., eds., *The Papers of Abraham Lincoln: Legal Documents and Cases,* 4 vols. (Charlottesville, VA, 2004).

   I prefer the last choice, even though it omits much material on lesser cases. The more selective approach more richly documents Lincoln's most important fifty cases, with the added bonus of excellent essays and sometimes maps on critical texts. The best secondary sources that early sprang from this primary-source feast included Brian Dirck's *Lincoln the Lawyer* and Mark E. Steiner's *An Honest Calling: The Law Practice of Abraham Lincoln* (both published in Dekalb, IL, 2009), plus the valuable essays in Roger Billings and Frank J. Williams, eds., *Abraham Lincoln, Esquire* (Lexington, KY, 2010).

2. Stephen Berry, *Lincoln & the Todds* . . . (New York, 2007), 197–98.
3. Wilson and Davis, eds., *Herndon's Lincoln*, 207.
4. Ibid., 203.
5. Henry C. Whitney, *Life on the Circuit with Lincoln* (Boston, 1892), 56–57.
6. Leonard Swett qtd. in Allen D. Spiegel, *A. Lincoln, Esquire* (Macon, GA, 2002), 45–46.
7. Zall, *Lincoln's Laughter*, xiv.
8. *CW*, 1:116.
9. Ibid., 2:81–82.
10. All qtd. in Steiner, *Honest Calling*, 40–43.
11. *HI*, 173.
12. Dirck, *Lincoln the Lawyer*, 38.
13. The vagueness by the usually precise Henry Pratt on this aspect of *Lincoln's Finances*, 25–57, indicates that only guesses are possible. Sensible estimates are in Spiegel, *A. Lincoln*, 34; and Burlingame, *Lincoln*, 1:333.
14. Zall, *Lincoln's Laughter*, 47. Donald, *Lincoln*, 104–6, well describes the Circuit.
15. Zall, *Lincoln's Laughter*, 90.
16. Rufus Rockwell Wilson, *Intimate Memories of Lincoln* (Elmira, NY, 1945), 105.
17. *HI*, 348–49.
18. Pease, ed., *Illinois Election Returns*, 159.
19. Wilson and Davis, eds., *Herndon's Lincoln*, 126.
20. *CW*, 1:108–15.
21. Stowell et al., eds., *Lincoln's Legal Documents*, 2:1–43, best illuminates the *Matson* case. See also Steiner, *Honest Calling*, 103–36; and Charles R. McKirdy, *The Matson Slave Case* (Jackson, MS, 2011). On Lincoln's attempted use of writ of habeas corpus technical logic, see Duncan T. McIntyne, "Lincoln and the Matson Slave Case," *Illinois Law Review* 1 (1906–7): 390–91.

7. The Rise and Turbulence of a Marriage

1. Joshua F. Speed, *Reminiscences of Abraham Lincoln* . . . (Louisville, 1884), 21–22.
2. Ibid., 23.
3. Michael Burlingame, ed., *An Oral History of Abraham Lincoln: John G. Nicolay's Interviews and Letters* (Carbondale, IL, 1996), 22–23; Wilson and Davis, eds., *Herndon's Lincoln*, 123.
4. Burlingame, *Lincoln*, 1:175.
5. *HI*, 443.
6. Ibid., 253.
7. Ibid., 256.
8. Ibid., 262.

9. Ibid.

10. Lincoln to Mary Owens, May 7, 1837, in *CW,* 1:78.

11. Lincoln to Owens, August 16, 1837, in *CW,* 1:94.

12. *HI,* 263.

13. Lincoln to Mrs. Orville H. Browning, April 1, 1838, in *CW,* 1:117–19.

14. Excellent studies of Mary Todd Lincoln include Stephen Berry, *House of Abraham: Lincoln and the Todds, a Family Divided by War* (New York, 2007); Ruth Painter Randall, *Mary Todd Lincoln: Biography of a Marriage* (Boston, 1953); Jean H. Baker, *Mary Todd Lincoln: A Biography* (New York, 2008); and Catherine Clinton, *Mrs. Lincoln: A Life* (New York, 2009).

15. *HI,* 263.

16. Ibid., 623.

17. Douglas L. Wilson, "Abraham Lincoln and the Fatal First of January," *Civil War History* 38 (1992): 101–30.

18. Martinette Hardin McKee to John Hardin, January 22, 1841, Hardin Papers, Chicago Historical Society; *HI,* 133, 475; Lincoln to John T. Stuart, January 23, 1841, in *CW,* 1:229.

19. Douglas L. Wilson, *Honor's Voice: The Transformation of Abraham Lincoln* (New York, 1998), is among the finest recent Lincoln books, featuring a convincing analysis of honor's part in a tortured domestic reconciliation. Wilson's book also exemplifies a rare and much-appreciated quality of the recent Lincoln editorial revolution: Many of the best editors of primary-source materials have also published some of the best secondary historical accounts.

20. Wilson and Davis, eds., *Herndon's Lincoln,* 151.

21. Ibid., 153.

22. Lincoln to Joshua Speed, October 5, 1842, in *CW,* 1:303.

23. Donald, *Lincoln,* 159.

24. *HI,* 443; Justin G. and Linda Levitt Turner, *Mary Todd Lincoln: Her Life and Letters* (New York, 1972), 293; Baker, *Mary Todd Lincoln,* 108.

25. Burlingame, *Lincoln,* 1:175.

26. Ibid.

27. Ibid., 1:202.

28. Harold Holzer, *Lincoln President Elect: Abraham Lincoln and the Great Secession Winter* (New York, 2008), 45.

8. A Congressional Aspirant's Rise

1. Henry C. Blair and Rebecca Tarshis, *The Life of Col. Edward D. Baker . . .* (Portland, OR, 1960), 18–19 (citing *Sangamo Journal,* June 5, 1840, p. 3, col. 1), is the most convincing version of this sometimes dubiously described event and the best source on Baker, Lincoln's most amusing opponent. Best on John J. Hardin is Amy S. Greenberg, *A Wicked War . . .* (New York, 2013).

2. Miller, *Lincoln,* 2:92–94.

3. Michael Holt, *The Rise and Fall of the Whig Party . . .* (New York, 1999); Daniel Walker Howe, *The Political Culture of the American Whigs* (Chicago, 1979); Howe, *What God Hath Wrought: The Transformation of America, 1815–1860* (New

York, 2007); Joel Sibley, "Always a Whig in Politics: The Partisan Life of Abraham Lincoln," *Papers of the Abraham Lincoln Association* 8 (1986): 21–42, all place Lincoln's Whiggery in national perspective.

4. *CW,* 1:205.
5. Ibid., 1:180.
6. Ibid., 1:202.
7. Ibid., 1:318.
8. Ibid., 1:315.
9. Ibid., 2:126.
10. Ibid., 1:319.
11. Ibid., 1:322.
12. Lincoln to Hardin, February 7, 1846, in *CW,* 1:360–65.
13. Robert Bray, *Peter Cartwright, Legendary Frontier Preacher* (Urbana, IL, 2005).
14. *CW,* 1:382.
15. *HI,* 506. This pivotal antebellum exchange points historians toward necessarily ambiguous formulations on Lincoln's fatalism. As James McPherson convincingly argues in "A Passive President?," *Atlantic Monthly* 276 (1995): 134–41, David Donald's otherwise excellent *Lincoln* cannot make a careful activist, in the personal responsibility vein, wholly understandable as a passive philosopher, in the impersonal determinist vein. One must find Lincoln's imprecise mix of personal responsibility and impersonal fatalism, perhaps the one that Richard Carwardine skillfully circles around in his *Lincoln,* 39–44, and/or the slightly different version here.
16. A point well made in Allen C. Guelzo's excellent "Abraham Lincoln and the Doctrine of Necessity," *Journal of the Abraham Lincoln Association* 18 (1997): 57–81.

9. The Congressional Fall

1. Lincoln to Mary Todd Lincoln, April 16, 1848, in *CW,* 1:465.
2. Lincoln to Mary Todd Lincoln, June 12, 1848, in *CW,* 1:477–78.
3. Samuel C. Busey, *Personal Reminiscences and Recollections . . .* (Washington, DC, 1895), 27.
4. Zall, *Lincoln's Laughter,* 4.
5. *CW,* 1:480–92, esp. 481, 489.
6. Lincoln to Albert G. Hodges, April 4, 1864, in *CW,* 7:281; Lincoln to Joshua Speed, August 24, 1855, in *CW,* 2:320.
7. Lincoln to Mary Speed, September 27, 1841, in *CW,* 1:259–60.
8. Lincoln to Joshua Speed, August 24, 1855, in *CW,* 2:320.
9. *CW,* 2:126.
10. Ira Berlin, *Generations of Captivity: A History of North American Slavery* (Cambridge, MA, 2003), is a fine synthesis, especially admirable for its careful tracing of change over time, an important phenomenon often absent from slavery studies.
11. Lincoln to Joshua Speed, August 24, 1855, in *CW,* 2:320.
12. *CW,* 1:75.
13. Illinois *House Journal,* 1837, 198; Illinois *Senate Journal,* 1837, 297.
14. *CW,* 1:75.
15. Ibid., 1:271–79.

16. William W. Freehling, *The Road to Disunion*, 2 vols. (New York, 1990, 2007), 1:287–352; William Lee Miller, *Arguing about Slavery . . .* (New York, 1996).

17. Lincoln to Williamson Durley, October 3, 1845, *CW*, 1:347–48.

18. *Speech of Henry Clay, at the Lexington Mass Meeting, 13 November 1847 . . .* (New York, 1847).

19. *CW*, 1:421–42.

20. *HI*, 691.

21. *Congressional Globe*, 30th Cong., 2d sess., January 10, 1849, 212. Lincoln's never-introduced resolutions are more conveniently available in *CW*, 2:20–22.

10. The Union's Economic Rescue

1. Lincoln so later exclaimed to Billy Herndon (Wilson and Davis, eds., *Herndon's Lincoln*, 188). For the uncertainty about when the Lincolns visited Niagara Falls and a description of their 1848 Great Lakes trip home, see John Fagant, *The Best of the Bargain: Lincoln in Western New York* (Bloomington, IN, 2010), chap. 1.

2. Jason Emerson, *Lincoln the Inventor* (Carbondale, IL, 2009).

3. Johannsen, *Douglas*, 314. John F. Stover's massive *History of the Illinois Central Railroad* (New York, 1975) remains the best history. Also helpful are Paul Wallace Gates, *The Illinois Central Railroad and Its Colonization Work* (Cambridge, MA, 1934); and Martin J. Emill, "The Illinois Central and the Development of Illinois," master's thesis, Loyola University, 1933.

4. Burlingame, *Lincoln*, 1:333.

5. Pratt, *Lincoln's Finances*, 123–24.

6. The latest rendition is George R. Deckle, *Abraham Lincoln's Most Famous Case: The Almanac Trial* (Santa Barbara, 2014). Splendid source material is reprinted in Stowell et al., eds., *Lincoln's Legal Documents*, 4:1–48.

7. Since Lincoln's speech to the jury was never recorded, I here flavor his beginning with a couple of his favorite renditions of similar events, as surviving in *HI*, 12, and in *CW*, 1:320.

8. *HI*, 173.

9. Burlingame, *Lincoln*, 1:221; Wayne C. Temple, *By Square and Compass: Saga of the Lincoln Home* (Mahomet, IL, 2002), esp. 89–116, 271–74.

10. A point well made in Stephen Hahn, "'A Self-Made Man'. . .," *New York Times Book Review*, May 13, 2016.

11. *CW*, 4:438.

11. Three Climactic Railroad Cases

1. Lincoln to Thomas R. Webber, September 12, 1853, in *CW*, 2:202.

2. *HI*, 529.

3. The best and excellent source on *Barret* is Stowell et al., eds., *Lincoln's Legal Documents*, 2:172–210.

4. *CW*, 1:398.

5. Stowell et al., eds., *Lincoln's Legal Documents*, 2:207.

6. Ibid., 2:375–415.

7. Ibid., 2:395–401, esp. 396, 401.
8. The latest narrative is Brian McGinty, *Lincoln's Greatest Case: The River, the Bridge, and the Making of America* (New York, 2015), but my favorite source is again Stowell et al., eds., *Lincoln's Legal Documents,* 2:308–82.
9. Burlingame, *Lincoln,* 1:337.
10. An excellent account of this dismal Lincoln incident is ibid., 1:339–41.
11. Lincoln's closing argument is in Stowell et al., eds., *Lincoln's Legal Documents,* 2:359–65.
12. *Mississippi & Missouri Railroad v. Ward,* 67 U.S. (2 Black) 485, esp. 496.

12. The Peoria Address and the Strategy of Defense

1. Francis B. Carpenter, "Anecdotes and Reminiscences of President Lincoln," in Henry Jarvis Raymond, *Life and Public Services of Abraham Lincoln . . .* (New York, 1865), 752.
2. *CW,* 1:130.
3. Ibid., 1:132.
4. On the importance of the colonization dream to American exceptionalism, see my *The Reintegration of American History: Slavery and the Civil War* (New York, 1994), 138–57. The point is exceptionally well developed in David Brion Davis, *The Problem of Slavery in the Age of Emancipation* (New York, 2014); and in Eric Foner, "Lincoln and Colonization," in *Our Lincoln: Perspectives on Lincoln and the World,* ed. Foner (New York, 2008), 135–66.
5. *CW,* 1:130.
6. Ibid., 2:382–83.
7. *HI,* 181, 197.
8. Alan Nevins, *Ordeal of the Union,* 2 vols. (New York, 1947), 2:101; Johannsen, *Douglas,* 411.
9. I more extensively document the important tale of Douglas, Atchison, Benton, and the F Street Mess in *Road to Disunion,* 1:537–600. See also Roy F. Nichols's seminal article "The Kansas-Nebraska Act: A Century of Historiography," *Mississippi Valley Historical Review* 43 (1956): 187–212.
10. *CW,* 2:317–18.
11. George Fitzhugh, *Sociology for the South, or the Failure of Free Society* (Richmond, VA, 1854), 94, 177–78, 182. For more on the intriguing Fitzhugh, see my *Road to Disunion,* 2:35–39.
12. Lincoln to Robertson, August 24, 1855, in *CW,* 2:317–18.
13. Lincoln to Speed, August 24, 1855, in *CW,* 2:322.
14. Donald, *Lincoln,* 178.
15. *CW,* 2:255, 275, 271, 276. The best book on the Peoria Address is Lewis E. Lehrman, *Lincoln at Peoria . . .* (Mechanicsburg, PA, 2008).
16. *CW,* 2:230, 255–56.
17. Ibid., 2:266.
18. Ibid., 2:276.
19. Ibid., 2:255.
20. Ibid., 2:248, 260.

21. Ibid., 2:270.
22. Ibid., 2:266.
23. Ibid., 2:256.
24. Ibid., 2:266–67.

13. The 1855 Setback

1. William E. Gienapp's fine *The Origins of the Republican Party, 1852–1856* (New York, 1987), is especially telling on the several moral issues that had to be sorted out before Republicanism could be primarily, much less all, about slavery.
2. Richard H. Sewell, *Ballots for Freedom: Antislavery Politics in the United States, 1837–1860* (New York, 1976), and James Oakes, *The Scorpion's Sting: Antislavery and the Coming of the Civil War* (New York, 2014), both illuminate the leftward side of the mainstream political struggle—not as far out as abolitionist extremists but much more radical than Abraham Lincoln.
3. Lincoln to Joshua Speed, August 24, 1854, in *CW*, 2:323.
4. Lincoln to Owen Lovejoy, August 11, 1854, in *CW*, 2:316.
5. *CW*, 3:350.
6. Ibid., 2:300.
7. Edward Magdol, *Owen Lovejoy: Abolitionist in Congress* (New Brunswick, NJ, 1967); William F. and Jane Ann Moore, *Collaborators for Emancipation: Abraham Lincoln and Owen Lovejoy* (Urbana, IL, 2014).
8. William F. and Jane Ann Moore, eds., *His Brother's Blood: Speeches and Writing, 1838–64* (Urbana, IL, 2004).
9. Victor B. Howard, "The Illinois State Republican Party," *Journal of the Illinois Historical Society* 64 (summer and autumn, 1971): 125–60, 185–311.
10. Lincoln to Ichabod Codding, November 27, 1854, in *CW*, 2:288.
11. Lincoln to Thomas J. Henderson, November 27, 1854, in *CW*, 2:288; Matthew Pinkster, "Senator Abraham Lincoln," *Journal of the Abraham Lincoln Association* 14 (summer 1993): 1–21, tells this story of this election very well.
12. See, for example, Lincoln to Elihu B. Washburne, December 19, 1854, in *CW*, 2:295.
13. Lincoln to Jesse Norton, February 16, 1855, in *The Collected Works of Abraham Lincoln: Second Supplement, 1848–1865*, ed. Roy P. Basler and Christian O. Basler (New Brunswick, NJ, 1990), 9–11.
14. Horace White, *The Life of Lyman Trumbull* (Boston, 1913); Mark M. Krug, *Lyman Trumbull, Conservative Radical* (New York, 1965).
15. The twin ballots can be followed in Illinois *House Journal*, 1855, 348–61.

14. The Lost/Found Speech

1. *CW*, 2:262–63.
2. Freehling, *Road to Disunion*, 2:73, 75.
3. *The Transactions of the McLean County Historical Society* 3 (1900): 3–184, is the best source on the Decatur Editors' Convention, esp. 30–43, 68. For the convention's resolutions, see *Daily Illinois State Journal*, February 27, 1856.

4. On the general phenomenon, see Harold Holzer's excellent *Lincoln and the Power of the Press* (New York, 2014).
5. Here as everywhere, the best general history of the gathering storm is David H. Potter, *The Impending Crisis: America before the Civil War* (New York, 1976).
6. *The Transactions of the McLean County Historical Society* 3 (1900): 3–184, is the best source on the May 29 Bloomington no less than on the February 22 Decatur Convention.
7. Wilson and Davis, eds., *Herndon's Lincoln,* 236.
8. Henry Clay Whitney's remembrance of the only never-lost sentence in the speech, as recorded in Elwell Crissey, *Lincoln's Lost Speech* (New York, 1967), 180. Whitney's sentence came in his reconstruction of the entire speech, published forty years later—the only such attempted reconstruction by an original witness in Major's Hall. I agree with most Lincoln scholars that Whitney's overall reconstruction does not *sound* like Lincoln and conflicts at too many points with other listeners' recollections. In contrast, Whitney's never-lost sentence precisely matches both a Lincoln sentence at Galena, fifty-five days later (see *CW,* 2:355), and the account by two other original witnesses in Major's Hall (see Crissey, *Lincoln's Lost Speech,* 196, 200).

15. The *Dred Scott* Case and the Kansas Finale

1. *Proceedings of the First Three Republican National Conventions of 1856, 1860, and 1864 . . .* (Minneapolis, MN, 1893), 63–64.
2. Robert S. Eckley, *Lincoln's Forgotten Friend, Leonard Swett* (Carbondale, IL, 2012), 53–54.
3. *HI,* 731–32.
4. Lincoln to Henry C. Whitney, July 9, 1856, in *CW,* 2:347.
5. Lincoln to David Davis, July 7, 1856, in *Collected Works of Abraham Lincoln: First Supplement,* 1832–1865, ed. Roy P. Basler (Westport, CT, 1973), 27.
6. Lincoln to John Bennett and to Hezekiah G. Wells, August 4, 1856, in *CW,* 2:358.
7. Ibid., 2:384–85.
8. Ibid., 2:354–55.
9. Ibid., 2:362–63.
10. For the best overall history of this case, see Don E. Fehrenbacher, *The Dred Scott Case: Its Significance in American Law and Practice* (New York, 1978). For how the case evolved among the Court's southern judges, see my *Road to Disunion,* 2:109–22.
11. Stephen Arnold Douglas, *Remarks of the Hon. Stephen Douglas, on Kansas, Utah, and the Dred Scott Decision* (Springfield, IL, 1857), esp. 7–11.
12. *CW,* 2:405, 408–9.
13. Ibid., 2:404.
14. Ibid., 2:405, 408.
15. Ibid., 2:409.
16. Ibid., 2:401.
17. Ibid., 2:406.
18. Ibid., 2:405.

16. The Great Debates

1. William H. Herndon to Elihu Washburne, April 10, 1858, Washburne Papers, Library of Congress.
2. Abraham Lincoln to Lyman Trumbull, December 28, 1857, in *CW*, 2:430.
3. Ibid., 3:482; 3:394; *HI*, 731. Don E. Fehrenbacher, *Prelude to Greatness: Lincoln in the 1850s* (Palo Alto, CA, 1962), is among the finest Lincoln books.
4. "Draft of a Speech," circa August 1858, in Abraham Lincoln, *Speeches and Writings*, selected and with notes by Don E. Fehrenbacher, Library of America Edition, 2 vols. (New York, 1984), 1:488–94. This best two-volume edition of Lincoln's orations is hereafter cited as *Lincoln's Speeches and Writings* and is cited whenever possible for the Great Debates.
5. *Lincoln's Speeches and Writings*, 1:426.
6. Ibid., 1:431.
7. Ibid., 1:427, 430.
8. Ibid., 1:432.
9. Ibid., 1:433.
10. Ibid., 1:434.
11. *Groves v. Slaughter*, 40 US 508–9 (1841). Several recent "might-have-been" historians have suggested that *if* New York State's important *Lemmon* case had been appealed to Taney's U.S. Supreme Court near the end of the antebellum period, the Court *might* have overturned New York's right to abolish slavery in its own jurisdiction. I find the speculation more plausible when guessing whether the case might have landed in Taney's lap than in guessing that the chief justice would then have canceled state-decreed emancipation. The Marylander, having freed all his own slaves, was hardly some fanatical Great Enslaver, likely to reenslave some 250,000 Yankee free blacks. Nor was this southern moderate some Great Disunionist, likely to shatter the Union with a judgment that northerners could never accept. Nor was this ardent state's-righter (and champion of his own *Groves v. Slaughter*) likely to somersault into the provocation that a Yankee state had no right to decide on its own labor system. Taney looked like an awful secessionist fanatic, as much as Lincoln looked like an uneducated country bumpkin. In both cases, appearances deceived.
12. Wilson and Davis, eds., *Herndon's Lincoln*, 244; *HI*, 574–75.
13. John L. Scripps to Lincoln, June 22, 1858, Lincoln Papers, Library of Congress.
14. Lincoln to Scripps, June 23, 1858, in *CW*, 2:471.
15. John C. Forney, *Anecdotes of Public Men*, 2 vols. (New York, 1873), 2:179.
16. *Lincoln's Speeches and Writings*, 1:461–62.
17. Ibid., 1:533, 553–54, 660, 755.
18. Ibid., 1:446, 470.
19. Ibid., 1 447.
20. Ibid., 1:810–11.
21. Ibid., 1:808.
22. Ibid., 1:717–18.
23. Ibid., 1:458.

24. Ibid., 1:506.

25. Ibid., 1:595–6.

26. "Speech of Douglas in Springfield, July 17, 1858," in George Haven Putnam, *The Political Debates between Abraham Lincoln and Stephen A. Douglas . . . ,* 2 vols. in 1 cover (New York, 1912), 1:143–46. This fuller edition of the debates has the advantage of including the early July 1858 "pre-debate" debates in Springfield and Chicago. It does not, however, include the June 1857 "pre-debate" debate in Springfield, as I believe the fullest edition should.

27. *CW,* 2:399.

28. *Lincoln's Speeches and Writings,* 1:807.

29. Ibid., 1:511.

30. Ibid., 1:458.

31. Ibid., 1:512.

32. Compare his Freeport answer (ibid., 1:539) with every other time he touched the subject in these debates (for example, ibid., 1:447, 603, 704, 798, 808).

33. For the most important examples of his compromised Radical Republican formulas, see his answers to Douglas at Freeport, ibid., 1:538–41.

34. Ibid., 1:539.

35. Ibid., 1:514–15.

36. Ibid., 1:677–8.

37. Ibid., 1:806.

38. Ibid., 1:508.

39. The raw voting figures are at State House and Senate Records, 1858, Illinois State Archives, microfilm reels 130–45. The most salient figures are in Exercise 5, "Who Voted for Whom," in the "Primary Sources" section of a superb aid to teaching the Great Debates: Allen C. Guelzo, ed., "House Divided; Lincoln, Douglas, and the Political Landscape of 1858," *Teaching the Journal of American History* 94, no. 2 (September 2007), online at archive.oah.org/special-issues/teaching/. Guelzo's excellent history of the debates, *Lincoln and Douglas: The Debates That Defined America* (New York, 2008), can usefully be supplemented with John Burt, *Lincoln's Tragic Pragmatism: Lincoln, Douglas, and Moral Conflict* (Cambridge, MA, 2013); William Lee Miller, *Lincoln's Virtues, An Ethical Biography* (New York, 2002); and especially Harry K. Jaffe, *Crisis of the House Divided: An Interpretation of the Issues in the Lincoln-Douglas Debates* (Chicago, 1959).

40. Lincoln to Anson G. Henry, November 19, 1858, in *CW,* 2:339.

17. The Cunning Revisions

1. *Lincoln's Speeches and Writings,* 1:542, 551–52.

2. *CW,* 3:390, 384.

3. Ibid., 3:453.

4. Ibid., 3:454.

5. Ibid., 3:404, 482.

6. Ibid., 3:463. Highlights of Lincoln's ensuing screech against Douglas are in 3:409, 423–24, 431.

7. Ibid., 3:369.
8. Illinois Republican State Committee, *Public Record of . . . Douglas on the Slavery Question* (n.p., n.d. [1860]), 11.
9. *CW,* 3:470.
10. Ibid., 3:459, 462–63, 468–69, 477–80.
11. *HI,* 57.
12. *CW,* 3:468–69.
13. David Brown, *Hinton R. Helper and the Impending Crisis of the South* (Baton Rouge, 2006); Freehling, *Road to Disunion,* 2:246–68.
14. Ibid., 2:496, 502.

18. The Cooper Union Address

1. James A. Briggs to Abraham Lincoln, October 12, 1859, Abraham Lincoln Papers, Library of Congress.
2. Briggs to Lincoln, February 15, 1860, Lincoln Papers, Library of Congress.
3. The best history of this major oratorical event is Harold Holzer, *Lincoln at Cooper Union: The Speech That Made Abraham Lincoln President* (New York, 2004).
4. Joshua Zeitz, *Lincoln's Boys: John Hay, John Nicolay, and the War for Lincoln's Image* (New York, 2014), 56.
5. The Cooper Union Address is reprinted in many places, including *CW,* 3:522–50. "*Enough*" cascades at 535.
6. Ibid., 3:546–47.
7. Ibid., 3:536.
8. Ibid., 3:535, 537–38.
9. Ibid., 1:538, 541.
10. Ibid., 3:547–50.
11. Ibid., 3:550.
12. Donald, *Lincoln,* 239; Burlingame, *Lincoln,* 1:587.
13. James A. Briggs to Lincoln, February 29, 1860, Lincoln Papers, Library of Congress.
14. Jason Emerson, *Giant in the Shadows: The Life of Robert T. Lincoln* (Carbondale, IL, 2012).
15. Lincoln to Mary Todd Lincoln, March 4, 1860, in *Collected Works: First Supplement,* ed. Basler, 49.
16. *CW,* 4:5, 18.
17. Ibid., 4:24.
18. Ibid., 4:25.
19. Ibid., 4:24–25.

19. The Presidential Election and the Fruits of Revision

1. Lincoln to Judd, December 14, 1859, in *CW,* 3:509.
2. Mark A. Plummer, *Lincoln's Rail-Splitter: Governor Richard J. Oglesby* (Urbana, IL, 2001), 41–44.
3. Gary Ecelbarger, *The Great Comeback: How Abraham Lincoln Beat the Odds to Win the 1860 Nomination* (New York, 2008), 260n, makes a convincing case

for this (disputed) wording. The best book on Lincoln's climb to the Executive Mansion is William C. Harris, *Lincoln's Rise to the Presidency* (Lawrence, KS, 2007).

4. Lincoln to Theodore Caninius, May 17, 1859, in *CW,* 3:380.
5. Burlingame, *Lincoln,* 1:599–600.
6. *CW,* 4:50.
7. R. Craig Sauter and Edward M. Burke, *Inside the Wigwam: Chicago Presidential Conventions, 1860–1996* (Chicago, 1996), 3–14.
8. These days, historical research is sometimes more profitably conducted on the Internet than in books. Witness Chicago's screw jack revolution. Start with two websites with good information and superb illustrations: chicagology.com/prefire/raising; and livinghistoryofillinois.com/raisingchicago/. Then back to the books for broader environmental history, especially William Cronon's awesome *Nature's Metropolis: Chicago and the Great West* (New York, 1991).
9. *CW,* 3:551–2.
10. Lincoln to Samuel Galloway, March 4, 1860, in *CW,* 4:33–34.
11. Convention ballots figures and colorful reporting on Wigwam scenes are in William B. Hesseltine, ed., *Three Against Lincoln: Murat Halstead Reports on the Caucuses of 1860* (Baton Rouge, LA, 1960), 167–70.
12. Burlingame, *Lincoln,* 1:626.
13. *CW,* 4:50.
14. Hesseltine, ed., *Three Against Lincoln,* 175.
15. David L. Smiley, *Lion of White Hall: The Life of Cassius M. Clay* (Madison, WI, 1962); H. Edward Richardson, *Cassius Marcellus Clay: Firebrand of Freedom* (Lexington, KY, 1976); Freehling, *Road to Disunion,* 2:227–30.
16. Walter Dean Burnham, *Presidential Ballots, 1836–1892* (Baltimore, 1955), 247–57.

20. The Erratic Interregnum

1. Fine studies of Lincoln's interregnum include David Potter, *Lincoln and His Party in the Secession Crisis* (Baton Rouge, LA, 1942); Kenneth M. Stampp, *And the War Came: The North and the Secession Crisis, 1860–1861* (Baton Rouge, LA, 1970); William J. Cooper, *We Have the War upon Us: The Onset of the Civil War, November 1860–April 1861* (New York, 2012); Harold Holzer, *Lincoln President-Elect: Abraham Lincoln and the Great Secession Winter, 1860–1861* (New York, 2008); and Russell McClintock, *Lincoln and the Decision for War: The Northern Response to Secession* (Chapel Hill, NC, 2008).
2. William W. Freehling, *Prelude to Civil War: The Nullification Controversy in South Carolina, 1816–1836* (New York, 1964).
3. John B. O'Neall, *Biographical Sketches of the Bench and Bar in South Carolina,* 2 vols. (Charleston, 1859), 1:181.
4. Freehling, *Road to Disunion,* 1:515–23, 2:352–426.
5. Nicolay and Hay, *Lincoln,* 2:306–14.
6. Freehling, *Road to Disunion,* 2:476–89.
7. Lincoln to William Kellogg, December 11, 1860, and Lincoln to Elihu B. Washburne, December 13, 1860, both in *CW,* 4:150–51.

8. Lincoln to Pennsylvania's James T. Hale, January 11, 1861, and Lincoln to Indiana's John D. Defrees, December 18, 1860, both in *CW,* 4:172, 155.
9. *HI,* 499.
10. Dan Crofts's *The Other Thirteenth Amendment* has given new importance to this passing incident.
11. "Resolutions . . . for the Republican Members of the Senate Committee of Thirteen," Lincoln to Trumbull, December 21, 1860, and Seward to Lincoln, December 26, 1860, all in *CW,* 4:156–58, leave no doubt about Lincoln's input.
12. *CW,* 4:270.
13. Gilmer to Lincoln, December 10, 1860, Lincoln Papers, Library of Congress; Lincoln to Gilmer, December 15, 1860, in *CW,* 4:152.
14. Ibid., 4:266.
15. John Townsend, *The South Alone Should Govern the South, and African Slavery Should Be Controlled by Those Friendly to It* (Charleston, SC, 1860), 12.
16. *Charleston (SC) Mercury,* October 11, 1860.
17. I have written at more length about irrepressible divisions between democratic and despotic political systems, as a partial cause of the Civil War, in *Road to Disunion,* 2:531–34. Also critical in blowing slavery issues beyond control were the irrepressible economic divisions between free labor and slaveholding economic systems, especially illuminated in Eric Foner's *The Fiery Trial* and in his *Free Labor, Free Soil, Free Men: The Ideology of the Republican Party Before the Civil War* (New York, 1970).
18. *CW,* 4:125–85.
19. Ibid., 4:191.
20. Ibid., 4:204, 211, 216.
21. Ibid., 4:241.
22. Lincoln to Peter H. Silvester, December 22, 1861, in *CW,* 4:160.
23. *CW,* 4:195. The same *CW* page features my next paragraph's "Free-love arrangement."
24. Ibid., 4:242.
25. The Lincoln-Bedell rendezvous in Westfield, New York, February 16, 1861, is recorded in ibid., 4:219–20, along with their October 15–19, 1860, exchange of letters.
26. *CW,* 4:202.
27. Ibid., 4:217.

21. The Troubled Inaugural Address

1. *CW,* 4:249–62. The quoted words in this and the next paragraph are at 256–58.
2. James D. Richardson, ed., *A Compilation of the Messages and Papers of the Confederacy . . . ,* 2 vols. (Nashville, TN, 1905), 1:32–36.
3. *CW,* 2:115–16.
4. At ibid., 4:434n83, editor Roy Basler skillfully demonstrated that Lincoln suppressed his four critical lines against a slaveholders' right of revolution. Thomas J. Pressly's "Ballots and Bullets: Lincoln and the Right of Revolution," *American Historical Review* 67 (1962): 647–62, is an outstanding essay that would have been even better with a clear-cut response to Basler's point (see Pressly's wobble at 659n).

5. *CW,* 4:254.
6. Ibid., 4:261.
7. Michael Burlingame, ed., *Oral History of Abraham Lincoln,* 109–10.
8. Browning to Lincoln, February 17, 1861, Lincoln Papers, Library of Congress.
9. Seward's some four dozen slight suggestions are also in the Lincoln Papers for February 1861. Roy Basler helpfully traces the fate of each Seward suggestion in *CW,* 4:249–61. Seward's suggestion for the First Inaugural's last paragraph is quoted and discussed in Douglas Wilson's enlightening *Lincoln's Sword: The Presidency and the Power of Words* (New York, 2006), esp. 65.
10. *CW,* 4:271.

22. Forts Sumter and Pickens and the Emergence of an Impressive Administrator

1. I built my somewhat different tale of the two forts atop fine previous versions, especially by Potter, Stampp, McClintock, and Cooper in books cited above, chapter 20, note 1, and Richard N. Current, *Lincoln and the First Shot* (Philadelphia, 1963). I have found Kenneth Stampp's emphasis on Lincoln's "Strategy of Defense" at Fort Sumter even more widely illuminating than he realized, and especially in understanding Lincoln's antislavery tactics, at Peoria in 1854 and thereafter until the Final Emancipation Proclamation, January 1, 1863.

    My additions to previous studies of the forts during the secession crisis include more emphasis on Fort Pickens, especially in the beginning of the tale, on the important "fizzle" (Lincoln's perfect word) in the middle of the story, and on the president's bluff at the prewar climax. These additions usually derive from the sources I have used somewhat more than my predecessors, especially the diaries, recollections, and letters of Lincoln's underemphasized key aides in plotting this episode: Gus Fox, Monty Meigs, and Erasmus Keyes.
2. George F. Pearce, *Pensacola during the Civil War: A Thorn in the Side of the Confederacy* (Gainesville, FL, 2000), 1–67, is very helpful on the Fort Pickens side of the story.
3. For the terms of "The Truce of Fort Pickens," see *Official Records of the Union and Confederate Armies,* 128 vols. (Washington, DC, 1880–1901), 1:355–56; hereafter cited as *OR.*
4. Burlingame, *Lincoln,* 2:60.
5. Montgomery Meigs Diary, entry for March 31, 1861, in "General M. C. Meigs on the Conduct of the Civil War," *American Historical Review* 26 (January 1921): 285–303. Meigs reports that Lincoln told him about the March 5 oral orders and March 11 written orders on March 29.
6. E. D. Townsend ("by command of Lieutenant-General Scott") to Israel Vogdes, March 12, 1861, in *OR,* 1:360.
7. Harry J. Carman and Reinhardt H. Luthin, *Lincoln and the Patronage* (New York, 1943), remains the best study of its subject.
8. Alexander K. McClure, *"Abe" Lincoln's Yarns and Stories . . .* (Philadelphia, 1901), 355–56.

9. Frank Blair Sr. to Montgomery Blair, March 11, 1861, Lincoln Papers, Library of Congress.

10. Fox retrospectively detailed his plan and his participation in the Sumter episode in Alfred Gilman, ed., "G. V. Fox in the War of Rebellion," *Contributions of the Old Residents' Historical Association, Lowell, Mass.* 2 (1883): 33–60. For a good biography, see Ari Hoogenboom, *Gustavus Vasa Fox of the Union Navy* . . . (Baltimore, 2008).

11. Fox's important letters during the crisis are in Robert Means Thompson and Richard Wainwright, eds., *The Confidential Correspondence of Gustavus Vasa Fox* (New York, 1920). For Big Byte Books' paperback edition, see *Gustavus Vasa Fox in the Civil War* (Bellevue, WA, 2014). For Fox's March 28 memo, see Fox to Lincoln, March 28, 1861, Lincoln Papers, Library of Congress.

12. On the newspaper rumors and the "necessary inference" cascading around Washington since the truth "could not [yet] be known," see Nicolay and Hay, *Lincoln*, 3:434.

13. Erasmus D. Keyes, *Fifty Years Observation of Men and Events, Civil and Military* (New York, 1884), 378.

14. On the Scott/Lincoln meeting, predinner on March 28, see Meigs Diary, March 29 and 31, 1861, recording what Lincoln told Meigs (including the president's "cold shock" upon hearing that his senior general wished to evacuate Fort Pickens); and Keyes, *Fifty Years*, recording what Scott told Keyes on March 29.

15. Welles to Lincoln, March 29, 1861, Lincoln Papers, Library of Congress.

16. Russell F. Weigley, *Quartermaster General of the Union Army: A Biography of M. C. Meigs* (New York, 1959); Robert O'Harrow Jr., *The Quartermaster: Montgomery C. Meigs* . . . (New York, 2016).

17. The best source on the first, March 29 meeting of Meigs and Lincoln is again Meigs Diary, March 29, 1861.

18. I found no record of when the Vogdes to Scott letter, March 21, 1861, in *OR*, 1:363–64, arrived in Washington. But my best guess is that the corrective report traveled the sea route, putting a guesstimate of its arrival early the next month. By then, the correction no longer much mattered, which is probably why the Vogdes letter received scant if any notice, public or private.

19. Meigs Diary, March 31, 1861; Keyes, *Fifty Years*, 381–83.

20. Lincoln to Scott, April 1, 1861, Lincoln Papers, Library of Congress; Lincoln to Officers of the Army and Navy, April 1, 1861, in *CW*, 4:315.

21. Michael Burlingame, ed., *With Lincoln in the White House: Letters, Memoranda and Other Writings of John G. Nicolay, 1860–65* (Carbondale, IL, 2000), 32.

22. Keyes, *Fifty Years*, 377–401.

23. Gilman, ed., "Fox in the War of Rebellion," 45.

24. Thompson and Wainwright, eds., *Fox Correspondence*, 39.

25. *CW*, 4:317–18.

26. Ibid., 4:316–17.

27. Gilman, ed., "Fox in the War of Rebellion," 46.

28. Nicolay and Hay, *Lincoln*, 4:62.

29. James P. Jones, "Lincoln's Courier: John L. Worden's Mission to West Florida," *Florida Historical Quarterly* 41 (1962): 145–53; Russ Dodge, "Henry Allen Adams," findagrave.com/415680206.

30. Lincoln to Robert Chew, April 6, 1861, in *CW*, 4:323–24.
31. Grady McWhiney's splendid "The Confederacy's First Shot," *Civil War History* 14 (1968): 5–14, contains the full text of Jefferson Davis's pivotal letter to Braxton Bragg, April 3, 1861, 10–12.
32. Wainwright and Thompson, eds., *Fox Correspondence,* 33.
33. Henry A. Adams to Welles, April 14, 1861, in *OR*, 1:376.
34. Montgomery Meigs to J. G. Totten, April 25, 1861, in *OR*, 1:393–99.
35. Lincoln to Fox, May 1, 1861, in *CW*, 4:350–51.
36. Theodore Calvin Pease and James G. Randall, eds., *The Diary of Orville Hickman Browning* (Springfield, IL, 1925), 476 (entry for July 3, 1861).
37. *CW*, 4:431–32.
38. William H. Seward to Frances Seward, June 5, 1861, in *William H. Seward,* 3 vols., ed. Frederick W. Seward (New York, 1893), 2:590. Doris Kearns Goodwin, *Team of Rivals: The Political Genius of Abraham Lincoln* (New York, 2005), provides a colorful and useful account of Lincoln's relationship with his advisors.
39. Gilman, ed., "Fox in the War of Rebellion," 37.
40. Burlingame, ed., *With Lincoln in the White House,* 19.
41. *CW,* 4:421–41, esp. 426, 438.

Epilogue: (Slowly) Becoming a Coercive Emancipator

1. All the full-scale Lincoln biographies cited above, pp. 327-28, concentrate (arguably overconcentrate) on the wartime years. Of the Lincoln books dwelling exclusively on the presidential period, my favorite is Philip Shaw Paludan, *The Presidency of Abraham Lincoln* (Lawrence, KS, 1994). Of the slew of monographs on aspects of the war years, the three most relevant to this book, all excellent, are Edward L. Ayers, *The Thin Light of Freedom: The Civil War and Emancipation in the Heart of America* (New York, 2017); William C. Harris, *Lincoln and the Border States; Preserving the Union* (Lawrence, KS, 2011); and Christopher Phillips, *The Rivers Ran Backward: The Civil War and the Making of the American Border* (New York, 2016).
2. Baker, *Mary Lincoln,* 187; Randall. *Mary Lincoln,* 233–36.
3. Burlingame, *Lincoln,* 2:271.
4. David Donald, "Whig in the White House," chap. 5 of Donald's stimulating *Lincoln Reconsidered: Essays on the Civil War Era* (New York, 1956), and Orville Vernon Burton's outstanding *The Age of Lincoln* (New York, 2007) offer fine perspectives on Lincoln's belated Whig triumph.
5. *CW,* 7:221–22.
6. Ibid., 8:332–33.
7. *HI,* 506.
8. Lincoln to Orville Browning, September 22, 1861, in *CW,* 4:532.
9. James Oakes, *Freedom National: The Destruction of Slavery in the United States* (New York, 2013), traces Radicals' escalating pressure skillfully. The problem is that telling the story through the Radicals' unchanging eyes makes all the difficult mainstream changes seem far easier than they were. The nation's coming to terms with slavery was a slow, agonizing process, and Lincoln, I think, offers the best guide to the tortuous complications.

10. *CW,* 5:388–89.

10. *CW,* 5:388–89.
11. Ibid., 5:144–46.
12. Eric Foner, "Lincoln and Colonization," in *Our Lincoln,* ed. Foner, is a balanced, informed essay on a fortunately no-longer-neglected subject.
13. *CW,* 5:518–37. For a fuller discussion of Lincoln's revealing last-minute efforts to preclude the necessity for coercive emancipation, see my *The South vs. the South: How Anti-Confederate Southerners Shaped the Course of the Civil War* (New York, 2001), 104–14.
14. Theodore Calvin Pease and James G. Randall, eds., *The Diary of Orville Hickman Browning,* 2 vols. (Chicago, 1927), 1:591 (entry for December 1, 1862).
15. Lincoln to John A. McClermand, January 8, 1863, in *CW,* 6:48–49.
16. Ibid., 5:28–30.
17. Foner, *Fiery Trial,* 241, presents a splendid map, illuminating where Lincoln's army could (and could not) emancipate immediately.
18. *CW,* 6:149–50.
19. E. D. Townsend (writing "General Orders . . . by order of the President"), October 3, 1863, in *OR,* ser. 3, 3:860–61.
20. John David Smith, "The Recruitment of Negro Soldiers in Kentucky," *Register of the Kentucky Historical Society* 72 (1974): 364–90.
21. For more on the South divided, racially and geographically, see my *South vs. South.* For Lincoln measuring the opportunity, see Paul D. Escott's fine *"What Shall We Do with the Negro?": Lincoln, White Racism, and Civil War America* (Charlottesville, VA, 2009).
22. *CW,* 5:423.
23. Ibid., 6: 30.
24. Ibid., 7:164.
25. Lincoln to Hahn, March 13, 1864, in *CW,* 7:243.
26. Ibid., 8:399–405.
27. Qtd. in Louis Masur's excellent *Lincoln's Last Speech: Wartime Reconstruction & The Crisis of the Negro* (New York, 2015), 12.

Illustration Credits

Pages ii and xii: Photographs by Frank Dina

Pages 19 (left), 71 (top left), 271, 310 (top right), and 318: Courtesy of the Abraham Lincoln Library and Museum, Harrogate, Tennessee. (Page 271, Frederick Hill Meserve Lincoln Portrait no. 101; page 318, Frederick Hill Meserve Lincoln Portraits nos. 1, 29, 100)

Pages 19 (right), 71 (top right, bottom left and right), 94, 130, 278, and 310 (top left and bottom left): Courtesy of the Abraham Lincoln Library and Museum, Springfield, Illinois

Pages 214, 215, and 310 (bottom right): Courtesy of the Library of Congress, Prints and Photographs Division

Pages 120 and 121: Copyrighted art by Lloyd Ostendorf, republished courtesy of the Ostendorf family, Daniel L. Ostendorf, agent

Page 133: Copyrighted drawing by Lloyd Ostendorf, republished courtesy of www.abelincoln.com, the Abraham Lincoln Collection of the late Phil Wagner, Springfield, Illinois, Donna Ashenbrenner, agent

Page 270: Courtesy of the University of South Carolina Library, University of South Carolina, Columbia, S.C.

Maps by Bill Nelson

Index

Davis, David (judge): image of, *71;*
Lincoln as lawyer and, *71, 72–75,* 190;
in presidential campaign and election
(1959–60), 245–47, 252–55; Senate
race (1856) and, 185; as U.S. Supreme
Court justice, 75, 247
Davis, David Brion, 336n4
Davis, Jefferson, 40, 141, 281, 299, 301–3,
306, 346n31
Davis, Robert O., 328–29n4
Dayton, William, 189–90, 254, 255
debt. *See* indebtedness
Decatur, Illinois: Anti-Nebraska newspaper editors' meeting in (1855), 182–84,
294; Lincoln migration to, 24–25, 182,
244; state Republican convention of
1860 in, 244–45
Decatur Resolutions, 183, 185, 186
Deckle, George R., 335n3
Declaration of Independence, 154–56,
159–60, 162–65, 183, 192, 196, 197, 217,
281, 282, 307
Democrats: in Cavalcade campaign
(1836), 54–55; corruption touted,
in presidential campaign of 1860,
246–47; Illinois, ex-Democrat
Anti-Nebraska faction in, 175–79, 186;
Jacksonian Democracy, 42, 43, 45–46,
48, 54, 55, 57, 76, 94–95, 104, 311–12;
on National Bank, 94, 95, 166, 311;
National Democratic Conventions
(1860), 257; railroad development
and, 123–24; in southern Illinois, 168
Des Moines (locomotive), 141
determinism. *See* fatalism of Lincoln
Donald, David, 334n15, 346n4
Don't Care-ism of Douglas, 153, 154, 159,
208, 221, 226, 238
Douglas, Adele, 212, 215
Douglas, Stephen A.: appearance of,
212–14, *214,* 272; Cooper Union
Address, quoted in, 236; Don't Care-
ism of, 153, 154, 159, 208, 221, 226, 238;
Douglas-Taney conspiracy alleged by
Lincoln, 203–5, 207, 210, 216, 226, 229,
274; on *Dred Scott* decision, 196–99;

early life and education, 56; on equality,
196, 211, 218, 219, 227; at first inauguration, 5, 162; John Hardin as political
rival of, 92–93; on House Divided
Address, 211, 216–17; Illinois, Lincoln's
move to, 24; as Illinois Supreme Court
justice, 58, 123; jealousy of Lincoln
regarding, 58, 123, 149; Kansas-Nebraska Act and, 149–53, 156, 174; on
Lecompton Convention, 200, 203;
Lincoln's father resembling, 17, 26; as
"Little Giant," 5, 56; nationalization of
slavery, Lincoln's beliefs regarding, 4–5,
204–5, 209, 240; political rise of, 58,
123–24; on Popular Sovereignty, 149,
181, 182, 200, 203, 233; in presidential
campaign of 1860, 257–58; presidential
election of 1860 and, 4, 225–26; as railroad tycoon, 117, 123–24; Republicans
and, 202–3; results of 1858 Senate race,
222, 223, 340n39; senatorial election
against Lincoln, 4; as state legislator,
55–58, 123; John Todd Stuart's congressional campaign against, 68, 202; Mary
Todd and, 87. *See also* Lincoln-Douglas
Debates; Peoria Address
Dred Scott decision (1857), 194–99;
Buchanan and, 194, 195–96, 204, 207;
Douglas-Taney conspiracy, Lincoln's
belief in, 203–5, 207, 210, 216, 226,
229, 274; Douglas versus Lincoln
on, 196–99; Freeport Question,
Lincoln-Douglas Debates (1858),
223–24; *Matson* case compared, 79,
210; McLean dissent to, 249; nationalization of slavery, Lincoln's beliefs
regarding, 4–5, 204–5, 209, 226
Dresser, Charles, 89, 90
Dubois, Jesse, 186
duel with James Shields, 88–89

Early, Jacob M., 40, 54
Ecelbarger, Gary, 341–42n3
education (formal and self-acquired) of
Lincoln, 10–11, 17, 19, 21, 38–39, 43, 45,
64–66, 69

Henry, Anson, 88

"hereafter acquired" proposal, 264–66

Herndon, William "Billy": as biographer of Lincoln, 327n2; on children of Lincoln, 180–81; on determination of Lincoln, 48; on Douglas, 202; on Great Lakes excursion by Lincoln family, 335n1; on House Divided Address, 211; as law partner, 67, 70–72, *71*, 73, 75, 81–82, 180–81, 232, 233; on Lost/Found Speech, 187; on Spot Address, 114

Heseltine, William B., 342n11

Hill, Samuel H., 31, 42, 48, 83

Hoffman, Francis, 186

Hofstadter, Richard, 328n2

Holzer, Harold, 338n4, 341n3, 342n1

"Honest Abe," Lincoln as, 32, 36, 39, 93, 162, 246–47, 248, 255

Hoogenboom, Ari, 345n10

horse, Lincoln kicked in head by, 20, 24, 28, 98

House Divided Address (Lincoln, 1858), 55, 96, 155, 161, 205–11, 216–17, 226, 283, 313

House of Representatives (U.S.), Lincoln in, 92–116; bowling lane, contacts made at, 103–4; Circuit Court contacts and, *74*, 74–75, 99–100; family and marital issues, 102–3; Illinois Whigs, Lincoln's party organization of, 93–96; long session, 102, 103, 112, 114; maiden oration on internal improvement, 104–5; Pekin Agreement, 97–98, 158–59, 178; resolutions to end slavery in Washington, DC, introduced by Lincoln, 114–16; rivals in Illinois Seventh Congressional District, 92–93, *94*, 97–98, 101; short session, 102, 114–15, 116; silence on slavery issues in long session, 105–12; Spot Address (1848), 113–14; victory in 1846 election, 98–101

Houston, Sam, 262

Hurd, Jacob, 140, 142, 145

Hurd et al. v. Rock Island Bridge Company (1857), 140–46, 177, 249, 312

Iles, Elijah, 40

Illinois: Anti-Nebraska Party in, 166–72, *169, 170,* 175–79, 182–86; economic prosperity stimulated by railroads, 124–27; free blacks entering state, fine for, 163; geographic divisions of, 167–71, *169, 170;* Tom and Abraham Lincoln's move to, 23, 24–25; in presidential elections (1856), 193; Radical Republicanism in, 172–74; railroads, by 1850, 125, *126;* slavery in, 77–79, 110, 175–76; Whigs, Lincoln's state party organization of, 93–96. *See also* Bloomington; Chicago; Decatur; New Salem; Springfield

Illinois (steamer), 304

Illinois and Michigan Canal, 51–53, 56–57, 61, 104, 105, 117, 120, 122, 127, 247

Illinois Central Railroad, 56, 122–25, 127, 139–40, 185, 202, 257–58, 272

Illinois Central v. McLean County (1853–56), 139–40, 146

Illinois Daily State Journal, 283

Illinois state legislature. *See* state legislator, Lincoln as

Illinois Supreme Court: Douglas on, 58, 123; Lincoln declared qualified to practice law by judges on, 66; Lincoln's cases before, 69, 136–37; *Matson* case, judges involved in, 78–79; railroad cases, 137–40; *State Bank v. People* (1843), 140; *Willard* decision (1843), 78

immigration, immigrants, and nativism, 166–67, 171, 176, 191–92, 218–19, 248, 276

income and assets of Lincoln: from Cooper Union Address, 234, 239; economic prosperity, response to, 128–31, 134; estate left by (1865), 128; indebtedness, Lincoln's struggles with, 31–33, 42, 44, 48, 64, 67, 82; Iowa lands received after Black Hawk War,

Lincoln, Abraham (*continued*)
Republican Party and (*see* Republicans); as river flatboat worker, 26–29; self-education of, 17; Senate ambitions of, 4 (*see also* Senate); sister's death, 21–23, 24, 84; as state legislator, 47–63 (*see also* state legislator, Lincoln as); stepmother, relationship with, 19–20, 131; stovepipe hat worn by, 5, 43, 47, *278, 279*, 280; unbrushed hair of, 91, 214–15, *215*, 234, *271*; unionism of, 1–2 (*see also* unionism of Lincoln); as vice-presidential candidate, 189–90; as Whig (*see* Whigs); women and pursuit of marriage, 81–91 (*see also* Lincoln, Mary Todd; women and Lincoln)

Lincoln, Abraham, images of: aging of Lincoln, images showing (1846–47, 1860, 1865), *318, 319*; Matthew Brady photo (1860), 234, 235; with Pinkerton, at Antietam (1862), *278*; profile image, hair unbrushed, *271*; reading to son Tad, *310*; at renovated home in Springfield (1860), *134*; Augustus Saint-Gaudens, *Standing Lincoln* (1887), *ii, xii,* 1, 2, 319, 327nn1–2; with self-rescuing vessel design, *120, 121*; standing image, ca. 1860, *215*; in white suit at "Almanac" trial (1858), *130*

Lincoln, Abraham, writings and speeches: Address to the Springfield Washington Temperance Society (1842), 109–10, 115, 160; Appomattox, speech at (1865), 323; "The Chronicles of Reuben," 22–23, 84; Clay, Henry, eulogy for (1852), 148, 154, 166; "Communication to the People of Sangamon County" (1832), 34–35; Final Emancipation Proclamation (1863), 48, 313, 317, 319–22; First Inaugural Address (1861), 5, 267, 268, 280–85, 53; Gettysburg Address (1863), 5, 11, 70, 206, 313; "Handbill Replying to Charges of Infidelity" (1846), 99–100; House Divided Address (1858), 55, 96,

155, 161, 205–11, 216–17, 226, 283, 313; Indiana poem, 15, 22; lightning rod speech, as state legislator (1836), 55, 93; Lost/Found Speech (after Bloomington Anti-Nebraska Convention; 1856), 186–88, 192, 237, 338n8; "Notes for a Law Lecture" (1850), 69; Peoria Address (1854), 147–65; "The Perpetuation of Our Political Institutions" (Lyceum Address, 1838), 75–77, 78, 79, 108, 140, 145, 185, 194, 209, 210, 317; Preliminary Emancipation Proclamation (1862), 317–19, 321; "Rebecca" lampoons, 88–89, 177; Robertson, George, letter to (1855), 155–56, 260, 272; Second Inaugural Address (1865), 5, 70, 206, 313–15, 319, 322; Spot Address (1848), 113–14. *See also* Cooper Union Address; Lincoln-Douglas Debates; Peoria Address

Lincoln, Abraham (grandfather), 8, 32
Lincoln, Edward Baker "Eddie" (son), 5, 90, 102, 103, 132, 180, 239
Lincoln, Hannaniah (cousin), 9
Lincoln, Isaac (uncle), 9
Lincoln, John ("Virginia John"; great-grandfather), 8, 25
Lincoln, Mary Todd (wife): broken engagement of Lincoln with, 88, 246; character of, 87; children born to, 89–90; courtship and marriage, 87–89; failed Senate bid and, 177, 178–79; family background and early life, 86; financial and emotional binges of, 91, 280–81, 309–11; as first lady, 309–11, *310;* home in Springfield, 90–91, 132–34, *133;* on Lincoln as dancer, 83; marital relationship, 90, 91, 103, 239, 311; Oregon, proposed move to, 118; political aspirations of, 86, 87, 88–89, 92, 102–3; potential suitors, 86–87; presidential election results announced to, 91; public appearance during travel to inauguration, 275–76; "Rebecca" lampoons, involvement in, 88–89, 177

Lincoln, Mordecai ("Uncle Mord"; uncle), 8, 9, 11, 13, 20, 24

Lincoln, Mordecai, Jr. (2x great-grandfather), 7–8

Lincoln, Mordecai, Sr. (3x great-grandfather), 7

Lincoln, Nancy Hanks (mother), 9, 18–19, 84

Lincoln, Robert Todd "Bob/Bobby" (son), 89–90, 102, 103, 132, 180, 239–40, 280, 283–84, *310*, 311

Lincoln, Samuel (4x great-grandfather), 7, 8, 12

Lincoln, Sarah (sister), 9, 10, 15, 18, 19, 21–22, 24, 84

Lincoln, Sarah Bush Johnston (stepmother), *19*, 19–20, 25, 131

Lincoln, Thomas, Jr. (brother, died in infancy), 10

Lincoln, Thomas "Tad" (son), 26, 90, 132, 180–81, 239, *310,* 311

Lincoln, Tom (father): appearance of, 16–17, *19;* death and funeral, Lincoln not present for, 26, 131; difficult relationship with son, 16–18, 20, 21, 24–26, 45, 131–32; home purchased by Lincoln for, 20, 25, 131; in Illinois, 24–25; in Indiana, 12–13, 14–23; in Kentucky, 8–13, 43; as storyteller, 35; wife and children not introduced by Lincoln to, 25–26, 131

Lincoln, William Wallace "Willie" (son), 90, 132, 180–81, 239, *310*, 311, 314

Lincoln-Douglas Debates (1858), 202–22; Chicago/Springfield unofficial debates, 212; compendium project, 224; Douglas-Taney conspiracy, Lincoln on, 203–5, 207, 210, 216, 226, 229; on equality and nativism, 218–19; Freeport Question, 223–24, 340n32; House Divided Address accepting senate nomination, 55, 96, 155, 161, 205–11, 216–17, 226, 283, 313; process, locations, and style of, 211–16, *213–15;* on Radical Republicanism and slavery in territories, 219–20; results of Senate

race, 222, 223, 340n39; revision of positions for presidential campaign, 223–31; on state's rights, 217; on territorial slavery, 219–20, 257, 265; on "ultimate extinction" of slavery, 216–17, 220, 221, 226; on unionism, 221

Lincoln Forum, 327n1

Literary and Debating Society, New Salem, Illinois, 38

Little Pigeon Creek, Illinois (childhood/teenage home), 12, 22–23, 26

Logan, Stephen A.: in Black Hawk War, 40; as floor manager in Lincoln's 1855 Senate bid, 178; Herndon studying under, 81–82; as law partner, 66, 69–70, *71*, 72, 75, 157, 245, 294; Spot Address affecting, 114; as state legislator, 63; whittling of, 69, 70, 114, 122, 145

log-cabin birth of Lincoln, 9–10, 13, 27

logrolling, 57–58

Long Nine (1836), 54–55, 57, 72

Lost/Found Speech (Lincoln, 1856), 186–88, 192, 237, 338n8

Louisiana Purchase, 149, 150

Lovejoy, Elijah, 76, 173

Lovejoy, Owen, 173–74, 175, 182, 186, 190–91

Luthin, Reinhardt H., 344n7

Lyceum Address ("The Perpetuation of Our Political Institutions," Lincoln, 1838), 75–77, 78, 79, 108, 140, 145, 185, 194, 209, 210, 317

malaria, 25

Manny, John, and Manny Reaper case, 143–44, 323

Masur, Louis, 347n27

Matson, Robert, and *Matson* affair (1840s), 77–80, 136, 176, 210

Mattson, Joel, 177–78, 246–47

McClintock, Russell, 342n1, 344n1

McCormick Harvesting Machine Company, 127, 143, 225

McGinty, Brian, 336n8

McIntosh, Francis L., 76

McLean, John, 141, 143, 144, 249

McLean County case (1854), 139–40

McNamar, John (partner of Samuel Hill and fiancé of Ann Rutledge), 83–84

McPherson, James M., 328n2, 334n15

McWhiney, Grady, 346n31

Meigs, Montgomery "Monty," 295–98, 300, 301, 304, 305, 344n1, 344n5, 345n14

melancholy of Lincoln: aging of Lincoln and, *318,* 319; broken engagement with Mary Todd and, 88; David Davis on, 73; early struggles and, 244; as father, 90; as lawyer, 73, 75, 90; as president, 273, 319; Ann Rutledge's death and, 84, 88; strength derived from, 1, 63, 324; as young man, 17, 21, 23

Mentelle, Charlotte, 86, 90, 91

Metzker, Pres, 129–30

Mexican War (1846–48), 98, 105, 111–14, 162, 290

milk-sick, 18, 23, 25

Miller, William Lee, 340n39

Missouri Compromise (1820), 149, 150, 152, 159–60, 167, 172, 183, 195, 207, 270

Morris, Buckner, 193

National Bank: under Republicans, 312; Second National Bank of the United States, 49, 95; Whigs versus Democrats on, 94, 95, 166, 311

National Road, 11, 26, 49

Native Americans: American relocation of, 148; Black Hawk War (1832), 40–44, 46, 65, 69; Chicago, etymological origins of, 250; Sauk and Fox, 40; Shawnee, Kentucky encounter of Lincolns with, 8, 20

nativism and nativists (Know-Nothings): American Party (Know-Nothing Party), 167, 186, 191–93, 248, 258; Fremont presidential campaign (1856) and, 191–93; in interregnum period, 274, 276; during presidential

campaign, 218–19, 248, 255; Senate race (1855) and, 166–67, 171, 176

natural right to choose another government, 281–83

Neale, Thomas, 40, 43

Necessity, Doctrine of. *See* fatalism of Lincoln

New England, post–Cooper Union speeches in, 240–42

New Salem, Illinois: Chicago compared, 29; commercial dreams for, 29, 30; general store run by Lincoln in, 29–31, 42; Literary and Debating Society, 38; milldam, boats stuck on, 28–29, 31, 50, 123; postmaster, Lincoln as, 42–43; surveyor, Lincoln as, 40, 43–45

New York Central Railroad, 128

New York City Gridiron Fraud, 247, 255

New York Evening Post, 232, 235

New York Tribune, 202, 232, 234, 238

Niagara Falls: the Great Blondin crossing, 147, 260; Lincoln at, 119, 335n1

Nichols, Roy F., 336n9

Nicolay, John G., 327n2

Norris, James, 130

Northern Cross Railroad, 56, 59, 61, *62*

northern expansion of slavery, Lincoln's fears regarding, 153, 162–64, 172, 194–95, 203–11, 225–26

northern states, political geography of, 168–71, *169,* 253–56, 259

Northwest Ordinance (1787), 106, 110, 175, 176

Norton, Jesse, 175

"Notes for a Law Lecture" (Lincoln, 1850), 69

Oakes, James, 337n2, 346n9

Offutt, Denton: and Jack Armstrong, Lincoln's brawl with, 36–37; debtors' troubles of, 30, 32, 34, 35, 42, 53, 246; flatboat business of, 27–29, 121; as horse whisperer, 28; New Salem, Illinois, commercial plans for, 29–30

Oglesby, Richard J., 244–46

Ohio Republicans, 224–25, 229

Seward, William H. (*continued*)
(as Secretary of State), 292, 293, 295–99, 303, 305–6
Sewell, Richard H., 337n2
Shakespeare, William, 11, 17, 38, 78
Shawnee, Kentucky encounter of Lincolns with, 8, 20
Sherman, John, 230
Sherman, William Tecumseh, 230
Shields, James, 88–89, 91, 161, 174, 176, 177, 180
Short, "Uncle Jimmy," 42, 44, 45, 64, 82, 83, 135, 245
Sinking Spring Farm, Kentucky (Lincoln's birthplace), 9
Sirens, 122–23
Slave Power arguments, 153–54, 194, 209, 264, 305, 315
slavery and antislavery movement: in Border South, Middle South, and Lower South states, 150–52; "bread" argument of proslavery advocates, 198–99; Clay on, 148; Cassius Clay on, 256; coerced emancipation, Lincoln's conversion to, 316–22; colonization proposals, 148, 317, 321, 322; consent to abolition, Lincoln's belief in need for, 2, 106, 108–10, 115–16, 153, 161–64, 171, 185, 197, 205, 253, 260, 267, 269, 272, 275, 316–17, 319, 322; Don't Care-ism of Douglas, 153, 154, 159, 208, 221, 226, 238; equality, southern extremism rejecting, 154–56; in First Inaugural Address, 281–83, 284; flatboat worker, Lincoln's encounters with slavery as, 27, 105–6; free labor, Lincoln on, 192, 227–29; free-soil arguments, 76, 79, 153–54, 155, 168, 183–84, 192, 228, 241, 245, 264, 274; Fugitive Slave Law, 224, 264; gag rules on slavery, 111; gradualism, Lincoln's espousal of, 2, 106–7, 148, 160–61, 204–5, 272, 316–17; gradualism, Lincoln's pessimism regarding, 155–56; House, silence of Lincoln in, 105–12; Illinois, slavery in, 77–79, 110, 175–76;

Illinois Anti-Nebraska Party, 166–72, *169, 170,* 175–79, 182–84; Illinois state legislature 1837 resolutions on abolitionism, 108–9; individual states, abolition of slavery by, 106–7; interregnum, rejection of any expansion of slavery in, 265–66; Kansas, first elections in (1855), 181–82; lynchings in Mississippi, 76; *Matson* affair (1840s), 77–80; Missouri Compromise (1820), 149, 150, 152, 159–60, 167, 172, 183, 195, 207, 270; northern expansion of slavery, Lincoln's fears regarding, 4–5, 153, 162–64, 172, 194–95, 203–11, 225–26; opposition of Lincoln to slavery, 99, 105–6, 109, 225–26, 247, 281; in "The Perpetuation of Our Political Institutions" (Lyceum Address, Lincoln, 1838), 76, 108; presidency, antislavery messages during, 313, 314; presidential campaign, rejection of any expansion of slavery in, 225–26, 227, 229, 236; slaveholders, Lincoln on, 160–61; Texas, annexation of, 111–12; Thirteenth Amendment, 3, 6, 266–67, 321–22; three-fifths clause, 153–54; tyrants, folly of seeking consent from, 155–56, 319; union versus slavery, 162, 306–7, 316; Washington, DC, resolutions introduced by Lincoln to end slavery in, 114–16, 162, 267. See also *Dred Scott* decision; emancipation proclamations; Kansas; Kansas-Nebraska Act; Peoria Address; Radical Republicans; southern proslavery extremism; territories, slavery in; "ultimate extinction" of slavery
Slemmer, Adam, 288, 297
slung shot, 129, 130
Smith, Ann Todd (sister-in-law), 280
Smith, Clark, 280–81
Smoot, Coleman, 48
South Carolina: on federal appointments in southern states, 269–70, 272–73; Fort Moultrie, 262, 263, 286; notice of reinforcement of Fort Sumter sent to,

Washington, George, 36; birthday of, 182, 184, 233, 274
Washington Aqueduct, 296
waterways, Lincoln's focus on, 119–23
Webster, Daniel, 144
Weed, Thurlow, 247
Welles, Gideon, 295–97, 299–301, 304, 305
Whigs: Baker as, 5; Black Hawk War and, 40; in Cavalcade campaign (1836), 54–55; collapse of, 166, 168, 171, 172, 174, 177, 178, 183–84, 312; economic nationalism of Lincoln and, 48, 49, 104–5; Illinois Seventh Congressional District usually electing a Whig, 92; Illinois state party organization of, 93–96; Lincoln's early allegiance to, 11; on National Bank, 94, 95, 166, 311; New Salem dominated by, 42; newspapers of, Lincoln's access to, 42; patronage position, Lincoln seeking, 116–17; Pekin Agreement at Whigs' Illinois Seventh District convention, 97–98, 158–59, 178; in "The Perpetuation of Our Political Institutions" (Lyceum Address, Lincoln, 1838), 76–77; railroad development and, 123–24

white snakeroot, 18
Whitney, Henry Clay, 338n8
Wide-Awakes, 246, 258
Wigwams (temporary convention halls), 245, 249–50, 252, 254, 269
Willard decision (1843), 78
Wilmot Proviso, 112
Wilson, Douglas L., 328–29n4, 333n19, 344n9
Wilson, William, 78–80
Winter of the Deep Snow, the, 25, 28, 30, 182, 244
women and Lincoln, 81–91; courtship of Mary Owens, 84–86, 87; engagement to Ann Rutledge, 83–84, 88; female company, Lincoln in, 82–83, 84–85, 87; prostitute's fee, story about, 36; shared beds in crowded inns, Lincoln on, 73. *See also* Lincoln, Mary Todd
Woodbury, Levi, 292

Young Indians, 116–17
Young Men's Central Republican Union, New York City, 232. *See also* Cooper Union Address
Young Men's Lyceum of Springfield, 75

Zall, Paul M., 330n3

Previous Civil War Books by William W. Freehling

Prelude to Civil War: The Nullification Controversy in South Carolina,
1816–1836

The Road to Disunion, Volume 1: Secessionists at Bay, 1776–1854

The Road to Disunion, Volume 2: Secessionists Triumphant, 1854–1861

The South vs. the South: How Anti-Confederate Southerners Shaped the Course
of the Civil War

The Reintegration of American History: Slavery and the Civil War

Secession Debated: Georgia's Showdown in 1860 (coedited with
Craig M. Simpson)

Showdown in Virginia: The 1861 Convention and the Fate of the Union
(coedited with Craig M. Simpson)